POLITICS IN EIGHTEENTH-CENTURY WALES

POLITICS IN
EIGHTEENTH-CENTURY
WALES

Peter D. G. Thomas

UNIVERSITY OF WALES PRESS
CARDIFF
1998

© Peter D. G. Thomas, 1998

British Library Cataloguing-in-Publication Data
A catalogue record for this book is available from the British Library.

ISBN 0–7083–1444–9

Published with the financial support of the Arts Council of Wales

Typeset at the University of Wales Press
Printed in Great Britain by Bookcraft (Bath) Ltd, Somerset

Contents

Preface

THIS book is intended to be both a study in Welsh history and a detailed example of British political history, between the Glorious Revolution of 1688 and the French Revolution of 1789. The political structure of Wales is set in the general context of British politics, and due cognisance is taken of the Welsh aspects of Jacobitism, early reform movements, and other manifestations of public opinion.

During forty-five years of study, on and off, of Welsh politics in the eighteenth century I have incurred many obligations. Early guidance at Bangor was received from Professors Glyn Roberts and A. H. Dodd, and Mr E. G. Jones. Subsequent help has been given by Margaret Escott, Andrew Hanham, Clyve Jones, Heather Mountjoy, R. D. Rees, and Eryn White, and others whom I fear I have forgotten. I am also grateful to anonymous readers of the University of Wales Press and the Arts Council of Wales for their constructive comments, and to the Council for a grant in aid of publication.

For authority to use manuscripts I am grateful for the gracious permission of Her Majesty the Queen, and the permission of the Marquess of Bute; the Earl of Harrowby; the Earl of Malmesbury; Olive, Countess Fitzwilliam and the Wentworth Settlement Trustees; the Syndics of Cambridge University Library; the Trustees of the British Library; and the County and City of Swansea.

For help with my research I am indebted to the staffs of the National Library of Wales; the British Library; the Public Record Office; the History of Parliament Trust; the Institute of Historical Research; Hampshire County Record Office; the former Dyfed County Record Office; the Library, University of Wales, Bangor; and the Library, University of Wales, Aberystwyth. Research and production of the book have been assisted by a grant from the Sir David Hughes Parry Award fund of the University of Wales, Aberystwyth. Dorothy Evans has converted my holograph into a text fit for the printer.

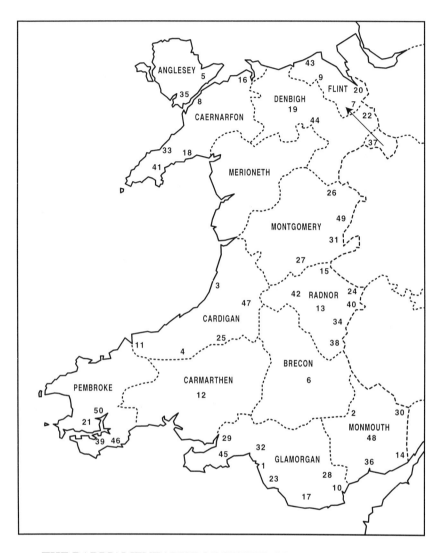

THE PARLIAMENTARY BOROUGHS OF WALES 1660–1832

Key to Map of Parliamentary Boroughs in Wales

1	Aberavon	26	*Llanfyllin* (1728)
2	*Abergavenny* (1685)	27	*Llanidloes* (1728)
3	Aberystwyth	28	Llantrisant
4	Adpar	29	Loughor
5	Beaumaris	30	Monmouth
6	Brecon	31	Montgomery
7	Caergwrle	32	Neath
8	Caernarfon	33	Nefyn
9	Caerwys	34	New Radnor
10	Cardiff	35	*Newborough* (1730)
11	Cardigan	36	Newport
12	Carmarthen	37	Overton
13	Cefnllys	38	*Painscastle* (1690)
14	*Chepstow* (1689)	39	Pembroke
15	Cnwclas	40	*Presteigne* (1690)
16	Conway	41	Pwllheli
17	Cowbridge	42	Rhayader
18	Cricieth	43	Rhuddlan
19	Denbigh	44	Ruthin
20	Flint	45	Swansea
21	Haverfordwest	46	Tenby
22	Holt	47	*Tregaron* (1730)
23	Kenfig	48	Usk
24	Knighton	49	*Welshpool* (1728)
25	Lampeter	50	Wiston

By 1730 the boroughs italicized had been disenfranchised or finally omitted at the dates indicated. The others participated until 1832.

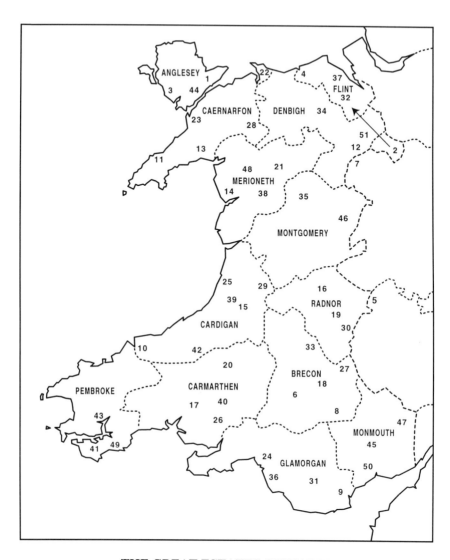

THE GREAT ESTATES OF WALES

Key to Map of the Great Estates of Wales

1	Baron Hill	27	Gwernyfed
2	Bettisfield	28	Gwydir
3	Bodorgan	29	Hafod
4	Bodrhyddan	30	Harpton Court
5	Brampton Bryan	31	Hensol Castle
6	Brecon Priory	32	Leeswood
7	Brogyntyn	33	Llanelwedd
8	Buckland	34	Lleweni
9	Cardiff Castle	35	Llwydiarth
10	Cardigan Priory	36	Margam Abbey
11	Cefnamwlch	37	Mostyn
12	Chirk Castle	38	Nannau
13	Clenennau	39	Nanteos
14	Corsygedol	40	Newton (Dynefor)
15	Crosswood (Trawscoed)	41	Orielton
16	Cwmhir	42	Peterwell
17	Cwmgwili	43	Picton Castle
18	Dderw	44	Plas Newydd
19	Downton	45	Pontypool Park
20	Edwinsford	46	Powis Castle
21	Glanllyn	47	Raglan Castle
22	Gloddaeth	48	Rhiwgoch
23	Glynllifon	49	Stackpole Court
24	Gnoll	50	Tredegar Park
25	Gogerddan	51	Wynnstay
26	Golden Grove		

MORGAN OF TREDEGAR

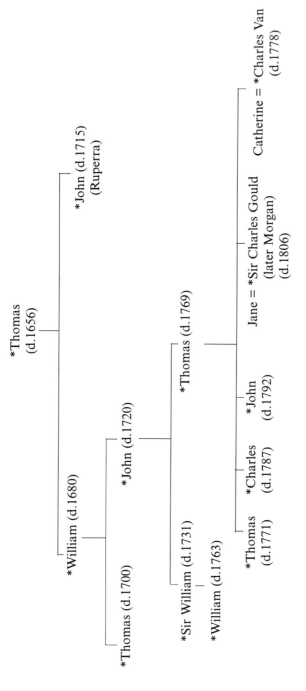

*Thomas
(d.1656)

*William (d.1680)

*John (d.1715)
(Ruperra)

*Thomas (d.1700)

*John (d.1720)

*Sir William (d.1731)

*William (d.1763)

*Thomas (d.1769)

*Thomas
(d.1771)

*Charles
(d.1787)

*John
(d.1792)

Jane = *Sir Charles Gould
(later Morgan)
(d.1806)

Catherine = *Charles Van
(d.1778)

* = MP

OWEN OF ORIELTON

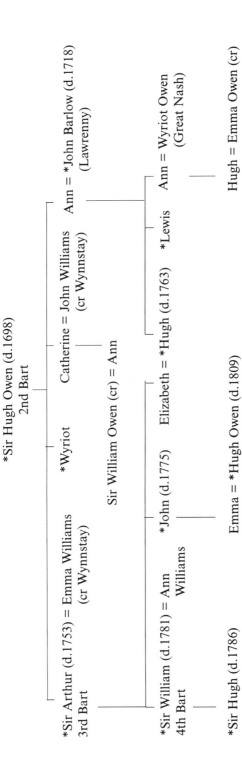

*Sir Hugh Owen (d.1698)
2nd Bart

*Wyriot

Catherine = John Williams
(cr Wynnstay)

Ann = *John Barlow (d.1718)
(Lawrenny)

Sir William Owen (cr) = Ann

*Sir Arthur (d.1753) = Emma Williams
3rd Bart   (cr Wynnstay)

*John (d.1775)

Elizabeth = *Hugh (d.1763)

*Lewis

Ann = Wyriot Owen
(Great Nash)

*Sir William (d.1781) = Ann
4th Bart   Williams

Emma = *Hugh Owen (d.1809)
(later Barlow)

Hugh = Emma Owen (cr)

*Sir Hugh (d.1786)
5th Bart

* = MP

cr = cross-reference to other
family trees

BULKELEY OF BARON HILL

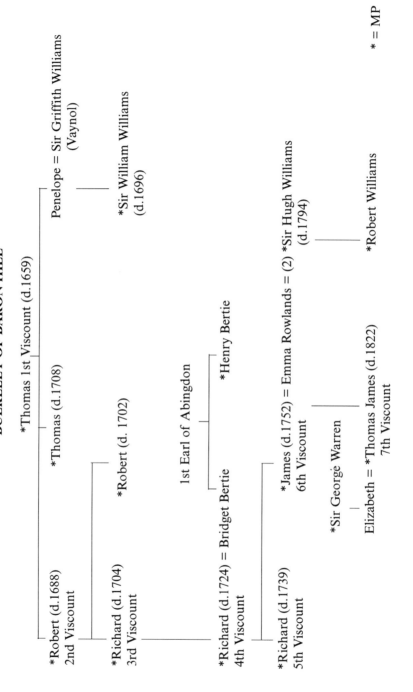

*Thomas 1st Viscount (d.1659)

Penelope = Sir Griffith Williams
(Vaynol)

*Thomas (d.1708)

*Sir William Williams
(d.1696)

*Robert (d.1688)
2nd Viscount

*Robert (d. 1702)

*Richard (d.1704)
3rd Viscount

1st Earl of Abingdon

*Henry Bertie

*Richard (d.1724) = Bridget Bertie
4th Viscount

*James (d.1752) = Emma Rowlands = (2) *Sir Hugh Williams
6th Viscount   (d.1794)

*Richard (d.1739)
5th Viscount

*Sir George Warren

*Robert Williams

Elizabeth = *Thomas James (d.1822)
7th Viscount

* = MP

WYNN OF WYNNSTAY

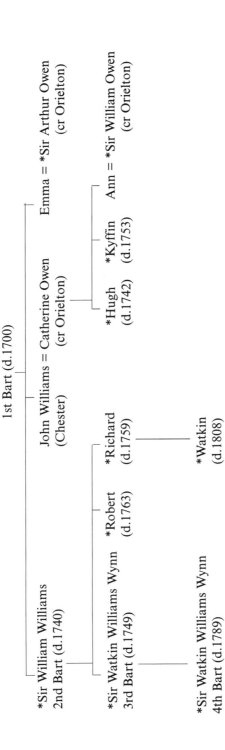

*Sir William Williams
1st Bart (d.1700)

*Sir William Williams
2nd Bart (d.1740)

John Williams = Catherine Owen
(Chester)   (cr Orielton)

Emma = *Sir Arthur Owen
              (cr Orielton)

*Sir Watkin Williams Wynn
3rd Bart (d.1749)

*Robert   *Richard
(d.1763)   (d.1759)

*Hugh   *Kyffin
(d.1742)   (d.1753)

Ann = *Sir William Owen
            (cr Orielton)

*Sir Watkin Williams Wynn
4th Bart (d.1789)

*Watkin
(d.1808)

* = MP
cr = cross-reference to other
        family trees

CHAPTER 1

The Political Structure of Wales in 1700

'THAT country where . . . the great families, though they did not exercise it as arbitrarily, had as much weight with their dependants as the chieftains in Scotland.'[1] So did that percipient English observer, Horace Walpole, write about Wales in 1778. In the period between the Glorious Revolution of 1688, that sent James II into exile, and the era of reform launched by the French Revolution in 1789 the rule of the Welsh squire-archy was virtually unchallenged by the Crown, an aristocracy or a middle class. The abolition of the Council of Wales in 1689 removed the main instrument of royal power. Wales had always lacked a resident nobility in any numbers. Of the two dominant peerage houses of the late seventeenth century, the Dukes of Beaufort lived at Badminton in Gloucestershire, while the Powis Castle family maintained a low profile even after recovery of the estate forfeited for loyalty to James II. English peers who married Welsh heiresses tended not to live in Wales. Very few Welshmen were elevated to the House of Lords during the century after 1688. The honours obtained by Welsh MPs and other squires were knighthoods, baronetcies, and Irish peerages, none of which precluded their recipients from sitting in the House of Commons or distanced them unduly from the other gentry.

The absence of a resident aristocracy was matched by the lack as yet of any middle class to pose a political challenge. A few entrepreneurs were harbingers of the Industrial Revolution, notably the Mackworths of Gnoll in Glamorgan and the ironmaster Hanburys of Pontypool in Monmouth-shire; but these men were squires who had diversified into industry rather than a new breed. Many other gentlemen enhanced their incomes by industrial and commercial ventures, most obviously in mining, but they remained landed proprietors. Nor was any conflict of class interest signified by the need or desire of squires, whether MPs or impecunious younger sons of gentlemen, to become officers in the army and navy, lawyers and

---

[1] Walpole, *Last Journals*, II, 214.

1

merchants. A few Welsh estates were acquired by wealthy incomers, such as 'nabobs' with fortunes gained in India, but such men were easily assimilated into landed society, and no threat to the existing political system.

Parliamentary elections now provided the battleground for the determination of where political power lay in Wales. Twenty-seven MPs were returned to Westminster from the Principality, one for each of the thirteen Welsh counties except that Monmouthshire, being deemed part of England, returned two. Representation of the local shire was more prestigious, and so more highly prized, than tenure of a borough seat. Wales had thirteen borough constituencies, supposedly comprising the 'ancient boroughs' of Wales. There was one for every county except Merioneth, and Haverfordwest returned an MP by virtue of its status as a county borough. From the Glorious Revolution of 1688 Parliament met every year, and elections became a recurrent feature of the political scene, required by the Triennial Act every three years between 1694 and 1716, and thereafter by the Septennial Act at least every seven years. Each general election was spread over a period of several weeks, depending on the arrival of election writs in the constituencies. There was no time-limit for elections contested by a poll, which might last from a few hours to a fortnight or more, until candidates conceded or ran out of voters. It was possible, and not uncommon, for candidates to fight two or more constituencies – for insurance, prestige, or to have a spare seat to oblige a friend. Candidates under the legal age of twenty-one were occasionally returned for constituencies where no questions would be asked, as Lewis Pryse was for Cardiganshire in 1701, but could not be risked when there was opposition, as in Brecon in 1722 and Beaumaris in 1727.

That there were fifty Welsh towns which during the period from 1660 to 1740 claimed to participate in the thirteen borough constituencies is misleading in a social and political context. For these towns, sometimes mere villages, were small, often artificial creations rather than the natural product of favourable economic conditions. Far from affording parliamentary representation to any middle class, they were as much under the control of the squirearchy as the counties. Less than a dozen had as many as 2,000 inhabitants in 1700, and ironically the largest town in Wales, Wrexham, with over 3,000, was not a parliamentary borough. But in any case franchise restrictions and admission of non-resident voters both, in opposite ways, destroyed any correlation between the sizes of electorates and populations. Beaumaris had perhaps 1,000 inhabitants but only 24 voters, whereas the little town of Lampeter, with a population of some 300, had voters by the thousand in the later eighteenth century, drawn from England as well as many parts of Wales. Swansea in 1831 had a population of over 13,000, but only 64 freemen.

The control of the landed gentry over the twenty-six parliamentary constituencies of Wales was therefore virtually unchallenged from above or below. This was more evidently so in the thirteen counties, where a uniform franchise qualification of a forty-shilling freehold provided electorates ranging from 500 to 2,000 voters, sometimes expanded during contests by the splitting of freeholds and creation of leaseholds, practices often deemed reprehensible and eschewed by scrupulous candidates. The weight of each squire's 'interest' lay in the number of tenants and dependants whose votes he could command.

A different system of power-play operated in the thirteen borough constituencies. Precedents supposedly determined which boroughs in each of twelve counties, all except Merioneth, should share the representation with the county towns. Already three county towns had secured an exclusive right to the parliamentary seat, a privilege also enjoyed by Haverfordwest, a county-borough enfranchised in its own right. Most boroughs were under patron control, usually exercised by local squires as lords of the manor, but sometimes as a result of Crown appointments, as to the constableship of the town castle. A minority were disputed between rival aspirants for control, and a few were seemingly independent of any patrons. When boroughs in the same constituency group were in the hands of rival patrons the situation often led to competitive creation of voters, a uniquely Welsh phenomenon that did not exist elsewhere in the British political system. If some such constituencies had thousands of voters, others had tiny electorates, few voters being easier to manage than many if there was firm patron control. That of Brecon fell from 200 in the early eighteenth century, when rival families fought for control, to a mere nineteen in 1809.[2]

That the total Welsh electorate rose in the eighteenth century to about 25,000 is not therefore a meaningful statistic. The increase owed little to population growth, and did not imply a greater degree of popular participation in politics. Rather was it caused by a variety of dubious expedients and downright malpractice by candidates in county and borough alike, and balanced to some extent by deliberate restriction of electorates in certain boroughs. There were no official electoral rolls, and one factor in any polls was the power of the returning officers to decide on the validity of individual votes. Sometimes such officials connived at last-minute alterations of the time or place of an election. Chicanery by a returning officer, who may have been coerced or bribed, was one hazard at an election. Another was violence, either deliberate to prevent opponents

---

[2] Thomas, 'Parliamentary Elections in Brecknockshire 1689–1832', *Brycheiniog*, 6 (1960), 101, 105, 108.

voting, or spontaneous as when supporters of rival candidates engaged in brawls. Partiality by officials at elections, and other misdemeanours, could be either confirmed or corrected by the House of Commons, where its Committee of Elections or the House itself constituted a court of appeal in election disputes, and whose often partisan decisions added another element of uncertainty to many a contest.

The political power of the squirearchy was maintained by a mixture of stick and carrot. Tenants were expected to vote in accordance with their landlord's wishes, as Mrs Victoria Kynaston made clear to a recalcitrant tenant in the Montgomeryshire contest of 1774: 'It is always customary for tenants to go along with their landlords and landladies.'[3] Coercion of tenants need not imply the crude and cruel weapon of eviction, although that was sometimes actually carried out as well as being merely threatened. Lesser menaces were deployed, such as loss of grazing privileges or of access to fuel. Nor were coercive tactics confined to dependants. Supposedly independent freeholders could be bullied by such economic pressures as loss of business, by social ostracism, and by the imposition of onerous unpaid tasks like that of village constable. The power and behaviour of Welsh squires was noted with some astonishment by Englishman John Meller in about 1720, soon after he had acquired the Erthig estate in Denbighshire: 'This whole country is governed by fear and the lesser gentry are as much awed by those of better estate as the poor people are.'[4]

That was the dark side of electoral politics. But the cultivation of local popularity and goodwill was necessary, for not even the greatest landowners could carry a county by their own tenants and dependants. In Glamorgan, precise calculations after a 1745 by-election poll of 1,329 showed that the Mansel family, the most powerful in the county, had controlled 216 voters.[5]

Challenges to a sitting member or a dominant interest therefore triggered off election campaigns that might be prolonged over a year or two. An early start could yield a tactical advantage, since promises were deemed binding and voting was public: electoral correspondence was full of apologies to candidates for premature pledges to their opponents. Some challenges were merely a preliminary sounding of local opinion by a press announcement of an anonymous candidate, and a subsequent canvass might be abandoned at any moment right up until the actual day of election. It is misleading to assume that only polls signified election campaigns. Late withdrawals were made to avoid causing supporters

---

[3] Peniarth MSS 418D.
[4] *Erthig Chronicles*, I, 230–1.
[5] Kemys Tynte MSS 1/83.

needless inconvenience and expense, and to save the candidates themselves heavy costs. For polls were troublesome affairs. All voting, for county and borough elections alike, had to be conducted at a single location, usually the shire town. Candidates therefore incurred the cost of transport and accommodation, for a poll might last several days, even a week or longer. It was also during the actual conduct of a poll that most of the expenditure of plying voters with food and drink would be incurred. Direct bribery of voters was rare, as being too expensive and transparently illegal, but the consumption of alcohol at elections was often prodigious. It was common to allow a gallon of ale for each voter, and in 1784 Paget supporters in Anglesey also averaged two bottles of spirits each. Lavish provision of coloured ribbons, to denote partisanship, and of musical and other entertainments helped to create what must sometimes have been a carnival atmosphere. Such contests might cost a candidate a great deal of money, though not the enormous amounts that were often formerly conjectured. At the Flint Boroughs election of 1734 Sir John Glynne spent £4,000, not the £35,000 once suggested.[6] The Montgomeryshire contest of 1774 may have been the most expensive Welsh election of the century, with Powis Castle spending £5,400 and Wynnstay £4,800.[7] The largest amount spent on behalf of a single candidate was probably the £8,373 by Lord Paget of Plas Newydd in 1784 when his brother wrested the Anglesey seat by seven votes from the hitherto dominant Baron Hill interest.[8] This was money well spent, for thereafter Pagets held the county until the Reform Act of 1832.

That such a contest could decide control of a seat for decades was what made electoral sense of such lavish expenditure. When Valentine Morris challenged the dominant Morgan of Tredegar interest at a 1771 Monmouthshire by-election, he complained publicly that Tredegar was willing to spend £10,000 to prevent his election. Victory actually cost Tredegar £5,600.[9] Such expenditure guaranteed the seat for the indefinite future. The costs for the next Monmouthshire elections, shared by two unopposed candidates, were £316 in 1774, £369 in 1780 and £351 in 1784.[10]

The electoral dominance of the great families in the counties was based on deep purses as much as on the massed ranks of tenant voters. Smaller squires who aspired to cut a parliamentary figure in Georgian times often

---

[6] Thomas, 'Sir George Wynne and the Flint Borough Elections of 1727–1741', *Flintshire Historical Society Journal*, 20 (1962), 51.

[7] Thomas, 'The Montgomeryshire Election of 1774', *Montgomeryshire Collections*, 59 (1965–6), 127. Humphreys, *Crisis of Community*, p. 211, has a total of £6,800 for Powis Castle.

[8] Plas Newydd MSS I, 1, 2; IV, 5266.

[9] Tredegar MSS 53/294; 228.

[10] Tredegar MSS 228, 259, 260, 261.

paid a high price for their ambition; sometimes, as with John Owen of Presaddfed in Anglesey, the loss of the family estate. Greater wisdom or caution was displayed by Thomas Kyffin of Maenan in Caernarfonshire, who canvassed that county more than once in George III's reign, without venturing to a poll, and confined his political ambitions to an active role in the reform movements of the 1780s. Wealth likewise reinforced patron control in the borough constituencies. In addition to treating and transport costs, a fee was payable on every burgess admission.

Often deployed also was the contention that contests were undesirable because they disturbed 'the peace of the county', that the question of parliamentary representation should be decided at a general county meeting or by a formal agreement among the leading squires. Such arguments, used almost always by those who wished to control such matters, were losing their efficacy by the dawn of the eighteenth century. Richard Jenkins of Hensol, mounting a challenge in Glamorgan in 1708, contended that 'the election was no man's birthright, and that opposition of this nature was very common in other parts of this kingdom'. So the sheriff reported to Thomas Mansel of Margam, who had sought to avoid a confrontational situation, with the comment that 'I very much dread the ill consequences the great concourse of people may have especially where disputed elections are so new'.[11]

County meetings called to decide on parliamentary representation remained the common practice throughout the eighteenth century. Increasingly they became a formality, to endorse the candidature of the dominant local squire, although sometimes they were the preliminary to a contest. An uncontested election customarily cost a candidate no more than £300, to provide suitable celebrations on election day, and sometimes a great deal less.[12] In 1768 a Flintshire gentleman noted the 'parsimony' of two local candidates. Denbighshire MP Sir Lynch Cotton was 'chaired by his own servants, and the whole expense, I am told, amounted not to ten pounds, five of which were squeezed out of him, with prodigious reluctance, towards a ball for the Denbigh ladies'. Cotton was surpassed in meanness by Flint Boroughs MP Sir John Glynne, who bought four voters 'a pint of ale apiece' and, including the cost of bell-ringing, spent under £2 altogether.[13]

Every Welsh constituency did go to the poll at least once during the eighteenth century. But if nowhere was a local power structure unchallenged, the desirability of avoiding contests was obvious even where the

---

[11] Penrice and Margam MSS L1443.
[12] For some such Tredegar election bills concerning Breconshire, Brecon and Monmouthshire see Tredegar MSS 228, 254, 257, 143/68.
[13] *HMC Kenyon*, p. 500.

balance of interests was undetermined. Conflicting parties, rather than face polls the outcome of which might be uncertain and which would always be expensive, frequently came to compromise arrangements, perhaps involving successive elections or several constituencies. That was especially the practice during the two decades after the Triennial Act of 1694, when general elections took place on average every two years. There is evidence for that period of such formal arrangements in Cardiganshire, Caernarfonshire, Flintshire and Monmouthshire, and others doubtless explain the frequent rotation of MPs elsewhere at the time; but this practice was effectively killed by the Septennial Act of 1716. Already by that time fewer constituencies were being disputed as the great families of Wales had begun to impose an oligarchic hold on the parliamentary seats.

The pace of politics was becoming too hot for the lesser squires who in earlier times might have expected to take their turn at Westminster. During the later seventeenth century the character of Welsh politics was being altered by the social and economic differentiation of the landowning class. The decline of the lesser gentry was often actual as well as relative. The majority had been Royalist in the Civil War, suffering fines and forfeitures from which many never recovered. And there were the usual factors of human frailty and misfortune. But if numerous estates declined into mere farms or went under altogether, others received injections of wealth. Some squires exploited mineral resources on their land, as did the Mansels in Glamorgan and the Mostyns in Flintshire. A few made money elsewhere, from the law or trade; several members of the Jeffreys family of mid-Wales were prosperous City men. Salvation was more commonly achieved by marriages to heiresses – the vast complex of Wynnstay estates in north Wales being the most spectacular product of such expedient betrothals. By 1700 there was a clear divide between the hundreds of squires who now aspired only to be magistrates, and the small number of leading families, already no more than forty or fifty altogether, who controlled and contested the parliamentary representation.

Patchy information, derived from both unreliable contemporary estimates and scholarly modern research, suggests that an income of several thousand pounds was already essential to support sustained parliamentary pretensions. Tredegar was thought to be worth £7,000 a year in 1700.[14] The pre-eminent Margam estate in Glamorgan was deemed to have an income of £10,000 in 1706, but a modern estimate is of £5,000 in

[14] Luttrell, *State Affairs*, IV, 719.

1740.[15] The Golden Grove income in Carmarthenshire rose from £3,200 in 1737 to nearly £8,000 by 1790. Stackpole Court, with £2,800 in 1725, had, at over £15,000, the largest estate income in south-west Wales by 1793. Its Pembrokeshire rivals of Orielton and Picton Castle then had incomes of £9,300 and £5,600 respectively. In Cardiganshire Gogerddan was deemed to be worth £3,000 in 1745. Crosswood (Trawscoed) from £2,000 in 1691 dipped to barely £1,000 in 1741 through mismanagement, but rose to £4,300 by 1798.[16] In North Wales the rent-roll of the Wynnstay estates was estimated at £15,000 in mid-century.[17] Robert Myddelton, who was in a position to know, put the income of his Chirk Castle estate at £6,700 in about 1718, but a contemporary estimate at his death in 1733 stated it to be 'near £12,000'.[18] The other great Wynnstay rival, Powis Castle in Montgomeryshire, was calculated to be worth £14,000 a year in 1779.[19]

Electoral influence appertained to such estates, not to individuals or families. The demographic lottery, which was such a marked phenomenon among the Welsh gentry at this time, with about one-third failing in the male line in each generation, did not therefore have the political impact that might be supposed.[20] If a major estate passed intact to a resident owner, whether a distant cousin or a son-in-law, the political interest would survive, and quite often the process of political inheritance was completed by the adoption by the new owner of the old family name. Margam remained the leading interest in Glamorgan long after the Mansel male line ended in 1750.

There was never an exact correlation between landed wealth and political influence. Personal popularity, vigorous campaigning, and tactical alliances were factors that could turn the balance of power in a county. Scope for successful challenges existed, especially if the leading family suffered a minority, or found the weight of government influence pitted against it. Increased competition for parliamentary seats in the half-century or so from 1688 created a situation where dominant interests became established in virtually all the Welsh constituencies. The great electoral contests of mid-century, Denbighshire in 1741, Monmouthshire in 1771, and Montgomeryshire in 1774, arose from attempts to overthrow established interests. The overall trend was a steady fall in the number of contests until very few polls took place in Wales at each general election,

---

[15] Luttrell, *State Affairs*, V, 110; Jenkins, *Making of a Ruling Class*, p. 68.
[16] Howell, *Patriarchs and Parasites*, pp. 12, 231–2.
[17] Ramage, *Portraits of an Island County*, p. 271.
[18] Chirk Castle MSS E.388; *Gent. Mag.*, III (1733), 214.
[19] NLW General MSS 9071E.
[20] The findings of Jenkins, *Making of a Ruling Class*, pp. 38–44, have been confirmed by Howell, *Patriarchs and Parasites*, pp. 16–18, 212–14, and Humphreys, *Crisis of Community*, pp. 99–101.

and the number of families there with credible parliamentary ambitions had fallen to about twenty at the time of the French Revolution.

It is time to ask a different question: why did these prosperous landowners choose to forsake a comfortable lifestyle at home and become MPs? Most of them were among Sir Lewis Namier's 'predestined Parliament men'. In many cases, it was expected of them, and the motive was a sense of family duty rather than political ambition. John Vaughan of Golden Grove caused much local astonishment when in 1784 he violated this implicit code of conduct and voluntarily gave up his Carmarthenshire seat, thereby plunging his family interest into terminal decline.[21] Membership of the House of Commons symbolized the pre-eminence of the family interest. To this motive of prestige was added that of patronage, essential if the MP's family was to maintain its local importance. In Wales the absence of a resident aristocracy meant that the MPs themselves often claimed the shire posts of lord lieutenant and custos rotulorum. Until 1760 the lieutenancy of most north Wales counties was held by non-resident English noblemen; but from then on, as in South Wales throughout the period, a lord lieutenant was appointed from and for each county. The lord lieutenant was the formal representative of the sovereign, and also had command when necessary of the county militia. The office was often held together with that of custos, a post usually denoting chairmanship of the county bench of magistrates, and involving consultation with the Lord Chancellor when new commissions of the peace were periodically issued, an opportunity to reward friends and vex enemies. MPs also claimed the leading voice in government patronage in their area, such as church livings and customs posts. Unless an MP obtained such favours for his friends and supporters his reputation would suffer and his influence decline. MPs likewise forwarded to ministers requests for army commissions, posts in the central government service, and so on. Opposition MPs were at an obvious disadvantage in this respect, and could not aspire to posts themselves; but even avowedly 'independent' MPs were expected to play the patronage game. Hence this stricture by Sir Charles Hanbury Williams in 1756 on his brother Capel Hanbury. 'He has been fifteen years an independent member of Parliament without having done the least good to him or any one friend in all that time.'[22]

There was a specifically Welsh dimension to the patronage system. A small group of posts came under the old structure of the Principality of

[21] Cwmgwili MSS 174.
[22] Hanbury Williams, *Works*, III, 102.

Wales, mostly appertaining to the revenue, and some were held by Welsh MPs. In 1780 Edmund Burke therefore sought to abolish the whole structure as part of his attack on government patronage.[23] His measure also sought to reduce the patronage potential of the distinctive judicial system in Wales, the Court of Great Sessions, which comprised four legal circuits, that altogether met twice a year in each Welsh county. Each circuit had a cluster of posts, an attorney-general, a chamberlain and chancellor, a prothonotary and clerk of the Crown, and two judgeships. These Welsh judgeships were much valued, for the holders, unlike English judges, could sit in Parliament and practise at the English Bar. Only three Welsh MPs held such judgeships during this period, but another dozen altogether at some time held posts in the Welsh legal system, as also did some of their friends and relatives.[24]

This variety of motives impelled the foremost squires of Wales to go to Westminster. Personal ambition and political zeal also played their part, albeit only for a minority. Few Welsh MPs evinced any inclination or ability to play an active role in Parliament or government. The great majority of them never spoke at all in debate, and those who made any sort of mark in national politics were very few indeed. A handful were ministerial politicians of the second rank: Thomas Mansel in Queen Anne's reign; John Campbell in the earlier Hanoverian period; George Rice and the first Earl of Lisburne under George III; and a few others also briefly held junior posts in various ministries. But no Welsh MP sat in the cabinet between 1711, when Robert Harley quit his Radnor seat for the Lords, and 1822, when Charles Watkin Williams Wynn attained that status. This undistin-guished political record affords a sharp contrast to the prominence of Welshmen in the seventeenth century. In part it can be attributed to the 'country' tradition of politics so prevalent among the Welsh gentry. The two most prominent Welsh MPs in the half-century after the Hanoverian Succession in 1714 both made their name in the parliamentary opposition, Sir Watkin Williams Wynn and Sir John Philipps. And the Welsh MP who spoke most often in the first half of George III's reign was an independent member, Sir Herbert Mackworth.

What of the political context created by the new party divide of Whig and Tory in the later seventeenth century? Clearly it provided an extra dimension to local rivalries that in many instances had long preceded it. Electoral alignments were often described in party terms, especially, though, it should be noted, by 'Whig' candidates appealing for govern-ment help to that busy electoral manager the Duke of Newcastle in the

[23] Almon, *Parl. Reg.*, XVII, 406–7, 756; Debrett, *Parl. Reg.*, I, 499–503.
[24] Williams, *Welsh Judges*, pp. 15–23, and passim.

mid-eighteenth century. Electoral alliances often spanned county boundaries, as did many great estates. But family links, personal friendships, or simple tactical advantages overrode party labels. Even when party terminology was much in vogue, as in the reign of Queen Anne (1702–14) or during the ministry of Sir Robert Walpole (1721–42), local Whigs and Tories did not scruple to make electoral alliances that cut across party lines.

In Wales professed Whigs were thin on the ground until after the onset of Whig supremacy in 1714. Examination of the Welsh political scene serves to show why that was so. Wales lacked precisely those political ingredients that by traditional analysis constituted the basis of Whiggery – aristocracy, commerce and religious dissent. In Wales Whiggism was very much a minority viewpoint, dependent for parliamentary representation before 1714 essentially on the three great family interests of Tredegar in Monmouthshire, Orielton in Pembrokeshire, and Golden Grove in Carmarthenshire. Elsewhere in Wales Whigs faced an uphill fight, and even in the Hanoverian era after 1714 it took three general elections with government support before in 1727 acknowledged Whigs secured a majority of the Welsh seats. The squirearchy, so dominant in Wales, was, after all, the traditional backbone of the old Tory party. The main Welsh political legacy from the seventeenth century was loyalty to the Crown, manifested at one level in parliamentary Toryism and at another in the long persistence of Jacobite sentiment. That other key element of Toryism, championship of the established Church of England, was an attitude that came naturally to Welsh squires. Memory of the Interregnum made Dissent unpopular with this Welsh ruling class, and its seeming reappearance in the guise of Methodism met with widespread persecution. Religious toleration was not a live issue in Welsh politics until the late eighteenth century, when in the 1780s Carmarthen MP John George Philipps proved a Welsh champion of that cause.[25] The public voice of Welsh Whigs centred on support of the Glorious Revolution and loyalty to the House of Hanover.

No longer did Welsh MPs constitute a lobby at Westminster. There were, indeed, no specific Welsh interests to pursue there: the Irish Sea, for example, was now regarded as safe, despite occasional Jacobite plans to land in Wales and the Fishguard fiasco of 1797. More significant was the changing attitude of the Welsh MPs. Increasingly anglicized, often with English wives, necessarily resident in London for much of each year, involved in the politics of Britain, seldom were they moved by sentiment or self-interest to champion the cause of Wales. An early storm of Welsh protest came in 1695 when William III bestowed the Denbighshire

[25] Cwmgwili MSS 226, 242a, 291.

Lordships of Denbigh, Bromfield and Yale on Hans Bentinck, Earl of Portland. The King was already unpopular for showering gifts on such Dutch favourites, but what gave particular offence was that those lordships customarily belonged to the Prince of Wales. The outcry against a 'Dutch Prince of Wales' was masterminded by Beaumaris MP Sir William Williams, a former Commons Speaker. On 31 January 1696 Denbighshire squire Thomas Yale wrote from London to a neighbour: 'That you may see what champions you and the rest of us have and that our British courage is not quite lost I have enclosed sent you Sir William Williams' discourse to the Lords of the Treasury. . . Some of the first rank in Town was pleased to compliment us with the title of an honest stout people.'[26] The next day the House of Commons unanimously voted an Address of protest to the King, who reluctantly rescinded the grant.[27]

In 1728 a specifically Welsh reaction arose from concern about the implication for other Welsh borough constituencies of a ministerial decision to disfranchise the Montgomery out-boroughs on the technical ground that they no longer contributed to the borough MP's wages. Fifteen Welsh MPs vainly opposed this, including five habitual supporters of the ministry, and so did the government's own law officers. Watkin Williams Wynn drafted a speech that reflected Welsh indignation about 'my injured country'. The decision was a breach of the Union between England and Wales, 'a Union made betwixt the Ancient Britons, the first possessors of this island, a people who never owned any allegiance to the King of England, except when overnumbered with numbers'.[28]

If there was an anti-government cutting edge to these Welsh protests, there can be no doubt concerning the self-interest behind the storm over a Treasury Warrant of 1778 instituting an inquiry into the state of Crown lands in Wales. That would reveal large-scale encroachments, and other malpractices by the squires. There resulted an outcry that the proposal was unfair and an insult to Wales, and under the cover of this proto-nationalist smokescreen Welsh landowners blocked the scheme. Protest meetings were staged in most of the Welsh counties, and every Welsh MP bar one, probably Whitshed Keene, brother-in-law to the Prime Minister Lord North, formed a delegation to the Treasury that forced a government climb-down. Subsequently Welsh MPs, anxious to preserve their own patronage enclave, also foiled attempts by Edmund Burke in 1780 and 1782 to include Wales in his plans for administrative reform.[29]

[26] *Erthig Chronicles*, I, 47.
[27] Baxter, *William III*, p. 334.
[28] Wynnstay MSS Box 85, nos. 1, 11.
[29] Thomas, 'A Welsh Political Storm: the Treasury Warrant of 1778 concerning Crown Lands in Wales', *WHR*, 18 (1997), 430–49.

Throughout the eighteenth century Welsh MPs, and their fellow squires generally, adopted an ambivalent attitude to their nationality. A certain pride in being Welsh, members of an old, brave, independent race, was manifested from time to time. Phrases like 'true Cambrians' and 'Ancient Britons' were deployed approvingly, by English flatterers and by Welshmen themselves. Welshmen in London celebrated St. David's Day and joined appropriate societies, notably the Cymmrodorion after its foundation in 1751. Yet they would also refer to themselves as English in a way Scotsmen would never have done. Being Welsh was not part of their political culture, except on the rare occasions when it proved to be a useful propaganda weapon.

Few men can ever have possessed the power in Wales exercised by the first Duke of Beaufort in the 1680s. President of the Council for Wales, and also lord-lieutenant of every county, his role was virtually that of a viceroy. At the general election of 1685 his success in controlling Wales on behalf of James II was symbolized by the return of his eldest son, the Marquess of Worcester, for four Welsh seats as well as for Gloucestershire. After the Glorious Revolution, the Duke's power shrank to his personal influence as a landed magnate. Even so, his electoral interest in south-west England and south Wales probably matched any in the kingdom. In Wales the Duke had considerable influence in both Glamorgan constituencies and some in Breconshire, but Monmouthshire, where the Duke had seats at Raglan and Troy, was the real centre of Beaufort power in Wales.

In the seventeenth century that county was dominated by three family interests – those of Raglan, the Earls of Pembroke, and the Morgans of Tredegar. But the Pembroke influence fell dormant after the death of the seventh earl in 1683 left a young heiress daughter. In 1704 she married Thomas Windsor, Viscount Windsor in the peerage of Ireland, but he soon sold most of the Monmouthshire inheritance, being content with the 'Cardiff Castle' interest in Glamorgan, and the Pembroke interest never recovered its former importance in Monmouthshire. To dispute ascendancy with the Dukes of Beaufort there remained the Morgans of Tredegar, and their long rivalry was sharpened by its initial guise as a party struggle, Tredegar succeeding the Earls of Pembroke as champion of the Whig interest.

The Duke ruled the east of the county from Raglan. Control of Monmouth Borough came to him with the nearby family estate of Troy, and he was also lord of the manor in the two out-boroughs of Newport and Usk. But the evolution of the borough constituency into a safe Beaufort seat was delayed for several decades, for the Tredegar family, headed since 1680 by Thomas Morgan, acquired influence in Newport by the large-scale purchase of property there.[30] The extensive estates of Tredegar and Machen gave the Morgans supremacy in the west of the county, and the family also held valuable estates elsewhere. Thomas Morgan's father had married the heiress of the Dderw estate in Breconshire, with an important interest there in both county and borough. And his uncle John Morgan, who had made a fortune in London as a merchant, had recently purchased the Ruperra estate in Glamorgan.

In Monmouthshire the Morgans possessed the advantages of continuous residence and accordingly close ties with many local squires, and by the 1690s they had created a sufficiently formidable interest to ensure one of the two county seats for their family. The centre of political interest in Monmouthshire was the preservation of the Beaufort influence, with the Duke preferring concession and concord to conflict. His eldest son shared the county representation with Thomas Morgan until 1695, when he was succeeded by Sir Charles Kemys, a Court Whig who had previously sat for the borough. At the next election, in 1698, Kemys gave way to a Court Tory, Sir John Williams. It is probable that these arrangements met with the approval of both Raglan and Tredegar, but more doubtful whether the borough elections of two Whigs, John Arnold in 1695 and Henry Probert in 1698, were in accordance with Beaufort wishes.[31] In 1700 the deaths occurred of both Thomas Morgan, who was succeeded in estate and seat by his brother John, and the Duke, whose heir was an under-age grandson. During this minority the electoral interest of Raglan reached its nadir, for the borough seat was taken in January 1701 by John Morgan of Ruperra, known as 'the merchant' to distinguish him from his namesake nephew. But battle between Raglan and Tredegar had not yet been joined.

Glamorgan at the end of the seventeenth century seemed to have fallen under the domination of the house of Mansel, seated at Margam with a junior branch at Briton Ferry. The Mansel family, long foremost in that county, had monopolized the shire seat since 1679 and the borough representation from 1689. The Mansel estates gave direct control of about one-sixth of the county electorate of 1300, and the Margam branch also ruled the parliamentary borough of Kenfig. But the superficial impression of Mansel hegemony is misleading. The political structure of Glamorgan was more complex than that of any other Welsh shire. The borough constituency of Cardiff included no less than seven out-boroughs, as well as the county town. Many squires of wealth and ambition lived in

---

[30] Havill, 'The Parliamentary Representation of Monmouthshire and the Monmouth Boroughs', MA Wales, 1949, pp. 40–4.
[31] Jenkins, 'Party Conflict and Political Stability in Monmouthshire 1680–1740', *Historical Journal*, 29 (1986), 565–6.

Glamorgan: twenty-eight became MPs between 1700 and 1750, fifteen of them for constituencies outside Glamorgan. The peerage interests of Raglan and Cardiff Castle each had considerable influence in both constituencies. The Raglan estates ensured for the Dukes of Beaufort a county interest of over a hundred votes, and control of the boroughs of Swansea and Loughor. The Cardiff Castle interest acquired by Lord Windsor was potentially the most significant in the borough constituency. It gave control of Cardiff, Cowbridge and Llantrisant, and only in these boroughs, and in Kenfig, was the mass creation of burgess voters possible; but not until the end of the eighteenth century was that advantage to be exploited. Influential among the local gentry was Sir Humphrey Mackworth, who in 1686 had married the heiress of the Gnoll estate. Mackworth developed coal mines and copper-smelting at Neath, and had mining ventures in Cardiganshire. Although he represented that county in Parliament, and also sat for Totnes in Devonshire, Mackworth made no bid for a Glamorgan seat. But by the early years of the eighteenth century he had so strengthened the Gnoll influence in Neath and Aberavon as to establish a fourth important interest in the borough constituency.

Despite this multiplicity of interests, astute political management had enabled the Mansels to enjoy an unchallenged hold on both county and borough seats since the Glorious Revolution. The head of the family, Sir Edward Mansel of Margam, had now retired from Parliament. His son, Thomas, already the leading political figure in Glamorgan, sat for the borough from 1689 to 1698, when he made way for his brother-in-law Sir Edward Stradling of St Donats. The county was held by old Bussy Mansel of Briton Ferry, who had fought for Parliament in the Civil War, from 1689 until his death ten years later. The vacancy was filled by Thomas Mansel, who gave up the seat, however, in January 1701 to Bussy's grandson and heir, also Thomas. A further reshuffle occurred at the election of December 1701, when Thomas Mansel took the county seat again, and his namesake of Briton Ferry moved to the borough, displacing the indignant Stradling. Mansel arrogance was soon to reap a harvest of resentment.[32]

In contrast to prosperous Glamorgan, the two inland counties of south-east Wales, Breconshire and Radnorshire, contained few resident families of wealth and importance, and were open to the manipulation of outsiders. Throughout the seventeenth century the Harley family of Brampton Bryan in neighbouring Herefordshire had been extending its influence in Radnorshire, and Sir Edward Harley had been MP for Radnor Boroughs from 1661 to 1679. One local family that raised itself to political importance by making money in London was that of Jeffreys, headed by the brothers

---

[32] *Glamorgan County History*, IV, 394–9; Jenkins, *Making of a Ruling Class*, passim.

Jeffrey and John. Tory in politics, both were prosperous tobacco merchants. Jeffrey, knighted in 1699 when he was rumoured to be worth £300,000, in about 1688 purchased from a less affluent relative the chief family estate of the Priory, Brecon, which gave him a strong interest in that borough. John in 1701 bought Pencoed in Breconshire and Caerwent in Monmouthshire.[33] The most active politician in the area was Sir Rowland Gwynne, a prominent Whig in the House of Commons when he could secure election there. He had sat for Radnorshire in the three Exclusion Parliaments of 1679 to 1681 and again in the Convention Parliament of 1689. Sir Rowland owned the estates of Llanelwedd in Radnorshire and Tymawr in Breconshire, and other branches of the Gwynne family held Garth in Breconshire and Glanbran in Carmarthenshire. The Gwynne family suffered from the electoral disadvantage that their scattered estates gave them no dominant interest in any one constituency, and they never became part of the ruling oligarchy in Wales. But in 1688 prospects looked bright for Sir Rowland, who obtained for himself the Crown appointment of Steward of the royal manor of Cantref Maelienydd. This lordship extended over a large part of Radnorshire, and contained all of the out-boroughs bar one; in each the Steward had authority to admit burgesses. The other out-borough of Cefnllys was disregarded as being of no importance, since custom confined the franchise there to the few residents, but another centre of power was New Radnor. Although now supplanted by Presteigne as county town, this borough was controlled by a co-optive corporation and its bailiff was returning officer.

Sir Rowland Gwynne would seem to have made some form of rotation agreement with Richard Williams of Caebalfa, borough MP in 1689 and twice before county member. For in 1690 Williams took the county, and Gwynne stood for the borough. He was opposed by Sir Edward Harley's son Robert. Gwynne was returned with a majority of 251 to 173, but he owed this to votes from Presteigne and Painscastle. The claims of these boroughs were disallowed on petition to the House of Commons, which awarded the seat to Harley.[34] The next year Harley consolidated his position in the constituency by contriving to secure the transfer to himself of the Stewardship of Cantref Maelienydd, and his tenure of the seat was never challenged in the twenty years he sat thereafter in the Commons. Robert Harley, the supreme political manager of the time, used the same skills to establish his family's control of both Radnorshire seats as he did to create his 'New Country Party' in the House of Commons. His tact and political dexterity can be discerned from his correspondence with

[33] Luttrell, *State Affairs*, IV, 530–1, 574; V, 81, 343; VI, 494.
[34] *CJ*, X, 355, 426, 469.

Radnorshire squires.[35] Harley even conciliated the fiery Thomas Lewis of Harpton, who attacked him with a sword at New Radnor in 1693. The incident probably stemmed from Harley opposition to the attempt by Lewis to gain the county seat at a 1692 by-election on the death of Richard Williams.[36] The vacancy was filled by wealthy John Jeffreys, until Robert Harley replaced him with his cousin Thomas Harley of Kinsham in 1698. Both Harleys retained their seats without opposition at the two general elections of 1701.[37]

Even before his 1690 defeat in Radnor Boroughs, Sir Rowland Gwynne had turned his attention to Breconshire. Here four families were disputing control of the parliamentary representation, the Morgans of Tredegar, through their Dderw estate, and three resident in the county, Williams of Gwernyfed, Jones of Buckland, and Jeffreys of the Priory. The MP elected in 1685 and 1689 was Edward Jones of Buckland, a staunch supporter of the now exiled James II. Gwynne therefore decided to stand for Breconshire as well as Radnor Boroughs in 1690, explaining his motive to fellow-Whig Thomas Morgan of Tredegar:

> You know very well how Mr. Edward Jones voted all the last Parliament, and I do therefore intend to offer my services for Radnorshire . . . It is of the last consequence that we get good men chosen for this Parliament, otherwise the nation will be in great danger of ruin.[38]

Gwynne was returned for Breconshire without a contest, but at the next election in 1695 Edward Jones, with the assistance of Jeffrey Jeffreys, defeated him by 812 votes to 717 after a six-day poll. Sir Rowland petitioned in vain, but subsequently found a seat in Beeralston; and so, when Jones died in 1696, the vacancy was filled by Sir Edward Williams of Gwernyfed, who defeated Marmaduke Gwynne of Garth in a 1697 by-election. Sir Rowland avenged these family setbacks by recovering the seat in 1698 and retaining it until the end of William III's reign in 1702.

The borough constituency comprised only the county town of Brecon, controlled by a co-optive corporation. Already borough elections had become a duel between the Morgan and Jeffreys families. Thomas Morgan defeated Jeffrey Jeffreys in 1689, but when he moved to Monmouthshire in 1690 his younger brother Charles lost to Jeffreys, who retained the seat until 1698. Thomas Morgan, although assured of being returned for

[35] BL Add. MSS 70247, passim.
[36] Howse, 'The Harley v Lewis Affray at Radnor in 1693', *Radnorshire Historical Society Transactions*, 26 (1956), 50–3.
[37] BL Add. MSS 70247, T. Lewis to R. Harley, 1 Aug. 1698; *HMC Portland*, IV, 12, 28.
[38] Penrice and Margam MSS L1385.

Monmouthshire, then stood for Brecon also, defeating Jeffreys by ninety-six votes to sixty-four; about forty other burgesses did not vote. Morgan died before a petition by Jeffreys was considered in Parliament, and since his brother and successor John paid little attention to Breconshire the Tredegar interest there suffered a temporary eclipse. Sir Jeffrey Jeffreys regained the borough seat in 1701 and held it until his death in 1709. The future Morgan hegemony in both Breconshire constituencies achieved by mid-century would not have been anticipated by an observer in 1700.[39]

The political structure of south-west Wales differed from that of south-east Wales, and also that of north Wales, because there were clear-cut electoral interests based on party alignments in all three counties of Cardiganshire, Carmarthenshire and Pembrokeshire. But the superficial appearance of an embryonic party system at the local level is deceptive. Tory squires assisted Whig candidates, for personal or tactical reasons, and Whigs sometimes backed Tories. Nevertheless the existence in each county of powerful Whig families does impart more depth to the electoral scene than would a mere struggle for power among local squires.

In Cardiganshire the most influential family ever since Tudor times had been the Pryses of Gogerddan, now not merely Tory but Jacobite in sympathy, whose estates had long given them pre-eminence in the shire, although a contest of 1710 was to show that Gogerddan could not quite defeat all the other leading squires combined together! By the end of the seventeenth century the Pryses had gained effective control of the borough constituency. Here they had long controlled the nearby out-borough of Aberystwyth, and soon after the death in 1693 of Hector Phillips, the Whig borough MP since 1679, they acquired from his family the Cardigan Priory estate, which gave control of the co-optive council of the county town. There were three other out-boroughs, but no putative patron ever sought to exploit Adpar, and it faded into insignificance. Tregaron was a manorial borough on the Nanteos estate, acquired through marriage in about 1700 by William Powell. Powell was a Tory and a natural ally of Gogerddan, for his father was the Sir Thomas Powell whom James II had knighted, appointed to the Council of Wales, and made a Judge of King's Bench, and who had resigned his judgeship in disapproval of the Glorious Revolution.[40] The other out-borough of Lampeter passed to a local Whig, Walter Lloyd of Voelallt, in about 1713 on his marriage to the heiress of the Peterwell estate. Subsequent owners of Nanteos and Peterwell were to exploit their control of Tregaron and Lampeter, but before 1714 the borough seat was a makeweight in arrangements or disputes over the county representation.[41]

[39] Thomas, 'Parliamentary Elections in Brecknockshire', *Brycheiniog*, 6 (1960), 99–103.
[40] Williams, *Welsh Judges*, pp. 109–10.
[41] Thomas, 'Eighteenth-Century Elections in the Cardigan Boroughs Constituency',

The Whig interest in Cardiganshire was headed by John Vaughan of Crosswood, whose grandfather Sir John Vaughan and father Edward had represented the county from 1661 until the latter's death in 1683. Sir John had raised an old Cardiganshire family to importance, being appointed Chief Justice of the Court of Common Pleas in 1668 and bequeathing an estate of £1,200 a year.[42] In 1689 John Vaughan sought to re-assert this new family claim to the shire seat by challenging the sitting member John Lewis of Coed Mawr, now resident in Berkshire. Although a Whig at Westminster, Lewis was sponsored by Sir Carbery Pryse of Gogerddan, but defeated Vaughan only by 385 votes to 363. This narrow margin of victory may explain why Pryse himself stood in 1690 against Vaughan. The poll began in Aberystwyth, but was adjourned on the second day to Cardigan, nearly forty miles away. Vaughan refused to accept this change of venue, and petitioned after Pryse was returned with a majority of 185 to 91. Only by a majority of one did the House of Commons uphold his return. When Pryse died in 1694 without a direct heir, he was succeeded by an uncle, Edward Pryse. Vaughan seized the chance to take the seat at the by-election and retained it in 1695, the year he received an Irish peerage as Viscount Lisburne.

At this point the political scene in Cardiganshire was complicated by the advent of Sir Humphrey Mackworth, who in 1698 paid over £16,000 to Edward Pryse for the Gogerddan share in what was now reconstructed as the Company of Mine Adventurers formed to exploit lead and silver on Gogerddan land. The Mackworth money revived Gogerddan's political power, and the general election of 1698 saw Lord Lisburne displaced without a contest by John Lewis. But Mackworth soon fancied his own chances of the county seat and, though a Tory, cut across party alignments, seeking the favour of both Lord Lisburne and William Powell by the offer of cheap coal from his mines in Glamorgan. His candidature was pushed by the veteran Tory politician, the Duke of Leeds, better known as the Earl of Danby, who was chairman of the Company of Mine Adventurers. He urged support of Mackworth on both Powell and young Lewis Pryse, who had succeeded his father Edward in the Gogerddan estate in 1699 at the age of sixteen. Powell at first held out little hope in view of John Lewis's extensive local connections, but in the end Lewis moved to the borough seat to allow Mackworth the county at the general election of January 1701. Sir Humphrey was to be a disruptive influence in Cardiganshire politics for over a decade.[43]

Ceredigion, 5 (1964–7), 402–4.

[42] J. G. Williams, 'Sir John Vaughan of Trawscoed, 1603–74', *NLWJ*, 8 (1953–54), 33–48, 121–46, 224–41.

[43] Thomas, 'County Elections in Eighteenth-Century Cardiganshire', *Ceredigion*, 11 (1991), 239–42. For Mackworth see Ransome, 'The Parliamentary Career of Sir Humphrey Mackworth', *Birmingham Historical Journal*, 1 (1948), 232–54.

Carmarthenshire was a Whig stronghold in a predominantly Tory Wales. Political control lay with the Vaughan family, headed by the Earls of Carbery at their seat of Golden Grove, with several cadet branches. From 1661 to 1689 Vaughans had sat for both the shire and the county borough of Carmarthen. Richard Vaughan of Derwydd was unopposed as borough member from 1685 until his death in 1724. But by 1689 there was no Vaughan candidate for the shire, since the third Earl of Carbery, who had succeeded in 1687, lacked a male heir. The Golden Grove interest ensured the unopposed tenure of the county seat by a local Whig squire Sir Rice Rudd of Aberglasney, from 1689 until he died in July 1701, but that vacancy gave rise to a contest at the general election of December 1701. A Tory squire, Sir Thomas Powell of Broadway, came forward to oppose the Whig sponsored by Golden Grove, but the appearance of a straight party fight is misleading. The Whig candidate was Griffith Rice of Newton: ancestors of his had sat for both county and borough, and the family boasted descent from the princely house of Dynefor. Rice's supporters included not only such men as Sackville Gwynne of Glanbran, who was to fight Breconshire in 1705, but also undoubted Tories like Sir Edward Mansel of Stradey Park and William Brigstocke of Kidwelly. On the other side, Powell's chief ally was his Whig cousin Nicholas Williams of Edwinsford, and he also had the backing of such influential Tories as Thomas Cornwallis of Abermarlais, Rawleigh Mansel of Abercyfor, and John Laugharne of St Bride's in Pembrokeshire. Rice won at a poll, and was not to be challenged again until 1710.[44]

Pembrokeshire was also dominated by a Whig family, the Owens of Orielton, one so jubilant at the Glorious Revolution that they henceforth adopted orange as their political colour. Orielton had held the county seat from the Restoration of 1660 until the Parliament of 1681, and Sir Hugh Owen resumed it in 1689, giving way in 1695 to his son and heir Arthur, who inherited the baronetcy and estate in 1699. Yet Owen power depended on a coalition of allies, foremost among whom was Sir John Philipps of Picton Castle, a firm Whig, but a man increasingly preoccupied with religious and philanthropic movements. The Orielton interest at the turn of the century also included Sir Arthur's uncle John Barlow of Lawrenny, and two prominent Tory squires, John Meyrick of Bush and John Laugharne of St Bride's.[45] These men were moderate Tories, not disposed to join the Jacobite-tinted Tory interest in the county headed by the brothers Sir George Barlow of Slebech and John Barlow of Colby. Laugharne was to be an active partisan of Owen in 1701, the same year he supported Tory Sir

---

[44] Mackworth MSS 910–16. Thomas, 'County Elections in Eighteenth-Century Carmarthenshire', *Carm. Antiquary*, 4 (1962), 32–3.
[45] NLW General MSS 12172.

Thomas Powell in Carmarthenshire. In the Pembroke Boroughs constituency, partisans of Orielton ruled the two chartered boroughs of Pembroke and Tenby and Owens had held the seat from 1676 to 1695, when Sir John Philipps took over. A third borough of Wiston, a mere village, represented a latent threat to Orielton, for control lay with Lewis Wogan of Wiston, a member of the Barlow faction. The divide in Pembrokeshire politics, at least as Orielton depicted it, was between those who favoured the Revolution Settlement and a Jacobite party, and there was much to support that view in the behaviour of malcontents in the 1690s.[46]

A third Pembrokeshire constituency was the county borough of Haverfordwest. Here an electorate of 400 resident voters was difficult for any would-be patron to control, but since 1685 the seat had been held by Sir William Wogan of Llanstinan. His decision to give up this seat and contest the county on the Barlow interest in January 1701 was just one more puzzling twist in a career that baffled the political analysts of the time. Orielton propaganda depicting Sir Arthur Owen's opponents as Jacobites was reinforced by physical violence at the poll, when Wogan supporters were evidently prevented from voting. The official result, a majority for Owen of 426 votes to 5, out of a county electorate of 1,000 freeholders, gave credence to the charge of foul play in the petition vainly submitted to Parliament on Wogan's behalf.[47] Orielton faced no further challenge in the county until 1710.

North Wales provided a marked contrast to south Wales. Here the few local Whigs were nowhere yet able to challenge for any seat with any prospect of success. During the later seventeenth century the parliamentary representation was often genuinely settled in an old-fashioned manner, by general agreement of the gentry, and contests were rare. Electoral arrangements in the six counties were still sometimes being made without regard to the precise pecking order of family interests within a particular constituency. But by the reign of William III this political ethos was changing. The great county families were achieving monopolistic representation of constituencies.

Foremost among them were the Bulkeleys of Baron Hill, probably the most powerful family in Wales at the turn of the century, with the leading voice in four constituencies. Dominant in their own island county of Anglesey, they also possessed the foremost interest in nearby Caernarfonshire. Tradition and the largest estate in Anglesey had long given the Bulkeleys a firm hold on the shire seat, and the third Viscount Bulkeley had

---

[46] Jones 'Disaffection and Dissent in Pembrokeshire', *T.H.S. Cymm.* (1946–7), pp. 216–20.
[47] NLW General MSS 12172; *CJ*, XIII, 22.

been the MP since 1690. The borough constituency consisted only of Beaumaris, a Bulkeley pocket borough through control of the corporation electorate of twenty-four. But in 1689 confusion caused by James II's revocation of the borough charter led to common burgesses voting in the parliamentary election. The Bulkeley candidate still won, and in 1698 an alternative weapon was deployed by enemies of Baron Hill – revival of the alleged rights of the former county town of Newborough. Owen Hughes, its mayor, took about thirty Newborough burgesses to vote for him at Beaumaris. Lord Bulkeley, presumably to avoid a precedent, conceded the seat to Hughes without a contest. Baron Hill control of the constituency was resumed in 1701, and the MP at the end of William III's reign was Lord Bulkeley's younger brother Robert.[48]

In Caernarfonshire the management of the Baron Hill interest had been entrusted since 1660 to Lord Bulkeley's uncle Thomas Bulkeley, who had married a local heiress. Here Bulkeley power depended on an understanding with four influential families. The Wynns of Gwydir and the Griffiths of Cefnamwlch both lived in the county. The Mostyns of Flintshire owned the Gloddaeth estate in the east, while Clenennau in the south was held by the Owen family of Brogyntyn in Shropshire. Between them these five families had monopolized both Caernarfonshire seats, county and borough, since 1661, but by the reign of William III there had occurred a shortage of candidates from among them. The direct male line of the Gwydir family ended with the death of Sir Richard Wynn in 1674, and the Gwydir interest, hitherto so important in Caernarfonshire politics, faded into insignificance when Sir Richard's heiress married the non-resident first Duke of Ancaster in 1678. The concern of the Mostyn family was now with Flintshire, and even Cheshire, not Caernarfonshire. When John Griffith of Cefnamwlch died in 1687 his heir William was only a year old. Sir Robert Owen of Brogyntyn, borough MP from 1689, died in 1697, leaving an eight-year-old son William. A second vacancy arose that year through the death, without an heir, of the county MP Sir William Williams of Vaynol, another uncle of Lord Bulkeley. Thomas Bulkeley himself became county MP again, as he had been four times already, and the borough went to an experienced MP seeking another seat, Sir John Wynn, scion of a junior branch of the Gwydir family and, as owner of the Watstay estate in Denbighshire and that of Rhiwgoch in Merioneth, one of the great landowners of north Wales.

The ruling oligarchy of Caernarfonshire was evidently determined to maintain a monopolistic hold on the parliamentary representation, and Thomas Bulkeley contrived to manage the borough constituency as well as

[48] NLW General MSS 1548, f. 33; Thomas, 'Anglesey Politics, 1689–1727', *TAAS* (1962), pp. 35–7.

the county. Here there existed potential for instability, five boroughs with the right to create non-resident voters. In the county town of Caernarfon the mayoralty was attached to the constableship of the castle, a Crown appointment; but Caernarfon in fact had no mayor, for the Earl of Radnor, constable since 1692, had not taken out a patent. The borough was controlled in practice by Thomas Bulkeley himself, and had only about forty burgesses.[49] The out-borough of Conway had no mayor and apparently no patron, but in the three other out-boroughs hereditary mayoralties gave control to different families. The owners of Brogyntyn ruled Cricieth, while Thomas Wynn of Bodfean and his relative Richard Vaughan of Corsygedol, MP for Merioneth from 1701, were respectively patrons of Nefyn and Pwllheli. Thomas Wynn was already by 1700 a young man of importance in Caernarfonshire through his marriage to the heiress of the Glynllifon estate; but as yet he made no attempt to exploit his position by the creation of burgesses: Nefyn at this time had a mere twenty-four and Pwllheli thirty-six.[50] Within the next decade he was to do so, but for the moment he was content to bide his time and bow to the arrangements made by old Thomas Bulkeley.

Merionethshire, the only Welsh county without a borough constituency, was in the eighteenth century to provide a classic example of the hegemony of a single family, the Vaughans of Corsygedol. During the seventeenth century the leading interest was that of the Wynns of Rhiwgoch, but resentment against this situation is indicated by an electoral agreement made by a dozen leading squires on the death in 1671 of Henry Wynn, MP since 1661. This provided for lots to be drawn to fill the vacancy. Wynn's heir John had not been present. He met signatories of the agreement early in 1673, and although one of them, William Price of Rhiwlas, was returned at the long-delayed by-election that year, Wynn, now Sir John, took the seat at the next general election in 1679 and apart from the brief Parliament of 1681 remained MP until 1695. Then he reluctantly made way for Hugh Nanney of Nannau, another of the 1671 signatories, and son-in-law of William Vaughan of Corsygedol. Nanney died in 1701 without a male heir, and the parliamentary seat and Nannau interest passed to his brother-in-law Richard Vaughan, whose son William consolidated the Corsygedol interest by marrying Nanney's eldest daughter.[51]

Denbighshire had long been dominated by two powerful families, the Myddeltons of Chirk Castle and the Salusburies of Lleweni. Sir Richard

---

[49] Llanfair and Brynodol MSS 96.
[50] Glynllifon MSS 1988.
[51] *Cal. Wynn Papers*, no. 2663; *Arch. Camb.* (1919), 220. Thomas, 'The Parliamentary History of Merioneth during the Eighteenth Century', *Journal of the Merioneth Historical and Record Society*, 3 (1958), 128–9.

Myddelton was in unchallenged possession of the county seat from 1685, for in the previous year the direct Lleweni male line ended with the death of Sir John Salusbury, whose estate passed to his brother-in-law Sir Robert Cotton of Combermere. Head of a Whig family in Cheshire, which he represented in Parliament from 1679 to 1702, Cotton evinced no ambition to sit for Denbighshire, where political attention in the last years of the seventeenth century focused on the borough constituency. This became the first to experience the competitive mass creation of the non-resident voters in different boroughs. The two out-boroughs of Holt and Ruthin were under the thumb of rival families, which were also disputing control of the shire town. The Cotton family inherited control of Holt with the Lleweni estate, while Ruthin was a manorial borough in the lordship of that name owned by the Myddeltons. In Denbigh itself the Myddelton family sought to maintain a precarious control; for while burgesses were admitted by the town council of twenty-five, vacancies on that body were filled not, as in many boroughs, by co-option but by election from the general body of burgesses, a procedure more difficult for any patron to manage.

At the general elections of 1689 and 1690 Myddelton and Cotton evidently united to secure the success of local squire Edward Brereton against William Williams, namesake son of the former Commons Speaker. Some Denbighshire squires had made their support of Myddelton in the shire conditional on his opposition to the Williams campaign in the borough constituency; while a 1690 petition on behalf of Williams complained of the creation of non-resident voters in Cotton-controlled Holt, 'a small open village', who had then polled for Brereton.[52] But from 1698 their interests clashed. Edward Brereton, the Myddelton candidate, then defeated Sir Robert Cotton's son Thomas by 523 votes to 219.[53] After this election Sir Robert Cotton enrolled 400 strangers as burgesses of Holt on 25 August, and over 400 more on 28 September, but Brereton later obtained a legal verdict against the mayor of Holt for irregularities.[54] Chirk Castle retaliated by creating 401 new burgesses at Denbigh on 5 June 1699.[55] Cotton was informed that Sir John Wynn of Watstay, Sir Richard Myddelton and Edward Brereton had then taken 'many hundreds of the meaner sort of people from their neighbourhood' to Denbigh for this purpose.[56] At the next general election, in January 1701, Brereton again defeated Thomas Cotton, who in his petition claimed a 'considerable majority' for himself, clearly based on non-resident Holt burgesses.[57] This

[52] Dodd, *Studies in Stuart Wales*, p. 229; *CJ*, X, 359, 428, 544–5, 568.
[53] Chirk Castle MSS E. 1040, 3393.
[54] *CJ*, XIII, 353–4.
[55] Chirk Castle MSS C.6.
[56] *Erthig Chronicle*, I, 59–60.
[57] *CJ*, XIII, 334, 353–4.

case was never heard by the Committee of Elections, and the Cotton family abandoned its attack in the constituency for over a decade.

The Flintshire political scene during the later seventeenth century witnessed the temporary withdrawal from parliamentary elections of the leading family in the county, as the Mostyns of Mostyn devoted their attention to rehabilitation of the family fortunes, so shattered in the Civil War period, by development of the mineral wealth and other resources of their estates. Sir Thomas Mostyn, second baronet, was the only Mostyn to sit at Westminster between 1660 and 1688, and he represented not a Flintshire constituency but Caernarfon Boroughs, in the three Exclusion Parliaments. Events were to show that the Mostyns had not sacrificed any electoral advantage, but their absence had left the way clear for the Conways of Bodrhyddan and Hanmers of Hanmer to take the lead, while such other families as the Pulestons of Emral, Whitleys of Aston Hall and Ravenscrofts of Broadlane also participated in the parliamentary representation. Just as none of these five families possessed a dominant influence in the county, so did the nature of the borough constituency render difficult effective control by any patron. The franchise was vested in five boroughs, for Rhuddlan, Overton, Caergwrle and Caerwys had all been added to Flint. Rhuddlan was a manorial borough under Bodrhyddan influence, but in none of the other three out-boroughs did any family possess such power; while in Flint, as in Caernarfon, the mayoralty was identified with the Constableship of the castle, a Crown appointment.[58] Throughout the eighteenth century the constituency was to remain the most independent of the Welsh boroughs.

The county and borough seats in Flintshire were both open to the claims of several squires, and electoral politics there in the reign of William III still followed a rotation system by amicable agreements among the local gentry. Sir John Hanmer represented the borough in the Convention Parliament of 1689, but then went off to Ireland. Sir Roger Puleston was county member from 1689 to 1695, when he moved to the borough, replacing Thomas Whitley, who had succeeded Hanmer there in 1690. That both Puleston and Whitley were Whigs at Westminster does not appear to have had an adverse effect on their electoral prospects in this Tory county. Puleston had made way for Sir John Conway, who now sat until December 1701. The death of Puleston in March 1697 led to the only contest of the decade, between Thomas Ravenscroft of Broadlane and Sir John Hanmer, seeking to regain his former seat. The bailiffs of Flint, returning officers for the constituency, protracted the poll for eight days before reluctantly

---

[58] Dodd, 'Flintshire Politics in the Seventeenth Century', *Flintshire Historical Society Journal*, 14 (1953–4), 22–46.

returning Ravenscroft as elected by 510 votes to 250.[59] He died the next year, and this, together with the death of Whitley as well as Puleston in 1697, ended the parliamentary pretensions of all three families. Flintshire politics henceforth followed the pattern already being established elsewhere in Wales, with a few influential families engrossing the seats to the exclusion of lesser squires. Only the Mostyn, Hanmer and Conway families remained to dispute the parliamentary representation. Sir Thomas Mostyn's younger son Thomas took the borough seat at the elections of 1698 and January 1701. In December 1701 the county was taken by his brother Sir Roger, who had succeeded his father as third baronet, and the borough by Sir Thomas Hanmer. A leading Tory politician in Queen Anne's reign, Hanmer had succeeded his uncle John in title and estate earlier in the year, but his chief sphere of influence lay in East Anglia, where he had married the heiress of the Lord Arlington who had been one of the celebrated Cabal ministry of Charles II. Hanmer had already sat earlier in the year for the Suffolk borough of Thetford, and on being re-elected there vacated the Flint seat in favour of Sir John Conway.

Montgomeryshire enjoyed the quietest electoral history of all the Welsh shires: when a contest did occur in 1774 legend then made it a 'virgin county'. The reason for the pacific story lay in the long-standing alliance of the two most powerful families in the county, the Herberts of Powis Castle and the Vaughans of Llwydiarth, whose combined estates amounted to well over half the shire. The traditional lead lay with Powis Castle, but the first Marquess of Powis accompanied James II into exile in 1688. His forfeited estates were recovered by the second Marquess in 1722, and the local electoral scene was not affected by this temporary hiatus. Edward Vaughan of Llwydiarth, county member since 1679, continued to represent Montgomeryshire until his death in 1718.

By contrast the Montgomery Boroughs constituency had had a stormy history since 1660, resulting from repeated attempts by the county town of Montgomery to disfranchise the three out-boroughs. In part this was a political conflict. Montgomery was controlled by the Montgomery Castle line of Herberts, headed since 1678 by the fourth Baron Herbert of Chirbury. A strong Whig, Lord Herbert had little in common with his Tory relatives of Powis Castle, in whose estate lay the boroughs of Welshpool and Llanfyllin, nor with his Tory neighbour of Llwydiarth, who controlled the third out-borough of Llanidloes. After a Commons resolution of 1685 confirmed the rights of the out-boroughs Lord Herbert no longer disputed the borough elections, and neither, after his death in 1691, did his Whig

---

[59] Taylor, 'Flint Borough Election, 1697', *Flintshire Historical Society Journal*, 11 (1925), 88–90.

nephew and successor, Francis Herbert. The joint interest of Powis Castle and Llwydiarth returned Price Devereux of Vaynor from 1691 until he became the ninth Viscount Hereford in 1700. The seat was then taken, for the next three parliaments, by Edward Vaughan's brother John.[60]

From the Glorious Revolution Parliament was in annual session, no longer a body called at the whim or need of the sovereign. By 1700 the consequently increased rivalry for seats was already having its effect on the political structure of Wales, as the great squires perceived the enhanced advantages of membership of Parliament. In the counties competing interests were based on landed estates; but in the borough constituencies, although much the same families were usually involved, two key criteria were the nature of the franchise and the number of boroughs that established a right to participate. The Welsh parliamentary borough constituencies formed a distinctive part of the British electoral system.

---

[60] Thomas, 'The Montgomery Borough Constituency, 1660–1728', *Bulletin Board of Celtic Studies*, 20 (1963), 293–8.

CHAPTER 2

The Parliamentary Borough Constituencies of Wales from Restoration to Reform (1660–1832)

WALES, unlike England, should have had a uniform borough constituency system: for whereas the diversity of the English parliamentary boroughs resulted from the piecemeal bestowal of representation over several centuries, the Welsh system was created by the enfranchising legislation of Henry VIII. Statutes of 1536 and 1544 specified that borough MPs should be chosen by the burgesses of the county town of each shire and of the 'cities, boroughs and towns' that contributed to the wages of such MPs. Merionethshire was excluded from this arrangement, and the other anomaly concerned Haverfordwest, which was given its own MP when its ancient status of county borough was restored by an act of 1543. Subsequent practice in the Welsh borough constituencies in Tudor and Stuart times as to which boroughs should participate was inconsistent, even in the same constituencies, partly because of the disadvantage for out-boroughs that all elections took place in the county town. There is a veil of obscurity over what happened; in many instances it is simply not known how frequently or which contributing boroughs then took part in parliamentary elections. Often contributory boroughs were not named in returns of MPs until 1660, and by then the payment of parliamentary wages was coming to an end. Many of the ancient boroughs of Wales never participated, fear of expense being an obvious deterrent. Conflicting precedents resulted from this confused situation, ready to be exploited in an age of growing competition for parliamentary seats. There was ample scope for manœuvre and dispute in the doubts, real and alleged, that arose over the composition of Welsh borough constituencies.[1]

To this uncertainty as to which boroughs should participate in parliamentary elections there was added ambiguity as to the meaning of

[1] 27 Henry VIII, C26; 34 Henry VIII, C26; 35 Henry VIII, C11. For a fuller discussion, see Roberts, 'Parliamentary Representation of the Welsh Boroughs', *BBCS*, 4 (1927–9), 352–60.

the designation 'burgesses'. The 1544 Act enfranchising the out-boroughs used the words 'inhabitants' and 'burgesses' interchangeably in a clause that, when the payment of wages had ceased, provided a ground for some county towns to claim that out-boroughs should no longer participate in parliamentary elections.

> Forasmuch as the inhabitants of all cities and boroughs in the twelve shires within Wales and in the county of Monmouth, not finding burgesses for the Parliament themselves must bear and pay the burgesses wages within the shire-towns . . . [be it enacted that] the burgesses shall have like voice and authority to elect name and choose the burgesses of every the said shire town like and in such manner as the burgesses of the said shire towns have or use.

If it was then the apparent aim to confine the franchise to resident burgesses, the practice soon developed of interpreting the word 'burgesses' to cover all freemen, whether or not they lived in the relevant boroughs. When after 1660 the parliamentary franchise came to be seen as a desirable right rather than a potentially expensive burden, these weaknesses of the enfranchising legislation, the failure to define which boroughs and what burgesses should vote, both became frequent grounds of dispute.

Problems were compounded, and opportunities enhanced, by the right of the House of Commons to decide disputed election cases. Too often its rulings were based on political or personal partisanship rather than on the merits of a case or the historical evidence, and bias could also be effectively demonstrated simply by not considering petitions at all if favoured candidates had been returned. Decisions sometimes contradicted earlier ones for the same constituency. In 1729, however, a clause explicitly asserting that any franchise decision of the House of Commons should be irrevocable was added to an Election Act aimed at preventing corruption that had been introduced by the first Watkin Williams Wynn.[2]

By 1730 it had been established which Welsh boroughs should participate in parliamentary representation. Of the fifty boroughs which from 1660 at some time or other put forward claims to do so, nine failed to establish or maintain their rights. For over a century before the Reform Act of 1832 the number of Welsh parliamentary boroughs remained fixed at forty-one. Two did not participate on a regular basis. Adpar in Cardiganshire became defunct, ceasing to participate in mid-century. The claim of Wiston in Pembrokeshire was intermittently accepted for much of the period, but its validity was confirmed in the early nineteenth century.

[2] Porritt and Porritt, *Unreformed House of Commons*, I, 8–9.

Five Welsh boroughs by 1730 returned an MP by themselves. Haverford-west did so by virtue of its status as a county borough, and so did Carmarthen when it became one in 1604. The others were Beaumaris, Brecon and Montgomery. In the other eight borough constituencies the number of out-boroughs varied from two to seven.

That a uniform franchise had been created in the Welsh borough constituencies was formerly the assumption of historians. At one time it was believed that an inhabitant householder franchise had been established.[3] Then scrutiny of the legislation led to the opinion that there was a freeman franchise, with the right of election in duly admitted burgesses.[4] That definition did not cover the variant practices, and avoided the key question of residence. The simple fact is that a pattern of uniformity did not long prevail. In Beaumaris the franchise was restricted to the corporation by a charter of 1562. In Haverfordwest, after a ruling of 1663 was altered in 1715, there were three categories of voters: freeholders, burgesses, and inhabitant ratepayers. Residence was necessary in Brecon and established for Monmouth Boroughs in 1680. The franchise was restricted to inhabitant ratepayers in Flint Boroughs in 1728, and to resident freemen in Denbigh Boroughs in 1744. But the customary non-resident freeman franchise was confirmed in five constituencies – Radnor Boroughs in 1690, Pembroke Boroughs in 1712, Carmarthen and Montgomery in 1728, and Cardigan Boroughs in 1730: later, however, a 1764 charter established a residence qualification in Carmarthen. It also existed in the two constituencies where no decision was made, Cardiff Boroughs and Caernarfon Boroughs. Altogether the seven constituencies where non-resident freemen could vote contained twenty-seven of the forty-one surviving boroughs.

The size of the electorate in each constituency depended on the political situation within it. In those with a single borough under the control of a patron there would be few voters, well under a hundred in Brecon and Montgomery in the later eighteenth century. In multi-borough constituencies patrons who had come to an agreement about the representation also found it in their mutual interest to restrict the size of the electorate. But where boroughs were under the control of rival patrons, large-scale creations would result. Contests were decided by the total number of votes cast and not, as in Scotland, by the number of boroughs favouring each candidate, and so a single borough could out-poll all the others in the group. In both the Cardigan and Caernarfon constituencies in the later eighteenth century thousands of freemen were eligible to vote.

---

[3] Porritt and Porritt, *Unreformed House of Commons*, I, 107–8.
[4] Roberts, 'Parliamentary Representation of the Welsh Boroughs'.

Creation of voters was constrained by cost, and not merely the prospect of transporting and entertaining such legions of supporters. A 1698 Stamp Act imposed a duty of one shilling on each burgess admission, and this was raised to two shillings in 1765, four shillings in 1783, £2 in 1808, and £3 in 1815. Another constraint was the need for forward planning after the so-called Durham Act of 1763 imposed a year's delay before new burgesses could vote.

Such measures did not prevent the growth of patron control. The often elaborate constitutions of the parliamentary boroughs of Wales served only to conceal the hold of patrons. Usually they were lords of the manor containing the borough. In six some influence was bestowed by the Crown, three in the Radnorshire manor of Cantref Maelienydd; in Caernarfon and Flint, where the constable of the castle was mayor, and in Haverfordwest, where the sovereign named the lord lieutenant. One way or another, few boroughs lacked a patron by the early eighteenth century.

Which towns enjoyed the privilege of enfranchisement? Who could vote in them? How many? Who exercised political control in these boroughs? The single-borough constituencies are the simplest to elucidate. As shire town for Anglesey, Newborough had returned the island county's first borough MPs, until Beaumaris took over in 1549. A charter of 1562 restricted the franchise to a co-opting council of twenty-four, comprising the mayor, two bailiffs, and twenty-one capital burgesses. In the first council the named mayor was Sir Richard Bulkeley, a favourite of Elizabeth I, and the council included three other Bulkeleys and fourteen of their tenants. Thereafter Beaumaris was a Bulkeley pocket borough, and the only example in Wales of a corporation borough.

In the late seventeenth and early eighteenth centuries there were several challenges to this Bulkeley hold on the borough seat. The 1689 precedent of the wider franchise of all Beaumaris burgesses remained solitary, while the 1698 concession of the seat to Newborough's mayor without a poll failed to create a precedent of that borough's participation. A more sustained attempt to establish Newborough's claims began in 1708, when Henry Bertie, brother-in-law of the current Lord Bulkeley, defeated Sir Arthur Owen by sixteen votes to one of the capital burgesses, after a claim by Newborough burgesses to vote was rejected.[5] A petition was submitted, claiming that the burgesses of Newborough and the common burgesses of Beaumaris both had the right to vote. But in July 1709 the House of

---

[5] Penrhos MSS V, 25.

Commons Committee of Elections decided in favour of the Beaumaris corporation franchise, a resolution confirmed in 1710 by the House itself.[6]

Even this ruling did not end the matter. The return of Henry Bertie in 1722 was merely the preliminary to a petition from his defeated opponent William Bodfel that repeated the claims that the burgesses of Newborough and the common burgesses of Beaumaris both had a right to vote and stated that they had given him a majority. This was backed by a Newborough petition, but the Committee of Elections never reported the case.[7] A third challenge came in 1727, when the electoral arrangements made by Bodfel seem to have been designed as a test case. Watkin Williams Wynn, standing in for an under-age fifth Viscount Bulkeley, was returned after polling twelve capital burgesses. Forty-eight votes were tendered for Bodfel, twenty-four as burgesses of Beaumaris, and twenty-four as burgesses of Newborough. He could therefore claim a majority if either interpretation of the electorate was accepted by the House of Commons, and separate petitions were accordingly submitted to cover both eventualities. The House of Commons did not hear the case until 3 March 1730. The Newborough petition was then disallowed on the ground of improper signatures, and that borough's claim lapsed by default. Counsel for the Beaumaris petition contended that all householders there could vote, but he was arguing against both law and practice, no mention being made of the 1689 precedent. The House confirmed the existing corporation franchise, and thereafter it was unchallenged until 1832. It is evident that in all these attempts to change the Beaumaris franchise the opponents of the Tory Bulkeleys hoped for a partisan decision from a Whig House of Commons, and a copy of Bodfel's 1727 case survives among the papers of Prime Minister Walpole. Certainly Lord Bulkeley feared the worst in 1730. But the Beaumaris evidence was so clear-cut that even a Whig House of Commons notorious for partisan electoral decisions then accepted it without voting on the issue.[8]

For the county borough of Haverfordwest there had never been any question of out-boroughs, and the sole point at issue was the nature of the franchise. The 1543 legislation restored a sheriff, who was the returning officer, and established a mayor and co-optive town council of twenty-four, that had the right to admit burgesses. From 1554 this freedom was restricted to residents. The dispute in a double return of 1661 was whether

---

[6] Baron Hill MSS 6745; NLW General MSS 1548, f.33; *CJ*, XVI, 21, 323–4.

[7] *CJ*, XX, 25, 230, 235.

[8] Cholmondeley Houghton MSS 68, 6A; *HMC Egmont Diary*, I, 11; *CJ*, XXI, 29, 35, 48, 421, 472–3. For fuller information, see Roberts, 'The Parliamentary History of Beaumaris, 1555–1832', *TAAS* (1933), pp. 97–109; and Thomas, 'Anglesey Politics, 1689–1727', *TAAS* (1962), pp. 36–7, 41–2, 48–9, 52–3.

the franchise lay only in the burgesses or also in the inhabitants paying scot and lot, the local rates. The right of the latter also to vote was confirmed by the House of Commons in 1663.[9] But in 1715 the Committee of Elections, before considering a petition, declared that 'the right of election was agreed to be in the freeholders, burgesses, and inhabitants, paying scot and lot, and not receiving alms'. The petition had not even mentioned freeholders, but the complaints had included voting by 'foreigners' for the MP returned and who now lost his seat.[10] There were now three distinct categories of voters, all with a residence qualification. For in 1726, just after his first election for Haverfordwest, Erasmus Philipps of Picton Castle wrote a memorandum on the constituency.

> The number of good voters for a member of Parliament for Haverford-west, is reckoned to be about four hundred; those who have a right of voting are the burgesses, those who have a freehold in the town, and the scot and lot men.

He then added that 'there are about seventy out burgesses and freeholders', implying that they did not have the vote.[11] Haverfordwest was very much a constituency where local goodwill was of paramount importance. No candidate from outside Pembrokeshire was elected after 1677, and no contest took place between 1741 and 1812. Although the Philipps family had the most influence, there was no dominant interest, and the chief beneficiaries of this pacific state of affairs were the Edwardes family of Johnston, who represented the borough for seventy-three of the ninety-six years between 1722 and 1818.[12]

Another county borough was created in Wales when Carmarthen in 1604 was given the status of a 'town and county borough'. Although at least nine Carmarthenshire contributory boroughs had been named in earlier election returns, these precedents were not used later as a basis to challenge Carmarthen's monopoly thereafter of the borough representation. A charter of 1546 had established a mayor and a council of twenty, with power to admit burgesses, who could apparently be non-resident: vacancies on this council were filled by burgess election, not co-option. For over a century Carmarthen had a quiet history, with political control in the Vaughan family of Golden Grove, but from 1725 its parliamentary representation became a matter of dispute, and the nature of the franchise an issue. After a petition consequent on a contest at the general election of

[9] *CJ*, VIII, 396, 491.
[10] *CJ*, XVIII, 138, 199.
[11] NLW General MSS 23276, f. 3.
[12] For more detail, see Thorne in *Pembrokeshire County History*, III, 348–54.

1727, the House of Commons resolved in 1728 that the right of voting was in 'the burgesses', presumably non-resident as well as resident, and rejected an amendment to add 'and in the inhabitants, paying scot and lot', as in Haverfordwest.[13] Control of the borough corporation was now the key, and from 1746 until the issue of a new charter in 1764 there were two rival corporations, one Whig and one Tory, with the ministry sending all election writs to the former.

The charter of 1764 named a mayor and forty burgesses, who were to choose a common council of twenty. There would seem to have been an attempt to establish a residence qualification for burgess-ship, since three possible categories were specified: freeholders of £4 property in the town, and any men apprenticed for seven years to a burgess, could claim freedom as a right, while any person paying a rent of £10 could be admitted at the discretion of the council.[14] One consequence was a sharp fall in the size of the electorate. Whereas 320 had voted in 1741, only ninety-four were polled in 1768. In 1770, the House of Commons rejected a claim to vote by twenty old burgesses, admitted before 1764.[15] But by the early nineteenth century the residence provision was being evaded by the practice of subdividing land within the borough into £4 lots to be held in succession for the minimum qualifying period of three years. Of the 754 who voted in 1818, only a quarter lived in the borough.[16]

Brecon was the other Welsh single-borough constituency in 1660. There is no obvious reason why this should have been so. Indenture returns at the end of the sixteenth century had mentioned 'other boroughs' without specifying any by name, but there was no attempt after 1660 to assert the claims of any out-boroughs. By a charter of 1555 the borough was ruled by a co-optive corporation of fifteen common councilmen, including a bailiff, who was chosen annually and acted as parliamentary returning officer. The franchise lay in the corporation and in any burgesses admitted by it. Although the 1555 charter stipulated residence as a qualification, that proviso had been ignored since 1573. Such a constituency was ripe for the rule of a patron, and by the late seventeenth century control was being disputed by two families, Morgan of Tredegar and Jeffreys of the Priory, the latter championing the exclusive right of inhabitants to vote, in petitions of 1713, 1723 and 1727, none of which were heard by the House of Commons.[17] In 1727, however, a test case against one non-resident

---

[13] *CJ*, XXI, 90, 94.

[14] For a copy of the charter, see Cawdor MSS 42/5826.

[15] *CJ*, XXXII, 762–3.

[16] Cragoe, 'The Golden Grove Interest in Carmarthenshire Politics, 1804–1821', *WHR*, 16 (1993), 472, 485–6.

[17] *CJ*, XVII, 481; XX, 232; XXI, 26.

burgess resulted in a ruling by the House of Lords that residence was necessary under the charter, the claim of usage being disallowed. In 1740, after a narrow Tredegar by-election win by thirty-one votes to twenty-eight, the Morgan family obtained legal advice that enabled it to circumvent the obvious intention of this judicial decision. Barrister John Talbot, then the borough MP, pointed out that since neither the charter nor the common law fixed any length of time for residence, this would only be necessary at the time of admission into burgess-ship.[18] The Morgans took advantage of this opinion to maintain control of the borough. The number of burgesses was kept to the minimum necessary for management of the borough, a mere twenty-one in 1831, inclusive of the corporation. Although in 1818 there was an abortive move based on a claim that all inhabitant householders should vote, no parliamentary contest took place again before 1832.[19]

Montgomery became a fifth Welsh single-borough constituency when in 1728 an earlier parliamentary decision of 1685 was reversed. Throughout a long period of dispute the definition of the electorate was always 'the burgesses', and no question of disqualifying non-resident voters arose. But attempts by the county town of Montgomery, whose two bailiffs acted as returning officers, to disfranchise the three out-boroughs of Welshpool, Llanidloes, and Llanfyllin began in 1661. The successful candidate then was returned by Montgomery alone without notice to them, and his opponent failed to pursue the matter. At a 1665 by-election, however, the patron of Montgomery specifically acknowledged the rights of the out-boroughs when his brother was returned without a contest; and at another by-election, in January 1679, the successful candidate owed his victory to the out-borough voters having out-polled those from Montgomery. Contrary precedents were then established at the elections to the three Exclusion Parliaments in February and October 1679 and March 1681, when the returns were all made on the basis of Montgomery alone. The Committee of Elections upheld the first of these, as against another return based on the out-boroughs, and the Commons lacked time to consider the other two cases. At the election for the next Parliament, that summoned by James II in 1685, a candidate standing on the exclusive right of Montgomery was again returned by that borough's bailiffs, but petitions led to consideration of the case by the House of Commons on 26 June. The election was declared void, after the House had resolved that the burgesses of the three out-boroughs had a right to vote for the Montgomery borough

[18] Tredegar MSS 34/63.
[19] Jones, *History of Brecknockshire*, II, 186–7; Thomas, 'Parliamentary Elections in Brecknockshire 1689–1832', *Brycheiniog*, 6 (1960), 100–8.

members, and not those of Montgomery alone.[20] This decision appeared final, and during the reigns of William III and Anne no attempt was made to challenge the rights of the out-boroughs, even though the return to the Convention Parliament of 1689 was by the Montgomery burgesses only, or so it was asserted in 1728. There were about 700 voters in the constituency, over 120 in Montgomery itself, so it was stated after only seventy-one had polled in 1705.[21]

The changed political situation after the Hanoverian Succession led to a revival of the exclusive claim of Montgomery by Francis Herbert, patron of the county town. In 1715 he submitted a petition to that effect against the return of Tory MP John Pugh, obviously hoping for support from the Whig ministry appointed by George I.[22] The case was never heard, and no petition followed another contest in 1722, even though the three out-boroughs were under Tory control. Welshpool and Llanfyllin lay in the estate of Powis Castle, and Llanidloes in that of Llwydiarth, inherited by Watkin Williams Wynn in 1718. But the general election of 1727 led to a final confrontation. Robert Williams, a younger brother of Wynn, was sponsored also by Lord Powis, while Henry Arthur Herbert, who had succeeded his father Francis in 1719 and had a safe seat himself at Ludlow, put forward a Shropshire ally, William Corbett. A double return was made, by one bailiff each, for while Williams had a majority at the poll of 475 to 128, Corbett had a lead of 107 to twenty-nine in Montgomery itself. The case led to one of the most notorious election decisions ever made by the House of Commons.

Counsel for Corbett, arguing before the Committee of Elections that the right of election lay only in the burgesses of Montgomery, cited such appropriate precedents as he could produce; but the real basis of the claim was the technical argument that by the legislation of Henry VIII the out-boroughs enjoyed only a conditional right of voting, conditional on contributing to the wages of MPs, which they had now forfeited. Two witnesses were produced on this point. One stated by hearsay that Montgomery had paid wages under Charles II. The other was a former borough MP Charles Mason, who claimed that Welshpool had refused to pay him wages after he had been elected MP in 1705, when, he said, he had excused Montgomery. Since the practice of the payment of wages to MPs had lapsed, the weakness of this argument is obvious. It would have implied the disfranchisement of every out-borough in Wales. Counsel for Williams replied that the burgesses of Llanidloes, Llanfyllin and Welshpool

---

[20] Wynnstay MSS Box 85; *CJ*, VIII, 262; IX, 571, 579–80, 640, 707, 732.
[21] *CJ*, XV, 8–9, 14–15, 94–5; XXI, 137.
[22] *CJ*, XVIII, 36; XXI, 138.

had contributed to wages when they had been taken; and he had no difficulty in showing that all the recent precedents were in favour of the rights of the three out-boroughs. They were mentioned in every return from 1690. But Henry Arthur Herbert possessed considerable influence with the Walpole ministry, and despite the evidence the Committee of Elections resolved that the right of elections lay 'in the burgesses of the said shire town only'.

The Committee's report was challenged when it was made to the House of Commons on 16 April 1728. No record of any debate survives, but the draft of a speech by Watkin Williams Wynn exists among his papers.[23]

Mr Speaker. The matter in debate now before you is a matter of that consequence to the Principality of Wales and to the whole realm in general in regard to its ancient constitution that I should think I neither deserved the name of a Briton and unworthy of a seat within these walls, were I to be silent on this occasion . . . I must beg leave to observe to gentlemen that if a right of election supported by two Acts of Parliament founded upon the Union betwixt England and Wales, several ancient returns evidently admitting the right, several resolutions made upon a formal hearing at the Bar of this House in the year 1685, strongly corroborated by resolutions of this House in other constituent boroughs of the same nature, an uninterrupted usage agreeable to these resolutions ever since the year 1685, and parole evidence as strong as the distance of time will admit, is to be broken through, I must appeal to gentlemen, whose seat in this House can be secure. I question whether any of the boroughs in England have such strong united confirmations of an established right as these boroughs in Wales have hitherto.

Ministerial pressure secured a majority of 145 to 119 for the resolution, and Corbett was awarded the seat. But the minority included the ministry's own law officers, the Attorney-General and the Solicitor-General, as well as fifteen of the twenty-five MPs then representing constituencies in Wales, five of them habitual administration supporters.[24] The resolution put the constituency entirely under the control of Herbert and his heirs; in 1745 he could refer to Montgomery as 'one of my boroughs'.[25]

Wynn was concerned about the implications of such a decision. 'This is but a leading card, and hereafter will no doubt of it be made use of as a precedent.' This fear was echoed on subsequent occasions. In 1734 Glamorgan Tories at first thought that the candidature of Thomas

[23] Wynnstay MSS Box 85, no. 11.
[24] Wynnstay MSS Box 85, no. 1; *CJ*, XXI, 136–8.
[25] BL Add. MSS 32704, f. 445.

Mathews might be intended to secure a majority in Cardiff and disfranchise the out-boroughs.[26] And in both 1741 and 1747 Caernarfonshire
Tories believed that MP Thomas Wynn of Glynllifon would welcome an
opposition so that with the aid of a compliant Whig majority in the
Commons 'he could have destroyed the contributory boroughs, and fixed
the right of returning members in Caernarvon only, and so consequently
make the borough hereditary in his own family'.[27] None of these fears or
hopes were to be realised, and the Montgomery precedent was not
followed.

In Monmouthshire there had already been an attempt to secure a
monopoly of the borough representation for the county town. In the
sixteenth century at least five out-boroughs had been named in returns –
Abergavenny, Caerleon, Chepstow, Trellech and Usk; and by 1660 Newport
also participated. But in 1679 the Marquess of Worcester, later the first
Duke of Beaufort, sought to consolidate his hold on the constituency by
restricting the franchise to the burgesses of Monmouth, where the Troy
estate gave him control of the common council of fifteen capital burgesses.
This move was foiled by a 1680 House of Commons resolution confirming
the rights also of Newport and Usk. In 1681 Abergavenny and Chepstow
were also named in the return, and Chepstow again in 1685; but from 1689
the 1680 ruling was the accepted designation of the constituency.

The 1680 resolution had also, inexplicably, imposed a residence
qualification for the franchise, declaring the right of election to be in 'the
burgesses, inhabitants' of Monmouth, Newport and Usk.[28] This stipulation
was evidently ignored at first, for when the county rivalry of the Morgans of
Tredegar and the Dukes of Beaufort resulted in a 1715 borough contest,
1,972 burgesses then voted, and 1,336 of them came from Usk, which even
at the 1801 census had only 700 inhabitants. At that election the Tredegar
candidate, with majorities in Newport and Usk, defeated the Beaufort
nominee, but thereafter Tredegar agreed to support Beaufort candidates as
part of a compromise arrangement in the county.[29] Beaufort control was
unchallenged for a century, and the electorate had dwindled to 137 resident
freemen by the next contest, in 1820. The Beaufort candidate, still with
Tredegar support, defeated radical John Moggridge by ninety votes to forty,
and creations of new burgesses deterred any challenges in 1826 and 1830.[30]

---

[26] Kemys Tynte MSS 1/8.
[27] Brogyntyn MSS 35, 37.
[28] *CJ*, IX, 663.
[29] Havill, 'The Parliamentary Representation of Monmouthshire and the Monmouth
Boroughs', MA Wales, 1949, pp. 40–4, 87–93.
[30] Havill, 'Parliamentary Representation', pp. 113–25; David, 'Political Electioneering
Activity in South-East Wales, 1820–52', MA Wales, 1959, pp. 38–41.

A residence stipulation was also imposed on the Denbigh Boroughs constituency. Here there was never any doubt that Ruthin and Holt shared participation with Denbigh in the borough constituency, but control of boroughs by rival families led to competitive mass creations of voters from the late seventeenth century. The Cotton family of Lleweni controlled Holt, and the Myddeltons of Chirk Castle, Ruthin, also maintaining a precarious hold over Denbigh. In 1690 both allied to defeat William Williams, whose petition, never considered by the Commons, put forward a claim for a resident franchise.[31] Circumstances alter cases. It was to be his own son, the first Sir Watkin Williams Wynn, who was to be outraged by the Commons decision of 1744 to establish such a franchise.

From 1698 Lleweni and Chirk Castle clashed in the borough constituency, each side deploying non-resident voters, with the Myddeltons being successful except in 1713, when the mayor of Denbigh, John Wynne, played them false after a Cotton promise of the seat for himself. Otherwise control of Denbigh meant selection of two Myddelton nominees as bailiffs, and thus returning officers, who in 1715, for example, disallowed enough Holt voters to ensure victory for the Chirk Castle nominee by 773 votes to 610, leaving a frustrated Wynne vainly to claim a majority of '59 good votes'.[32] But only sixty of 222 resident Denbigh burgesses had supported Chirk Castle, and the Cotton family therefore now sought to break the Myddelton hold on the county town by challenging the right of non-resident burgesses to vote in elections to the common council. That right was upheld by a legal decision of 1717, a verdict that confirmed Chirk Castle control of a second borough with power to make in both as many burgesses as would be necessary 'to put the borough out of dispute'.[33]

This proved not to be so, after two quiet decades of Myddelton control. In preparation for the 1741 election Sir Watkin Williams Wynn, in retaliation for a Myddelton attack on his county seat, arranged with the Cotton family for the admission as Holt burgesses of a vast number of his tenants, one estimate being 1,500: certainly 635 were admitted on 17 October 1740 alone.[34] The Myddeltons were quite unable to match this total, and had to resort to a different tactic. At the poll the Denbigh bailiffs admitted to vote only the resident burgesses of the three towns, arbitrarily adopting a new definition of the electorate; for by this time control of Denbigh and Ruthin had given the Myddeltons a majority of the resident burgesses in both boroughs. Only forty-five votes were accepted from Holt,

---

[31] *CJ*, X, 359, 428, 544–5, 568.
[32] Chirk Castle MSS E945, 945A, 947, 4055–60; *CJ*, XVIII, 36.
[33] Chirk Castle MSS E946, 5318, 5912–22, 5928.
[34] Chirk Castle MSS C31, 40.

and the Myddelton candidate was returned with a majority of 282 votes to 139.[35]

That was to Wynn an injustice almost comparable with the disfranchisement of the Montgomery out-boroughs and not a matter he was disposed to let rest. After repeated petitions, the case was heard by the House of Commons on 7 February 1744. Counsel for the sitting member rested his case simply on the enfranchising legislation, which could arguably be interpreted as intending the franchise to be in inhabitants; and in defiance of all the evidence of past practice the House took the partisan decision of resolving, by a majority of one vote, 175 to 174, that the right of election lay only in the inhabitant burgesses.[36] This decision made permanent the control of the Chirk Castle family. The constituency was to be represented by a Myddelton without opposition until the extinction of the male line in 1796 set the scene for a new struggle among the husbands of the Myddelton heiresses.

Another restrictive alteration of a franchise took place in the Flint Boroughs constituency, one reducing it to inhabitant ratepayers. This constituency comprised five boroughs, a matter about which there was no dispute. Rhuddlan, Overton, Caergwrle and Caerwys were the out-boroughs added to Flint, with only Rhuddlan under any family influence, that of the Conways of Bodrhyddan. Agreements among the local squirearchy prevented the contests that might otherwise have arisen in such an open constituency. In 1697, the only known poll of the later seventeenth century, the 760 voters were drawn from non-resident as well as resident burgesses of all five boroughs. It is true that the unsuccessful candidate Sir John Hanmer submitted a petition complaining that his opponent had won by polling 'many foreigners, who had no right to vote'. But he had himself been intending to bring voters from Chester, and withdrew the petition before it came under consideration.[37] There was no dispute over the borough franchise in a contest of 1722.[38] Yet that became the point at issue when the comparative political calm was shattered in 1727 by two disruptive factors: the appearance of a wealthy political adventurer, albeit a local man, George Wynne of Leeswood; and the intervention of the Walpole ministry. Wynne's opponent was Salusbury Lloyd, a protégé of Liverpool MP Thomas Brereton, a man well in with Sir Robert Walpole.

[35] Chirk Castle MSS C38, 40, 46; E5407, 5833, 5837.

[36] *CJ*, XXIV, 28, 347, 486, 549–50.

[37] *CJ*, XII, 2–3, 45; Taylor, 'Flint Borough Election, 1697', *Flintshire Historical Society Journal*, 11 (1925), 89–90.

[38] *CJ*, XX, 33–4, 235; XXI. 173; Roberts, 'The Boroughs of North Wales: Their Parliamentary History from the Act of Union to the first Reform Act 1536–1832', MA Wales, 1929, pp. 172–7.

Lloyd had property in Flint town, but Wynne controlled the borough machinery, and his electoral preparations included the admission of several hundred non-resident burgesses there.[39]

Disputes over the franchise took place during the poll itself. Lloyd asserted that only resident burgesses, paying the local taxes, scot and lot, could vote. Wynne claimed that all precedents showed that the franchise lay in 'the burgesses at large'. At the close of the poll, Wynne had a majority of 685 to 312, but 397 had been queried as non-resident, 335 of them from Flint. The two Flint bailiffs sent in separate returns, one for each candidate, and the case went to the Committee of Elections, which made its report on 21 May 1728. Wynne's claim for 'the burgesses at large' was found to include not all non-resident burgesses, but non-residents in Flint and residents in the out-boroughs, a curious interpretation particularly favourable to his influence in the county town. Lloyd maintained that only ratepayer inhabitants could vote, producing as his chief evidence the charters of Flint, Rhuddlan and Overton; since Caerwys and Caergwrle were boroughs by prescription, they had no charters. This franchise was familiar to MPs, being common in England, but had no historical or legal basis in the Flint constituency. Yet it was accepted by both the Committee and the House of Commons. This case, like the Montgomery one, was decided not on its merits but by ministerial pressure on MPs. Walpole's papers include a document headed 'Flint Election: Lists', clearly a list of rebellious customary supporters, seventy of whom were 'absent' and thirty-nine 'against', four Welsh MPs being absent and three against.[40]

For Wynne, deprived thus of his seat, there was an ironic sequel at the next election, in 1734. Now a baronet, he was the ministerial candidate against local squire Sir John Glynne. He was returned by the Flint bailiffs after they disallowed twenty-four votes for Glynne, who had won at the poll by 270 to 258. When the case was eventually heard by the House in 1737 the Commons ruled that inhabitants whose landlords paid their rates for them could not vote, a decision that served to check the rise of any future borough patron. The election of Wynne was confirmed, even though Glynne calculated a majority of 231 to 188 legal votes for himself.[41] For the 1741 election Sir Watkin Williams Wynn put up a younger brother Richard Williams. Wynne was accused of creating fictitious residents by use of barns, stables and, mockingly, pigsties, and certainly the marked increase in the number who claimed to be resident ratepayers at the poll, which Wynne

---

[39] Glynne of Hawarden MSS 4952.
[40] Cholmondeley Houghton MSS P66/2; *CJ*, XXI, 27, 173–6.
[41] Glynne of Hawarden MSS 5166, 5174, 5194, 5235; *CJ*, XXII, 823, 832, 835, 839–41, 864, 866–7.

won by 320 to 280, gives credence to the charge of fraudulent voters.[42] Wynne lost the seat on petition, finding a hostile majority in the House of Commons after Walpole's fall, and management of the borough seat reverted to the local squires.[43]

Of the thirteen Welsh borough constituencies only five survived with both contributory boroughs and a franchise of 'burgesses' without a residence stipulation. In them competitive mass creation of voters remained a possibility until 1832. In three of these five – Cardigan, Pembroke and Radnor – there were parliamentary decisions as to the number of boroughs that comprised each constituency, but with an illogical situation in Radnor Boroughs that residence was necessary to vote in Radnor but not in the out-boroughs. The Caernarfon and Cardiff groups of boroughs entirely escaped any parliamentary definition of either the franchise or the constituency.

For Radnorshire there was no mention by name of the out-boroughs before 1680. In the county town of New Radnor, a charter of 1562 had established a corporation of twenty-five capital burgesses. This governing body filled its own vacancies by co-option; chose annually from among themselves a bailiff who was returning officer for the constituency; and admitted other burgesses, but only from among the inhabitants. At the general election of February 1679 this body sought to arrogate the franchise to itself, on the model of Beaumaris, excluding the other freemen of New Radnor as well as those of the out-boroughs; or so it was alleged in a petition that named Cefnllys, Cnwclas, Knighton and Painscastle as the aggrieved boroughs.[44] Apart from New Radnor, the other centre of power in the constituency was a Crown appointment, Steward of the royal lordship of Cantref Maelienydd, for this contained all the out-boroughs apart from Cefnllys, and in each the Steward could hold manorial courts to admit burgesses, whether resident or not. Cefnllys was regarded as being of no account, for by tradition the franchise was confined to the small number of resident burgesses: but custom in the end was not to prove sacrosanct.

After 1679 New Radnor made no attempt to disfranchise its out-boroughs, but which exactly they were became a matter of dispute at the election of 1690. Sir Rowland Gwynne then defeated Robert Harley, but he owed his majority to votes from Presteigne and Painscastle, Harley seeking no votes in either. The Committee of Elections awarded Harley the seat

[42] Wynnstay MSS L751, 812–21, 857.
[43] Wynnstay MSS L758, 807–9; *CJ*, XXIV, 26, 29, 133, 136–7, 144–5.
[44] Adams, 'The Parliamentary Representation of Radnorshire, 1536–1832', MA Wales, 1969, pp. 13–16.

after resolving the right of election to be 'only' in 'the burgesses' of New Radnor, Rhayader, Knighton, Cnwclas and Cefnllys.[45] Harley became Steward of Cantref Maelienydd in 1691, and his control of the constituency was unchallenged until after the Hanoverian Succession in 1714.

Harley control was destroyed by a coup in 1715, when the Bailiff of New Radnor, acting on behalf of Thomas Lewis of Harpton, usurped the corporation's power by creating 251 new burgesses there himself, and so overturned the majority of ninety among the old burgesses anticipated by the Harley candidate. After an unopposed election in 1722 the same tactic was repeated in 1727, when the Bailiff admitted over 200 new freemen, and Lewis retained his seat by a poll majority of 651 to 497. Since the population of New Radnor at the 1801 census was only 329, these mass creations show that, as elsewhere, the residence stipulation was being circumvented, by an interpretation that it applied only at the actual time of admission. In 1734 the Bailiff polled seventy votes for Thomas Lewis and allowed only one for his opponent. On all these occasions, 1715, 1727 and 1734, petitions from opponents of Lewis were never heard by the House of Commons. The ambition of the Harpton family now developed from temporary electoral success to permanent control of the constituency, by seeking an alteration of the franchise. On 3 February 1735 a petition from 'the Bailiff and capital burgesses' of New Radnor was presented, asserting that only inhabitants of the outboroughs could be made burgesses thereof. Such an interpretation would have checked the potentially superior significance in the constituency of the Steward of Cantref Maelienydd, for Knighton, Cnwclas and Rhayader were small towns. This claim was refuted in a petition from the outboroughs on 4 March, and the Committee of Elections never considered the matter.[46]

Although thwarted in this respect, Thomas Lewis strengthened his position in the borough constituency by obtaining a new charter for New Radnor in 1739. This charter, virtually a repetition of that of 1562, placed control of the borough firmly in the Harpton family: their friends formed a majority of the new council of twenty-five capital burgesses and any vacancies were filled by co-option.[47] There was no contest at the elections of 1741 and 1747, and the Harpton hold on the constituency became even more secure when in 1746 Thomas Lewis obtained the Stewardship of Cantref Maelienydd for his brother Henry. Before the election of 1754 Thomas Lewis, aware of an intended opposition, reminded his brother on 6 January that 'there are out-boroughs as well as Radnor where I can name

[45] *CJ*, X, 355, 426, 469.
[46] Harpton MSS C44; *CJ*, XVIII, 39, 493, 652; XXI, 29, 189; XXII, 329, 346, 401–2, 506, 539.
[47] Williams, *History of Radnorshire*, pp. 124–8.

500 burgesses whenever I thought fit, and no one else has any authority to make one single person . . . I can make as many as I please there likewise'. At the poll, however, objections were vainly lodged against the votes of non-resident freemen.[48]

Thomas Lewis had retained the seat throughout the reigns of George I and George II, but the Harpton hold on the constituency depended on the Stewardship being in friendly hands. Its transfer back to the Harley family opened a dispute over the franchise, after the Lewis family twice lost the seat by simple carelessness. In 1761 it was neglect to pay stamp duties for burgess admissions that caused Thomas Lewis to concede the seat to London merchant Edward Lewis.[49] Technical errors before the 1768 election then caused his nephew John to lose the seat on petition by Edward Lewis, after winning the poll by 547 to 440: the most notable of them was the failure of John's father Henry to register his patent as Steward of Cantref Maelienydd at the beginning of George III's reign in 1760, an omission which thereby invalidated many burgess creations.[50]

The decisive event in the future electoral history of the constituency was the appointment of the fourth Earl of Oxford as Steward in February 1768, a month after the death of Henry Lewis. Although the Durham Act prevented him from creating voters for the 1768 contest, he would obviously do so on future occasions. In 1770 Thomas Lewis therefore took up the idea floated in 1735, restriction of the franchise to resident freemen. On 2 March he suggested to John Lewis that he make out a case based on the 1544 Act and on various resolutions of the House of Commons, presumably those concerning Denbigh and Flint. But he advised his nephew to consult with MPs like Sir William Owen and Sir John Wynn, both of whom wished to retain the right to make as many non-resident freemen as possible in the Pembroke and Caernarfon constituencies respectively.[51]

The Radnor Boroughs election of 1774 was therefore avowedly fought on that point. On 1 October John Lewis issued a public notice announcing his intention to use resident voters only. Edward Lewis, now evidently the Harley candidate, pointed out that the Harpton family had in the past constantly relied on non-resident voters. John Lewis retorted that in 1754 and 1761 'foreigners were formally objected to on the poll'. John Lewis now polled 201 residents, as against seventy for Edward Lewis, who also polled 549 non-residents to claim victory by 619 to 201: but the Bailiff

---

[48] Harpton MSS C29, 143–4.
[49] BL Add. MSS 32985, f. 413.
[50] PRO 30/8/53, ff. 203–4; *CJ*, XXXII, 29, 36, 227, 235, 242, 257–8, 293–4.
[51] Harpton MSS C49.

returned John Lewis as duly elected.[52] Before Parliament met John Lewis rashly published an Address to the Radnor burgesses that championed the exclusive rights of resident freemen in all the Welsh boroughs.[53]

> You have now placed me in that situation which calls upon me to protect your privileges and assert your rights. I promise you I am both ready and willing to do it and should it become necessary shall meet with pleasure that question in Parliament in which not only your rights but those almost of every borough in the Principality of Wales are in some measure interested.

Thomas Lewis reproved his nephew for this indiscretion. 'Surely you should have omitted making every borough member in Wales your opposer, . . . most of whom are chosen by outlyers'. He named in particular Sir William Owen and, curiously, Herbert Mackworth, who never faced a contest in the Cardiff constituency.[54] Thomas Lewis was exaggerating: by now only six other Welsh borough constituencies had non-resident voters.

The case was one of the first heard by a small Election Committee established under an Election Act of 1770 and comprising fifteen MPs chosen, for fairness, by lot. Counsel for John Lewis cited the 1544 Act that used the words 'inhabitants' and 'burgesses' as evident equivalents, and reminded MPs that after similar statutory evidence a residence franchise had been established in the 1744 Denbigh Boroughs case. He also argued that when the House had, in contradiction to the 1544 Act, confirmed the voting rights of non-resident freemen, the words 'at large' had been deliberately added to 'burgesses', as in the Cardigan Boroughs case of 1730. No such expression had been used in the Radnor Boroughs case of 1690, when the issue had been that of contributory boroughs, and not residence: the poll then had been so small as to suggest that non-residents had not then voted. The third argument for a resident franchise was based on the 1739 New Radnor borough charter. The admission of freemen was confined to inhabitants, who alone could vote: it would be unreasonable if the shire town was restricted more than the contributory boroughs. Counsel for Edward Lewis replied that in 1690 the word 'burgesses' covered both residents and non-residents. If a resident franchise had been intended, the word 'inhabitants' would have been added to 'burgesses'. Moreover, in such other Welsh borough constituencies as Cardigan and Pembroke, the right of voting had been established by the House of Commons in

---

[52] *Gloucester Journal*, 10 October 1774; Adams, 'Parliamentary Representation of Radnorshire', 363–6.

[53] *Gloucester Journal*, 31 October 1774.

[54] Harpton MSS C.92.

non-residents despite the legislation of Henry VIII. The Committee awarded the seat to Edward Lewis, but made no resolution concerning the right of election, in its report to the House on 20 February 1775.[55]

That omission left open the issue of residence, a situation highlighted by an advertisement of 22 September 1776 offering Cefnllys for sale at public auction on 17 October as a borough with a right to make burgesses for the constituency. Cefnllys was purchased by a Benjamin Walsh from Berkshire, but the Walsh family did not immediately exploit the right to create non-resident voters.[56] The issue of residency remained the centre of controversy. On 14 May 1779 the House of Commons received a petition from New Radnor, asking that the admission of burgesses in the contributory boroughs should be confined to residents, claiming that before the 1774 election over 700 burgesses had been presented at Rhayader, and 426 of them sworn, only seventeen of whom had been resident.[57] The House of Commons took no action on this petition, but it set the scene for the election of 1780. The two candidates then stopped the poll by mutual consent, when John Lewis had a majority of fifty to thirty among the resident freemen, and Edward Lewis one of sixty to fifty altogether. Again the seat was awarded to Edward Lewis without any resolution on the right of election.[58] The illogical situation remained of residence being required in New Radnor but not in the out-boroughs, an anomaly the House of Commons evidently preferred to ignore rather than resolve.

The Lewis of Harpton family gave up that point, and left the Harley family in control of the constituency. In 1790 Lord Oxford dropped Edward Lewis in favour of a relative, David Murray, who defeated Lewis by 609 votes to 313. There is some evidence that Edward Lewis now in turn took up the cause of the resident freemen.[59] On Oxford's death later that year the Stewardship of Cantref Maelienydd passed to his nephew and heir, but the fifth Earl of Oxford chose not to exploit his power. No freemen at all were created in his three boroughs between 1799 and 1824, when management of the Stewardship seemingly reverted to the Harpton family. By default control of the constituency was contested by local squires, and Richard Price of Knighton, MP from 1799 to 1847, initially with Harley support, twice, in 1812 and 1820, defeated Perceval Lewis of Downton, son of Edward Lewis. By 1820 the Walsh family had belatedly

---

[55] Douglas, *Elections*, I, 318–38; *CJ*, XXXV, 134–5.

[56] Adams, 'Parliamentary Representation of Radnorshire', pp. 39–44.

[57] *CJ*, XXXVIII, 399.

[58] *CJ*, XXXVIII, 12, 136, 156; Adams, 'Parliamentary Representation of Radnorshire', pp. 395–8.

[59] Oldfield, *History of the Boroughs*, III, 49–50. There is no petition in the *Commons Journals*.

made Cefnllys a power in the constituency with 190 voters, only sixteen of whom were resident.[60]

In the Pembroke Boroughs constituency the question of disfranchising non-resident voters never arose, and the sole point at issue was the claim of Wiston to participate in elections. It was a small village but a manorial borough in the possession of the Wogan family, whose steward appointed the bailiff and named the twelve burgesses of the leet jury that admitted other freemen. Wiston represented a threat to the control of the constituency by the Owen of Orielton family that ruled the other two boroughs. Under a charter of 1485 Pembroke was governed by a mayor and co-opting council of twelve. In Tenby, by a charter of 1581, power lay with a mayor and common council of thirty. Both councils could admit burgesses.[61] The claim of Wiston had been first made in 1621, and was revived in the late seventeenth century, the borough being mentioned in returns of 1681, 1689, 1690 and 1695. Notice of elections was sent to its mayor in 1701 and 1702 but this ceased, and in 1708 Wiston submitted a petition to the House of Commons complaining about this omission.[62] Confrontation came in 1710, after the unopposed return of Owens or their nominees since 1679. Lewis Wogan of Wiston, a Tory evidently anticipating the favour of a Tory House of Commons against the Whig Owens, challenged Sir Arthur Owen. The mayor of Pembroke polled only burgesses from Pembroke and Tenby, and returned Owen with a majority of 207 to 124. Wiston burgesses were prevented from entering the town hall, but the names of 239 Wiston voters for Wogan were recited outside. When the Committee of Elections reported to the House on 23 February 1712 its decision that Wiston was a contributory borough was upheld by the Commons and Wogan was awarded the seat.[63]

This decision was regarded as a great injustice by the Owens, who did their best to ignore it when a Whig ascendancy followed the Hanoverian Succession in 1714. Some Wiston burgesses did vote in 1715, when Pembroke and Tenby submitted a petition denying the right of that borough.[64] But the Commons did not consider the issue, and if necessary the Owens forcibly excluded Wiston voters, as in 1741, when complaint of this behaviour was never examined.[65] The latent threat that borough posed to Owen hegemony, deployed in 1761 to influence the county election,

[60] Harpton MSS C401.

[61] Jones, 'The Parliamentary Representation of Pembrokeshire, the Pembroke Boroughs and Haverfordwest', MA Wales, 1958, pp. 31–40.

[62] *CJ*, XVI, 22.

[63] *CJ*, XVI, 420; XVII, 4, 108–11.

[64] NLW General MSS 12171, John Barlow to Lord Harcourt, 14 February 1715; *CJ*, XVIII, 37.

[65] *CJ*, XVIII, 37; XXIV, 23, 72, 340, 404.

became a reality after Lord Cawdor purchased the manor of Wiston in 1794. Hundreds of voters were created there, and after an abortive challenge of 1812 the outcome of the threat to Orielton hegemony was a compromise of 1816 whereby Lord Cawdor was to be allowed to nominate the borough MPs for the next two elections, Orielton control being resumed at the third one in 1826.

In the Cardigan Boroughs constituency there was an apparent attempt in 1661 to disfranchise the four out-boroughs of Aberystwyth, Adpar, Lampeter and Tregaron; for the return of James Phillips was declared void in 1662 for want of notice to them.[66] Phillips was owner of the Cardigan Priory estate, which then gave effective control of the county town, governed by a co-optive council of thirteen including the mayor, who was returning officer, and who chose the juries that created new burgesses. By the end of the seventeenth century the estate had passed to the Pryse family of Gogerddan, which already ruled the borough of Aberystwyth by appointment of its mayor and other officials. Lampeter was a manorial borough within the estate of Peterwell, Tregaron one in that of Nanteos, both being managed by portreeves. In the fifth borough of Adpar there was apparently no patron.

The mass creation of borough voters after 1720 was the consequence of a situation where boroughs were controlled by rival families at a time when two minorities in the Pryse family led to a power vacuum in the constituency. In 1725 Thomas Powell of Nanteos won a contested by-election against a Gogerddan candidate, and he repeated the feat in 1729 by 1,224 votes to 924. Cardigan supplied over 500 votes for Gogerddan, but Powell had created 800 in Tregaron during 1728. At this election the right of Tregaron to be part of the borough constituency was challenged, while Powell, though polling non-residents, claimed that only resident burgesses could vote: for an earlier Pryse alliance had given him many resident voters in Cardigan and Aberystwyth. These issues led to a double return, and the various petitions were heard by the Committee of Elections. Evidence was produced of Tregaron's participation in ten of the twelve elections from 1701, but none for the period between 1663 and 1701. The Committee ruled against Tregaron, and then also against Powell's claim that the right of election lay in 'the resident burgesses only'. On the contrary, the Committee resolved that it lay 'in the burgesses at large of the boroughs of Cardigan, Aberystwyth, Lampeter and Adpar only', a decision confirmed by the House of Commons on 7 May 1730.[67]

---

[66] *CJ*, VIII, 417.

[67] *CJ*, XXI, 387–8; Thomas, 'Eighteenth-Century Elections in the Cardigan Boroughs Constituency', *Ceredigion*, 5 (1964–7), 402–8.

The exclusion of Tregaron reduced the electorate to about 1,000, according to the sitting member Richard Lloyd of Mabws in 1734.[68] But such an estimate meant little when unlimited creation of voters was possible. Prior to the election of 1741 Thomas Pryse of Gogerddan, now of age and determined to regain the seat for his family, resorted to mass creations at Cardigan, and won by 1,034 to 697. The poll-book shows that 694 voted from Cardigan, 469 from Aberystwyth, 298 from Adpar, and 270 from Lampeter. Only 11 per cent of the voters lived in the borough for which they were voting. Within a year Adpar lost its corporate structure. No new burgesses could be created there, and the borough sank into effective disfranchisement. It became impossible for existing burgesses to vote, for two who attended a contest in 1769 could not produce evidence of their admission.[69]

The possibility of voter creation in any of the three remaining boroughs rendered the political situation in the constituency extremely volatile. The death of Pryse in 1745 led to the second long Gogerddan minority and the prospect of another challenge for control of the constituency, this time based on control of Lampeter by the Lloyd family of Peterwell. After a borough contest in 1746 Peterwell was given the county seat in 1747 and 1754 on condition of ceding the borough to Gogerddan, an arrangement reversed in 1761. Finally, when no compromise was possible at a 1769 by-election, the Gogerddan nominee defeated Sir Herbert Lloyd of Peterwell by 1,950 votes to 1,704, the size of the poll demonstrating the large-scale creation of voters on both sides. At the general election of 1774 a similar success of Gogerddan over Peterwell, by 1,488 votes to 980, was reversed on petition, when on 7 December 1775 the House of Commons accepted the report of the Committee of Elections on the invalidity of many votes.[70] Control of Cardigan borough then passed successively to the Johnes family, whose various estates included Hafod, and the Vaughans of Crosswood, who held the borough seat from 1796 to 1818 in the face of Gogerddan hostility, manifested by support of a Herbert Evans who challenged John Vaughan in 1812. Vaughan, who created numerous burgesses at Cardigan, won by 588 votes to 508, despite Gogerddan creations at Aberystwyth and others at Lampeter by the then owner of Peterwell, Richard Hart Davis. But he did not relish another contest after Davis created 600 freemen at Lampeter in 1814, and at the 1818 election Pryse Pryse resumed Gogerddan tenure of the seat, holding it for over thirty years.

---

[68] Cholmondeley Houghton MSS no. 2212.

[69] Thomas, 'The Cardigan Boroughs Election of 1741', *Ceredigion*, 6 (1968–71), 128–9.

[70] Douglas, *Elections*, III, 184–229.

No parliamentary decision was taken on either the Caernarfon or Cardiff borough constituencies yet in both boroughs were in the hands of rival patrons, and the former was the scene of bitter rivalries. From the sixteenth century it comprised five boroughs – Caernarfon, Conway, Cricieth, Nefyn and Pwllheli. During the later seventeenth century there were no contested elections, the constituency being managed on behalf of the local squirearchy by Thomas Bulkeley, brother and uncle of successive Lords Bulkeley. Lack of conflict meant few burgess creations; in the early eighteenth century Caernarfon had about forty burgesses, Nefyn twenty-four and Pwllheli thirty-six.[71] But the potential for strife lay in the distribution of power. In Caernarfon itself the mayoralty was attached to the Constableship of the castle, a Crown appointment. The mayoralty of Nefyn was hereditary in the Wynn of Glynllifon family, by virtue of their Bodfean estate; that of Pwllheli in the Vaughans of Corsygedol, a Wynn ally; and that of Cricieth in the Owens of Brogyntyn, a Bulkeley ally. In Conway there was no mayor, and control lay with minor local squires. After the death of Thomas Bulkeley in 1708 Thomas Wynn prepared the ground for a challenge by the gradual admission of non-resident burgesses, a manœuvre somehow concealed from the ruling Bulkeley-led oligarchy. By 1713 Nefyn had acquired 689 new ones and Pwllheli 174, and at the general election of that year, in a poll for which no totals are known, Wynn defeated William Owen of Brogyntyn, whose petition was not heard by the House of Commons.[72]

This coup established Glynllifon control of the constituency for over seventy years, although that was not immediately apparent. Owen chose not to fight in 1715, fearing the verdict of a Whig House of Commons in favour of Whig MP Wynn. In 1722 Wynn defeated William Price, candidate of the local Tory squires, by 1,025 votes to 572. A poll-book incomplete by forty-four of Wynn's voters showed that only 272 of the 1,553 known voters were resident. Price polled 477 from Cricieth, 285 of them non-resident. Wynn polled at least 795 non-residents, 651 of them from Nefyn and Pwllheli. The poll from Caernarfon itself was low, Wynn winning there by ninety-six to eighteen.[73] Thereafter there was no contest for over sixty years, with the Wynns supposedly desiring one so as to make Caernarfon their pocket borough by disfranchising the contributory boroughs, on the example of Montgomery.[74] They were not given the opportunity. The next contest was a fratricidal conflict in 1784.

[71] Glynllifon MSS 1988; Llanfair and Brynodol MSS 96.
[72] *CJ*, XVII, 486–7.
[73] Brogyntyn MSS 1126; Porth yr Aur MSS 12543.
[74] Brogyntyn MSS 35, 37.

The sitting member Glyn Wynn, grandson of Thomas Wynn, resisted the claim of his elder brother Lord Newborough to what was now deemed a family seat. He arranged for his own nominee Richard Howard to be appointed Constable of Caernarfon Castle in 1782, and formed an alliance with Lord Paget of Plas Newydd to obtain a supply of voters. Burgess admissions in Caernarfon totalled 329 in 1782, 362 in 1783, and sixty-four in 1784, when the supply even from Lord Paget's Anglesey estate was running out. The seventh Lord Bulkeley, an Anglesey rival of Lord Paget, took up the cause of Lord Newborough, with 235 burgess admissions in Cricieth in 1782, and 200 in 1783. The result of all this activity was successful pressure by the Pitt ministry on Lord Bulkeley to drop his opposition to Glyn Wynn.[75] This meant that the Bulkeley tenants were not polled, and Wynn won by 490 to 410, totals well below the new creations. Wynn, to save trouble and expense, may have merely polled enough votes to secure a safe margin of victory. Lord Newborough had a majority of resident burgesses by ninety-three to forty-one, but that issue was never raised in this constituency. Wynn soon discovered that his role had been that of a Trojan Horse for the admission of Paget control. At the next election, in 1790, Wynn was deprived of the seat, which was held by members of the Paget family until 1830. Doubtless fearing Paget wealth, the patrons of the out-boroughs did not challenge Paget control by mass creations of voters. There was a steady decline in the size of the electorate, with only 200 voters being admitted in Caernarfon in the first three decades of the nineteenth century.[76]

In Glamorgan the Cardiff Boroughs constituency had a quiet history after several contests in the reign of Charles II, when the only known poll totalled 145 in 1661. It comprised eight boroughs, which by 1700 had come under the control of only four patrons. Since they preferred to decide the parliamentary representation by consultation rather than conflict the story of the constituency is not one of competitive mass creations of voters as in Caernarfon and Cardigan. Dormant for most of the eighteenth century but potentially dominant was the 'Cardiff Castle interest', which prevailed in Cowbridge, Llantrisant and in Cardiff itself, when the two bailiffs acted as returning officers. In 1704 this passed to the Viscounts Windsor. Only in these three boroughs and in Kenfig, purchased in 1668 by the Mansels of Margam, was the large-scale creation of voters possible: in the other four boroughs burgess-ship involved such extensive material privileges that creation of freemen for electoral purposes was difficult and unpopular.

[75] Plas Newydd MSS II, 216.

[76] For details and documentation, see Thomas, 'The Parliamentary Representation of Caernarvonshire in the Eighteenth Century, Part I, 1708–1749', *T. Caerns. H.S.*, 19 (1958), 42–8; 'The Parliamentary Representation of Caernarvonshire in the Eighteenth Century, Part II, 1749–1784', 20 (1959), 80–6.

Swansea and Loughor were controlled by the Dukes of Beaufort, and Neath from 1686 by the Mackworths of Gnoll, who were also contesting control of Aberavon with the Mansels. Only four boroughs, Cardiff, Cowbridge, Neath and Swansea, had councils, small and co-optive: the others, Aberavon, Kenfig, Llantrisant and Loughor, were manorial boroughs ruled by courts leet.[77]

In the late seventeenth and early eighteenth centuries Mansel control was maintained by astute political management of what was a group of Tory patrons. During the Walpole ministry the Glamorgan Whigs disputed this hegemony, Thomas Mathews of Llandaff being defeated in 1727 and 1734 respectively by Bussy Mansel and Herbert Windsor; the poll figures are not known for either contest. When Windsor succeeded to his father's peerage in 1738 the other patrons agreed on the candidature of Herbert Mackworth. He represented the constituency from 1739 until his death in 1765, when he was succeeded by his namesake son. Neither Mackworth faced any contest, but their long tenure of the seat was due to the acquiescence of the other patrons and not to the significance of Neath. In 1790, much to his indignation, the younger Mackworth was obliged to surrender his seat to the son of Lord Mountstuart, later the first Marquess of Bute, who had acquired the Cardiff Castle estate by marriage to the Windsor heiress in 1766. Power politics had replaced a gentlemanly arrangement. For the Cardiff Castle interest ruled three of the four boroughs where mass creation of freemen encountered no problems, and Lord Mountstuart had obtained a promise of support from Thomas Mansel Talbot, patron of the fourth, Kenfig. As a precaution Lord Mountstuart during 1789 arranged for the admission of 111 new freemen in Cardiff and forty-three in Llantrisant, and thereafter the Cardiff Castle interest returned the borough MPs.[78]

There was a token opposition in 1818, when Lord Bute's brother Patrick James Stuart won by forty-five votes to seventeen out of an electorate of 500. But then a political quarrel between the Tory Lord Bute and his Whig brother led Stuart to move in 1820 to a family seat in Scotland. For Cardiff Bute returned Wyndham Lewis with a majority of 457 to 245 over Ebenezer Ludlow, Bute's original candidate and whose large majorities from Swansea and Loughor, totalling 109 to 4, demonstrated Beaufort support. Kenfig supplied the significant majority of 146 to 4 for Lewis. By now there was widespread resentment at Bute's high-handed behaviour, as manifested in Cowbridge anger at his use of non-resident voters. Stuart, a

---

[77] John, 'The Parliamentary Representation of Glamorgan, 1536–1832', MA Wales, 1934, pp. 19–80, 207–8.

[78] For detail and documentation, see Thomas in *Glamorgan County History*, IV, 394–429.

popular figure in Glamorgan, made a triumphant return to the constituency in 1826, C. R. M. Talbot of Margam putting the Kenfig votes at his disposal and Lewis withdrawing before the poll. It is this election, rather than the often misinterpreted one of 1820, that was a defeat for the Cardiff Castle interest.[79]

The history of the unreformed borough constituencies was basically one of unscrupulous power struggles among local patrons. That some electorates were for that time comparatively large did not signify any independence of the voters: rather had burgess creations produced supplies of electoral cannon-fodder. No holds were barred in these contests. Attempts were made by shire towns to shed their contributory boroughs once their participation became a political privilege and not a financial liability. There were efforts in several constituencies to disfranchise large sections of the electorate. In others legal, or illegal, evasion of the residence stipulations took place. Violence at a poll was not uncommon. How many of these devices and manœuvres succeeded depended on arbitrary decisions of the House of Commons, according to the political flavour of the moment. If the decisions concerning Montgomery, Denbigh and Flint were the most obvious injustices, other decisions, like those concerning Tregaron and Wiston, appear questionable to a modern eye. That the overall trend was to ever tighter patron control was symbolized at the general election of 1790, when three peers, Mountstuart in Cardiff, Oxford in Radnor, and Uxbridge in Caernarfon, each installed their own relatives in the place of sitting members who had served their purpose.

---

[79] David, 'Political Electioneering Activity in South-East Wales, 1820–52', MA Wales, 1959, pp. 23–6, 35–6; John, 'The Parliamentary Representation of Glamorgan, 1536–1832', MA Wales, 1934, p. 247.

CHAPTER 3

The First Age of Party (1688–1714)

THE period between the Glorious Revolution of 1688 and the Hanoverian Succession in 1714 was one of political metamorphosis. The decades since the restoration of the monarchy in 1660 had seen the formation of organized political parties in Parliament, and especially had they been forged in the Exclusion Crisis of 1679–81, when Charles II foiled the vigorous attempts of majorities in three successive parliaments to prevent the succession to the throne of his Roman Catholic brother, the future James II. The Tories were defenders of the Crown, and the established order in state and church, the Whigs the opponents of government. That had been the political divide before the accession of James II in 1685 soon forced Tories to choose between church and monarchy, and only a small minority of them then gave preference to their King.

But if before the exile of James II in 1688 the Whigs had been the 'Country' or opposition party and the Tories the 'Court' party, after the accession of George I in 1714 this situation had become reversed. Exactly how and when this change occurred has long exercised the minds of historians, with the most recent arguments being focused on whether, how far, and how long the old antagonism of 'Court versus Country' remained a more significant divide in politics than the newer one of 'Whig versus Tory'. The latter from 1688 was now based on such current issues as the primacy in state as well as church of the Anglican faith, and the conduct of foreign policy, with the Whigs being more European-orientated than the Tories. And over the whole political scene there loomed the question of the succession to the throne, a matter brought to the forefront of attention again after 1700 when it became clear that the direct Stuart line would end on the death of Anne.

These new political issues soon came to overshadow the original party dispute over the extent of royal power. The Revolution Settlement of 1689 ended the danger of a direct royal autocracy, that might ignore Parliament and set aside the rule of law, such as had happened in several European monarchies: but there soon developed the fear that unscrupulous sovereigns might achieve virtually the same power by manipulation and corruption of Parliament and other institutions. The new 'country programme', while still embracing the older fear of a permanent army, was concerned to prevent any such development by preventing office-holders, 'placemen', from sitting in Parliament, insisting on frequent elections, and so on. The broad aims behind these proposals were to reduce the influence of the executive over the legislature, and to increase the dependence of the legislature on the electorate. These remained basic opposition principles for much of the century after 1689, but such issues were especially hard-fought in the reigns of William III and Queen Anne. For at a time when sovereigns wielded real power these matters were regarded by many MPs as of paramount concern, and the Court-Country split often cut across the Whig–Tory one that resurfaced in a new guise in the reign of William III.

The Whigs possessed the organizational advantage of good leadership by a small band of able men, the famous Junto, who soon made the Whigs an obvious party of government. The more numerous Tories, most of them country squires, lacked such a focal point, and clustered in loose groups around such peers as the Earls of Danby and Nottingham. The key political personality of the period was Robert Harley, MP for Radnor Boroughs from 1690 until he took a peerage as Earl of Oxford in 1711, for he responded positively to the new political situation. Himself of a Whig and Presbyterian family, Harley in the 1690s created a 'New Country Party' that embraced some former Whigs as well as many more Tories looking for a cause. This gradually fused with the 'Church of England' Tories to form a reshaped Tory party by about 1700, but both before and after that date the broader Court–Country divide could still produce some cross-voting, with the few remaining Country Whigs opposing a Whig Junto ministry on some issues, while conversely that ministry might enjoy the support of Court Tories.

How did Wales fit into this political system? The country had been strongly Royalist in the Civil War, and was to return an overwhelming majority of Tory MPs during the reign of Queen Anne. But the deduction that there was a political tradition linking these two situations does not stand up to detailed examination. Indeed, at the time of the Exclusion Crisis of 1679 there was strong Welsh sympathy for the embryonic Whig party. Whig leader Lord Shaftesbury, in his classification of the first Exclusion Parliament, expected support from fifteen of the twenty-seven Welsh MPs. Of the others he deemed six only as courtiers, three as doubtful, and three were not classified at all.[1] When it came to the actual

---

[1] J. R. Jones, 'Shaftesbury's "Worthy Men"', *BIHR*, 30 (1957), 238, 241.

vote, the Welsh MPs aligned twelve to seven for exclusion, with eight being absent.[2] Many of the names on each side were as would be expected from the later behaviour of themselves or their families as Whig or Tory. The dozen for exclusion included Bussy Mansel, Rowland Gwynne, Edward Vaughan of Crosswood, and two Owens of Orielton. The seven against included three Bulkeleys of the Baron Hill family, Sir John Wynn of Watstay, Edward Vaughan of Llwydiarth, and William Wogan from Pembrokeshire. But the traditional orthodoxy of political analysis, that Exclusionism presaged Whiggery, overlooks the consideration that much of the strength of that movement was drawn from the tap-roots of future Toryism, support of the Church of England, and country hostility to the Court. There is palpable continuity between the strength of Exclusionism in Wales and the Tory dominance there a generation afterwards.

Ten years later, the Convention Parliament of 1689–90 included only nine of those twenty-seven Welsh MPs. For this brief Parliament there survive only two minority voting lists. One is for 5 February 1689, when extreme Tories, including ten Welsh MPs, voted that James II had not vacated the throne; the other is of 147 extreme Whigs, three Welsh MPs among them, for a vote on 12 January 1690.[3] Collation of these lists with local, earlier and later evidence makes it possible to categorize eleven Welsh MPs as Whig and fourteen as Tory.[4] The former Speaker Sir William Williams appears in both lists, and his case, albeit that of a careerist, exemplifies the political confusion of the time. Having been the Speaker in the Exclusion Parliaments he had made his peace with James II, from whom he obtained a baronetcy in 1688 after his role as prosecuting Solicitor-General in the famous trial of the Seven Bishops. After initial snubs he became reconciled with William III, but ended his career as a country Tory, sitting twice for Beaumaris as nominee of the Tory third Lord Bulkeley.

At the general election of 1690 Wales returned thirteen Whigs and Tories apiece. Montgomery MP Charles Herbert is excluded from this computation, for he was an army officer serving in Ireland, where he was killed in 1691. That such party designations were not always meaningful in a local context is shown by the reaction to a Radnorshire by-election of 1692, which was a nominal Tory gain as merchant John Jeffreys replaced the deceased Richard Williams. Local comment on the result portrayed it as the triumph of 'a Presbyterian interest', since Robert Harley had

[2] Browning and Milne, 'An Exclusion Bill Division List', *BIHR*, 23 (1950), 215, 224–5.

[3] *White and Black Lists*, pp. 4–5; Browning, *Danby*, III, 72. The former list, with variations, is analysed in Cruickshanks, Ferris and Hayton, 'The House of Commons Vote on the Transfer of the Crown, 5 February 1689', *BIHR*, 52 (1979), 37–47.

[4] Two, Sir John Williams and Charles Herbert, were apparently absent.

sponsored Jeffreys, and as the election of 'a stranger against their own countryman': for a resident squire, Edward Lewis of Mynachdy, backed by Sir Rowland Gwynne, had opposed Jeffreys until he abandoned the poll when losing by 271 votes to 120.[5] In 1690, too, the replacement of Court Tory Sir John Hanmer by Thomas Whitley meant that predominantly Tory Flintshire was fortuitously represented in this Parliament by two Whigs. Otherwise north Wales returned eight identifiable Tories, but south Wales only five out of its sixteen MPs. That was due to the balance of family interests, for the only seat decided by overtly political considerations was Breconshire, where Whig Sir Rowland Gwynne had deliberately driven out Jacobite Edward Jones.[6]

That 'the rage of party' had not yet taken hold of national politics is implied by the absence of any Whig–Tory division-lists for the whole Parliament of 1690 to 1695. The Court–Country divide was the customary alignment of Parliamentary dispute, for William III himself was the centre of government. The Court party, whether its members were nominally Whig or Tory, supported both the predominantly Tory ministry of the Earls of Danby and Nottingham, and its Whig Junto replacement in 1694. Government lists of supporters tend to be merely those of placemen, and are singularly devoid of Welsh MPs. A 1692 list of 103 office-holder MPs included only Sir William Wogan of the Welsh members, as a 'Judge in Wales'.[7] That most Welsh MPs were of the country persuasion is suggested by an obviously incomplete list of 170 potential opposition MPs for the session 1694–5. The ten Welsh MPs include country Whigs Sir Roger Puleston and Richard Vaughan, Robert Harley, and seven Tories.[8]

Nor were party considerations significant in Wales at the general election of 1695, except perhaps in the revenge defeat inflicted in Breconshire by Tory Edward Jones on Whig Sir Rowland Gwynne, who retreated to a Devonshire constituency. A modern classification of this Parliament, based on analysis of three division-lists of 1696, has revealed that the balance of Welsh politics was now tilting in favour of the Tory–Country alliance being forged and fostered by Radnor MP Robert Harley. The Whig Junto ministry could rely on firm support from only six of the twenty-seven Welsh MPs: the Monmouthshire trio of Thomas Morgan, Sir Charles Kemys and John Arnold, together with old Bussy Mansel in Glamorgan, and the two MPs from Cardiganshire, Lord Lisburne and John Lewis. Six others were independent or 'country' Whigs, liable to vote in opposition on

[5] Adams, 'The Parliamentary Representation of Radnorshire, 1536–1832', MA Wales, 1969, pp. 185–6.
[6] Penrice and Margam MSS L1385.
[7] Browning, *Danby*, III, 176–8, 184–7.
[8] Rubini, *Court and Country*, pp. 262–7.

appropriate topics: these were the Pembrokeshire pair of Arthur Owen and John Philipps, the two MPs from Carmarthenshire, Sir Rice Rudd and Richard Vaughan, Flint MP Sir Roger Puleston, and, surprisingly, the new MP for Merioneth, Hugh Nanney, despite his Tory relatives and connections. The other fifteen Welsh MPs were Tory or country MPs, notably Harley himself.[9]

Temporary political salvation for the Junto came with the 1696 Fenwick plot to assassinate the King. The ministry launched the "Association for the Defence of William III", refusal to sign which could be construed as disloyalty. This enabled the ministry to drive a wedge between its opponents, a division of basic loyalties that in some sense foreshadowed the Tory split over the succession at the end of Anne's reign. Nineteen Welsh MPs signed the Association, including Lord Bulkeley, after an initial refusal, and even two, Edward Vaughan and Sir William Wogan, who in 1689 had voted against declaring the throne vacant. Eight Welsh MPs refused to sign, six of them having also been against giving the Crown to William in 1689: Edward Brereton, Edward Jones, Thomas Mansel, Sir Richard Myddelton, Sir John Wynn, and Sir William Williams, the last objecting not on principle but on the specious excuse that it had once cost him £8,000 to sign a document in the House, when a Speaker prosecuted by the Crown, and that he would not sign another![10] The other two were Sir John Conway and Jeffrey Jeffreys. The group did not foreshadow the future shape of Jacobitism in Wales. In the 1690s, indeed, apart from local disorders such as those in Pembrokeshire caused by malcontent partisans of the exiled James II, Jacobitism was not an active political movement, for at this time the continuity of the Stuart monarchy through the progeny of Anne was still anticipated.[11]

The end of that assumption in 1700 on the death of Anne's last child stimulated a discussion on the succession question that was to wreck the Toryism that had by then emerged as the majority political attitude in England and was to dominate Welsh politics until the end of Anne's reign and beyond. The diversity of attitudes within the new Toryism was fully reflected in its Welsh dimension. Although a strong Jacobite element was to emerge, the Tory party in Wales essentially comprised independent-minded Anglican squires, sympathetic to the 'country' ideas of Robert Harley, however much they might suspect and even dislike a man of Whig and

[9] Burton, Riley and Rowlands, 'Political Parties . . .', *BIHR, Special Supplement* No. 7 (1968), 41–2, 46, 51. This wrongly classifies Owen, Philipps and Vaughan as Tories, not as Country Whigs. The error concerning Owen is corrected, ibid., 36.

[10] *HMC Hastings*, p. 259.

[11] For the Pembrokeshire disorders, see F. Jones, 'Disaffection and Dissent in Pembrokeshire', *T.H.S. Cymm.* (1946–7), pp. 216–20.

Presbyterian background. Some Welsh MPs had more specific political associations. Family ties brought both the Bulkeleys and the Mostyns into the orbit of Lord Nottingham. Too much has been made of such connections by historian Robert Walcott, who erroneously included Edward Brereton in the Nottingham group on the tenuous ground that he was an uncle of a cousin of Nottingham's deceased first wife. For the Bulkeley family held Jacobite views at odds with those of Nottingham.[12] In south Wales Robert Harley was to build up something of a personal following, Thomas Mansel of Margam being an early recruit and soon a close associate.

As by the late 1690s the British political system settled into a clear Whig–Tory polarity, so was more attention paid in the constituencies to the political conduct of MPs. No longer would personal esteem or electoral agreements secure the election of Whigs for strongly Tory areas, as had happened in Flintshire and Merioneth. It was to the obvious disadvantage of Welsh Whiggery that elections became more directly related to the behaviour of MPs at Westminster. But this change did not manifest itself at the general election of 1698. Local circumstances resulted in Whig gains as well as losses: Owen Hughes took the Beaumaris seat by a coup, and Sir Rowland Gwynne regained Breconshire from the Tory successor to the deceased Edward Jones. But in Monmouthshire Court Tory Sir John Williams replaced a Whig, and a reshuffle in Cardiganshire meant a net Whig loss; when borough MP John Lewis replaced another Whig Lord Lisburne in the county, his seat was taken by a country Tory, Sir Charles Lloyd. That local rivalries might still have little relation to national politics was shown by the Radnorshire election. Here John Jeffreys, though a Tory at Westminster, had now deserted the Harleys and allied with Whig Sir Rowland Gwynne. Robert Harley therefore put forward his cousin Thomas Harley, who won after a lively campaign that failed, however, to culminate in a poll.[13] In 1698 there was no challenge to such Whig strongholds as Carmarthenshire, Monmouthshire and Pembrokeshire, and altogether Wales returned twelve Whigs and fifteen Tories.

At Westminster, now that the end of the French war in 1697 had released the pent-up fury of MPs at its cost and apparent futility, the Whig Junto ministry faced increasing hostility on 'country' issues. This initially focused on the traditional grievance that a permanent army was both expensive and a putative threat to liberty. That was an issue on which country Whigs would oppose the ministry, as Owen Hughes did. Fourteen Welsh MPs were named in a list of 209 expected to vote for a reduction of the army,

[12] Walcott, *English Politics*, pp. 58–9, 209.
[13] Adams, 'The Parliamentary Representation of Radnorshire', pp. 197–8, 200–1.

which was carried in January 1699 by 221 votes to 154.[14] Only four voted for government, Sir Rowland Gwynne, Sir John Philipps, Sir Rice Rudd and Court Tory Sir John Williams.[15]

The parliamentary weakness of the Whig Junto caused William III gradually to replace them in office by Tories. Robert Harley was elected Speaker after the general election of January 1701, and retained that post, then of political significance in the guidance of debate, for three parliaments, until 1705. There were two general elections in 1701. Since the first resulted in a strongly 'country' House of Commons William III dissolved it for a December election of what proved to be his last Parliament, for the King died in March 1702. The elections of 1701 demonstrated that party considerations were now an important influence in elections, to the disadvantage of Welsh Whigs, who ended the reign with only seven MPs as against twenty Tories.[16] In Merioneth the death of Whig Hugh Nanney led to his replacement in May by his Tory kinsman Richard Vaughan of Corsygedol. December 1701 saw Tory Henry Lloyd replace Whig John Lewis as Cardigan Boroughs MP. Even in their strongholds Whigs came under attack. In January Sir Arthur Owen defeated a Tory challenge in Pembrokeshire, and new MP Griffith Rice had to defeat a Tory to gain his Carmarthenshire seat in December. Sir John Philipps still sat for Pembroke Boroughs, and Carmarthen MP Richard Vaughan had now long since shed his pre-1688 Tory past. In Monmouthshire it was fortunate for the Whig cause that the Beaufort interest was at its nadir, so that the Morgans of Tredegar held two seats. Sir Rowland Gwynne retained his precarious hold on Breconshire. The Whigs of Wales were to have a hard time of it in the Tory atmosphere of Queen Anne's reign.

The accession in 1702 of a monarch who was a devout Anglican and of evident Tory predilections seemed to betoken a golden Tory future at the local level in Wales as well as at Whitehall and Westminster. Many Tory squires doubtless shared the hopes voiced by young Lewis Pryse of Gogerddan, anxious for revenge on his Cardiganshire Whig rival Lord Lisburne, who had contrived, through Lord Carbery, to engross official favour under William III: on 21 April Pryse wrote to fellow Tory William Powell of Nanteos:

---

[14] Hayton, 'The Country Party in the House of Commons', *Parliamentary History*, 6 (1987), 147–60.

[15] Browning, *Danby*, III, 213–17.

[16] Snyder, 'Party Configurations in the Early Eighteenth Century House of Commons', *BIHR*, 45 (1972), 37–72. This modern analysis is confirmed for Welsh MPs by a list in Harley's papers for the end of William III's reign. BL Harleian MSS 7556, ff. 96, 100.

I am now in great hopes of putting my Lord Lisburne's nose out of joint in his arbitrary government in this country . . . We shall take all care imaginable in settling the officials of our country in order to improve our interest; and I don't question but we shall meet with such a favourable compliance from the government as shall answer our expectation.[17]

Queen Anne was guided by the Duke of Marlborough, who had Lord Godolphin appointed Lord Treasurer to run the home government while he was busy with the war in Europe. Satisfied about Tory determination to win the French war, they accepted the evident wish of their sovereign for a Tory ministry. It was headed by High Tories like Nottingham and Rochester, and some Welsh MPs associated with them shared in minor spoils of office: Robert Bulkeley, Thomas Bulkeley and Sir Roger Mostyn, who in 1703 was to marry one of Nottingham's daughters.[18] There were few places for the moderate Harleyites, and Welsh MPs of that group bided their time for office.

Popular sentiment and government influence combined to make the general election of 1702 a sweeping Tory triumph, but in Wales there was little scope for gains. Two of the seven Whig MPs lost their seats, one by defeat, the other by personal choice. Sir Rowland Gwynne lost in Breconshire to John Jeffreys, the former Radnorshire MP and brother of the member for Brecon Borough. Jeffreys won by seventy-seven votes, a poll-book complete except for the hundred of Talgarth showing a majority for him of 433 to 399.[19] So passed from the parliamentary scene one of the notable Welsh MPs of the late seventeenth century, who had been chairman of the Commons Committee of Elections from 1698 to 1702. Gwynne had held office virtually throughout William III's reign, as Treasurer of the Chamber, and then a sinecure at the Board of Green Cloth. He now spent much of Anne's reign abroad, and never regained a Commons seat. Sir John Philipps, anxious to concentrate on his philanthropic activities, gave up his Pembroke Boroughs seat to another Orielton nominee, Tory John Meyrick of Bush, while Sir Arthur Owen's other leading Tory ally in Pembrokeshire, John Laugharne, now secured the Haverfordwest seat, until his death in 1715. Though Meyrick was a High Churchman, both he and Laugharne were soon drawn into the Harley network of influence in south Wales. Elsewhere Welsh Whigs were as yet firmly entrenched on strong family interests. Griffith Rice and Richard Vaughan continued to represent Carmarthen county and borough on that of Golden Grove, while in

---

[17] Nanteos MSS L53.
[18] Luttrell, *State Affairs*, V, 180, 250–1, 315–16.
[19] Penpont MSS 2395.

Monmouthshire the Tredegar interest enabled the two John Morgans to share the representation with Sir John Williams. Here, as in Pembrokeshire, political opponents at Westminster were electoral allies.

The only other Welsh contest of 1702, in Flintshire, arose from personal rivalry among the Tory squires. Sir John Conway, who had sat in every Parliament since 1695 for county or borough, was unwilling, so Sir Thomas Hanmer informed a friend, 'to be out of Parliament once in ten years when other gentlemen require to have their turn of serving . . . he is forming an interest against that which Sir Roger Mostyn and I shall jointly prosecute on our behalf. The county I shall appear for, and Sir Roger for the borough, both mutually assisting one another'.[20] Hanmer defeated Conway for the county by 510 votes to 308. The determination of the victorious coalition to keep Conway out of Parliament was underlined when Mostyn vacated the borough seat by opting to represent Cheshire, where he had also been returned; for at the by-election in December he was succeeded by his brother Thomas, who had sat from 1698 to 1701.

Cardiganshire was the only other Welsh seat to change its MP in 1702. Here Sir Humphrey Mackworth again represented the county, warmly supported by the associates in his mine venture, the retiring member Lewis Pryse, still under age, and William Powell of Nanteos.[21] Elsewhere the elections seemingly passed off without incident, and the situation in Denbighshire was doubtless typical. The county MP Sir Richard Myddelton sent out his canvassing letters on 5 July, a mere month before the election, and next day Sir William Williams of Llanforda, namesake successor of the Speaker, wrote to Sir John Wynn of Watstay:

> I signified my readiness by letter to serve worthy Sir Richard Myddelton with my voice and interest the next election. And in compliance with your request am disposed to promote Mr Brereton's election for the borough.[22]

Brereton, returned again on 5 August, developed a connection with Lord Treasurer Godolphin, and after accepting a minor but lucrative office in 1703 he became, like Sir John Williams, a Court Tory.[23]

Events during the ensuing Parliament soon demonstrated that disputes within Tory ranks during the next few years were to be more significant than the divide between Tories and Whigs, now a twenty-two to five split among Welsh MPs. For before the next election in 1705 the moderate Harleyites, six Welsh MPs among them, were to unite with Whigs in a

---

[20] *HMC Kenyon*, p. 428.
[21] Nanteos MSS L57.
[22] Chirk Castle MSS E 1021–8, 6130–1.
[23] Chirk Castle MSS E 1028; Luttrell, *State Affairs*, V, 336.

ministry confronted by a Tory opposition. The realignment came about partly over conduct of the war, partly over religion, the determination of the Tory majority to exclude Protestant Dissenters from office by enforcing the Anglican monopoly prescribed by the Test Act of 1673.

Before that sequence of events unfolded there occurred one of those incidents that enabled Whigs to brand Tories as Jacobites. The Hanoverian Succession to the throne on the death of Anne had been established by the 1701 Act of Settlement; but a vote in the House of Commons on 13 February 1703 was nevertheless portrayed in Whig propaganda as having been in reality on the succession issue. The House divided on a technical motion concerning the loyalty oath, carried only by 118 to 117. The division was widely regarded as having been a trial of strength before the next clause, one establishing the penalty of treason for opposing the Hanoverian Succession, and which was then carried without a vote. The minority, which included the third Lord Bulkeley, Thomas Mansel of Margam, and Sir Roger Mostyn, were blacklisted for Jacobite sympathies. The incident had a particular interest for Wales, because of the Orielton tradition that the clause had been about to fail by one vote when Griffith Rice and Sir Arthur Owen, in that order, belatedly entered the House and redressed the balance. The Owen family claimed the credit for thereby saving the Hanover Succession! Both men were listed as voting then, as was John Morgan of Tredegar.[24]

Political attention subsequently focused on the Tory fight, led by the Nottingham group from within the ministry, for an Occasional Conformity Bill to exclude from office Dissenters who took the Anglican sacrament the minimum number of times, perhaps only once a year, to avoid the legal disability imposed by the Test Act of 1673, and, for local government, the Corporation Act of 1661. Tory indignation at such evasion had been brought to a head by an incident involving Sir Humphrey Edwin, a wealthy London merchant and Dissenter who founded a new political dynasty in Glamorgan by his purchase of the Llanvihangel estate. Edwin, on his first Sunday as lord mayor of London in 1697, provocatively made a formal procession in the full panoply of office to a 'conventicle'.[25] The Occasional Conformity Bill was intended to prevent any such behaviour by penalties of fines and forfeitures of office, and twice, in 1702 and 1703, it passed the Commons only to fall at the barrier of the Whig-Court majority in the Lords.

By 1704 there was a clear divide between the moderate Tories and the High Tories, over religion and over the conduct of the war, which as a

---

[24] *White and Black Lists*, 8–11; Phillips, *Orielton Memoirs*, 58–9.
[25] Luttrell, *State Affairs*, IV, 303.

decade earlier again cost Nottingham his post as Secretary of State. In May 1704 he was replaced by Robert Harley, who also still remained Speaker. In the previous month Thomas Mansel of Margam succeeded Sir Edward Seymour as Controller of the Royal Household, part of the same political change. The showdown came in November, when the High Tories resorted to the device of tacking the Occasional Conformity Bill to the land tax, seeking by this dubious manœuvre to take advantage of the constitutional principle that the House of Lords could not reject a finance measure. This tactic rebounded on their heads when on 28 November the Commons rejected it by 251 votes to 134. Many Tories abstained or voted against the Tack. Only eight Welsh MPs supported it. Three were connected with Nottingham – Thomas Bulkeley, Sir Thomas Hanmer and Thomas Mostyn, whose brother Sir Roger, then a Cheshire MP and Nottingham's son-in-law, was also in the minority. The other five were country Tories, the brothers Edward and John Vaughan from Montgomeryshire, Sir Humphrey Mackworth and Henry Lloyd from Cardiganshire, and old Sir John Wynn. All contemporary lists agree on the names of the Tackers, but majority lists are so suspect as to have 335 names for the 253 voters. They include three Welsh Whigs – John Morgan, Griffith Rice and Richard Vaughan – three Harleyites – Robert and Thomas Harley and John Laugharne – and five Welsh Tories.[26]

'Queen Anne is turned Whig.' So wrote Sir Rowland Gwynne about the reconstructed ministry of Harleyites and Whigs.[27] But such electoral coalition as resulted in 1705 did not benefit Gwynne, who had hoped thereby to regain his Breconshire seat. In a letter of 15 May to his old enemy Robert Harley he announced that intention. 'If I am not chosen there, perhaps I may be elsewhere.'[28] Any reply cannot have been encouraging, for Sir Rowland left Breconshire to be contested by his kinsman Sackville Gwynne of Glanbran, and stood himself unsuccessfully for Cambridgeshire on the interest of the Earl of Orford, whose niece he had married in 1703.[29] The Breconshire MP John Jeffreys did not stand again, preferring to resume a seat at Marlborough, but Sackville Gwynne was defeated by Sir Edward Williams of Gwernyfed, the Tory displaced by Sir Rowland in 1698. In nearby Radnorshire the revival of an important but long dormant interest was portended when Richard Fowler of Abbey Cwmhir canvassed the county.[30]

---

[26] For various lists, see *White and Black Lists*, pp. 32–4; Oldmixon, *History of England*, 346–7; Chandler, *Debates*, IV, Appendix; Cobbett, *Parl. Hist.*, VI, 362–7.

[27] Feiling, *Tory Party*, p. 379.

[28] *HMC Portland*, IV, 181.

[29] Luttrell, *State Affairs*, V, 338.

[30] Adams, 'Parliamentary Representation of Radnorshire', pp. 204–8.

The realignment in national politics meant that the alliance in Pembrokeshire between the Whig Owens of Orielton and moderate Tories John Meyrick and John Laugharne was no longer an anomaly; both retained their borough seats, but Sir Arthur Owen retired from the county in favour of his brother Wyriot. Next year the Harleyite–Whig alliance did bear electoral fruit: for on the death of Thomas Mansel of Briton Ferry in 1706 the Margam family nominated a local Whig, Sir John Aubrey of Llantrithyd, to succeed him as MP for Cardiff Boroughs.[31] How positive this alliance was in other constituencies is unclear. In 1705, a friend of Robert Harley clearly assumed he would support the Whig Morgans in the first Monmouthshire contest between the great interests of Tredegar and Raglan.[32]

Here the young second Duke of Beaufort, who only came of age in April 1705, had already made clear his determination to reassert his family influence in both constituencies. The death of Sir John Williams in November 1704 raised the question of the county representation. The Duke met the Morgans face to face, and his understanding was that they would make no move without consultation. But by January 1705 the two John Morgans, uncle and nephew, were canvassing the county, and the Duke of Beaufort indignantly countered this Tredegar attempt to win both shire seats by sponsoring two rival candidates, Sir Hopton Williams of Llangibby, brother and successor of Sir John, and Sir Thomas Powell, the defeated Carmarthenshire candidate of 1701, then residing on his Monmouthshire estate of Coldbrook.[33] The background of alleged treachery and the even balance of interests made this a bitter contest, especially when, nine days before the county election, the Duke succeeded in replacing the elder Morgan as borough member by Powell. At what may have been the first ever poll for the county, 1,398 freeholders voted. John Morgan of Tredegar came top with 843 votes, but the second seat went to Sir Hopton Williams, who headed John Morgan of Ruperra by 696 votes to 659, Powell finishing well behind with 564.[34]

Altogether thirteen seats changed hands in Wales at the 1705 election, and although there were only three polls several MPs were forced out unwillingly. In Cardiganshire Lewis Pryse demonstrated Gogerddan power by both taking the borough seat himself and replacing Mackworth as county member by his Jacobite crony John Pugh of Mathafarn in Montgomeryshire, causing a disgruntled Sir Humphrey to find a seat at Totnes. A move to replace Edward Brereton, MP for Denbigh Boroughs

---

[31] Thomas, 'Glamorgan Politics, 1700–1750', *Morgannwg*, 6 (1962), 55–6.
[32] *HMC Portland*, IV, 195.
[33] Tredegar MSS 53/94–6.
[34] Tredegar MSS 255.

since 1689, with a representative more attuned to the political views of his fellow squires was more awkward to implement, but was also achieved without a contest. Brereton's connection with government may have rendered him suspect even before the issue of the Tack. His refusal to support that measure exposed him to bitter local criticism, and he accordingly wrote from London to Sir Richard Myddelton on 3 March.[35]

> I hear that some persons have aspersed me, and reported that I am turned a Whig. I cannot guess at the reason of it, unless it be that I did not stay in the House to vote for the tacking of the bill against occasional conformity to the land tax bill . . . I must not forget to acquaint you, that I was heartily zealous for the Bill itself against occasional conformity, and when the motion was made for leave to bring it into the House, twas vigorously opposed, and I divided for it; and afterwards I appeared for the Bill in all the steps which it made in the House (except in the tacking part) and now you have the history of my fanaticism; and I had rather be called a pickpocket rather than a Whig.

Myddelton, who had also missed the vote on the Tack and like Brereton had been listed as opposing it, answered that he would consult with Sir John Wynn, and they sent a tactful reply through an intermediary, stating, as acknowledged by Brereton, that 'the temper and inclinations of the country gentlemen are not so favourable to me as they could wish, and that they feared that it would be too difficult a task for them to serve me effectively in the next election'. Brereton failed to take this hint, announcing that he would stand if Wynn and Myddelton would support him.[36] But, together with Sir William Williams, they had already decided on another candidate, William Robinson of Gwersyllt, who had approached Myddelton under the impression that Brereton's office would disqualify him from standing again. This time their answer to Brereton led to his withdrawal.[37]

Discord appeared in North Wales only with a Whig challenge, as in Anglesey and Montgomery Boroughs. Elsewhere, any changes in representation were merely adjustments to suit the convenience or prestige of local squires. In Caernarfonshire Thomas Bulkeley and Sir John Wynn exchanged constituencies. In Flintshire the problem of three Tory baronets competing for two seats was now solved permanently, for Sir Thomas Hanmer was able to secure election for Suffolk on the interest of his wife's estate in that county. Sir John Conway and Sir Roger Mostyn could share

---

[35] Chirk Castle MSS E 4204.
[36] Chirk Castle MSS E6066.
[37] Chirk Castle MSS E 979, 6064–6.

the representation by amicable agreements for the rest of Anne's reign, in 1705 taking the county and borough seats respectively. But in Montgomery Boroughs the Tory squires were tricked by the device of a last-minute candidature, doubtless organized by Francis Herbert, Whig patron of the county town. No opposition to John Vaughan's re-election had been anticipated, but on the election day Charles Mason, a Shropshire Whig of unsavoury reputation, appeared and defeated Vaughan by forty-one votes to thirty, out of an electorate of 700. All legal formalities had been scrupulously observed, and Vaughan's petition to the House of Commons was rejected. Mason soon obtained a lucrative minor post, the only Welsh Whig MP to hold office under Anne.[38]

That result was an infuriating but temporary setback for Tory squires. Of more long-term significance was a Whig challenge to the hegemony of Baron Hill in Anglesey. Here, on the death of the third Viscount Bulkeley in 1704, the family title and estate, and also the county seat, had passed to his twenty-two-year-old Jacobite son. An arrogant and unpopular young man, the new Lord Bulkeley faced a challenge in 1705 from the leading Anglesey Whig, Owen Meyrick of Bodorgan. The rivalry of these men was to be the main theme of Anglesey politics for two decades, but in 1705 Meyrick declined to force a poll after a vigorous canvass had proved unfavourable.[39] In Beaumaris there was no attack on Baron Hill, and Lord Bulkeley, who had married a daughter of the Earl of Abingdon in 1703, gave the seat to his brother-in-law Henry Bertie, a moderate Tory.

The general election of 1705 confirmed the hold of Tory families in Wales, reinforced now by the revival of the Beaufort interest, for only five Whigs had been returned. At Westminster the overall result was deemed to be so finely balanced between ministry and opposition as to lead to a vigorous contest over the Speakership, now being vacated by Robert Harley. Whigs, Harleyites and courtiers combined to carry the ministerial candidate John Smith by 248 votes to 208, against the Tory William Bromley. Twenty-five Welsh MPs attended, the highest number known at any Commons vote before the nineteenth century. The two absentees were both Harleyites: Thomas Mansel of Briton Ferry was ill, but John Meyrick, a High Churchman, may well have stayed away. Ten Welsh MPs voted for Smith, the five Whigs, four Harleyites, and Sir Hopton Williams, who despite the Beaufort support at his election proved to be a Court Tory, like his brother. The other fifteen Welsh Tory MPs were in the minority, Sir

---

[38] *CJ*, XV, 8–9, 14–15, 94–5; Luttrell, *State Affairs*, X, 44, 49, 151; VI, 7, 294.
[39] Baron Hill MSS 5510.

Roger Mostyn speaking in the debate, as were, from outside Wales, Sir Humphrey Mackworth, John Jeffreys and Sir Thomas Hanmer.[40]

Only one other voting-list for this Parliament is known, that for the ministerial majority of 205 for a clause in the 1706 Regency Bill removing a prohibition in the 1701 Act of Settlement on office-holders sitting in Parliament after Anne's death. That such an aim had been an old country issue emphasizes the irony that Robert Harley, founder of the 'New Country Party' in the previous decade, now voted on the court side, as did his cousin, Sir Hopton Williams and three Welsh Whigs – Griffith Rice, Charles Mason, and Wyriot Owen.[41] The Harleyite–Whig alliance cut across both major political alignments, Court–Country as well as Whig–Tory, and proved short-lived. Pressure for more offices and greater power by the Whig Junto resentful of Harley's leading role emphasized the artificiality of the coalition and soon forced Lord Treasurer Godolphin to choose between Whigs and Harleyites, and Marlborough's preference for the positive Whig support of the war tipped the balance. The resignations of Robert Harley and his supporters, including Sir Thomas Mansel as he now was, took place in February 1708, before the general election of that year. Government influence and popular enthusiasm for a successful war made this election result the best one for Whigs between the Exclusion Parliaments and the Hanoverian Succession, but not in Wales. Welsh Whigs caught the mood by challenging several Tory seats, albeit without any success.

The Bulkeley interest in Anglesey and Caernarfonshire bore the brunt of this reaction, perhaps because of personal enmity to the fourth Viscount Bulkeley, regarded by his enemies as 'a gentleman that hath but very little of truth or honesty in him and less sense'.[42] In Caernarfonshire the death of old Thomas Bulkeley in March created a vacancy for the borough seat and removed the man who had so long dominated the county political scene. Even the ambitious young Whig squire Thomas Wynn of Glynllifon had deferred to his political management, but he had nevertheless been creating his own interest with the aid of his relative Richard Vaughan, the Tory MP for Merioneth, by playing on the resentment of smaller squires at Bulkeley control. Faced with this potential threat the Bulkeley party called a general county meeting on 22 April, which decided that Sir John Wynn should continue as shire member, while William Griffith of Cefnamwlch, a Tory squire of influence in the Lleyn peninsula, was to be returned for the borough. Ominously Thomas Wynn and his friends refused to sign this

[40] Speck, 'The Choice of a Speaker in 1705', *BIHR*, 37 (1964), 20–46.
[41] Walcott, 'Division-Lists of the House of Commons 1689–1715', *BIHR*, 14 (1936–7), 30–3.
[42] Penrhos MSS V, 101.

agreement, but they made no move to challenge these arrangements in 1708.[43]

The situation was very different in Anglesey, where there was now an ongoing feud between Lord Bulkeley and his enemies. Early in 1708 he sought to allay local resentment by offering a parliamentary seat to seventy-eight-year-old Nicholas Bagenal of Plas Newydd, who had sat for Anglesey from 1661 to 1679 as a Country MP. Bagenal declined on the grounds of age and infirmity, but, so Whig Owen Hughes gleefully informed a Tory squire John Owen of Penrhos, 'told his Lordship that he did not approve of his taking liberty to dispose of both the Parliament men in this country as he did'. Bagenal also announced that he would support any candidate chosen by the gentry of Anglesey.[44] The Tory squires did not respond to this plea to free their county from Bulkeley hegemony, but a Whig attack was mounted in both constituencies. Owen Meyrick of Bodorgan stood for the county, while Sir Arthur Owen of Orielton, whose island estate of Bodeon was the original Owen family home, came forward for the borough. Lord Bulkeley defeated Meyrick by 167 votes to 152 in a two-day poll, the first ever in the county, a margin of victory rendered precarious only by a partisan sheriff.[45] Afterwards Meyrick's supporters, anticipating the bias of a Whig House of Commons, came to regret that the sheriff had not returned him in disregard of the poll.[46] A biased parliamentary verdict, in favour of either Newborough's claim or that of the common burgesses of Beaumaris, was the only hope for Owen in the borough, where Bertie defeated him by sixteen to one in the corporation. At one meeting of the Election Committee matters became so heated that Lord Bulkeley struck Sir Arthur Owen, and the House had to order them not to fight a duel.[47] In this case political prejudice did not override legal precedents and chartered rights, the House confirming the Beaumaris corporation franchise.[48]

The other Whig challenge came in Cardiganshire. Here Lewis Pryse was again returned unopposed for the borough constituency on 20 May, but so fierce a Whig attack developed in the county, mounted by Lord Lisburne with Thomas Johnes of Llanfair Clydogau and of Hafod as candidate, that Pryse deemed his own candidature necessary to foil this onslaught. On the day of the county election, 2 June, he therefore replaced John Pugh and

---

[43] NLW General MSS 1548F.
[44] Penrhos MSS V, 101.
[45] Richards, 'The Anglesey Election of 1708', *TAAS* (1943), 23–34.
[46] Baron Hill MSS 5594.
[47] Luttrell, *State Affairs*, V, 538.
[48] *CJ*, XVI, 333–4. For more detail on both contests see Thomas, 'Anglesey Politics, 1689–1727', *TAAS* (1962), pp. 39–42.

defeated Johnes by 383 votes to 347 in a three-day poll. Johnes petitioned, but he was also to obtain no satisfaction from the Whig House of Commons.[49]

Altogether ten Welsh seats changed hands. Pugh moved to take the Montgomery Boroughs seat, where the Tory patrons removed the Whig interloper Charles Mason. In Flintshire Sir Roger Mostyn and Sir John Conway exchanged seats. Sir William Williams of Llanforda, who had evinced no parliamentary ambitions since his unsuccessful candidatures for Denbigh Boroughs in 1689 and 1690, now displaced William Robinson as that constituency's MP. For Monmouth Boroughs the Duke of Beaufort replaced Sir Thomas Powell by a man more to his Jacobite taste, Clayton Milbourne, a wealthy Gloucestershire landowner who retained the seat until the end of the reign. None of these changes were related to the national political scene, but that did influence the contest in Monmouthshire. Here Lord Windsor, a Tory MP for Bramber since 1705, had now decided to revive the old electoral interest of the Earls of Pembroke, but both current MPs were resolved to stand. The position of John Morgan of Tredegar was impregnable, but the Duke of Beaufort now withdrew his support from the courtier Sir Hopton Williams in favour of Lord Windsor as an opposition Tory. Analysis of the poll reveals not, as might be expected, an alliance between the two ministerial supporters, but rather a tacit understanding between the dominating Tredegar and Raglan interests. For Morgan obtained 212 votes in the Beaufort hundred of Skenfrith, as compared with only twenty-two in 1705; while Lord Windsor secured a majority of 258 to fifty-one over Williams in the Tredegar stronghold of Wentloog. Altogether about 1,600 freeholders voted in this three-sided contest between a Court Tory, an opposition Tory, and a Whig. Morgan headed the poll with 1,095 votes, Lord Windsor obtained 897, and Sir Hopton Williams only 605.[50]

If the national Whig resurgence did not lead to any Whig gains in Wales, the recent Whig–Harleyite split did have electoral repercussions. The long-standing alliance in Pembrokeshire between the Whig Owens of Orielton and the moderate Tories now ended. Two days after his defeat at Beaumaris Sir Arthur Owen displaced John Meyrick as Pembroke Boroughs MP, his brother Wyriot retaining the county. The breach at Westminster may also explain tentative Whig moves in the Harley preserve of Radnorshire. Rumours circulated that Richard Fowler was again, as in 1705, intending to challenge Thomas Harley in the county.[51] Thomas Lewis of Harpton,

---

[49] *CJ*, XVI, 267–9.
[50] Tredegar MSS 255.
[51] BL Add. MSS 70222, A. Davies to R. Harley, 10 March 1708.

whose namesake son was with Fowler to take the Radnorshire seats from the Harleys in 1715, informed Robert Harley on 10 March 'about the offers some persons lately made to oppose him [Thomas Harley], which I think will vanish. As for your part the obligations you have laid upon private families, and the great service you have done the public, make me esteem it an honour to have you as representative'.[52] Any threat to Harley power in Radnorshire was still-born.

Glamorgan was the scene of a vigorous controversy at this election, but as a form of political time-warp, since it originated from the earlier Whig–Harleyite alliance and ended with an ironic outcome. The Mansel nomination of Whig Sir John Aubrey at the Cardiff by-election of 1706 had sparked existing resentment at Mansel rule into open hostility. Before the end of that year a formidable opposition interest, including the Duke of Beaufort, Lord Windsor, and Sir Humphrey Mackworth, was supporting two rival candidates, Richard Jenkins of Hensol for the county and Sir Thomas Mansel's own brother-in-law Sir Edward Stradling for the borough. Mansel himself headed a powerful alliance of squires that included the Whig Morgans of Tredegar. That electoral alignment in Glamorgan during 1707 corresponded to the current national divide between supporters and opponents of the ministry. The resignation of the Harleyites in February 1708 was at once followed by attempts of the Glamorgan Tories to seek a compromise of the dispute. The Duke of Beaufort joined with Mansel in efforts at reconciliation. Jenkins was persuaded to withdraw, and Stradling forfeited all support when he declined to cast lots with Aubrey for the borough seat.[53] The result was a Mansel triumph – the unopposed return of the two previous members.[54]

Despite this fortuitous re-election of Sir John Aubrey the Whig Junto ministry enjoyed the support of only six Welsh MPs after the 1708 election, the others being Griffith Rice and Richard Vaughan from Carmarthenshire, the brothers Sir Arthur and Wyriot Owen from Pembrokeshire, and John Morgan of Tredegar. The twenty Welsh Tory MPs ranged in opinion from Harleyite to Jacobite, but all opposed the Junto. There was one seat to be filled, since Lewis Pryse had been returned for both Cardiganshire and Cardigan Boroughs, but he could not make his choice for the county until the House of Commons confirmed his election there by rejecting a petition from Thomas Johnes on 18 January 1710.[55] The attention of several Tory politicians unseated in 1708 had promptly turned to this safe borough seat. John Meyrick was the early favourite, but soon he was expected to

---

[52] BL Add. MSS 70247.
[53] *HMC Portland*, IV, 490.
[54] Thomas, 'Glamorgan Politics 1700–1750', *Morgannwg*, 6 (1962), 55–60.
[55] *CJ*, XVI, 267–9.

withdraw in favour of the bright young Tory hope Henry St John, the future famous Lord Bolingbroke. Then the rumbustious Sir Humphrey Mackworth, also out of Parliament, announced his candidature.[56] During the summer of 1709 he launched a vigorous campaign, Sir Thomas Mansel being informed that 'he makes some of the gentlemen believe that he will bring the white cloth trade from Shrewsbury into Cardiganshire, and that he will build them a quay at Aberystwyth . . . He will build them Cardigan Steeple, which fell some years since, and cast their bells anew'.[57] Pryse did not welcome Mackworth's return to Cardiganshire politics, and, on the solicitation of Robert Harley and Sir Thomas Mansel, decided to give the seat to the leading Harleyite lawyer Sir Simon Harcourt, who had been unseated for Abingdon in January 1709. Mackworth thereupon allied with local Whig Lord Lisburne and forced a poll at the by-election in February 1710, being defeated by 169 votes to sixty-nine.[58] But his behaviour boded no good for the Gogerddan interest in Cardiganshire.

The Tory leaders, despite the many adverse results at the general election of 1708, made great efforts to muster their friends for the beginning of the new Parliament in November. Sir Thomas Hanmer, who now sat for Suffolk until 1727, distributed a circular letter, a copy of which was forwarded from London by Chester MP Peter Shakerley to Sir Richard Myddelton with the hope that he would 'communicate it forthwith by special messengers to all the members, our friends, in Denbighshire, Flintshire, Caernarvonshire, Carmarthenshire, Merionethshire, Montgomeryshire, Anglesey and Shropshire'.[59] Sir Roger Mostyn also wrote to urge Myddelton to attend. 'Since the possibility of doing the country any service depends entirely upon the good appearance of honest gentlemen at first, it is most earnestly requested of you, and all such, to be there the very first day'.[60] This produced the sharp response from Sir Richard that he had 'always been as constant in my attendance at the opening of the Parliament as any member whatsoever, when my health did permit'.[61] Myddelton failed to attend. The first trial of strength between administration and opposition came on 22 November, when a Tory motion that, to prevent party bias, election cases in the House should be decided by secret ballot was defeated by the narrow margin of 178 votes to 169.[62] Sir William Williams thereupon wrote next day to Myddelton, 'I hope your self, and other worthy

---

[56] Penrice and Margam MSS L 612; *HMC Portland*, IV, 489, 494.
[57] Penrice and Margam MSS L 651.
[58] *The Post-Boy*, 4 March 1710; *HMC Portland*, IV, 33; *CJ*, XVI, 369, 395.
[59] Chirk Castle MSS E994.
[60] Chirk Castle MSS E995.
[61] Chirk Castle MSS E993.
[62] *CJ*, XVI, 7.

members, will hasten up, if you observe we come so near them in further divisions.'[63]

Tory hopes were to be disappointed. Whig control of the Commons was never threatened throughout the Parliament, but the popularity of the Whig ministry was gradually being eroded by war-weariness. The Whig fall from power in 1710, however, was caused primarily by measures that gave great offence to Anglican sentiment. Popular feeling was aroused by a Bill for naturalizing foreign Protestants, debated during February and March 1709. A list was published of those MPs thought to have backed the measure, including five of the six Welsh Whigs, all but Richard Vaughan.[64] This reaction was as nothing compared with the storm over the famous Sacheverell case in 1710, stemming from a ministerial decision to impeach that Tory clergyman for a fiery sermon, preached at St Paul's on 5 November 1709, that had in effect impugned the principles of the Glorious Revolution. Sir Simon Harcourt was the leading counsel for Sacheverell, and the return of the Cardigan by-election writ was deliberately delayed from 22 February until 7 March so that he could play that role. Party feelings ran high, and the alignment in Parliament was on a strictly Whig–Tory basis. Contemporary lists of MPs for and against Sacheverell were numerous. In general they merely confirm what is already known about the political views of the Welsh members, although Edward Jeffreys, a London merchant who had succeeded his father Sir Jeffrey as Brecon MP in 1709, is shown on both sides. He would seem to have soon become a Whig. The other six Whigs were always listed as supporting the impeachment, and nineteen of the twenty Tories as in opposition, John Pugh being the omission.[65]

The alignment in Parliament was to prove less significant than the public reaction during and after the trial, in February and March 1710. Mob demonstrations, notably riots in London, showed how strongly popular feeling was running against the Whig ministry. Sacheverell was given only a token punishment, and his subsequent journey to a living in the Welsh border became a triumphant tour. His passage through Wrexham was marked by bonfires and the ringing of church bells.[66] It was the evidence of public opinion that precipitated the Whig fall from power. Queen Anne was encouraged to indulge her own prejudices, and despite the Whig majority in the Commons she began a gradual dismissal of her Whig ministers. A Tory administration under Robert Harley was already in office when the Parliament was dissolved in September. Harley himself, the only head of a

---

[63] Chirk Castle MSS E991.

[64] *White and Black Lists*, pp. 12–14.

[65] *White and Black Lists*, pp. 15–22; Walcott, 'Division-lists of the House of Commons 1689–1715', *BIHR*, 14 (1936–7), 34–5.

[66] Dodd, *History of Wrexham*, p. 75.

ministry to sit for a Welsh constituency before Lloyd George, was First Lord of the Treasury, while Sir Thomas Mansel was appointed to the Treasury Board and Thomas Harley became a Secretary to the Treasury. At the general election the power of government was allied with the tide of public opinion, stemming from the Anglican backlash and the widespread desire for peace. The result was a Tory triumph more sweeping than in 1702. In Wales the basic weakness of Whiggery was starkly revealed. The failure to make gains in the favourable atmosphere of 1708 was now underlined in 1710, when four of the seven Welsh Whig MPs lost their seats.

The most spectacular Whig disaster was the fall of Orielton power in Pembrokeshire, where Sir Arthur Owen had good reason to rue the breach with his former Tory allies. A Tory candidate for the county appeared in the form of an old enemy John Barlow of Colby, whose earlier Jacobite sympathies waned after his marriage in 1708 to Sir Simon Harcourt's eldest daughter. As early as 2 June John Meyrick, already destined for the Cardigan Boroughs seat, wrote to inform Harcourt that Barlow's success could be assured by the support of Haverfordwest MP John Laugharne. 'Mr Harley and yourself, or at least one of you, should without loss of time make him a visit and desire his interest, which he will be proud to grant to either of you.' Meyrick also suggested that an attempt should be made to secure the long dormant interest of Stackpole Court, an estate that had passed in 1698 to Sir Alexander Campbell of Cawdor Castle in Scotland, after his marriage to the heiress of Sir John Lort. The Campbell family thereupon resided in Pembrokeshire throughout the eighteenth century. By 1710 the estate had passed to his son John, not yet of age, and Meyrick advised that an approach should be made to Robert Harley's son Edward, 'who governs entirely my Lady Campbell and her affairs'.[67]

Harleyite connections constructed a formidable threat to Sir Arthur Owen, who planned to defend the county seat himself. Shortly before the election he vainly sought to win over Meyrick by an offer of the Pembroke Boroughs seat for life.[68] At the poll on 17 October, Barlow defeated Owen by 492 votes to 189.[69] That the 'Church in danger' cry had reached Pembrokeshire is shown by the jubilant report of the contest in a Tory newspaper *The Post-Boy*: 'In this election the diligence of the clergy was remarkable, 50 of them polling for Mr Barlow. But there was a Judas among the Apostles; 7 of them polled for Sir Arthur.'[70]

[67] *HMC Portland*, IV, 542.
[68] Penrice and Margam MSS L695.
[69] NLW General MSS 6108. This 'state of the poll' was later dated 1714, and has been erroneously ascribed to 1713 by R. Thorne in *Pembrokeshire County History*, III, 343.
[70] *The Post-Boy*, 26 October 1710.

Four days earlier, Owen sought to insure against defeat in the county by retaining the borough seat. But the enemies of Orielton, anticipating the bias of a Tory Commons, now deployed the weapon long held in reserve, the disputed right of Wiston to share in the borough constituency election, Wiston patron Lewis Wogan himself being the candidate. Here is the partisan report in the same issue of *The Post-Boy*. 'Sir Arthur Owen had 283 voices and Lewis Wogan Esq. 335. But the Mayor, being a Dissenter, and the son of a Presbyterian preacher, does declare that he will return Sir Arthur Owen.' The mayor had in fact simply ignored the Wiston burgesses and polled only those from Pembroke and Tenby, returning Owen with a majority of 207 to 127. Owen sat as MP until 23 February 1712, when the case was reported to the Commons by the Committee of Elections. Wiston was deemed to be part of the borough constituency and Wogan was awarded the seat.[71]

Carmarthenshire was another traditional Whig stronghold to be stormed by a Tory candidate. Richard Vaughan was safe in the borough, but Griffith Rice, as in 1701, was challenged in the county by Sir Thomas Powell. Rice again had the hitherto dominant Golden Grove interest at his command, but to no avail. He suffered a defeat even more humiliating than that of Owen in Pembrokeshire. He presumably abandoned the poll early when he saw his cause was hopeless, for Powell won by 752 votes to 82.[72]

The fourth Whig seat lost was that of Cardiff MP Sir John Aubrey. In the circumstances of 1710 he could not have expected the support of Sir Thomas Mansel, and there is no evidence that he stood at the election. As early as May Mansel offered the seat to Sir Edward Stradling, who accepted with this dry comment: 'The Whig interest at present is very low in that county.'[73]

An early and incomplete analysis of the election returns sent to Hanover listed three Welsh MPs out of twenty-two as Whig. They were John Morgan of Tredegar, Sir Arthur Owen, and Edward Jeffreys, who retained his seat without incident.[74] Morgan was secure in Monmouthshire against any Tory resurgence, and the prolongation of negotiations before the elections there was caused by his hope of obtaining a seat for a Whig ally, Thomas Lewis of St Pierre. At first there was a threat of a third successive contest in the county, since Sir Hopton Williams hoped to regain the seat he had lost in 1708. The Duke of Beaufort displayed cold realism at that time of high political passion. Although a Tory loaded with favours by the

---

[71] *CJ*, XVI, 420; XVII, 4, 108–10.

[72] Mackworth MSS nos. 910–16; *The Post-Boy*, 21 October 1710.

[73] Penrice and Margam MSS L678.

[74] BL Stowe MSS 223, ff. 453–6. The listing of Richard Vaughan as a Tory doubtless refers to the Merioneth MP, not that for Carmarthen as stated.

new ministry the Duke chose not to attempt the return of a second Tory for Monmouthshire by pitting his Raglan interest against that of Tredegar. Instead he suggested to John Morgan that he should form a joint interest with Lord Windsor, 'who has served us, I hope, with unquestionable honour in this Parliament'. Morgan replied proudly that he was 'standing by myself and not joining with one more than the other'. But his Whig uncle Thomas Morgan of Ruperra was actively canvassing for Tory Lord Windsor, and the Duke wrote canvassing letters on John Morgan's behalf. Sir Hopton was deterred by this semblance of an alliance from pressing his candidature, but John Morgan raised with the Duke the matter of the borough seat:

> I have been in company with several gentlemen who were talking much of Mr Milbourne, and saying he was not a native of this county; and that they thought of my cousin Lewis of St. Pierre to be a proper person to be represented to your Grace for your interest, as he being a gentleman of this county and one of considerable estate.

The Duke of Beaufort replied that he had already recommended Milbourne for the borough, adding a veiled threat of opposing Morgan in the county if he backed Lewis. John Morgan disclaimed any intention of pressing the matter, and both borough and county elections passed off without further incident.[75]

One other Whig–Tory contest took place in Wales, but in a sense it was merely part of the ongoing Anglesey feud between Lord Bulkeley and his enemies. Here the dispute had been further embittered by the presentation to Lord Treasurer Godolphin in 1709 of a memorial of grievances against Lord Bulkeley, alleging abuse of various Crown appointments he still held at the height of Whig power: custos rotulorum of Anglesey and constable of Beaumaris Castle were merely two among several posts. The political temperature on the island was maintained by a series of county meetings about the memorial, even though the 1710 change of ministry dashed hopes of obtaining Lord Bulkeley's dismissal from any office. Owen Meyrick nevertheless again challenged him for the county seat, being defeated by 232 votes to 130.[76]

The most remarkable result in Wales at this general election was not any of these Whig defeats, but the triumph of Sir Humphrey Mackworth in Cardiganshire. By 1709 his Company of Mine Adventurers had become

[75] Tredegar MSS 53/97–103.
[76] Baron Hill MSS 5509; Thomas, 'Anglesey Politics, 1689–1727', *TAAS* (1962), pp. 42–6.

bankrupt in highly suspicious circumstances. While he had been absent from London at the Cardigan by-election of February 1710 a petition to Parliament from creditors and proprietors of the Company revealed dubious expedients adopted by Mackworth, such as the purchase of silver elsewhere and then the sale of it, in London, at a loss, as the product of the Cardiganshire mines. On 21 March the House of Commons voted Mackworth guilty of fraud, and legislation was introduced to transfer control of the Company to trustees and to prevent Sir Humphrey fleeing the country or alienating his estate.[77] But Parliament was dissolved before this became law. The case had made Mackworth notorious throughout Britain. 'Though a High Churchman his honesty in his mine adventure will hardly maintain his character' was the opinion of Robert Harley's sister Abigail.[78] Yet in 1710 he contrived to secure his election for Cardiganshire.

Here Lewis Pryse put forward John Meyrick for the borough and stood himself for the county. But Mackworth 'found means to unite the two most distant persons on earth in opinion', Whig Lord Lisburne and William Powell of Nanteos, who was a Jacobite. The inducements deployed by Mackworth were an agreement to cover the next two elections as well, and lavish disposal of money. Pryse himself did not help his cause by refusing to ally with one leading squire, Walter Lloyd of Voelallt, because of 'the objection of his being a Whig, which goes further with him than any man on earth'. Meyrick, already returned as borough member, explained Pryse's impending defeat to Sir Thomas Mansel while the county poll was still in progress.

Powerful gold has wonderfully operated in this affair. When I left Mr Pryse was foremost by about 30 but he had not above 30 more to poll, and Sir Humphrey had about a 100, so that he expected to lose it by forty, which will be no shameful defeat, since there was so strong a union of both parties against him.[79]

Only one other seat in Wales changed hands, when Sir William Williams retired after a mere two years in Parliament. His successor for Denbigh Boroughs, agreed on by Williams himself, Sir John Wynn, and Sir Richard Myddelton, was one of the lesser local squires, John Roberts of Hafod-y-Bwch. His nomination was approved by a meeting of the gentry on 28 September.[80] Elsewhere elections doubtless passed off as quietly as in

---

[77] *CJ*, XVI, 353, 358–69, 391, 395.
[78] *HMC Portland*, IV, 533.
[79] Penrice and Margam MSS L. 695; Thomas, 'County Elections in Eighteenth-Century Cardiganshire', *Ceredigion* 11 (1991), 243–4.
[80] Chirk Castle MSS E6128.

Radnorshire. Robert Harley was too busy to attend his own borough election, and left the matter to Thomas Lewis of Harpton, who reported that both county and borough elections had passed with 'perfect unity and satisfaction'.[81]

Twenty-three Tory MPs were elected in 1710 from Wales, as against four Whigs, one of whom, Sir Arthur Owen, was soon to lose his seat on petition. But Toryism embraced a variety of opinions. Since Anne had vetoed any ministerial offer to Lord Nottingham his faction, Sir Roger Mostyn among them, increasingly acted as a separate party. There was, moreover, a pressure group of High Tories, critical of Harley's moderation, formalized into an October Club whose membership list included seven Welsh MPs.[82] Country Tories and Jacobites alike would support the ministry against the Whig opposition, however, and Robert Harley found means to bind MPs to his administration. Sir Thomas Mansel and Thomas Harley already had posts at the Treasury. When Sir Simon Harcourt became Lord Keeper of the Great Seal in October 1710, John Barlow was named purse-bearer by his father-in-law.[83] John Meyrick was rewarded in February 1712 with a Welsh judgeship, and though he then chose to vacate his Cardigan seat the ministry received an assurance of support from his successor Owen Brigstoke, a Carmarthenshire squire.[84] Also in the ministerial orbit was Sir John Conway, whose financial problems led him to seek government assistance.[85]

A year after becoming head of the ministry Robert Harley left the House of Commons. The office of Lord High Treasurer was bestowed on him in May 1711, and before acceptance of this dignity he necessarily took a peerage, as Earl of Oxford. Since the change involved abolition of the Treasury Board Mansel's post disappeared, but the next month he resumed his former position as Comptroller of the Queen's Household. There was also a consequent by-election in Radnor Boroughs, the new peer's son Edward, now styled Lord Harley, succeeding his father.

In Parliament Tory majorities in both Houses did not guarantee the ministry immunity from problems, especially that of obtaining approval of the peace terms negotiated with France whereby Spain would after all have a sovereign from the French royal house of Bourbon, a decision contrary to the war aims of both Nottingham and the Whigs. They struck a bargain – Whig acceptance of the Occasional Conformity Bill in return for

---

[81] BL Add. MSS 70247, T. Lewis to R. Harley, 12 October 1710.
[82] Dickinson, 'The October Club', *Huntingdon Library Journal*, 32 (1969–70), 170–2.
[83] Luttrell, *State Affairs*, VI, 644.
[84] BL Add. MSS 70282, O. Brigstocke to Oxford, 1 November 1712.
[85] BL Add. MSS 70219, passim: undated letters. *HMC Portland*, V, 210. Conway was trying to sell some paintings to Queen Anne.

Nottingham's opposition to the peace. This last was defeated in the Lords, a circumstance that led to the creation of twelve new peers on 31 December 1711 to secure a ministerial majority in that House. The dozen included two Welsh MPs. Viscount Windsor received a British peerage as Baron Mountjoy, and Sir Thomas Mansel now became Baron Mansel. In Glamorgan, for the first time since 1670, there was no Mansel to take the county seat. The vacancy was filled by Robert Jones of Fonmon Castle, a Tory despite his family's Cromwellian antecedents. Lord Mansel was informed that 'he had given us great assurances he will be diligent and an honest voter'.[86]

In Monmouthshire matters were not so easily arranged. The balance of power between Raglan and Tredegar produced a delicate situation at the by-election there. The Duke of Beaufort sponsored James Gunter of the Priory, Abergavenny, and sought to forestall any Tredegar move by announcing the candidature as early as 29 December, even before Lord Windsor officially received his title. He then attempted to mollify John Morgan by this comment: 'I should have thought Mr Morgan the merchant a proper person but fear the gentlemen of the county will not like two out of one family.' John Morgan was annoyed, commenting to Gunter that the compliment to Thomas Morgan of Ruperra would have been better left unsaid, and declined to promise him support.[87] Morgan did not challenge Gunter's election, but after the new MP died early in 1713 the Tredegar Whig ally Thomas Lewis secured the seat at the further by-election in April.

Ratification of the peace treaty was merely delayed by the initial Lords defeat. But ministerial policy suffered a setback when on 18 June 1713 the Commons rejected by 194 votes to 185 a proposed trade treaty with Britain's old enemy, France. The majority was a coalition of Whigs with those Tories fearful not only for the British economy but also about the Hanoverian Succession if a political alliance with France should follow the trade agreement. Over half the Welsh MPs were absent, either Tory abstainers or already departed for home. Six voted on each side. Those for the ministry were Oxford's son and cousin, Sir John Conway, and three October Club men, Lord Bulkeley, Henry Bertie and Clayton Milbourne. The opposition included all four current Welsh Whig MPs – John Morgan, Thomas Lewis, Edward Jeffreys and Richard Vaughan, together with Nottinghamite Sir Roger Mostyn, and Sir Thomas Powell.[88]

---

[86] Penrice and Margam MSS L721.
[87] Tredegar MSS 531/105–6.
[88] *White and Black Lists*, pp. 23–30.

The general election of 1713 followed soon afterwards, but the course of events in Wales was not affected by these recent political matters. Party considerations, indeed, even in this 'first Age of Party' proved to be less important in electoral arrangements than family interests. Local Whigs and Tories often allied together, and several MPs owed their return to cross-party support. There was no prospect, however, of a Whig recovery from the setbacks of 1710, and no counter-attack was attempted in the traditional strongholds of Pembrokeshire and Carmarthenshire. In party terms there was no change in the overall Welsh parliamentary representation. Four Whigs and twenty-three Tories sat both at the dissolution and after the elections.

Even the great clash in Monmouthshire, where a Tory successfully challenged the two Whig members, was a battle of family interests as much as of party. Here, since the April by-election, the shire seats were held by John Morgan and his ally Thomas Lewis, but the Duke of Beaufort was resolved to recapture the one seat usually accorded to his family interest. The candidate he selected for this purpose was an influential Jacobite squire from Glamorgan, Sir Charles Kemys, a son and successor of the namesake Court Whig returned for Monmouthshire in 1695. So little did political considerations at first enter into this election that the Duke asked John Morgan to form a joint interest with Kemys, or at least to be neutral. Morgan replied that he had long ago promised to support Thomas Lewis, adding this curt comment. 'I look upon Sir Charles Kemys standing now to be of little purpose, because most people are engaged for Lewis.'[89] But circumstances were weighted heavily in Beaufort's favour. It was the turn of Monmouth to hold the election, a disadvantage Morgan sought to overcome by hiring thirteen hostelries in the town, to lodge over 400 freeholders.[90] More significant was the government support Beaufort obtained as he now played the Tory card, portraying his side as 'the Church interest in Monmouthshire'. On 6 September he reminded Lord Oxford of 'your Lordship telling Mr Milbourne you would help us to carry it for Sir Charles Kemys'.[91] It was the appointment of a partisan sheriff that gave Kemys the decisive advantage over Lewis. Instead of the usual six polling booths, one for each hundred, the sheriff permitted only one, thereby protracting the election over six days. Moreover, according to the abortive petition later submitted by Lewis, he admitted all the voters for Kemys before accepting any for Lewis. The narrow margin of victory by which Kemys defeated Lewis, 856 votes to 851, was therefore open to suspicion,

---

[89] Tredegar MSS 53/107–8.
[90] Tredegar MSS 53/5.
[91] BL Add. MSS 70282, Beaufort to Oxford, 6 September 1713.

but the House of Commons never examined the case. John Morgan's seat had not been in question, and he headed the poll with 1,196 votes.[92]

The restoration of the Tredegar interest in Brecon compensated Morgan for this setback. Here the rival Priory interest of the Jeffreys family had controlled the borough since 1701. Now in 1713 the Whig Morgans sponsored a Tory candidate, Roger Jones of Buckland, to challenge Whig Edward Jeffreys. Jones, a leading squire of the county and son of the Edward Jones who had earlier represented Breconshire, defeated the sitting member by 114 votes to 63. Jeffreys petitioned, but this case also was never heard by the Commons.[93]

Tredegar control of Brecon, though not unchallenged, was to continue until the 1832 Reform Act. More remarkable, but less permanent in its consequences, as lasting only seventy years, was a Whig coup in the Caernarfon Boroughs constituency. Here Thomas Wynn of Glynllifon now engineered the overthrow of Baron Hill power, having prepared the ground since 1707 by the creation of freemen in Nefyn and Pwllheli, the out-boroughs under his own control and that of his ally Richard Vaughan of Corsygedol. These admissions were made in groups of a dozen or twenty at a time, so as to avoid causing alarm; but by 1713 Wynn had a majority of votes in the constituency.[94] Somehow concealing his ambitions, Wynn also obtained influence in Caernarfon through the Earl of Radnor, a distant relative who had been constable of the castle since 1692: by increasing the number of freemen there to over a hundred Wynn secured the choice of two supporters as bailiffs, to serve as returning officers for the 1713 parliamentary election. Lord Bulkeley and his friends saw the danger too late. His nomination of two other bailiffs, after the creation of 140 more burgesses, was ruled invalid by the Court of Queen's Bench.[95] Lord Bulkeley's best hope of regaining his influence lay in wresting the post of constable from Lord Radnor, but Oxford, through policy or inertia, delayed that change until it was too late.

A further setback to the Bulkeley interest came with the desertion of William Griffith of Cefnamwlch, Tory borough MP by virtue of the 1708 agreement. Now threatened with the loss of his seat he decided to ally with the Whig Wynn on promise of the county. Here old Sir John Wynn was at last retiring from Parliament, and by the terms of that agreement, signed by Griffith himself, should have been succeeded by Sir Roger Mostyn. But at the election on 16 September Griffith was returned by the sheriff. A London newspaper reported his majority as 128 votes to 4, with 300 more

---

[92] Tredegar MSS 253; *CJ*, XVIII, 485.
[93] *CJ*, XVII, 481.
[94] Glynllifon MSS 1988; Baron Hill MSS 5609.
[95] Llanfair and Brynodol MSS 96.

freeholders in reserve.[96] Mostyn's reliance on the 1708 agreement had caused him to make no preparations for a poll! At the borough election two days later Wynn was returned after Lord Bulkeley put forward William Owen of Brogyntyn, the patron of Cricieth. Wynn claimed there was a poll. Owen denied this, saying that his friends had withdrawn for safety because of disorder. Neither his complaint nor a petition from Mostyn was heard by the Commons.[97]

The Caernarfonshire elections, lost by incredible complacency, aroused uneasiness among the Tory squires of north Wales.[98] There was also concern over that for Denbigh Boroughs, as marking the revival of the Lleweni interest now held by the Whig Cotton family. Here Sir Richard Myddelton, and his nephew John, had been consulting with the mayor of Denbigh, John Wynne of Melai. But Wynne, son-in-law of Sir William Williams and a substantial squire, cherished his own ambitions. In 1710 he had been rebuffed by the Myddeltons when the seat was vacant.[99] Now he played them false, for Sir Thomas Cotton in March 1713 publicly pledged Wynne his support at the next election. Since Wynne also had the goodwill of Sir John Wynn as well as that of his father-in-law, Sir Richard Myddelton acquiesced in his return, despite his own preference for the sitting member John Roberts.[100]

Elsewhere in Wales the election of 1713 was devoid of incident, but four other seats changed hands. The return of Thomas Johnes, the fourth Welsh Whig MP, for Cardiganshire in place of Sir Humphrey Mackworth was evidently the result of the nine-year agreement of 1710. Sir George Barlow of Slebech, elder brother of Pembrokeshire MP John, succeeded Owen Brigstocke as Cardigan Boroughs MP. In Flintshire, Sir John Conway and Sir Roger Mostyn again exchanged seats, for the earlier agreement had been renewed at a London meeting of Mostyn, Conway, Sir Thomas Hanmer, and Lord Bulkeley.[101]

Since Queen Anne died on 1 August 1714 this Parliament was to be short-lived, an obvious reason why so few election petitions were heard. Overnight the 'first age of party' became an era of Whig supremacy, or so convention has it. In Wales the change was not so complete or so sudden. Already personal ambition and family interests had frequently cut across local party alignments of Whig and Tory: and it was to be some time before

---

[96] *Flying Post*, 29 October 1713.

[97] *CJ*, XVII, 486–7; Thomas, 'The Parliamentary Representation of Caernarvonshire in the Eighteenth Century: Part I, 1708–1749', *T. Caerns. H. S.*, 19 (1958), 42–6.

[98] Wynnstay MSS Box C, no. 69.

[99] Chirk Castle MSS E6126–7.

[100] Chirk Castle MSS E3240, 4054–60.

[101] Bettisfield MSS 32.

Whigs gained a secure majority of Welsh seats. Never were they to hold as many as the Tories had under Anne.

Hitherto the relative strength of Whiggism and Toryism in Wales had depended on how many of the leading family interests belonged to each party; and, as in similar areas in England, the majority of Welsh squires were Tory. The Hanoverian Succession introduced the new factor of permanent government support for Whigs that enabled them to overcome their initial numerical weakness. Official assistance at elections, as by the choice of partisan sheriffs, and bestowal of patronage in between both enhanced the prospects of favoured candidates. So did the behaviour of a Whig House of Commons in election cases taken there on petition. It was often sufficient for the House simply to ignore cases where Whig candidates had been returned; in other instances, decisions given in face of the evidence were all too common. There was nothing new in such parliamentary bias, but now it was always the same way, and that it could be relied upon in advance encouraged unscrupulous behaviour by candidates. Another general factor in the political situation was that, as elsewhere in Britain, men and families of Tory background who nurtured political ambitions, or simply wanted official patronage to protect their local influence, would increasingly turn their faces to the sun of Whiggism. These were good reasons why Whigs flourished and Tory influence withered in a near half-century of Whig power from 1714.

CHAPTER 4

The Triumph of the Whigs (1714–1740)

It is time for everyone [who] has anything to lose to look about them since such unparalleled methods are taken to obtain a House of Commons. It not only shows they despair of the majority if the people be trusted to a free choice and that they have something extraordinary to do on a house of Parliament.[1]

L ORD Oxford's comment on 17 November 1714 to his son was to be especially true with regard to his personal fate – two years in prison without trial – and to the downfall of his family interest in Radnorshire and elsewhere. It also anticipated in general the unscrupulous behaviour Whigs employed to secure most of the parliamentary seats in Wales during the next two decades.

Destruction of Harley electoral power must have been especially sweet revenge for the Whig ministry appointed by George I and determined to consolidate its position by success at the general election of 1715. In Radnorshire the fall of the Harley interest was contrived by Lord Coningsby, long a Whig enemy of that family in the border counties. Appointed lord lieutenant of Radnorshire as well as Steward of Cantref Maelienydd, he was able to deploy the full weight of the government interest: but ultimately the decisive factor was to be the refusal of the Whig House of Commons to investigate the two dubious returns from Radnorshire. For the county Lord Coningsby set up the Richard Fowler who had canvassed it in 1705 and 1708, and whose cousin Edward Fowler was appointed sheriff. As returning officer he rejected the demand of sitting member Thomas Harley for a poll! The petition against Richard Fowler's return was buried in the Committee of Elections, as was that for

[1] BL Add. MSS 70382, f. 73.

the borough.[2] Here the Harleys had been betrayed by former allies. The rival candidate to Lord Harley was Thomas Lewis of Harpton's namesake son, who bore a personal grudge against the Harley family. 'Young Lewis plays the fool', Oxford warned his son on 29 November.[3] The Bailiff of New Radnor, Samuel Burton, hitherto a Harley adherent, now created 251 burgesses there on his behalf. The Harleys had calculated on a majority of ninety in the old electorate, but in this circumstance did not force a poll.[4] Both Fowler and Lewis were to be Whig MPs.

Other Whig gains took place in traditional south Wales strongholds. The death of the second Duke of Beaufort in 1714, leaving an heir aged only seven, gave rise to an opportunity in Monmouthshire of which local Whigs took full advantage. In the county there was no opposition to John Morgan and Thomas Lewis, while in the borough constituency another Whig, William Bray, defeated Andrews Windsor, younger brother of Lord Windsor, by 1,028 votes to 944. In Carmarthenshire Tory Sir Thomas Powell lost his seat to the Marquess of Winchester, who in 1713 had acquired control of the Golden Grove estate on marriage to the heiress of the last Earl of Carbery. Son and heir of the second Duke of Bolton, he had been a 1710 Whig casualty in Hampshire. With the Golden Grove interest buttressed by government support and the national upsurge of Whig sentiment, he defeated Powell by 699 votes to 493. The Orielton interest made a similar comeback in Pembrokeshire, gaining all three seats in 1715. The poll figures are not known for either the county, where Sir Arthur Owen unseated John Barlow in a contest marked by deliberate violence and dubious practice, or the borough. Here the Orielton candidate was a brigadier-general with local connections, Thomas Ferrers. Since Lewis Wogan had recently died, Ferrers was confronted by Sir George Barlow of Slebech, who was giving up his Cardigan Boroughs seat to another Tory, Stephen Parry. The mayor of Pembroke refused to poll many Wiston burgesses or even some new Tenby ones in the Barlow interest, and returned Ferrers. The Whig House of Commons declined to examine petitions about either election.[5] The third Orielton success, at Haverfordwest, came at a by-election after John Laugharne died the day after his re-election. At the poll on 3 May Sir George Barlow defeated John Barlow of Lawrenny, Sir Arthur Owen's cousin, by 222 votes to 181. But this time the Whig House of Commons promptly heard the complaint of the defeated candidate, and awarded him the seat after Sir George failed to defend the case.[6]

---

[2] *CJ*, XVIII, 38–9, 493, 652.
[3] BL Add. MSS 70382, f. 83; *Arch. Camb.*, 3rd s., 10 (1864), 32–4.
[4] *HMC Portland*, V, 505–6, 663.
[5] NLW General MSS 12171; Nanteos MSS L 32; *CJ*, XVIII, 37.
[6] *CJ*, XVIII, 138, 199.

Other Whig gains, then and later, were to ensue from changes of party allegiance by individuals and families. Brecon MP Roger Jones, hitherto a Tory, was henceforth deemed a Whig. He had recently married a Whig bride, and had John Morgan as his electoral patron.[7] That Caernarfonshire MP William Griffith, who died a month after his re-election, should have been succeeded by his brother and heir John proved to be a Whig gain. Another was caused by the decision of Lord Bulkeley, a Jacobite peevish about the Hanoverian Succession, to concede his Anglesey seat to Owen Meyrick. Another Jacobite, Lewis Pryse of Gogerddan, displayed his disgust at the new regime in different fashion. He unseated Whig Thomas Johnes in Cardiganshire, apparently in a contest, but then declined to attend Parliament, to avoid swearing allegiance to the new dynasty, or so his enemies alleged. He was expelled in consequence, but the Tory alliance of Gogerddan and Nanteos secured the 1717 by-election return of Tory Owen Brigstocke.[8]

Elsewhere in Wales the power of Tory magnates proved as yet impervious to the Whig tide and ensured the return at the general election of fifteen Tories as against twelve Whigs; but very soon the by-elections for Caernarfonshire and Haverfordwest led to two more Whig gains. Few other seats changed hands. The Denbigh Boroughs victory of former MP John Roberts over his successor John Wynne, by 773 votes to 610, was a contest between two Tories, and marked the restoration of the Chirk Castle control of that constituency. Another contest saw John Pugh defeat a Whig challenge in Montgomery Boroughs from Francis Herbert, patron of Montgomery. Herbert secured a majority of fifty-nine to fourteen in the county town, but his petition, based on the old claim of its exclusive right, was not heard by the Commons.[9] In Flintshire, under the 1713 agreement, Sir Roger Mostyn again exchanged seats with Sir John Conway, beginning the Mostyn tenure of the county that remained virtually unbroken until near the century's end. Mostyn, though a Tory, was a government supporter for two years, since the offer of ministerial posts to some Tories by George I had been accepted by his father-in-law Lord Nottingham, once again a Secretary of State, with Sir Roger himself holding a lucrative office as Teller of the Exchequer.

This Tory participation in government was ended by the political consequences of the Jacobite Rising in 1715, for sympathetic Tory responses to that episode, even if merely compassion for captured rebels, were portrayed by Whigs as evidence of disloyalty and provided a pretext for Tory removal

---

[7] Sedgwick, *House of Commons 1715–1754*, I, 184.
[8] Nanteos MSS L 34; *CJ*, XVIII, 40, 260, 367, 391, 411, 493, 654.
[9] *Flying Post*, 1 March 1715; *CJ*, XVIII, 36; XXI, 138.

from office in 1716. The Whig ministry did not need their support in Parliament, for at the 1715 general election 341 out of 558 MPs had been returned as Whigs, a number increased to 372 after the hearing of petitions. As with the Tories under Anne too large a majority led to internal divisions, and the structure of parliamentary politics for decades to come was to be one of Whig ministries opposed both by dissident Whigs and by Tories. But before the famous Whig Schism of 1717 established that pattern of politics the Septennial Act of 1716 provided a clear party vote between Whigs and Tories. Establishment of such a long interval between elections would provide greater political stability, ran the Whig government argument. It would remove Parliament further from popular opinion, said the opposition Tories, now becoming more clearly identifiable as a country party. The key vote took place on 24 April 1716, a day late enough in the session to highlight the opposition problem of attendance. Only five Welsh MPs voted in opposition, and they included Monmouthshire MP Thomas Lewis, who though rated a Whig always voted against government. Eleven Welsh Whigs voted for the ministry, and they included another Tory defector, Sir Edward Williams of Breconshire, once an October Club man but henceforth a Whig.[10]

What happened in 1717 was a double split: one within the ministry, when Lord Sunderland and James Stanhope were successful in the battle for royal favour, and Robert Walpole and Lord Townshend consequently led their Whig faction into opposition; and a quarrel between the King and the Prince of Wales, who thereupon formed a political alliance with the Walpole group. That event determined the parliamentary behaviour of Thomas Wynn, for he held household office under the Prince. The ministerial dispute was over policy as well as power, and the extent of religious toleration for Protestant Dissenters, a traditional Whig cause, became the focus of Parliament's attention early in 1719. A composite voting-list for January over the ministerial proposal to repeal the repressive Tory measures of Anne's reign, the 1711 Occasional Conformity Act and the 1714 Schism Act, provides information as to the Sunderland–Walpole divide among the Welsh Whigs. That only five Welsh MPs supported the measure, with thirteen opposed, may, however, reflect the intolerant Anglican attitude widespread among the Welsh squirearchy as much as support for Walpole. The five voting for the ministry included three Court Whigs, army officer William Bray, Radnor's Thomas Lewis, and Owen Meyrick, soon to be in receipt of money from Sunderland. The other two were Fowler, now Sir Richard, a Sunderland adherent, and the ever-tolerant Sir John Philipps, who had returned to Westminster as Haverfordwest MP on the death of John Barlow in 1718.

[10] Chandler, *Debates*, VIII, Addenda, 73–92.

The thirteen Welsh MPs against repeal included six Whigs, men like Sir Arthur Owen and Thomas Ferrers as well as Thomas Lewis and Thomas Wynn.[11]

The ministry carried that legislation, by a majority of forty-one on the key vote, but anticipated greater difficulty later that year over a more controversial measure, the Peerage Bill, designed to limit the number of new peerage creations so as to prevent the Prince of Wales on his accession from filling the Lords with his own men. James Craggs, the government manager in the Commons, therefore compiled a list of the House to ascertain prospective supporters; it serves as a reminder that changes of allegiance and representation had now altered the current political balance of Welsh MPs to fifteen Whigs and twelve Tories. He anticipated the support of thirteen Welsh MPs, all the Whigs except Richard Vaughan and Thomas Wynn: among them Sir John Philipps would be canvassed by Stanhope, and three others by Sunderland, Sir Richard Fowler and the two Monmouthshire MPs John Morgan and Thomas Lewis. Ten of the twelve Welsh Tories were expected to oppose, the two omitted being Sir John Conway and the new Montgomeryshire MP Price Devereux.[12] The calculations were optimistic. The Peerage Bill was to be heavily defeated by 269 votes to 177, only three Welsh MPs voting for it – Fowler, Meyrick and Radnor's Lewis.[13]

This setback for the Stanhope administration led to a Whig reconciliation, and by the time of the next general election in 1722 Walpole was beginning his long ministry. In parliamentary politics there was again a clear divide between government Whigs and opposition Tories, but at the local level of elections the picture was as usual more complicated. In Wales only five of the nine contests were between Whigs and Tories, two being fought by rival Tories and two between Whigs. The overall result was that Wales, as in 1715, again returned a Tory majority, this time of sixteen to eleven.

Lord Bulkeley was involved in three of the Whig–Tory contests. Owen Meyrick, despite a 1715 pledge, refused to hand back the Anglesey seat. In this county contest, which began in 1720, Meyrick was supported by Sir Arthur Owen, owner of the Bodeon estate, and by Lord Bulkeley's Caernarfonshire foe Thomas Wynn, but not by the influential Whig squire of Plas Newydd, Edward Bayly, who had succeeded his great-uncle Nicholas Bagenal there in 1712. Bayly was such an avowed Whig as to

---

[11] For lists of voters, see Sedgwick, *House of Commons 1715–1754*, I, 127. The most accessible list is in Chandler, *Debates*, VIII, Appendix, reprinted in Cobbett, *Parl. Hist.*, VIII, 585–8.

[12] BL Stowe MSS 247, ff. 184–99.

[13] Chandler, *Debates*, VIII, Appendix.

obtain a baronetcy in 1730, but he declined to assist Meyrick; and it was to Lord Bulkeley that he apologized that 'his conscience would not give him leave to vote for so worthy a man as your Lordship, . . . but being of different principles in policy he cant vote for him . . . He will stand neuter.'[14] The campaign lasted some eighteen months and, so it was alleged forty years later, cost Lord Bulkeley the improbable sum of £10,000 before he was elected in April 1722 by 217 votes to 148.[15] His expenses included defence against a petition submitted by Meyrick, whose complaint of bribery was so unconvincing that even the Whig House of Commons rejected it without a vote.[16] The challenge in Beaumaris was formal, an attempt by Caernarfonshire Whig William Bodfel to poll burgesses of Newborough against Henry Bertie. The Commons buried that weak case in Committee.[17] It may have been in retaliation that Lord Bulkeley thought of attacking the Whig hold on both Caernarfonshire seats.[18] Although the idea of a county challenge was soon dropped he put up a relative, William Price of Rhiwlas in Merioneth, against Thomas Wynn in the borough constituency. In a four-day poll, Wynn won by 1,025 votes to 572.[19] He gained a majority in four boroughs, all except Cricieth. Analysis of a poll-book incomplete by forty-four of Wynn's voters reveals that at least 795 of his voters were non-resident, but that he also had a majority of residents by 186 to 87.[20] A petition by Price was never heard by the Commons, and there was no further contest in the constituency until 1784.[21]

Montgomery Boroughs was the scene of a Whig challenge to a Tory MP, John Pugh, and one that marked the emergence onto the Welsh political scene of the man who was the most influential Whig in Wales for nearly half a century, Henry Arthur Herbert, later Lord Herbert and subsequently the first Earl Powis of the second creation. He had succeeded his father Francis Herbert of Dolgeog as patron of Montgomery in 1719, and was doubtless the sponsor of the unsuccessful rival candidate, Sir Charles Lloyd of Garth. Nothing is known of the poll, and, somewhat surprisingly, no petition was sent to Parliament. Tories held nine north Wales seats, all except those in Caernarfonshire, and the two Welsh contests fought

---

[14] Baron Hill MSS 5618.

[15] Baron Hill MSS 5737.

[16] *CJ*, XX, 30, 238, 334, 440–1.

[17] *CJ*, XX, 25, 230, 235. For more details on these Anglesey and Beaumaris contests, see Thomas, 'Anglesey Politics, 1689–1727', *TAAS* (1962), pp. 47–50.

[18] Penrhos MSS V, 236.

[19] Brogyntyn MSS 1519; Baron Hill MSS 5618.

[20] Porth yr Aur MSS 12543.

[21] *CJ*, XX, 38, 232, 347–8. For further details, see Thomas, 'The Parliamentary Representation of Caernarvonshire in the Eighteenth Century: Part I', *T.Caerns.H.S.*, 19 (1958), 46–8.

between Tories were in this area, Flint Boroughs and Denbighshire. In Flint Sir John Conway had been succeeded on his death in 1721 by Thomas Eyton of Leeswood, a member of that famous Jacobite club, the Cycle of the White Rose. In 1722 he was taken to a poll by an Edward Conway, presumably some kinsman of Sir John, who after his defeat petitioned without result.[22]

The Denbighshire contest was a sequel to the capture of the seat by Watkin Williams Wynn at a 1716 by-election consequent on the death of Sir Richard Myddelton. As Watkin Williams he then defeated Robert Myddelton by 840 votes to 644 in an overthrow of the hitherto long dominant Chirk Castle interest.[23] Myddelton was so determined to avenge this setback that he opened his campaign in 1720 and, although a Tory, secretly sought government help, as local Whig John Meller of Erthig knew full well.[24]

> There is now some apprehension that Mr Myddelton when in London kissed the King's hand, as in fact he did, and 'tis now industriously spread abroad that Mr Myddelton is turned Whig; which, if it was certainly known, would carry off a great number of the Tories who have already promised him their votes. But by good luck the story is not believed.

Whether or not Myddelton secured ministerial assistance, he did obtain the support of local Whigs like Meller, but that undoubted Whig Sir Robert Cotton of Lleweni, perhaps resentful of Chirk Castle control of the borough constituency, canvassed for Wynn, as he had done in 1716. The campaign was marked by lavish entertainments, as at Wrexham, where both candidates roasted oxen in December 1720, and also by coercion; one supporter assured Chirk Castle that 'tenants who have promised the other side and will not come over will be turned out'.[25] Wynn's margin of victory was similar to that in 1716, 856 to 673, and Chirk Castle did not challenge Wynnstay again until 1741.[26] A few days later Myddelton was returned for the borough without the contest Wynn had at one time threatened. Myddelton submitted a petition about the county election, hoping that 'the favour of the court' would obtain a sympathetic hearing, but he forfeited any chance of that by voting against the Walpole ministry.[27]

[22] *CJ*, XX, 33–4, 235; XXI, 173.
[23] Wynnstay MSS L1293.
[24] *Erthig Chronicles*, I, 233.
[25] Chirk Castle MSS E 971.
[26] Chirk Castle MSS C 12.
[27] Chirk Castle MSS C11, 14; E 401, 674, 3983–4, 4008, 4109, 5515; *CJ*, XX, 38–9. For more information, see Thomas, 'Wynnstay versus Chirk Castle', *NLW Journal*, 11 (1959), 108–11.

The two constituencies where Whig fought Whig were Radnorshire and Carmarthenshire. During 1721 a Walpole supporter, the Duke of Chandos, who owned a Radnorshire estate of £1,200 a year, replaced Lord Coningsby, a Sunderland man, in all his Radnorshire posts. He agreed to support both current MPs, and Thomas Lewis was returned for the borough without incident. The county was canvassed by Marmaduke Gwynne of Garth, seeking to revive the family interest created by Sir Rowland Gwynne. The Duke persuaded him to stand down, on promise of support at the next election; but a third Whig candidate, Sir Humphrey Howorth of Maesllwch, then conducted a two-month campaign so successfully that at the election on 10 April he defeated Fowler by 707 votes to 151. The low poll for Fowler lends credence to his complaint that his supporters had been intimidated from attending the election, but he withdrew his petition before the case was heard.[28]

The Carmarthenshire election, like that in Denbighshire, demonstrated the cross-party nature of electoral politics by 1722. Whereas in Denbighshire two Tory candidates each enjoyed the support of local Whigs, in Carmarthenshire the two Whigs both had Tory adherents. The contests of 1701, 1710 and 1715 had been fights between Whig and Tory candidates. Edward Rice of Newton, son of the former county MP Griffith Rice, was now the candidate sponsored by the Golden Grove interest, the former county MP the Marquess of Winchester having succeeded his father as third Duke of Bolton. But he was challenged by another Whig, Sir Nicholas Williams of Edwinsford. Rice was the candidate favoured by most local Whigs. Sir Arthur Owen was expected to provide him with 50 votes, and other leading Whigs in support included the Bishop of St David's, Grismond Philipps of Cwmgwili, and Walter Lloyd of Peterwell in Cardiganshire. Tory support for Rice came from Lord Mansel in Glamorgan, expected to supply twenty votes, and the retiring and incoming MPs for Cardiganshire, Owen Brigstoke and Francis Cornwallis of Abermarlais. Sir Nicholas Williams possessed impeccable Whig credentials, having been given a baronetcy in 1707, and had the support of the retiring MP Sir Thomas Stepney, a stop-gap when the Marquess of Winchester went to the Lords in 1717; but he relied heavily on the local Tories. Williams refused to accept an offer by the Duke of Bolton of support at the next election if he would give way to Rice, and was defeated in a week-long poll by 593 votes to 588.[29] Sir Nicholas promptly petitioned, complaining about the conduct of the sheriff in almost every respect, from appointing the venue of the election at Llandeilo, a village near Rice's

---

[28] Chandos Letter-Book 1721–1722; *CJ*, XX, 26, 227, 257.
[29] Edwinsford MSS 2907–8, 4197.

house, to protracting the poll and then closing it prematurely after Rice had instigated a riot by 'great number of rude persons armed with swords and clubs'. When the House eventually heard the case on 18 December 1724 it did not help Rice's cause that Williams was a Walpole man whereas the Duke of Bolton had sided with Sunderland in 1717. He offered no defence, and Sir Nicholas was awarded the seat.[30]

Breconshire was the scene of the other Welsh contest in 1722. William Morgan, who had succeeded his father in 1720 as master of Tredegar, was determined to establish control over both constituencies. His initial tactic was to persuade Roger Jones to resign the borough in return for support in the county, even though the Tory sitting member, William Gwyn Vaughan of Trebarried, who had taken the seat in 1721 on the death of Sir Edward Williams, was his uncle. Vaughan mildly commented to his Tory ally Lord Mansel that his nephew's behaviour was 'somewhat unexpected'.[31] Whether Morgan's motives were tactical expediency, personal antipathy or a political quarrel, this part of his scheme failed, Vaughan retaining the seat by a majority of 181 votes. The borough seat William Morgan wanted for his younger brother Thomas, who would not come of age until 7 May 1723. William Morgan therefore resorted to an elaborate manœuvre. He had himself returned for Brecon a week after his election also for Monmouthshire. There followed a sham petition, to enable him to postpone his choice of seat, and this was conveniently withdrawn on 16 May 1723.[32] William Morgan thereupon opted for Monmouthshire, but his brother was challenged at the by-election by John Pratt, who had married a daughter of Sir Jeffrey Jeffreys of the Priory. Thomas Morgan won by 113 votes to 69, since control of the borough machinery enabled Tredegar to admit sufficient non-residents to outnumber the resident majority for the Priory candidate, and Pratt petitioned in vain.[33]

William Morgan had himself been under age when his father John died in 1720, and the Monmouthshire vacancy had been filled by John Hanbury of Pontypool, an ironmaster with extensive estates in the county. In 1722 it was Thomas Lewis who gave way to Morgan as there began a long Whig alliance between Tredegar and Pontypool against which various Dukes of Beaufort were to pit the Raglan interest seldom and in vain. There may indeed have been a tacit compromise in Monmouthshire politics, for Beaufort control of the borough constituency was henceforth unchallenged until 1820. That seat, held by Andrews Windsor since William Bray's death

[30] *CJ*, XX, 35–6, 227, 333, 365.
[31] Penrice and Margam MSS 9018.
[32] *CJ*, XX, 45, 71, 216.
[33] *CJ*, XX, 232; Thomas, 'Parliamentary Elections in Brecknockshire 1689–1832', *Brycheiniog*, 6 (1960), 103–6.

in 1720, was now taken by Edward Kemys, another Tory, but also Bray's nephew. Elsewhere 1722 saw sitting members unchallenged and usually unchanged. Sir Charles Kemys had been MP for Glamorgan since 1716, on the death of Robert Jones. Tory Francis Edwardes became MP for Haverfordwest as Whig Sir John Philipps now finally retired from Westminster.

The ensuing Parliament is almost a closed book to historians. No significant voting-lists survive, and records of debates are poor; that Watkin Williams Wynn spoke once in 1727 is virtually all that is known about the political behaviour of Welsh MPs. The Parliament was brought to a premature end by the death of George I in 1727. At the consequential general election of that year Wales now returned an overall Whig majority, of sixteen to eleven, though one Whig was to vote against Walpole's ministry. Over half the Welsh constituencies, fourteen out of twenty-six, went to the poll, a remarkably high proportion that reflected the rising tide of Whig power in Wales. Six contests were fought between rival Whig candidates, and five arose from Whig attacks on Tory seats, three of which were successful. Two contests arose from Tory attempts to regain lost ground, and in Flintshire Tory fought Tory. Here Sir Roger Mostyn defeated a challenge from Thomas Puleston by 431 votes to 301. Examination of the poll-book reveals yet another situation in which rival candidates were each supported by both Whigs and Tories.[34] If Whig Sir Robert Cotton was among those who voted for Puleston, so were Denbighshire Tories Watkin Williams Wynn and the Myddelton family. Mostyn voters included retiring Tory borough MP Thomas Eyton, and Chester Tory MP Sir Richard Grosvenor, but also George Wynne of Leeswood, one of the two Whig candidates for Flint Boroughs, a seat that in party terms represented a fourth Whig gain in Wales. Wynne, who was fortuitously wealthy because of a lead mine on his estate, that reputedly yielded £20,000 a year for twenty years, intended to make a splash in politics, and had secured control of Flint Borough. At the poll, deploying 335 non-resident Flint voters, he obtained a majority of 685 to 312 over another local Whig Salusbury Lloyd. But Lloyd had ministerial support, through a connection with Liverpool MP Thomas Brereton, and Prime Minister Walpole's own papers show that pressure was put on MPs when Lloyd's petition was heard in the House of Commons. The House defied law and precedent to rule that only ratepayers in the five constituency boroughs had the right to vote. When calculations showed that Wynne still had a majority, witnesses alleged violence and intimidation by Wynne's miners; but one did admit under cross-examination that 'there never was

[34] Mostyn MSS 7884.

any election in Wales without mobbing and tumults'. Lloyd was awarded the seat.[35]

Far more notorious was the ministerial intervention in the Montgomery Boroughs election. Here, since John Pugh now retired, Robert Williams, a younger brother of Watkin Williams Wynn, was the Tory candidate on the joint interest of Powis Castle and Llwydiarth that controlled the three out-boroughs. Henry Arthur Herbert, patron of the county town, had a safe seat in Ludlow, but he put up a Shropshire Whig ally William Corbett as a rival candidate. Williams secured a majority of 475 to 129, but Corbett had a lead of 107 to 29 in Montgomery itself. When the case came before the Commons in 1728 the three out-boroughs were disfranchised on the ground that they did not contribute to the wages of the MP, a technical and archaic reason since the payment of parliamentary wages had now lapsed.[36] Corbett was awarded the seat, and Montgomery became a pocket borough under the control of Henry Arthur Herbert and his heirs.

Elsewhere in north Wales there were no contests outside Anglesey, with the incumbent MPs, Whigs in Caernarfonshire and Tories otherwise, all retaining their seats. The Anglesey county contest was a re-run of a 1725 by-election consequent on the death of the fourth Lord Bulkeley. His son and successor was under age, and to counter the continuing challenge of the rival Whig Bodorgan interest the Tory Baron Hill family itself then put up a Walpole Whig as its candidate, Hugh Williams of Chester, who possessed a small estate on the island and was a first cousin of Watkin Williams Wynn. Even Wynn was prepared to sacrifice political advantage at Westminster for electoral expediency, as he stated in a private canvassing letter. 'His principles I cannot say much for, but think him the only person at present in Lord Bulkeley's interest that can in all likelihood meet with success.'[37] Owen Meyrick of Bodorgan did not stand, and shrewdly put forward his popular nephew Thomas Lloyd of Llanidan. Lloyd, obtaining the support of the Bishop of Bangor and Edward Bayly of Plas Newydd, pressed the Baron Hill interest hard. Williams won the 1725 by-election only by 194 votes to 162, but achieved a greater margin of victory in 1727, 209 votes to 140.[38] The chief concern then of the Baron Hill family was to find a Beaumaris candidate who would stand down when the fifth Lord Bulkeley came of age, for current MP Henry Bertie refused to do so. Advantage was taken of William Bodfel's candidature as again the

[35] Cholmondeley Houghton MSS P66/2; *CJ*, XXI, 173–6; Thomas, 'Sir George Wynne and the Flint Boroughs Elections of 1727–1741', *Flintshire Historical Society Journal*, 20 (1962), 45–7.

[36] Wynnstay MSS Box 85, no. 1; *CJ*, XXI, 136–8.

[37] Penrhos MSS 1335.

[38] Baron Hill MSS 6803; Penrhos MSS V, 304; *Post-Boy*, 14 September 1727.

champion of Newborough's claim. Watkin Williams Wynn agreed to stand, for he could opt for Denbighshire when the borough election was resolved. The poll was formal. Wynn obtained twelve votes from Beaumaris corporation, Bodfel twenty-four each from the burgesses of Beaumaris and those of Newborough, and the dispute was referred to the House of Commons. The hope of Lord Bulkeley's opponents was evidently that the Commons would disregard law and precedent, as in the cases of Flint and Montgomery. But the House, when it eventually heard the case on 3 March 1730, confirmed the corporation franchise of Beaumaris, and Lord Bulkeley took the seat promptly vacated by Wynn.[39]

In north Wales Wynn provided a personal focus for an electoral network of opponents of the Whig government. In south-west Wales there was by now even a formal organization, the Society of Sea Serjeants, at the time and afterwards suspected to be a secret Jacobite club like the Cycle of the White Rose in north-east Wales. It was not Jacobite nor secret; but neither was it merely the social club portrayed by its then President Sir John Philipps when he was attacked over its treasonable aims in 1754 while a parliamentary candidate for Bristol. 'The intent, indeed, of our annual meeting (which is always at some sea-port town, whence we are called sea-serjeants) is to spend a week together in innocent mirth and recreation, as other gentlemen in England do at a horse-race.' That was its public face. The Society met openly, and its membership was widely known to contemporaries in south-west Wales. But the bond of unity was political as well as social: as the son-in-law of one Serjeant later recalled, 'this Society were all gentlemen in the country interest', and its members co-operated in electoral and other political activities in opposition to government. The Society is known to have existed from 1726 to 1763. It comprised twenty-five full members, and a few probationers. Geographically membership was centred on Carmarthenshire and Pembrokeshire, with a few from Cardiganshire and Glamorgan. Ten Sea Serjeants became MPs, two outside the years of its existence. Two represented English constituencies: Lewis Barlow of Lawrenny sat for Orford from 1734 to his death in 1737, and Velters Cornewall for Herefordshire for forty-six years from 1722. The others were elected for local constituencies in south-west Wales, where three other Serjeants were unsuccessful candidates.[40]

The first electoral move by the Society took place in Carmarthenshire, where in 1727 Sir Nicholas Williams was challenged by Serjeant Richard Gwynne of Taliaris, and a circular letter on behalf of 'our Brother

---

[39] Cholmondeley Houghton MSS 68, 6A; *CJ*, XXI, 29, 35, 48–9, 472–4.

[40] Fenton, *Historical Tour through Pembrokeshire*, pp. 462–8. For an account of the Society, see F. Jones, 'The Society of Sea Serjeants', *T.H.S. Cymm.* (1967), 57–91.

Gwynne' was sent to members of the Society, signed by its President William Barlow of Slebech and five other Serjeants, including secretary John Philipps of Kilgetty; the younger son of Sir John Philipps of Picton Castle, he apparently acted as secretary until he became president in 1752, and was the guiding figure of the Society throughout its existence.[41] Gwynne received enthusiastic assistance from fellow Serjeants during the campaign, and over a dozen personally voted for him at the poll, but he was defeated by 693 votes to 591.[42]

The Carmarthenshire contest was one of nine taken to a poll in south Wales. Only one took place in Pembrokeshire, where both borough seats had changed hands since the previous general election. In late 1722 Sir Arthur Owen's eldest son William began a first, twenty-five year, tenure of the Pembroke seat on the death of Thomas Ferrers, while in 1726 Erasmus Philipps, elder son of Sir John, quietly took the Haverfordwest seat after Francis Edwardes had died in 1725. Both were unchallenged in 1727, but in the county Sir Arthur Owen suffered his second downfall, again as in 1710 finding the government interest against him. Whereas then he had been defeated by a Tory, in 1727 Owen, an independent Whig, lost to a rival Whig who was a ministerial adherent, John Campbell of Stackpole Court. Sir Arthur found that the proud Orielton record of Whig loyalty availed him nothing, for Campbell was connected to such influential men as the Dukes of Newcastle and Argyll, and so had the sheriff on his side. Owen may have cried foul play after he lost the poll by 541 votes to 374, but a significant factor in his defeat was his personal unpopularity. His monopoly of local patronage had bred widespread resentment, especially with the sons of Sir John Philipps, Erasmus and John, who resented the way their father had been displaced as lord-lieutenant in 1715. Although Sir John himself remained loyal to Sir Arthur, his son John, with the connivance of Erasmus, led about a hundred tenants and supporters to vote for Campbell, and Erasmus noted in his diary that 'everybody owned that it was the Picton family that carried the election for Mr Campbell'.[43]

Elsewhere in south-west Wales there were two Whig gains. A power struggle was developing in Carmarthen Borough, where a century-long domination of the constituency by the Golden Grove interest had ended with the death of Richard Vaughan in 1724. At a 1725 by-election the seat was taken by local Tory James Philipps of Pentyparc. In 1727 he defeated by eighty-five votes to sixty-two the Whig Recorder of the borough Arthur Bevan, married to a niece of Vaughan, who petitioned the Commons. The

[41] Picton Castle MSS, Box 12.
[42] Dynevor MSS 160/2.
[43] NLW General MSS 23274, pp. 192–3, 197, 201–2, 204–7.

point at issue was the franchise, with Philipps championing the claim of inhabitants to share it with official burgesses, as in Haverfordwest. The House of Commons rejected this claim on 19 March 1728 and awarded Bevan the seat.[44]

In Cardiganshire a Whig opportunity that resulted in the gain of both seats arose from a quarrel between the leading Tory families, Pryse of Gogerddan and Powell of Nanteos. After the death of borough MP Stephen Parry, the Nanteos heir Thomas Powell defeated a Gogerddan candidate at a 1725 by-election. A temporary Tory reconciliation at the general election of 1727 involved the transfer of county MP Francis Cornwallis to the borough and Powell's candidature for the county; but the Tory interest there had been sufficiently weakened for the Whig second Lord Lisburne to defeat him by 404 votes to 340. However the death of Cornwallis in August 1728 gave Powell an opportunity to re-enter the Commons, and he enrolled 800 new burgesses at Tregaron in October. But the Gogerddan family followed the Bulkeley example in Anglesey by putting forward a Whig supporter of Walpole's ministry as a rival candidate, Richard Lloyd of Mabws, a Pryse kinsman. The by-election in May 1729 was disorderly, with swords being drawn on both sides, and one Lloyd supporter was killed in the rioting. Powell secured a poll majority of 1,224 to 924, but the mayor of Cardigan sent to the House of Commons a double return that made it clear Powell's majority depended on Tregaron votes. The Committee of Elections found little evidence of Tregaron participation in the constituency before 1701, and set aside its claim to do so. The amended poll gave Lloyd a majority of 918 to 465, and the House of Commons awarded him the seat when the Committee reported in May 1730.[45]

In south-east Wales it was the Whig Morgans of Tredegar who were under attack in both their seats. The Tredegar–Pontypool alliance in Monmouthshire made no allowance for the traditional influence of Raglan; and the Duke of Beaufort, although undisturbed in Monmouth Boroughs, where Edward Kemys remained MP, sponsored the candidature of a popular local squire, Robert Hughes of Trostrey. Standing single against John Hanbury and Sir William Morgan, a new Knight of the Bath, Hughes polled nearly all plumpers. He obtained majorities in the Beaufort hundreds of Raglan and Skenfrith, but lost by over 400 votes in the two-day poll at Newport, Morgan securing 1,186 votes and Hanbury 1,162 to the 740 for Hughes.[46] That was the last Beaufort challenge in Monmouthshire for nearly half a century, but Brecon Borough was not yet safe for

---

[44] *CJ*, XXI, 40–1, 90, 94, 96.
[45] *CJ*, XXI, 407, 571–4.
[46] Tredegar MSS 255.

Tredegar. Here Sir William Morgan's brother Thomas successfully defended his seat, this time against John Jeffreys, son of the 1702 county MP and standing on the Priory interest, by 105 votes to 61.[47]

In Glamorgan, where Tredegar now held the Ruperra estate, events were a portent of the future Whig threat to the long-standing Tory hegemony. An important newcomer to the county was Charles Talbot, Walpole's Solicitor-General and MP for Durham City, who had acquired by marriage the estates of Hensol and Castell-y-Mynach. Another influential Whig, now returned to Glamorgan, was a former naval man Commodore Thomas Mathews of Llandaff Court. In 1727 he stood unsuccessfully for Cardiff Boroughs against Bussy Mansel of Briton Ferry, who earlier that year had replaced the deceased young Edward Stradling. This was the first shot of the Glamorgan Whigs across the Tory bows.

Radnorshire, for a succession of reasons, had the liveliest electoral history of the eighteenth century. That there were contests in both constituencies in 1727 resulted from a vain attempt of the Duke of Chandos to establish a dominating interest there, based on his own estate and on such government patronage as the Stewardship of Cantref Maelienydd. He now opposed both sitting members, abandoning his 1722 alliance with borough MP Thomas Lewis for one with the Harley family, headed by the second Earl of Oxford, who as Lord Harley had been borough MP from 1711 until his defeat by Lewis in 1715. The formidable combination sponsored a Chandos nominee in the county and a Harley candidate for the borough seat. In 1722 the Duke had pledged himself to support Marmaduke Gwynne of Garth for the next county election, and now did so; but Sir Humphrey Howorth retained his seat by 529 votes to 447. In the borough Thomas Lewis was opposed by John Verney, Lord Oxford's cousin by marriage, who expected support from the Walpole ministry, whose patronage he had already enjoyed as MP for Downton, notably a judgeship in 1726 on the Brecon circuit. Before the election the Harley family was confident of success. 'Mr Verney has an undoubted majority of legal votes', Lord Oxford was assured on 8 September.[48] Verney made the same claim to Walpole himself.[49] But Thomas Lewis had an impregnable hold on New Radnor, where the Bailiff, his own brother-in-law Herbert Lewis, could make burgesses at will, and did so to counter Chandos creations in the out-boroughs. At the poll he returned Thomas Lewis with a majority of 651 to 497. Verney's petition was never heard by

---

[47] Tredegar MSS 33/38.
[48] BL Add. MSS 70381, ff. 12, 16.
[49] Cholmondeley Houghton MSS 1469.

the House of Commons.[50] Since he had retained his Downton seat, and Lewis was also an administration supporter, the ministry evidently deemed it expedient to let the matter rest. Lewis would have done himself no harm with Walpole by his enthusiastic support on 7 May 1728 for a motion promising repayment to the Crown of unaudited and unauthorized expenses incurred in the recent conduct of foreign policy.

> The duty I owe my country and my King makes me entirely for the motion. I dont pretend to as great an estate as many gentlemen that hear me have, but my little vineyard shall freely pay its share towards the conclusion of so good a work as a general peace, and the security of our navigation without which my vineyard will yield me nothing. I have that confidence in the King and those who administer under him that the money has been or will be well employed, that I shall expect no account of so small a sum which it may be dangerous and impolitic to require.[51]

The general election of 1727 was a resounding success for the Walpole ministry: after petitions had been decided, it enjoyed the support of 415 MPs as against 128 Tories and 15 opposition Whigs under William Pulteney. But while the next few years saw Sir Robert Walpole tighten his hold on power and policy-making at the heart of government, in Parliament there built up by 1730 a formidable group of about 80 opposition Whigs, among whom were numbered Erasmus Philipps and John Hanbury. Nor was any ministerial majority solid in the eighteenth century, on matters over which MPs felt strongly, or believed it expedient to temporize. John Griffith, Sir Humphrey Howorth, William Owen, Hugh Williams and Sir Nicholas Williams were five Welsh ministerial Whigs who rebelled over the Montgomery election case.[52] Howorth, Owen and Hugh Williams also voted against the Flint election decision, when Walpole also noted the abstentions of Lord Lisburne, Sir William Morgan, Thomas Wynn, and John Hanbury, evidently then still deemed a supporter.[53] None of these MPs, apart from Hanbury, were permanent defectors from the ministry.[54]

It was Walpole's Excise Bill of 1733, proposing such duties on wine and tobacco, that famously demonstrated the parliamentary limitations on his power: desertions and abstentions so reduced his Commons majority that he dropped the proposal. Two of his Welsh supporters defected, Arthur

---

[50] *CJ*, XXI, 29, 189.
[51] *Knatchbull Diary*, p. 124. This report was by Lord Egmont.
[52] Wynnstay MSS Box 85, no. 1.
[53] Cholmondeley Houghton MSS P66/2.
[54] This is shown by Commons division-lists for 1729 and 1730. Chandler, *Debates*, VIII, Appendix.

Bevan and Salusbury Lloyd. The other twelve voted with the ministry, Whigs Erasmus Philipps and John Hanbury with the opposition, who included seven of the eleven Welsh Tories, among them Lord Charles Noel Somerset, brother of the Duke of Beaufort, who had come in temporarily for Monmouthshire on the death of Sir William Morgan in 1731. Walpole's parliamentary support returned after the Excise Bill Crisis, and in 1734 Bevan and Lloyd were both among twelve Welsh MPs voting for the ministry when the opposition, just before the general election due that year, vainly proposed the popular measure of repeal of the Septennial Act.[55]

The anti-government reaction in the country aroused by the Excise Bill Crisis nevertheless had so boosted opposition morale that Tories and opposition Whigs alike made a determined effort to defeat Walpole. Anglesey diarist William Bulkeley of Brynddu noted on 30 April 1734 this news from Lord Bulkeley's agent.

> There was an association or confederacy betwixt 25 or 30 very great men, the Duke of Bolton, Earl of Chesterfield, . . . and several other Lords, Mr Watkin Williams Wynn, Mr Sandys of Worcester, Mr Pulteney, Sir William Wyndham and others to exert all their interest and power in all the parts of the Kingdom to get a majority if possible against the villain Walpole, and they hoped to get amongst them 270 members to sit in the House of Commons whose knee had not bowed to Baal.[56]

One obvious target was Hugh Williams, whose Anglesey seat was held on the Tory interest of Lord Bulkeley. Since he himself preferred the safe seat of Beaumaris, a Baron Hill candidate had to be found, and the problem was solved by the choice of not a Tory but an opposition Whig, Nicholas Bayly, son of Sir Edward Bayly of Plas Newydd. Hugh Williams sought Whig support to retain his seat, and obtained the Bodeon interest of Sir Arthur Owen, but gave up his campaign when even Owen Meyrick declared for Bayly, who was elected by acclamation on 9 May.[57]

Elsewhere in Wales Walpole's opponents achieved no success. In north Wales no challenge was mounted in the three Whig seats of Caernarfonshire, Caernarfon Boroughs and Montgomery, but a bitter contest occurred in Flint Boroughs. Here the Tory squires were determined to regain the seat, and on 8 September 1733 a formal written agreement was

---

[55] Commons voting-lists for 1733 and 1734 are also in Chandler, *Debates*, VIII, Appendix.
[56] Bulkeley Diary, I, 14.
[57] Bulkeley Diary, I, 7–9, 16–17; Penrhos MSS 1359–65.

signed by Sir Roger Mostyn's son Thomas, Thomas Puleston, and Sir John Glynne of Hawarden, a young newcomer to the local scene. This arranged that Mostyn should stand for the county instead of his father, and Glynne for the borough, all expenses to be equally shared; and Mostyn agreed to stand down next time if the other two both wished to be candidates. This agreement was confirmed by a county meeting.[58] It was doubtless a reaction to a canvass in both constituencies by a ministerial candidate, not the ailing borough MP Salusbury Lloyd but his former opponent, now Sir George Wynne since Walpole had given him a baronetcy in 1731.[59] Realizing that he would never break the hold of the Tory squires in the county, Wynne soon concentrated on the borough seat. He was Constable of Flint Castle, thereby controlling the shire town, and his wealth was an asset in a constituency with many independent voters. The Tory squires retaliated by threatening his supporters with eviction, and Wynne's personal character was traduced in a pamphlet that alleged ill-treatment of his father and stepmother. So bitter and violent was the campaign that a Glynne supporter was clubbed to death in Caergwrle on 2 April. The poll was prolonged over ten days from 6 May as the two returning officers, Flint bailiffs appointed by Wynne, examined every Glynne vote and rejected many. When Glynne nevertheless won by 270 votes to 258, the bailiffs struck off twenty-four of his voters and returned Wynne after a private scrutiny. The Walpole ministry repeatedly postponed consideration of Glynne's inevitable petition until the Commons finally heard the case on 24 March 1737. The proceedings then took over a month, and the trend of the evidence, whereby Glynne had hoped to establish a legal majority for himself of 231 to 188, was ignored when the House confirmed Wynne's election on 28 April 1737. The contest had cost Glynne £4,034, and Wynne doubtless a great deal more.[60]

South-east Wales was the scene of most electoral activity, with five contests in the eight constituencies, and one man busy in several of them was Thomas Morgan, controlling the Tredegar interest during the minority of his nephew William. He now transferred from Brecon to Monmouthshire, evidently by agreement displacing Lord Charles Noel Somerset, who took the Monmouth Boroughs seat from Edward Kemys. In Brecon, apparently this time without a contest, Morgan brought in John Talbot, a younger son of the Charles Talbot of Hensol in Glamorgan who at the end

[58] Glynne of Hawarden MSS 5198; Chirk Castle MSS E955, 4752.

[59] BL Add. MSS 32688, f. 332.

[60] Glynne of Hawarden MSS 1, 4920, 4926, 5146, 5166, 5174, 5194, 5235; Chirk Castle MSS E 4048; Wynnstay MSS L 711, 716, 770; *CJ*, XXII, 338, 498–9, 612, 637, 669, 698, 724, 823, 832, 835, 839–41, 864, 866–7. For more details, see Thomas, 'Sir George Wynne and the Flint Boroughs Elections', *J. Flints. H.S.*, 20 (1962), 48–51.

of 1733 had become Lord Talbot as Walpole's Lord Chancellor. Thomas Morgan was evidently on better terms than his brother Sir William had been with their uncle William Gwyn Vaughan, for he helped Vaughan, though a Tory, to defend his Breconshire seat against a Whig, the John Jeffreys who had fought Morgan himself in the borough in 1727. Vaughan had been that rarity among Welsh MPs, one who spoke in debate: he was probably the 'Mr Vaughan' who on 5 February 1730 'when no opposition was expected' objected to a resolution to pay foreign soldiers, and he certainly spoke on 5 February 1733 against the army estimates.[61] Jeffreys defeated Vaughan by 586 votes to 547, and in Parliament was to be an opposition Whig, a follower of William Pulteney.

In Glamorgan there took place a contest portrayed by the opposition as even more notorious than Flint. Here Sir Charles Kemys was retiring from the county and borough MP Bussy Mansel intended to succeed him, but the local Whigs fought both seats. The Tory candidate for the Cardiff Boroughs seat was Herbert Windsor, who had the 'Cardiff Castle interest' of his father Lord Windsor. He defeated Thomas Mathews, again the Whig candidate, in a poll for which the votes are unknown. The county election was a fight between the hitherto dominant Tory alliance and the Whig supporters of Walpole's ministry. Bussy Mansel was backed by the Duke of Beaufort, Lord Windsor, Sir Edward Stradling and Herbert Mackworth, who had succeeded his father Sir Humphrey in 1727, but Sir Charles Kemys, piqued by a quarrel with Mansel over shared election expenses in 1727, declared his neutrality. The candidate who challenged Mansel was Lord Talbot's heir William, and Thomas Mathews and Thomas Morgan were among those active on his behalf. The adherents of Talbot were Whig, those of Mansel Tory, and a political flavour dating from past party traditions was evidently imparted to the contest by the charge that the Tory candidate was hostile to Protestant Dissenters, for Mansel deemed it expedient to issue a 'Declaration to Dissenters' that was minimal in its reassurance.

> Whereas it has been invidiously represented in order to determine persons to oppose my interest in the ensuing election that I am an enemy to the religious and civil rights of my countrymen, I assure all gentlemen that have votes in this country and particularly the Protestant Dissenters, that if I have the honour to represent this county, I shall always have a tender regard to those just privileges they at present enjoy.

The Lord Chancellor appointed a partisan sheriff, William Bassett of Miskin, to ensure his son's success. At the poll, which lasted from 23 May

---

[61] *Knatchbull Diary*, p. 103; Chandler, *Debates*, VII, 272.

until 3 June, Mansel had a majority of 823 votes to 678, but sheriff Bassett queried so many that he declared Talbot the victor by 455 to 288. After a scrutiny demanded by Mansel, he announced on 10 June that Talbot had been elected by 658 votes to 577. The Whig House of Commons refused by a party vote to hear Mansel's petition on 28 January 1735, and the case was never reported from its Committee of Elections.[62]

In Radnorshire Sir Humphrey Howorth and Thomas Lewis, now cooperating in self-defence, again had to defend their seats. Herbert Lewis, once more Bailiff of New Radnor, returned his brother-in-law Thomas Lewis after polling about seventy voters, only one of them for the rival candidate Lord Bateman. Although Lord Bateman had been Whig MP for Leominster, Prime Minister Walpole had made it clear to the Duke of Chandos that he strongly favoured Lewis, and both the borough challenge and that in the county may have been instigated by the Harley family. Howorth's opponent was an unidentified 'Gwyn Vaughan', probably the son of William Gwyn Vaughan and whose cousin had married Edward Harley, soon to be the third Earl of Oxford. At the three-day poll at Presteigne Howorth won by only twelve votes, 567 to 555, a victory attributed to the partiality of the sheriff by subsequent petitions that were never considered by the House of Commons.[63] The sense of injustice bred threats and violence, which caused Howorth to ask Walpole to send soldiers to Knighton, where the sheriff and Thomas Lewis had been hanged in effigy, 'otherwise my poor country friends, and those who I am sure are true friends to the administration, must positively quit their homes, or be murdered or ruined'.[64]

The Prime Minister, concerned to prevent another contest between John Campbell and the Orielton family, also intervened in Pembrokeshire, the inducement being a safe Cornish borough seat for Sir Arthur Owen's second son John, as William Owen, returned again for Pembroke, reminded Walpole on 8 June after Campbell's 'quiet' election for the county. 'I fully performed my promises. Had I acted otherwise he [John Owen] should have been chosen in Pembrokeshire.'[65] John Owen, for whom Walpole was not able to provide at the general election, was given a seat at West Looe early in 1735. But at Haverfordwest Sir Arthur Owen sought vicarious revenge for his county defeat of 1727. Soon afterwards, as MP Erasmus Philipps noted with concern, Owen had had himself appointed custos rotulorum of

---

[62] Kemys Tynte MSS 1/9–12; Penrice and Margam MSS L 1158; *CJ*, XXII, 330–1. For further details and sources, see Thomas, 'Glamorgan Politics 1700–1750', *Morgannwg*, 6 (1962), 64–8.

[63] *CJ*, XXII, 344, 507, 744; Sedgwick, *House of Commons 1715–1754*, I, 380–1, 544.

[64] Cholmondeley Houghton MSS 2186, 2205.

[65] Cholmondeley Houghton MSS 2193.

Haverfordwest, 'with a view to strengthen his interest there and to do our family all mischief possible'.[66] The growing breach between Pembrokeshire's foremost families of Orielton and Picton Castle was becoming one of political enmity as well as local rivalry, for as the personal influence of old Sir John Philipps waned his sons Erasmus and John gravitated to the opposition. At the general election of 1734 Sir Arthur put forward his nephew Wyriot Owen of Great Nash. Erasmus Philipps won by 215 votes to 153 on 6 May, noting that 'the principal people of the town were for me (three excepted). The Dissenters and Quakers against me. A large appearance of county gentlemen on my side on this occasion, some of whom had votes, and others had none but there to countenance my side'. Erasmus did not attend the election himself. 'Being in London, my brother John represented me, and was carried in the Chair.'[67] Wyriot Owen must have threatened to petition, for John Philipps, exploiting a family relationship with the Walpoles, visited the Prime Minister on 4 June to solicit support. This resulted in the bizarre circumstance that the ministry contrived to prevent the hearing of a petition from an administration supporter against the election of one of its parliamentary opponents, for every recorded vote by Erasmus Philipps was against the government. Wyriot Owen petitioned three times against the alleged malpractice of the Haverfordwest sheriff, but the case was never heard by the House of Commons.[68]

In Cardiganshire Richard Lloyd, brought in for the borough seat in 1729 on the Pryse of Gogerddan interest, had proved to be a Whig Trojan Horse, creating a formidable interest of his own in both constituencies. Since the Whig county MP Lord Lisburne was busily ruining his Crosswood estate he was unable to prevent his own replacement by Lloyd's ally Walter Lloyd of Peterwell. In the borough Richard Lloyd defeated another Gogerddan candidate, Walter Pryse, who was supported by Watkin Williams Wynn, and wrote triumphantly to the Prime Minister. 'I have . . . succeeded both in town and county, the latter without opposition, and the former I got by a majority of no less than 300.'[69]

Despite the national campaign against the Walpole ministry and all the electoral excitement in Wales only one sitting Welsh MP was defeated at a poll in 1734, and he was a Tory, W. G. Vaughan, although two others, Lord Lisburne and Hugh Williams, had been unwillingly removed without one. Fifteen MPs had retained the same seats, and one had changed constituencies. Two sons had succeeded fathers, William for Richard Vaughan

[66] NLW General MSS 23274, p. 223.
[67] NLW General MSS 23274, pp. 265–6.
[68] Cholmondeley Houghton MSS 2191; Picton Castle MSS 1673; *CJ*, XXII, 332–3, 502, 717, 728.
[69] Cholmondeley Houghton MSS 2212.

in Merioneth, Thomas for Sir Roger Mostyn in Flintshire. Just as in Parliament Walpole's majority had hardly been dented – the new House of Commons would comprise 330 ministerial Whigs, 83 opposition Whigs and 145 Tories – so in Wales the opposition had made no headway at all. Fourteen government Whigs, two opposition Whigs and eleven Tories had become fifteen ministerial supporters, four opposition Whigs, and only eight Tories. Twenty years earlier, at the accession of George I, there had been twenty-three Tories and a mere four Whigs. Too much should not be made of this contrast. Some powerful Tory interests were in temporary eclipse, as those of Raglan in Monmouthshire and Gogerddan in Cardiganshire, and in Anglesey a Whig had again come in on the Tory interest of Baron Hill. Nor did contemporaries always conceive of elections in party terms. The Tredegar interest had supported Whigs in Glamorgan, Monmouthshire and Brecon, but a Tory in Breconshire. Detailed analysis of the political structure of individual constituencies usually reveals cross-party alignments, whether the motives were personal animosities, like the refusal of Sir Charles Kemys to assist his projected Tory successor in Glamorgan, or the more enduring one of family interest: in the Haverfordwest election the Prime Minister himself had given preference to a remote family connection ahead of the consideration of another parliamentary vote.

Tory Wales was nevertheless being brought into the Whig political system. There had been direct intervention by the Walpole ministry in several constituencies and, as ever, the House of Commons safeguarded doubtful Whig returns, this time in Flint Boroughs, Glamorgan, Radnorshire and Radnor Boroughs. Government electoral assistance, both in the constituencies and at Westminster, was boosting the influence of favoured Whig families. This support was supplemented by patronage, both local and national, and in 1739 an opposition list identified nine Welsh MPs who had been suborned by paid office, quite apart from such honours as county lieutenancies. John Campbell, thus listed, was an active politician rather than a placeman, speaking often in debate and accepting junior ministerial office in 1736 as a Lord of the Admiralty, with a salary of £1,300. Thomas Wynn was by contrast an obvious example of a placeman: a household official of George II when he had been Prince of Wales, Wynn after that monarch's accession held for life the sinecure post of Clerk of the Board of Green Cloth, with £1,000 a year, without ever speaking during his thirty-six years in the Commons. The inducements to other Welsh MPs varied enormously. William Corbet's father was on the Customs Board, and Thomas Lewis had 'several relations in the customs'. John Griffith was an army captain, worth £250 a year, while William Owen had three brothers as army officers. Walter Lloyd had £300 salary as Attorney-General for the

South-West Wales legal circuit, and Sir Nicholas Williams £500 as Chamberlain for the South-East Wales one. The inducement to Sir George Wynne had been a long lease of Flintshire mines.[70] Another name would soon be added to the list. Charles Hanbury Williams, later a famous diplomat, had succeeded his father John Hanbury as a Monmouthshire MP in 1735. He soon made his mark as a ministerial speaker, seconding the Address in 1736, and in 1739 was rewarded for his parliamentary services by the £2,000 post of Paymaster of Marines. It was he who proposed parliamentary acceptance in 1739 of the Spanish Convention, Walpole's vain attempt to avoid a war with Spain, the popular cry for which was taken up by the parliamentary opposition because of alleged Spanish depredations on and insults to British merchant shipping. Walpole narrowly won the Commons vote by 260 to 232. All fifteen Welsh ministerialists supported him, but three of twelve oppositionists were absent, among them Bussy Mansel, who by an ironic sequel to the 1734 Glamorgan election had taken the county seat when his former rival William Talbot succeeded to his father's peerage in 1737. Mansel had in fact paired with the British envoy to Florence, and the absent Lord Bulkeley died a week later: the only unexplained Welsh absentee was Sir Erasmus Philipps, as he had become on his father's death in 1737.[71]

The parliamentary success availed Walpole little, for Spain reneged on the agreement, and a Spanish war began later that year. The onset of hostilities, which spread throughout much of Europe when the War of the Austrian Succession began in 1740, marked the virtual end of the Walpole era. At the general election of 1741 the opposition made a final and eventually successful push to topple him from power, and the middle decades of the century witnessed a new political game. Factions flourished as the Court–Country divide became more evidently the touchstone of political attitudes than the party distinction of Whig and Tory.

---

[70] Chandler, *Debates*, XII, Appendix 1–8, reprinted from *Gent. Mag.*, IX (1739), 304–10.

[71] Chandler, *Debates*, XII, Appendix, 1–8. There were no changes of side by Welsh MPs recorded in a division-list for 29 January 1740 on a Place Bill. Ibid., 9–16.

CHAPTER 5

The Decline of Party and
Rise of Oligarchy (1740–1760)

THE general election of 1741 was perceived by Sir Robert Walpole's opponents as the opportunity for a final and eventually successful push to overthrow his ministry, the outcome being a bitter parliamentary struggle for several weeks before his resignation followed a succession of defeats in the House of Commons. In Wales his advantage of fifteen supporters to twelve opponents was exactly maintained at the elections themselves, but all seven contests won by ministerial candidates were victories achieved in suspect circumstances, and three were to be subsequently reversed on petition. Walpole did much to help his proven supporters, as by providing sheriffs favouring ministerial candidates in contested counties. And in two contests between opposition men, Anglesey and Denbighshire, the ministry assisted two former opposition MPs, Nicholas Bayly and John Myddelton, giving rise to suspicions that they had agreed to support Walpole on re-election. In contrast to 1734, south-east Wales was quiet, with only the seemingly inevitable contest in Radnorshire; but in south-west Wales six of the seven constituencies went to the poll, all fights between ministerial and opposition candidates, and four did so in north Wales. Much of this activity centred around John Philipps and Sir Watkin Williams Wynn, the two most prominent politicians in eighteenth-century Wales.

John Philipps, hitherto obliged to play second fiddle to his older brother Erasmus, now emerged as a dynamic electoral organizer, undoubtedly the man behind the Tory attacks launched on the three Whig seats of Carmarthen, Pembrokeshire, and Pembroke Boroughs in which members of the Society of Sea Serjeants played a prominent role. The ground for his own success in Carmarthen had been prepared by Sea Serjeant James Philipps of Pentyparc, namesake son and successor, in 1730, of the former Carmarthen MP; in 1743 MP John Campbell, who was his brother-in-law in that their wives were sisters, daughters of the late Lewis Pryse of Gogerddan, recalled that James Philipps had 'ruined the [Whig] interest at

Carmarthen and been the sole author of Sir J. P.'s power there'.[1] Eighty-five new burgesses were created at Carmarthen between 1738 and 1741, thirty-two of them current or future Sea Serjeants.[2] The result was that in 1741 John Philipps at last entered Parliament, defeating by 208 votes to 112 not the previous MP Arthur Bevan but the young local Whig Griffith Philipps of Cwmgwili. The contest attracted the attention of the London press. The *General Evening Post* of 26 May claimed that Griffith Philipps had had a majority of resident burgesses, who alone had the right to vote. That definition of the franchise was denied by the opposition *London Evening Post* of 9 June, which added that in any case John Philipps had polled 123 residents. Griffith Philipps lodged a petition with the House of Commons, claiming a majority of legal votes, and renewed it in November 1742.[3]

In Pembrokeshire the county campaign had begun by June 1740, when Sea Serjeant John Symmons of Llanstinan issued a canvassing letter.[4] Government support gave MP John Campbell the advantages of a poll at Pembroke, near both Stackpole Court and Orielton, and a favourable sheriff, Matthew Bowen. Family ties prevailed over political principles, for his brother-in-law James Philipps was for Campbell, who recalled that 'he made no scruple to declare he would have been for Mr Symmons if I (his brother-in-law) had not been the other candidate'. How much support he received from the Owens of Orielton is uncertain, for he was later to remind his son, 'how I was used for a long time after Mr Symmons declared, and what an expense that usage occasioned', alluding to 'that family which occasioned all the trouble I have already had'. Whether or not this reference was to the Owens, Campbell was on friendly terms with them by 1742.[5] The county poll lasted from 9 to 15 June, when the sheriff declared Campbell the victor by only twenty-nine votes, 556 to 527. A partisan report in the *London Evening Post* on 25 June claimed that all the voters allowed for Symmons were checked for payment of the 1740 land tax, but not those for Campbell. A petition from Symmons complaining of the sheriff's partiality was read in the Commons on 16 December 1741 and renewed in November 1742.[6]

The Tory attack in the Pembroke Boroughs constituency took the form of a revival of the claim of Wiston to be a borough, since the Owen hold on the old chartered boroughs of Pembroke and Tenby was too secure to be overthrown. The mayor of Pembroke, the Wyriot Owen who had been

---

[1] NLW General MSS 1352, f. 147.
[2] G. Roberts in *History of Carmarthenshire*, II, 34, 39.
[3] *CJ*, XXIV, 28, 340.
[4] Edwinsford MSS 2939.
[5] NLW General MSS 1352, ff. 57, 88, 97, 101, 147–8.
[6] *CJ*, XXIV, 28, 340.

the unsuccessful Orielton candidate for Haverfordwest in 1734, as usual sent no notice of the election to the mayor of Wiston: but he and other Wiston burgesses nevertheless attended to vote for Sea Serjeant Rawleigh Mansel, the candidate opposing William Owen. In his subsequent petition Mansel, claiming the putative support also of burgesses from Pembroke and Tenby, complained that none of his voters had been admitted into Pembroke Town Hall.

> They were obstructed and prevented from going into the said Hall, by a great number of persons, who were placed on the stairs leading to the said hall, armed with pitchforks, and other offensive weapons: that, during the whole time of the election, several persons, friends to the said William Owen, stood at the head of the said stairs with their back-swords or scimitars in their hands, and when any of the said burgesses (who attended with an intent to vote for the petitioner) attempted to go up into the Town Hall, to vote for the Petitioner, they called out to the other persons, so placed on the stairs as aforesaid, to knock them down, saying they are none of our friends: by which means the Petitioner's Electors were obstructed and hindered from going into the Hall, to give their votes for the Petitioner; whereby the said William Owen unfairly had all the hands in the Hall, and was by the said Mayor declared duly elected on view.

When this petition and one from Wiston were read in the House of Commons on 15 December the case was one of those deemed so reprehensible by the opposition majority in the House as to be selected for a hearing at the Bar of the House on 6 February 1742, and on 21 January Mayor Wyriot Owen was ordered to attend then. But on 1 February the case was postponed, and never heard that session. When the petitions were renewed on 22 November a motion to hear the case at the Bar was this time defeated.[7] The Owens of Orielton had meanwhile retaliated by putting up another of Sir Arthur's nephews, Hugh Barlow of Lawrenny, now also his son-in-law, in a second Haverfordwest challenge to Sir Erasmus Philipps, who won by 247 votes to 207. Petitions from Barlow and some Haverford-west burgesses complained that the sheriff had admitted voters for Philipps in disregard of a 1715 Commons resolution that the Common Council could not create burgesses on its own authority without 'the consent of the commonalty'. When the case was not heard, these petitions were also renewed in November 1742.[8]

---

[7] *CJ*, XXIV, 23, 52, 72, 340.
[8] *CJ*, XXIV, 19, 30, 340–1.

In Cardiganshire the ministry's supporters lost both seats, one on petition. Thomas Pryse of Gogerddan had come of age in 1737, and deployed his family interest to good effect, swamping the borough electorate by the mass creation of burgesses in Cardigan. At the poll he defeated MP Richard Lloyd of Mabws by 1,034 votes to 697. In the county the influence of Crosswood was paralyzed by a dispute over the inheritance, and the Whig interest constructed by Richard Lloyd fractured when the younger Thomas Johnes of Llanfair sought to oppose MP Walter Lloyd of Peterwell. This Whig quarrel was patched up by Prime Minister Walpole, but too late. The damage had been done. At a four-day poll, Thomas Powell of Nanteos finished ahead by 352 votes to 346, but the ministry-appointed sheriff then conducted a private scrutiny and returned Walter Lloyd as elected by 344 votes to 340. This was one of the notorious election results reversed by the opposition after Walpole's fall. Lloyd made no attempt to dispute the case, Powell being awarded the seat on 22 March 1742.[9]

In north Wales the election campaign had begun in 1739. Local Whigs, with ministerial backing, were already organizing an electoral coalition against Watkin Williams Wynn when their solidarity was threatened by the death of Caernarfonshire MP John Griffith in June 1739. Two Whig candidates came forward, John Wynn, son of borough MP Thomas Wynn of Glynllifon, and William Bodfel, the Beaumaris candidate of 1722 and 1727, by now an important landowner in his native Caernarfonshire. Watkin Williams Wynn, himself with estates there, saw his chance to make mischief. As early as 3 July John Myddelton of Chirk Castle, the challenger to Wynn in Denbighshire, was informed that he 'of late has been altogether engaged in Caernarvonshire in fixing the candidates'.[10] Wynn's aim may merely have been to strengthen his position in Denbighshire, since John Wynn had married the heiress of the Melai estate there; and in November Myddelton was warned that he might join Watkin in Denbighshire on being made 'easy in Caernarvonshire'.[11] The Walpole ministry foiled any such hopes by sending Ludlow MP Henry Arthur Herbert, already the government's North Wales manager, to resolve the problem. He reported complete success to Lord Chancellor Hardwicke in January 1740:

I have been so fortunate as to reconcile the two Whig gentlemen, for the support of the Whig interest, who were opposing each other with great warmth, and to disappoint the Tories, who were ready and endeavouring

[9] Wynnstay MSS L1219; *London Evening Post*, 11 and 25 June 1741; *CJ*, XXIV, 24, 31–2, 144.
[10] Chirk Castle MSS E90.
[11] Chirk Castle MSS E903.

to take all advantage of these differences between them, and to ruin that interest.[12]

The arrangement was evidently that John Wynn would be returned at the by-election that month, but give up the seat to Bodfel at the general election, when Wynn was to be the Myddelton candidate for Denbigh Boroughs.

Paradoxically, in 1741 both Watkin Williams Wynn and Henry Arthur Herbert supported the same Anglesey candidate, Nicholas Bayly, whose 1734 success had not been popular among squires resentful of Baron Hill arrogance, notably former Whig MP Owen Meyrick and ambitious Tory John Owen of Presaddfed. These two men came to an agreement that whichever of them could win the more promises of support in their canvasses would be the candidate. Owen was the more successful, 'upon scrutinising our lists', agreeing in turn to support Meyrick's son at the next general election.[13] Bayly had meanwhile obtained the reluctant support of James, sixth Viscount Bulkeley, who had succeeded his brother in title, estate and Beaumaris parliamentary seat in 1739. After three days of polling in May, Bayly conceded defeat when Owen was ahead by 232 votes to 127, with some thirty freeholders on each side unpolled.[14] This Anglesey contest should be seen as a successful revolt of local squires against Bulkeley hegemony rather than as part of the national election campaign. Watkin Williams Wynn canvassed on behalf of Bayly, though a Whig, as a sure opposition voter: 'His behaviour, I assure you, in Parliament has been unexceptionable, and we do not at this time abound so much in honest men as to spare a proved man.'[15] Yet the Walpole ministry made a last-minute intervention on behalf of Bayly. Henry Arthur Herbert appeared at the poll, sitting beside the sheriff, in constant consultation with him and Bayly, a circumstance hinting that Bayly had made some pledge of support to Walpole if re-elected. Certainly it gave rise to a fear of a false return of the minority candidate, such as had just happened in Denbighshire.[16] That was the most notorious event of the whole general election. Early in 1739 Sir Robert Walpole gave an interview to John Myddelton, who had succeeded his brother Robert at Chirk Castle and as Denbigh Boroughs MP in 1733. Ambitious to recover the shire seat for his family, he evidently made an agreement with the Prime Minister for government support to that end,

---

[12] BL Add. MSS 35600, f. 233.
[13] Penrhos MSS 1099.
[14] Penrhos MSS 1369, 1376.
[15] Penrhos MSS 1373.
[16] Bulkeley Diary, I, 439; *Morris Letters*, I, 54–5.

despite being an opposition voter at Westminster.[17] With his new Whig allies, who included Henry Arthur Herbert and the Wynns of Glynllifon, he negotiated with Sir Robert Cotton for the Lleweni interest. Cotton, elected Whig MP for Cheshire in 1727 but defeated there in 1734, insisted on being the shire candidate himself, but he soon backed down from fear of the cost. The hiatus of several months before Myddelton announced his own candidature in January 1740 gave Wynn a tactical advantage, and Myddelton's interview with Walpole enabled his enemies to launch a smear campaign, alleging that 'Mr Myddelton had become a Presbyter and a subverter of our religion, and that he had attended Sir Robert Walpole and joined with the government to burden the country with taxes'.[18] In his canvassing letter Myddelton sought to refute these charges.[19]

> My indisputable attachment to the Church of England on every occasion, and my whole behaviour in the House of Commons, together with the property I possess in the county from my ancestors, will, I hope, recommend me to that honour which they enjoyed, and at the same time leave no room to the most artful and designing to suggest me capable of any other bias in Parliament than that of the true interest of my country.

The campaign during 1740 was 'very warm', marked by mass creations of leasehold voters on both sides and by lavish entertainment, with one observer opining that 'whoever gives the last treat will carry the day, for the county freeholders make but little difference of party when well fed'.[20] Wynn retaliated for the county challenge by a cynical deal with Sir Robert Cotton, whereby he was to have the Lleweni interest in the county and support Cotton in the borough. Since Wynnstay would pay all costs, 'the old miser made a safe bargain'.[21] During 1740 over 1,000 new burgesses were admitted in Holt, controlled by the Cotton family, at Wynn's expense, and Lynch Cotton wrote triumphantly to his brother. 'At Holt there are now 1500 burgesses out of which Mr Myddelton cant influence 50; . . . nothing but foul play can prevent your being chosen, and should that be attempted no doubt an Old Whig will have the preference of his antagonists.'[22] Sir Robert refused the offer, conveyed personally by the First Lord of the Admiralty Sir Charles Wager, of an expenses-paid candidature for Montgomeryshire, then vacant on the succession of Price

[17] Chirk Castle MSS E529, 4650.
[18] Chirk Castle MSS E128.
[19] Penrhos MSS 1372.
[20] Chirk Castle MSS C31.
[21] Chirk Castle MSS E128, 5256, 5330, 5333, 5407.
[22] Chirk Castle MSS C26–38.

Devereux to his father's peerage. He did eventually accept a seat for the Cornish borough of Lostwithiel, but insisted on giving his county interest to Wynn, who became Sir Watkin on his father's death in October.[23] Wynn, who could also still command hundreds of Holt voters, produced another borough candidate in Arthur Trevor, son of the former Speaker Sir John Trevor.

The Denbigh Boroughs poll preceded that for the county. The bailiffs arbitrarily ruled, contrary to previous practice, that only resident burgesses could vote, and declared John Wynn elected by 282 votes to 139.[24] In the county the sheriff was William Myddelton, a relative of John. Despite what Sir Watkin's brother Robert described as 'the most scandalous barefaced partiality that ever was seen in a returning officer at any election' Wynn secured a majority of 1,352 to 933. 'We must prevail if numbers will do.'[25] They would not do, for the sheriff put a D against the names of 594 of Wynn's voters and 86 of those for Myddelton, and returned the latter as duly elected, even though he told Sir Watkin the D only meant doubtful, not disallowed.[26] Wynn would obviously petition, but there were initial fears of 'a false determination' by the Commons over the borough constituency, such as had happened in Montgomery and Flint. These doubts were removed by encouraging news of election results in England, and Trevor submitted a petition complaining of the conduct of the returning officers.[27] Sir Watkin meanwhile thwarted the ministerial plan to drive him from the Commons by securing an unopposed election for Montgomeryshire, replacing his brother Robert, who had been returned there at a by-election in December 1740.

Another notorious election occurred in Flint Boroughs. The 1734 candidates for shire and borough, Sir Thomas Mostyn and Sir John Glynne, who had shared the costs of the borough contest against Sir George Wynne, called a county meeting for October 1740,

neither of them being desirous of going to Parliament . . . Tis therefore hoped that gentlemen will consult together and think of the most proper means to support the Country Interest, in which the said two gentlemen have expended above £4,000 at the last election, a sum much too large for the private fortunes of any one or two persons.[28]

[23] Chirk Castle MSS C31; Penrhos MSS 1099; Glynne of Hawarden MSS 4065–6.
[24] Chirk Castle MSS C38, 40, 46.
[25] Nannau MSS 3578.
[26] Wynnstay MSS L910.
[27] Glynne of Hawarden MSS 5147; *CJ*, XXIV, 18–19, 28.
[28] Glynne of Hawarden MSS 5146.

Sir John Glynne did then reluctantly accept nomination to replace Mostyn for the county, and such was the prevailing political temperature that even though Glynne faced no opponent Mostyn later evicted a tenant who refused to promise his vote.[29] The Flintshire squires had great difficulty finding a candidate for the expensive and unpleasant task of challenging Sir George Wynne. Mostyn declined, but Richard Williams, another brother of Sir Watkin, was persuaded to stand. By now Sir George Wynne was himself in financial difficulties, since his mines were ceasing to be profitable. In a long letter of 12 February 1741 to the Prime Minister he claimed to have spent over £30,000 fighting Sir Watkin Williams Wynn, Mostyn and Glynne. He now needed £3,000 election expenses, double the £1,500 already offered by Walpole, and 'a handsome place or pension to make me safe'.[30] Sir George obtained enough assistance to stand the poll, when seventy-five voters for Williams were rejected by the Flint bailiffs, who returned Wynne by a majority of 320 votes to 280.[31] Not only had apparently valid votes for his opponents been refused, but many of Wynne's own voters, all deemed to be resident ratepayers, were suspect in the opinion of his opponent, some 'put into barns and stables to give them the appearance of inhabitants', and others rated for the first time in the election year. A petition from Richard Williams was inevitable.[32]

The quiet story of south-east Wales is a marked contrast to all this phrenetic activity. Local Whigs made no challenge to the Tory MPs in Glamorganshire, where Herbert Mackworth, in the absence of a candidate from the aristocratic patrons, had taken the borough seat in 1739 after Herbert Windsor succeeded to his father's peerage. Nor was there any change or contest in Monmouthshire or Breconshire, even though in 1740 John Talbot, seeking re-election after appointment as a Welsh judge, had retained his Brecon seat by only three votes, defeating William Scourfield from Pembrokeshire by thirty-one to twenty-eight.

Radnorshire politics as usual bore little relation to the national scene. The county contest resulted from a quarrel between the shire and borough MPs, both ministerial supporters, arising from a false rumour in 1740 that the Duke of Chandos had resigned the Stewardship of Cantref Maelienydd. Both applied to Walpole for the post.[33] Thomas Lewis, who needed it to prevent creations in the out-boroughs being made to outnumber his New Radnor voters, was so indignant about Howorth's application that he instigated the county candidature of Roderick Gwynne

[29] Glynne of Hawarden MSS 5141.
[30] Cholmondeley Houghton MSS 3085.
[31] Wynnstay MSS L812–21, 857.
[32] Wynnstay MSS L751; *London Evening Post*, 21 May 1741; *CJ*, XXIV, 26, 29.
[33] Cholmondeley Houghton MSS 2976, 2987.

of Glanbran, younger brother of the Marmaduke Gwynne of Garth who had challenged Howorth in 1727. Howorth thereupon complained to Walpole that this move split the Whig interest. 'I had, as I thought, secured my interest so well, that 'twas not possible for the Tories to have raised their hands; this has been my chief aim for many years, which has from time to time cost me at least £10,000 . . . Tis very true Mr Gwynne who is put up is a Whig, or at least in the last election acted with me on those principles.'[34] It is an ironic comment on Howorth's complaint that he would seem to have been saved from defeat by the traditionally Tory interest of the Harley family, guided by Gwyn Vaughan, his opponent of 1734: for on 4 March Roderick Gwynne assured his Carmarthenshire neighbour MP Sir Nicholas Williams, 'I have great reason to believe I shall be able in spite of all Vaughan's stratagems, to rout the Knight'.[35] But at the election on 12 May Howorth defeated him by 519 votes to 496.[36] The opposition *London Evening Post* condemned the sheriff's conduct as 'extremely partial' and alleged that Howorth's voters included 'two convicts for felony, brought out of prison on purpose to serve this occasion'.[37] In the borough Thomas Lewis faced no contest, even though the Duke of Chandos retained the Stewardship of Cantref Maelienydd until his death in 1744. The post was given two years later by the then Prime Minister Henry Pelham to Thomas Lewis, and held by his brother Henry.[38] With control of the out-boroughs now joined to the Harpton hold on New Radnor, Lewis control of the constituency was secure, until forfeited by incompetence early in the reign of George III.

Widespread electoral malpractice had for a time preserved a majority for Walpole in Wales of fifteen to twelve MPs. How many of these returns would be upheld or overturned depended on the political battle at Westminster. When the new Parliament met in December 1741 administration and opposition were evenly balanced, and the importance of election cases were evident. The opposition made great efforts to prevent dubious returns from being buried in the Committee of Elections, and with exemplary timing brought forward early the worst example of electoral skulduggery. Walpole's first defeat took place on 14 December over a motion to hear Sir Watkin Williams Wynn's petition at the Bar of the House. This was carried by nine votes, 202 to 193, the manifest injustice of the Denbighshire return sufficing to tilt the balance.[39] Some of Walpole's

---

[34] Cholmondeley Houghton MSS 3063.
[35] Edwinsford MSS 2945.
[36] Harpton MSS 2503.
[37] *London Evening Post*, 23 May 1741.
[38] BL Add. MSS 32969, f. 450.
[39] *CJ*, XXIV, 19.

usual supporters refused to back him in this and subsequent election cases and, though he secured narrow majorities on matters of policy, after a run of defeats he resigned on 2 February 1742. His fall was greeted by nation-wide rejoicing: here is a report to Thomas Pryse of the reaction in Carmarthen.[40]

> I congratulate you and the rest of the Patriots on your late victory. God grant you the like in everything. We burnt Bob Booty last Monday in effigy, treating the populace with liquor, . . . joy appeared in every countenance; even Griffith Philipps had so much the sincerity of a courtier, as to . . . say he was glad of the Minister's fall. The boy was a liar when at school, and now he continues the same and excellent person.

For a time confusion among administration adherents allowed their opponents to busy themselves with election cases. 'The chief affair has been the Denbighshire election', wrote Horace Walpole, son of the fallen minister. That case was heard on 22 and 23 February. Myddelton's counsel could put forward little defence of the return, but sought to amuse the House. 'It was objected to the sheriff, that he was related to the sitting member; but, indeed, in that country, Wales, it would be difficult not to be related.' The Commons resolved, without a division, that Wynn ought to have been returned, and sent sheriff William Myddelton to Newgate Prison, where he remained seven weeks; and in 1743 he suffered further retribution when Wynn was awarded £2,800 damages against him.[41]

Two other Welsh election cases were among those accorded priority. On 22 March, the same day that Thomas Powell was awarded the Cardiganshire seat, Sir George Wynne abandoned defence of his return for Flint Boroughs, after a hearing that had begun on 17 March, and Sir Watkin's brother Richard Williams was given the seat.[42] Their other brother Robert resumed tenure of the Montgomeryshire seat now vacated by Wynn. But Sir Watkin was unable to secure priority treatment for the Denbigh Boroughs case, which was to be eventually decided against his candidate in 1744.[43]

The fall of Walpole in 1742 did not, to the disappointment of many naïve Tories, lead to the overthrow of the Whig system of government. The ministerial reconstruction of that year brought some opposition Whigs like

---

[40] Gogerddan MSS Box 17B, J. Adams to T. Pryse, 11 February 1742.

[41] Walpole, *Letters* (Toynbee), I, 183–4; *CJ*, XXIV, 89–92; *Gentleman's Magazine*, XII (1742), 217; XIII (1743), 610.

[42] *CJ*, XXIV, 26, 29, 133, 136–7, 144–5.

[43] On this see Thomas, 'Wynnstay versus Chirk Castle: Parliamentary Elections in Denbighshire 1716–1741', *NLWJ*, 12 (1959), 119–21.

Lord Carteret and William Pulteney into the administration, alongside the Duke of Newcastle and his brother Henry Pelham. Two years later, they were out again, in another Whig reshuffle, and Henry Pelham was Prime Minister until his death in 1754. Of the Welsh MPs the only one to change sides in 1742 was John Jeffreys. As a follower of William Pulteney, now Lord Bath, he became Joint Secretary to the Treasury, a post worth £5,000 a year: since he was a notorious gambler, his lucrative appointment excited mirth and surprise, still more so when he retained it on Lord Bath's fall from power in 1744. The other Welsh Whigs were denominated 'Old Whigs', safe administration supporters rather than members of factions; the Welsh Tories maintained equally consistent opposition, apart from a brief and abortive flirtation of a few, including Wynn and Philipps, with the Pelham ministry for some months from the end of 1744.[44]

Earlier a multiplicity of election cases had remained outstanding when the new parliamentary session began in November 1742. Among the unfinished business the four constituencies of Carmarthen, Haverfordwest, Pembroke Boroughs and Pembrokeshire still awaited verdicts by the House of Commons, the first three involving franchise disputes. After the political re-alignments it was quite uncertain how rough would be the justice meted out in election cases. Past alliances, former promises, personal antipathies and tactical considerations were among factors blurring any line between administration and opposition. John Campbell later recalled that at first Henry Pelham and Chancellor of the Exchequer Samuel Sandys, a former oppositionist, would both have been 'glad to have had all petitions dropped', at least with respect to Wales. After all cases had been referred to the Committee of Elections, manœuvring began over their timing, postponement being to the advantage of sitting members. On 29 November Pelham was among those who argued successfully to defer the Pembrokeshire case to 'a long day', with Sir Watkin Williams Wynn complaining 'loudly' about the decision. Campbell thought that the opposition wanted to trade off Carmarthen, due to be heard early, against Pembrokeshire.[45]

Before the Carmarthen case was heard the withdrawal of all the petitions concerning Carmarthen and the three Pembrokeshire constituencies was proposed by the Picton Castle family, an arrangement that would

---

[44] For this, see the studies of Wynn and Philipps below. Evidence on the alignment of MPs at this time may be found in (a) A Cockpit list of 293 administration supporters, Oct. 1742. BL Add. MSS 32699, ff. 467–8. (b) A division-list on payment of Hanoverian soldiers, 10 Dec. 1742, printed Chandler, *Debates*, XIV, Appendix. All twenty-seven Welsh MPs are listed, thirteen for government (one absent), fourteen against (three absent). The names on each side are exactly as to be expected. (c) List of MPs for and against payment of Hanoverian soldiers, 11 April 1346. BL Add. MSS 33034, ff. 110–11. Fourteen were for (five absent) and ten against. Three others, all Tory, were omitted.

[45] NLW General MSS 1352, ff. 66C–D, 89, 100.

safeguard the Haverfordwest and Carmarthen seats of the Philipps brothers at the expense of their allies in the other two constituencies. Pembrokeshire MP Campbell was informed of this suggestion by Herefordshire MP Velters Cornewall, a Sea Serjeant. Lord Bath approved, and at the end of parliamentary business on 12 January 1743 Cornewall and the Philipps brothers discussed the idea with Sandys. Campbell declined to participate, since he would benefit from the arrangement, and guessed correctly from the subsequent facial expression of John Philipps that the ministry had rejected the proposal: 'I think it will come to nothing. I will only say if our friends reject this offer they should make sure of turning out both the Philipps's, or else we shall make a very ridiculous figure.'[46]

It soon became evident that the ministry had made a mistake. When the Committee of Elections discussed the Carmarthen case on 26 January, the opposition carried by 165 votes to 116 a decision that in Campbell's opinion was plainly against the evidence. He thought John Philipps was now 'quite sure of his seat, and probably Sir Erasmus too' in Haverford-west, where Hugh Barlow was petitioner. His pessimism was reinforced by events two days later, as he told his son Pryse.[47]

> We had no division for indeed we saw ourselves too weak to divide. The case is not ended, but there can be no doubt of our losing it, were it a much stronger case than it is. I wish Mr Barlow may have better fortune. I think him an honest good-natured man, and believe he has a strong case. But that will signify little if there is a strong party against him.

The ministry now hastened to conclude the bargain previously rejected. On 2 February an agreement, witnessed by Sir Watkin Williams Wynn among others, was made to withdraw all petitions concerning the four constituencies. Next morning John Symmons, Pembrokeshire petitioner against Campbell, refused his consent: but Wynn insisted on his compliance, and the petitions were withdrawn later that day. 'Considering how matters went it was certainly a good bargain on our side', wrote John Campbell, for Lord Bath, who had been neutral over the Carmarthen case, urging his supporters to stay away, 'was more for Sir Erasmus than for his brother. So if the petitions had gone on, Mr G. Philipps and Mr Barlow would have been put to further expense, and lost their causes, and next

---

[46] NLW General MSS 1352, ff. 99–102.
[47] NLW General MSS 1352, ff. 110–13.

session the petitions against Mr Owen and me might have been renewed, when we had nothing to set against them.'[48]

Later that year John Philipps unexpectedly came into the Picton Castle inheritance of title and estate. His elder brother Sir Erasmus died unmarried on 15 October at the age of forty-three, being drowned in the River Avon where he had been thrown by his horse. The immediate consequence was a by-election at Haverfordwest. Here the Picton Castle candidate was Sea Serjeant George Barlow of Slebech, son of former Tory MP John Barlow of Colby. But rumours soon reached John Campbell and Sir John Philipps, both in London for the parliamentary session, that 'the people of the town' wanted to elect Hugh Barlow, even though he had early on given up his own pretensions as a candidate and not only pledged his support to his namesake relative but even canvassed for him.[49] Why he should have done so is puzzling, unless this by-election was a harbinger of the *rapprochement* between Orielton and Picton Castle at the next general election.

The middle decades of the eighteenth century were a time when the old party terminology of Whig and Tory faded away into the actual political alignment of Court and Country. Ministerial supporters, especially when writing to the Duke of Newcastle, continued to emphasize their own Whiggery and the Toryism of their opponents; but the latter eschewed the name of Tory, preferring to call themselves 'the country interest'. In Wales the transition was almost an exact match, with every Tory an opposition voter and almost every Whig a government man, with breakaway Whig factions receiving little support. In this context the famous Glamorgan by-election of 1745 was an anomaly, a throwback to the old party divide in the county.

It was caused by the succession of Bussy Mansel to the family peerage in November 1744. First in the field was Whig Thomas Mathews of Llandaff, who had fought the borough seat in 1727 and 1734. He had resumed his naval career in 1736 and, as an admiral, commanded the British fleet at the indecisive battle of Toulon in February 1744. Public outcry at his failure then to defeat the French caused his recall, but despite this cloud over his head Mathews again sought to enter Parliament. Local Tories soon drafted a reluctant candidate in Somerset squire Sir Charles Kemys Tynte, who had inherited Cefn Mably from his uncle Sir Charles Kemys in 1735. The Tory magnates of Glamorgan, the Duke of Beaufort, the new Lord Mansel, Lord Windsor and Herbert Mackworth, rallied to the cause. This was the very time when Tories were negotiating with new Prime Minister Henry

---

[48] NLW General MSS 1352, f. 120; *CJ*, XXIV, 403–4.
[49] NLW General MSS 1352, ff. 165–6.

Pelham, and some of Tynte's friends hoped that ministerial pressure might be put on Mathews to withdraw. Pelham was persuaded to offer Mathews a seat then vacant at Portsmouth, but he declined to reply, and the Prime Minister refused to intervene directly in the contest.[50]

One reason why Mathews failed to respond to Pelham's approach was his political allegiance to Lord Bath, the former William Pulteney, recently pushed back into opposition in the 1744 reshuffle.[51] But ministerial Whigs headed by Thomas Morgan of Tredegar nevertheless maintained their county alliance with opposition Whigs like Lord Talbot in support of Mathews, and Morgan told Lord Chancellor Hardwicke on 25 December that Mathews 'stands very fair to be chose but I dont like to be so positive beforehand'.[52]

With the issue very much in the balance Charles Edwin of Llanvihangel, who sat as a Tory for Westminster and had so far refused to commit himself, now made a calculated move. He offered Tynte his interest in return for the support of the Glamorgan Tories at the next general election. Tynte's allies accepted this hard bargain, since it was thought to guarantee his success. Canvass registers promised a clear majority for Tynte, but the Tory magnates, with the painful memory of 1734, sought to insure against a partisan sheriff by procuring the attendance at the poll of Sir Watkin Williams Wynn and other gentlemen of influence. The Duke of Beaufort promised Tynte he would try to secure Wynn's presence, but Sir Watkin refused to go to Glamorgan, Somerset MP Thomas Prowse explaining his attitude to Tynte. 'The election was out of his province (North Wales), and therefore I believe an application to him to attend you will be to no purpose: and, to say the truth, a gentleman's appearance at a county election where he has not the least concern very often offends even that side he has come to support.' Lord Mansel disagreed. 'I know there is nothing so common, and I also know it would have been of service to you.'[53] Tory fears proved to be well-founded when at the poll in January 1745 the sheriff declared Mathews the victor by 688 votes to 641. Tynte could not afford the cost of a petition, and contended that he should not have to pay all his campaign expenses of £2,500.

> I am convinced that no one harbours so ill an opinion of me that I attempted to get into Parliament to gain any thing by my seat, therefore I think it extremely hard, that I should be expected to pay a greater share of the election expenses for offering myself to be a slave in Parliament, in hopes to serve poor England in general and the county of Glamorgan in particular.

[50] Kemys Tynte MSS 1/18–22, 47; Mackworth MSS 653.
[51] BL Add. MSS 33034, ff. 110–11.
[52] BL Add. MSS 35601, f. 348.
[53] Kemys Tynte MSS 35–7, 41–4, 47, 60.

Lord Mansel, Lord Windsor and the Duke of Beaufort agreed to share the burden according to their respective interests: 216 votes were attributed to Mansel, 125 to Beaufort, and the other 300 deemed independent or under Windsor influence, and the bill was therefore divided in these proportions.[54] Tynte entered Parliament only two months later. The Duke of Beaufort died on 24 February, to be succeeded by his brother, Lord Charles Noel Somerset, and Tynte was returned for the vacant Monmouth Boroughs seat. The victory of Mathews made him a marked man by the Tories, who exploited the parliamentary inquiry into the Toulon failure to launch a court martial that resulted in his conviction and disgrace.

The ministry of conciliatory Henry Pelham so lowered the political temperature from 1744 onwards that the general election of 1747 was a notable contrast to the heated campaigns of 1734 and 1741. By then there was no prospect of the opposition overturning the ministry. The dwindling group of Tories found Whig allies only in the small factions of Lord Bath and of Frederick, Prince of Wales, who had reverted to opposition in 1746. In Wales the election passed off quietly. In the only two constituencies that went to the poll sitting members defeated their challengers. Sixteen Welsh seats did change hands, but these were for the most part voluntary adjustments among the dominant families, as when three MPs moved to alternative Welsh seats and three others found seats elsewhere. These were merely reshuffles of a tightening oligarchy.

What was the most bitter election did not reach a poll. Anglesey Tory MP John Owen now honoured his 1741 promise to support the Whig Owen Meyrick junior of Bodorgan; but Tory Lord Bulkeley, retaining the Beaumaris seat for himself, again sponsored Whig Sir Nicholas Bayly, who had inherited his father's baronetcy. After a canvass showed only a narrow majority of a dozen for Meyrick, the Bodorgan family sought to play safe, signing an agreement with Lord Bulkeley to support Bayly or any other Baron Hill candidate next time if Bayly withdrew. John Owen was so indignant at this disregard of his own parliamentary pretensions that he offered his Presaddfed interest of thirty voters to Lord Bulkeley, who then reneged on the agreement with Meyrick. The Bodorgan family thereupon boycotted the election, Bayly being returned unopposed. 'Mr Meyrick was fairly bit by the Tories', commented local Whig observer William Morris, and Owen's perfidy achieved national notoriety.[55]

Across the Menai Straits Caernarfonshire was the scene of a fierce contest. By now the Glynllifon family had been well rewarded for their

---

[54] Kemys Tynte MSS 69, 78, 83. For a fuller account of this by-election see Thomas, 'Glamorgan Politics, 1700–1750', *Morgannwg*, 6 (1962), 71–6.

[55] Penrhos MSS 1377–8; *Morris Letters*, I, 115, 117–18.

Whig loyalty. Thomas Wynn in 1742 added a baronetcy to his lucrative post, while his son, the Denbigh Boroughs MP John Wynn, had become Deputy Treasurer of Chelsea Hospital in 1744. Since a Place Act of 1742 had made this virtual sinecure incompatible with membership of the Commons as from the next dissolution of Parliament, John Wynn did not stand at the general election, and at the request of Henry Pelham the Glynllifon family agreed to support the re-election of William Bodfel.[56] A canvass of the county by Sir Watkin Williams Wynn in 1746 gave notice of a Tory challenge, and one local squire asked William Owen of Brogyntyn 'whether it would not be proper to prepare private leases among our friends to make a certain number of new voters for the county. Sir Watkin is well acquainted with such proceedings.'[57] The candidate selected to challenge the Glynllifon interest was not a local squire but Sir Thomas Prendergast, a former Whig MP with government connections, who had acquired by marriage the Marle estate in the county. He was supported by the Tory grandees of north Wales, Sir Watkin, Lord Bulkeley and Sir Thomas Mostyn, all with Caernarfonshire estates: but his friends feared that 'his being a stranger will be an objection to the vulgar', and Bodfel defeated him by 279 votes to 185 at the poll in July.[58] This contest had an unpleasant aftermath. Prendergast told Mostyn on 13 August that since 'the adverse party is using its utmost endeavours to distress such as voted with us' he wanted his supporters to retaliate: 'that they may both exert their power against such as have broke their words, or been absent who had promised us, and also against such as are within their reach, who engaged against us.'[59]

There was no other contest in north Wales, but several seats changed hands. In Flintshire Sir Thomas Mostyn resumed the shire one almost as of hereditary right. Sir John Glynne was unwilling to remain an MP, and so for the borough Sir Watkin Williams Wynn replaced his brother Richard, a reluctant candidate in 1741, by his cousin Kyffin Williams, younger brother of former Anglesey MP Hugh Williams and brother-in-law of new Pembroke Boroughs MP Hugh Barlow. Like them he was a ministerialist Whig, even Sir Watkin on this occasion putting family above political considerations. Wynn retained his Denbighshire seat, and John Myddelton's son and successor Richard took what was now the safe Denbigh Boroughs seat, one that he was to hold for over forty years without a challenge. Whether or not his father had agreed with Walpole to back his administration in 1741, young Myddelton proved to be a ministerial

[56] BL Add. MSS 32919, f. 267.
[57] Brogyntyn MSS 35.
[58] Brogyntyn MSS 818, 1562; Llanfair and Brynodol MSS 4.
[59] Mostyn MSS 7840.

supporter, one especially cultivated by Prime Minister Pelham during the next few years.[60] In Montgomeryshire Sir Watkin's other brother Robert gave way to his Shropshire Tory ally Edward Kynaston. In the borough Henry Arthur Herbert, now Baron Herbert, brought in his cousin Henry Herbert for General James Cholmondeley, a relative of Sir Robert Walpole who had done his political duty and now wished to concentrate on his military career. Henry Herbert was replaced by his brother Francis on his death in 1748, the year Lord Herbert succeeded to the vast Powis Castle inheritance and was created Earl of Powis. This change in the balance of Montgomeryshire power was not to threaten Kynaston's tenure of the shire seat, for the new Lord Powis used him in negotiations with Shropshire Tories.

Radnorshire was the scene of the only contest in south Wales, and nothing is known of this except that Sir Humphrey Howorth was challenged by William Perry, the new lord lieutenant of the county who had broken with Henry Pelham over not having been given an Irish peerage.[61] In Monmouthshire both county MPs yielded to stronger family claims. Capel Hanbury, master of Pontypool and MP for Leominster since 1741, replaced his younger brother Sir Charles Hanbury Williams, while Thomas Morgan made way for his nephew William Morgan, since that young master of Tredegar was now of age, and moved to take the Breconshire seat, John Jeffreys finding one at Dartmouth. Sir Charles Tynte vacated the Monmouth Boroughs seat to represent Somerset, Wiltshire squire Fulke Greville, a relative of the fourth Duke of Beaufort, being the Duke's next nominee there.

In south-west Wales Sir John Philipps played the paradoxical role of possessing the decisive voice in several constituencies and of simultaneously losing his own seat: a paradox partly explained by his genuine if somewhat inexplicable desire to withdraw from Parliament at this election. In 1745 Sir John had been suddenly catapulted into a leading role in Cardiganshire politics by the death of Thomas Pryse of Gogerddan, who left a six-year-old heir John Pugh Pryse. Mindful of the events during his own minority Pryse had established a trust, including Sir John Philipps and Sir Watkin Williams Wynn, whose political aim was to preserve the electoral interest of Gogerddan for the young heir. For the 1746 borough by-election consequent on Pryse's death, they therefore agreed on Sea Serjeant John Symmons, the unsuccessful Pembrokeshire candidate of 1741, to fill the vacancy. Symmons was opposed by Whig Walter Lloyd, the

---

[60] Chirk Castle MSS E613. Newman (ed.), 'Leicester House Politics', *Camden Miscellany XXIII*, p. 164.
[61] Newman, 'Leicester House Politics', p. 165.

former county MP whose estate of Peterwell gave him control of the contributory borough of Lampeter, in a contest for which the poll figures are unknown. The Gogerddan trustees did not relish the prospect of an ongoing struggle in the Cardigan Boroughs constituency, where the absence of a residence stipulation made possible the mass creation of burgesses in any borough. For the general election of 1747 they arranged a compromise with the local Whigs whereby John Lloyd, who succeeded his father Walter as owner of Peterwell early that year, would take the county seat if there was no challenge to the Gogerddan nominee for the borough. But who that choice would be was disputed among the trustees. Wynn and Thomas Pryse's widow favoured the displaced county MP Thomas Powell. But Sir John Philipps feared that a local candidate might establish his own interest in defiance of Gogerddan, and prevailed on the trustees to return John Symmons again. After Wynn's death in 1749 Philipps was in undisputed control of the Gogerddan political interest.[62]

His own Carmarthen seat had meanwhile been lost in 1747 to an unscrupulous coup by Griffith Philipps, the defeated Whig candidate of 1741. At the town corporation election of 1746, by deploying mob violence, he secured the election of a rival Whig corporation alongside the existing Tory one controlled by Sir John. The aim behind this manœuvre became apparent at the general election, when the Whig ministry sent the borough election writ to this usurping Whig corporation. Sir John had lobbied vainly for delivery of the writ to the old corporation, intending Sea Serjeant James Philipps of Pentyparc to be his successor as Carmarthen MP. The Pelham ministry wanted young George Rice of Newton to take the seat, but Griffiths Philipps had another candidate in mind, and through William Owen warned off Rice from standing.[63] The man belatedly revealed as Whig candidate was Admiral Thomas Mathews, now conceding his Glamorgan seat without a contest to a Charles Edwin claiming his promise from that county's Tory patrons. This choice must have been as annoying to the ministry, since Mathews was a follower of Lord Bath, now in opposition, as it was galling to the local Tories: but Griffith Philipps himself was deemed 'a Whig, but not well with the Pelhams' in a later political survey made by Lord Egmont on behalf of the Prince of Wales.[64] James Philipps did not contest the election, but in September Admiral Mathews heard reports that there would be a petition by some Carmarthen burgesses about the irregular nature of his election, including charges that

---

[62] Thomas, 'Eighteenth-century Politics in the Cardigan Borough Constituency', *Ceredigion*, 5 (1964–7), 409–10.

[63] Cwmgwili MSS 34; G. Roberts in *History of Carmarthenshire*, II, 34–6.

[64] Newman, 'Leicester House Politics', p. 164.

he had paid £3,000 for the seat and had obtained possession of the election writ by bribery: nothing came of such rumours.[65]

In 1745 there had also been a by-election in Carmarthenshire on the death of Sir Nicholas Williams, when Whig John Vaughan of Derwydd was returned on the Golden Grove interest of his relative, the Duchess of Bolton. She was estranged from her husband, and on her death in 1751 bequeathed the estate to Vaughan, who had been unopposed in 1747, when there was a series of changes in Pembrokeshire about which little is known. In the county Sir John Philipps joined his old Orielton foes to replace John Campbell by William Owen: Campbell, now a Lord of the Treasury, retreated to the Nairnshire seat controlled by his family. Owen, who as a precaution had secured re-election for Pembroke Boroughs, gave up that seat to his cousin and brother-in-law Hugh Barlow of Lawrenny. At Haverfordwest William Edwardes of Johnston claimed the seat briefly held by his father Francis in the 1720s, and his family interest was so buttressed by wealth from his Kensington estate that in his constituency survey a few years later Lord Egmont noted that 'the best interest is in Edwards . . . Sir John Philipps has the next best interest, and Campbell of the Treasury has some.'[66] Certainly Edwardes, later to be but perhaps not yet a Sea Serjeant, was to retain the seat until 1784.

The use of party terms, still widely current at local level in the context of family traditions and alignments, was becoming an anachronism at Westminster. The government list of the new Parliament was headed 'For' and 'Against'. Fourteen Welsh MPs were in the former category, twelve in the latter, Mathews the only one of them with a Whig pedigree. There was a query against the name of Sir Nicholas Bayly, perhaps because of what had happened at the Anglesey election of 1741.[67] He was to be another opposition Whig, attached to the Prince of Wales.

Absence of political controversy, by removing one obvious motive for challenge, evidently served to strengthen local oligarchy. The creation of new electoral interests, by overturning established ones, was becoming more difficult to achieve, and normally awaited some favourable opportunity, such as a minority or a failure in the line of inheritance of a dominant family, perhaps only a vacancy in a constituency. The years of the ministry of Henry Pelham, who died in 1754, and those of the Seven Years War (1756–63) against France, were a period of quiescence in national politics. In Wales a more specific explanation for the calm that ensued until the accession of George III in 1760 created a new political

---

[65] Cwmgwili MSS 38.
[66] Newman, 'Leicester House Politics', p. 165.
[67] BL Add. MSS 33002, ff. 440–6; 33034, ff. 173–8.

environment was the departure from the Welsh scene of the two most active participants in recent elections. Sir Watkin Williams Wynn died in 1749, and Sir John Philipps mainly concerned himself with matters outside Wales.

On Wynn's death Henry Pelham, promising the full support of the ministry, urged young Richard Myddelton to 'push for the county and then you may bring in . . . any good man you think proper for the town of Denbigh. A minority, the divisions and distresses in the Williams family, will probably open a door for your easy entrance.'[68] But Myddelton displayed no ambition to recover the Denbighshire seat for Chirk Castle. Instead, he came to an agreement with Sir Lynch Cotton, who had recently succeeded his brother Robert in baronetcy and the Lleweni estate, whereby Cotton would vote for the ministry in Parliament if given Chirk Castle support at the by-election.[69] This arrangement was confirmed before the general election of 1754. 'County and town settled by agreement between them' is a note in the government's election analysis.[70]

Altogether twenty-one of the twenty-seven Welsh MPs sitting at the dissolution in 1754 were returned again for the same constituencies, and all but one of the six changes can be identified as the decisions of patrons. Carmarthenshire was the exception to this picture of electoral calm. The continued existence of rival Whig and Tory corporations in Carmarthen was merely one factor that raised the political temperature there. No sooner had Admiral Mathews been elected in 1747 than speculation began about his successor, for he was already seventy years old. John Campbell was soon informing his son Pryse that

> Griffith Philipps indeed seems very desirous to have you chosen, but the debt I had contracted by my contest with Mr Symmons made me so fearful of expense that I often told him I could not think of it, and indeed I had long ago told Mr Pelham so, upon which he had advised Mr Rice of Newton to offer, and that makes the difficulty now.

John Campbell admitted his own indecision, confessed his puzzlement at the offer, and expressed the fear that a Whig split would let in Sir John Philipps again.[71] Griffith Philipps was playing a deep game to ensure united Whig support for himself. In December 1749 a meeting of some forty Carmarthen burgesses decided to support him as prospective candidate, the claim of Pryse Campbell being studiously ignored. Sir John Philipps was

[68] Chirk Castle MSS E613.
[69] Chirk Castle MSS E593.
[70] BL Add. MSS 32995, f. 82.
[71] NLW General MSS 1352, ff. 296–7.

promptly informed of this resolution, but it was widely accepted that his influence had been destroyed by the usurping role of the Whig corporation.[72] Lord Egmont's constituency survey had this note on Carmarthen. 'I hear Sir John Philipps is entirely lost here which is not bad. That one Griffith Williams or Philipps . . . has the leading interest.'[73] As soon as news that Mathews had died on 2 October 1751 reached Carmarthen the Whig Mayor proclaimed Griffith Philipps as candidate. He was elected without opposition the next month, even though the idea had been floated that William Owen might join with his new Pembrokeshire ally Sir John Philipps to put up a rival candidate in his relative John Williams, currently the deputy judge on the Carmarthen circuit and younger brother of MP Kyffin Williams.[74]

Private animosities and personal ambitions nevertheless produced contests in both Carmarthenshire constituencies at the 1754 general election. John Vaughan of Golden Grove, a supporter of the Pelham ministry, proposed to retire from the county seat in favour of his son Richard. But an opponent appeared in George Rice, by now reconciled with Griffith Philipps, to whom he sent an optimistic account of his canvass.[75] The Duke of Newcastle, who at this election succeeded his deceased brother Henry Pelham as Prime Minister, evidently gave Rice the ministerial seal of approval, for his electoral list notes that Rice was supported by 'Mr P. and the Whigs' and that Griffith Philipps was being threatened by 'a Tory'.[76] Yet not only had the Golden Grove family an unimpeachable Whig pedigree, but the other candidate in the borough was a professed Whig supporter of the ministry, Sir Thomas Stepney of Llanelli: and the duke was sent this explanation of Stepney's candidature by Lovell Stanhope, formerly his law clerk when Secretary of State. 'Sir Thomas Stepney professes himself and I believe very sincerely a friend to the administration', but Griffith Philipps had wronged his family.[77] Despite this claim Stepney was in fact a Sea Serjeant and championing the cause of the Tory corporation. John Campbell, soon to become MP for Inverness Boroughs, expressed regret to Griffith Philipps that Stepney had allowed himself to be made use of, 'but I hope nothing will be able to break the Whig interest in that town'. He would use his 'best endeavours' to ensure that the writ was given to 'the legal sheriffs'.[78] A poll did take place, and

---

[72] Cwmgwili MSS 42.
[73] Newman, 'Leicester House Politics', p. 164.
[74] Cwmgwili MSS 43.
[75] Cwmgwili MSS 45.
[76] BL Add. MSS 32995, f. 81.
[77] BL Add. MSS 32734, ff. 365–6.
[78] Cwmgwili MSS 47.

Stepney petitioned about the return of Philipps, claiming a majority of legal votes and alleging partisan conduct by men usurping the office of sheriffs. Before the House of Commons could investigate the state of affairs in Carmarthen Stepney was persuaded to withdraw his petition.[79] The two rival corporations nevertheless continued in Carmarthen, and the party feud was maintained by legal actions and physical violence, as when in 1755 local Whigs blamed Sea Serjeants for bringing armed men from Pembrokeshire into the town.[80]

In the county contest Rice defeated Vaughan by 785 votes to 390, a remarkable triumph over the hitherto formidable Golden Grove interest, and a victory afterwards depicted as the triumph of the small freeholders over the county magnates.[81] Partisans of Rice were also involved in the attack on the Tredegar interest in nearby Breconshire.[82] Here county MP Thomas Morgan's eldest son Thomas took the safe borough seat while he himself fought Howell Gwynne of Garth, whose father Marmaduke had contested Radnorshire in 1727 and whose uncle Roderick Gwynne of Glanbran about this time bought the important Buckland estate from the widow of former MP Roger Jones. Morgan was sufficiently concerned about the challenge to obtain from the ministry the appointment of a friend as sheriff, but won the poll by a comfortable majority of 682 votes to 433.[83] Thereafter for the rest of the century the rule of Tredegar was as unchallenged in the county as in the borough.

Howell Gwynnne did not have to wait long for a seat, being returned in 1755 for Radnorshire. Here in 1754 both Sir Humphrey Howorth and Thomas Lewis faced challenges. Lewis, confident that he could create as many borough voters as he needed, was concerned only about the trouble and expense caused by an opposition raised by the third Earl of Oxford.[84] The press reported the result as 'Lewis 604, Mr Jennings of Suffolk 516'.[85] Howorth was again threatened with a poll by William Perry, but he failed to appear on election day, allowing Sir Humphrey to boast in the press that it was the sixth successive county contest he had won.[86] Nine months later he died, leaving the Maesllwch estate encumbered with £26,000 of debt. Two years earlier, in anticipation of his death, Henry Pelham and Lord Powis had fixed on Howell Gwynne as candidate, and George Rice now reminded Newcastle of that circumstance. But the Marquess of

---

[79] *CJ*, XXVII, 31, 116, 141–2, 145, 320, 429.
[80] G. Roberts in *History of Carmarthenshire*, II, 37–42.
[81] Cawdor MSS 1/42/5817, 5822.
[82] Cwmgwili MSS 45.
[83] BL Add. MSS 35604, ff. 125, 154; Tredegar MSS 33/40.
[84] Harpton MSS C29, 34–6, 38, 143–4.
[85] *Gloucester Journal*, 23 April 1754.
[86] *London Evening Post*, 21 May 1754.

Carnarvon, son of the Duke of Chandos, had also then had pretensions, and told Newcastle that having been supported on that occasion by Lord Oxford, he had promised to back Oxford's candidate next time. This candidate, Sir Richard Chase, declined the poll after Gwynne gained the Howorth interest.[87]

In the previous year Lord Powis had again, as in 1739, been obliged to resolve a Caernarfonshire dispute between the Glynllifon Wynns and William Bodfel. When Sir Thomas Wynn died in 1749 his son and successor Sir John, reluctant to give up his disqualifying office, had brought his uncle Sir William Wynn in for the borough, and promised him the seat again in 1754. He himself proposed now to take the shire seat, resisting ministerial pressure to give one seat to Bodfel, the current county MP. Lord Powis therefore brought Bodfel in for Montgomery, where he had intended to retain Francis Herbert. Sir William Wynn died within a month, whereupon Sir John, declining numerous offers for the safe seat, brought in an old electoral ally, Robert Wynne of Bodyscallen.[88] Nor did Bodfel see out the Parliament, dying in 1759, when Lord Powis gave the Montgomery seat to a Shropshire ally Richard Clive, father of the famous Lord Clive of India.

The only other Welsh contest of 1754 occurred in Anglesey. Here the younger Owen Meyrick, seeking revenge after the treachery of 1747, obtained in 1753 the promise of help from Prime Minister Pelham; but the local Whig interest was split, even ministerial supporter Sir William Owen giving Sir Nicholas Bayly his Bodeon interest. Meyrick, short of money, was defeated by 231 votes to 126.[89] The Beaumaris seat was put up for auction among the Tory squires of North Wales by Lady Bulkeley, who managed the Baron Hill interest from her husband's death in 1752 until her own in 1770: for John Owen, rewarded with it on Lord Bulkeley's demise in 1752, himself died before the election. The successful bidder was Richard Price of Rhiwlas in Merioneth, at a reputed price of £2,000.[90]

Sir John Philipps was now the leading figure in the Welsh political scene, but in 1754 he fought Bristol, after considering Haverfordwest, thereby raising ministerial hopes that he might drive William Edwardes from the opposition to the administration side in Parliament. Sir John did not neglect his home area, although in his own county of Pembrokeshire he

---

[87] BL Add. MSS 32852, ff. 388, 404; 32853, ff. 170, 301. *Gloucester Journal*, 4 March 1755. For more detail see Namier, *Structure of Politics*, pp. 254–5.

[88] BL Add. MSS 32734, ff. 297, 340; 32735, ff. 388–9; 32995, ff. 82, 110, 118, 126, 168, 180.

[89] Bodorgan MSS 1592; Pantperthog MSS 1113; BL Add. MSS 32731, f. 110; 32735, f. 76; *Morris Letters*, I, 259.

[90] *Morris Letters*, I, 284.

seems to have passively acquiesced in the re-election of all three current MPs. There was a brief threat to the electoral tranquillity when an anonymous newspaper advertisement asked electors in all three Pembroke-shire constituencies not to promise their votes until 'the sense of all those who have a right of voting can be taken at a general meeting'. It was published, however, after Edwardes and Sir William Owen, as he had become on his father's death in 1753, had already been adopted unan-imously as candidates at meetings on 5 and 2 February respectively, and no contests took place in Pembrokeshire.[91]

It was in Cardiganshire that Sir John played an active role, as Gogerddan trustee. Before the end of 1752 he was canvassing among his fellow trustees the claim of John Symmons to retain the borough seat. Herbert Lloyd of Peterwell, younger brother of county MP John Lloyd, vainly attempted to drive a wedge between them by promising future Peterwell support for Gogerddan heir John Pugh Pryse if he himself could now have the borough seat. Sir John would have none of that. As in 1747 he negotiated a compromise with John Lloyd by which both Symmons and John Lloyd would retain their seats unopposed. Since Thomas Powell of Nanteos had died in 1752 there was no Tory to put up in the county, so he commented to Powell's younger brother and heir the Reverend William Powell, who was disqualified from standing himself because he was a clergyman. He could see no purpose in jeopardizing Symmons's borough seat, and incurring expense for Gogerddan, by supporting one Whig against another in the county.[92] But next year the obvious tactic of allying the Gogerddan interest with that of Nanteos was foiled at a county by-election consequent on John Lloyd's death. Wilmot Vaughan, heir to the Crosswood estate and ambitious to regain his family's traditional Whig leadership in Cardigan-shire, was at odds with the other Whig families but contrived to establish an improbable but enduring electoral alliance with William Powell.[93] Sir John Philipps was reluctant to endorse Vaughan's by-election candidature, on both political and tactical grounds, as he explained to Powell.

> I should choose to be for an honest man, if 'tis practicable to bring such a one in . . . It is my desire to preserve your family interest, and that of Gogerddan . . . and to keep everybody out that would undermine either. This well deserves consideration, and you know where a man is once possessed of a seat, it is no very easy matter to remove him, especially if he is a time server as most men are now.

[91] *London Evening Post*, 12, 14, 21 February 1754.
[92] Nanteos MSS L114. Thomas, 'Eighteenth-Century Elections in the Cardigan Boroughs Constituency', *Ceredigion*, 5 (1964–7), 410–11.
[93] Nanteos MSS L133.

This was clearly directed against Vaughan as a potential adherent of the Newcastle ministry, but Sir John could find no alternative candidate. Sea Serjeant James Philipps of Pentyparc had sounded him out, with pretensions through marriage to a daughter of the late Lewis Pryse.[94] But Sir John did not deem him a viable opponent of Vaughan, who contrived to block any alternative Whig candidate by securing the support of Newcastle and thereby an unopposed return.[95]

Already before the general election Glamorgan had witnessed a landmark in its political history, the end of the house of Mansel on the death in 1750 of Bussy, fourth Baron Mansel. Margam was inherited by his nephew the Reverend Thomas Talbot, and Briton Ferry by his daughter Barbara, who in 1757 married George Venables Vernon, soon to be a Whig MP in his native Sussex. In 1754 the same two MPs had been returned for shire and borough, but the lack of traditional Tory leadership was highlighted by a county by-election of 1756 caused by the death of Charles Edwin. For the son of one former Whig foe fought the son-in-law of another. Thomas William Mathews, son and successor of the admiral, was confronted by not a Tory but Charles Van of Llanwern, son-in-law of the elder Thomas Morgan of Tredegar, but standing against the better judgement of the Morgan family. Mathews trounced him by 954 votes to 212, the Tory magnates of the shire evidently bearing no grudge against the son for his father's behaviour.

Altogether Wales at the general election of 1754 returned sixteen ministerial supporters out of its twenty-seven MPs, a number increased to eighteen before the end of the decade by the election of Mathews and that for Flintshire in 1758 of Sir Roger Mostyn at the death of his father.[96] For guided by his uncle General John Mostyn, a Whig MP for Malton in Yorkshire, he deserted the Tory tradition of his family. That such families as the Myddeltons and Mostyns, Tory since the first evolution of parties, should now support the Whig ministers of George II underlines the changing nature of contemporary politics. In Wales circumstances seem to have conspired against the former Tory families. The accidental death of Sir Watkin Williams Wynn in 1749 had been followed within a year by the end of the Mansel line. Those stalwart Tory families, Bulkeley of Baron Hill and Pryse of Gogerddan, both endured long minorities. The old Whig families by contrast flourished in every way: Morgan of Tredegar, Owen of Orielton and Wynn of Glynllifon had all been Whig in the dark days of

---

[94] Nanteos MSS L115.
[95] BL Add. MSS 32856, ff. 52–3, 612; 32857, ff. 115–16, 431. For more detail see Thomas, 'County Elections in Eighteenth-Century Cardiganshire', *Ceredigion*, 11 (1991), 248–50.
[96] BL Add. MSS 32995, ff. 158–69; 33034, ff. 173–5.

Queen Anne. New men coming to prominence after 1714 tended to be Whig, whatever their family tradition. But in 1760 the accession of George III led to a new political scenario, when the men deemed and dubbed Tory by the Duke of Newcastle, then Prime Minister, were no longer to be proscribed from royal favour and political power.

CHAPTER 6

Jacobitism in Wales

IN their exile after 1688 the Stuarts looked to Wales as well as to Scotland, Lancashire, and western England for their chief support; and if Scotland was naturally the main centre of Stuart hopes, Wales featured occasionally in Jacobite plans. A proposal of 1717 was for a landing at Milford Haven, and a scheme of 1738 envisaged simultaneous disembarkations there and in Scotland. Welsh Jacobites played a prominent part in negotiations with Stuart envoys in the years before the Forty-Five, and much attention focused on Wales during that Rising. But although Wales as a geographical area long remained a centre of Jacobitism, loyalty to the Stuart dynasty cannot be associated with any Welsh national aspirations.[1] The Welsh squires who cherished the Stuart cause were anglicized. Jacobitism generally lingered longer in the north and west of Britain, for these areas were more conservative and backward, less susceptible to changes of ideas and attitudes. The comparative strength of Jacobitism in Wales is primarily explained by the enduring support of many prominent Welsh families for the Stuart dynasty, as manifested earlier in the English Civil War, and also by the circumstance that the foremost Welsh politician of the time, the first Sir Watkin Williams Wynn, was a man zealous in the cause.

Pre-eminent among the Stuart sympathizers were the Dukes of Beaufort. The first Duke, as Lord President of the Council for Wales, had ruled the Principality on behalf of James II, but at the Glorious Revolution stayed in Britain and took the oaths of allegiance to the new sovereign William III and Mary II, albeit rather belatedly.[2] Despite his reconciliation to the court, he was suspected of complicity in the Fenwick Plot of 1696. His grandson Henry, the second Duke, displayed the same political principles by deliberately absenting himself from court until the Tory ministry of

---

[1] I have discussed this point in 'Jacobitism in Wales', *WHR*, 1 (1960–2), 279–80.
[2] *LJ*, XIV, 145.

1710, when he is reputed to have told Anne that 'he could then call her Queen in reality'. The third Duke, another Henry, continued the family tradition, being one of the acknowledged Jacobite leaders south of the Scottish border.[3] Closely associated with the Raglan family was the Sir Charles Kemys who was MP for Monmouthshire 1713–15 and Glamorganshire 1716–34. A famous story is told of Sir Charles as a Jacobite. On his European travels he had often visited Hanover, and became a personal friend of the Elector: but on the latter's accession as George I in 1714, Sir Charles declined the new ruler's pressing invitation to attend him at court: 'I should be happy to smoke a pipe with him as Elector of Hanover, but I cannot think of it as King of England.'[4] Kemys headed a small knot of Jacobites in Glamorgan and, until his death in 1735, was among those on whom the exiled Stuarts placed most reliance: in 1730 he was listed as one of the four Jacobite leaders in the west of Britain.[5]

Pembrokeshire long remained a stronghold of Jacobitism, under the influence of Colonel William Barlow of Slebech, a Catholic who had been elected county MP in 1685. During the reign of William III there were many instances of discontent in Pembrokeshire. Report was often made to the government of rash utterances and of the drinking of James II's health. In June 1693 Barlow and other squires assembled at Narberth with swords and pistols, 'the said William Barlow being a known enemy to their Majesties and their government'. In August legal proceedings were commenced against eight Pembrokeshire gentlemen who had been appointed magistrates in 1689 and had refused to take the requisite oaths or accept the office. In the same year eighteen prominent landowners in the county were presented by a jury for refusing oaths, and fifteen squires were still charged with this offence in 1696.[6] Twenty years later, at the time of the Fifteen Rising, local Jacobites used

> all the means that they could to make the common sort of the people to turn of the Pretender's side by telling them that the Pretender was the true owner of this Kingdom and that King George have no right to it;

and in October 1716 they wielded clubs to break up a loyalist meeting that was celebrating the defeat of the Rising.[7] A favourable report on Pembrokeshire was naturally included in the 'State of England' compiled in

[3] *Complete Peerage*, II, 51–4.
[4] Williams, *History of Monmouthshire*, p. 321.
[5] Stuart MSS 133/151.
[6] F. Jones, 'Disaffection and Dissent in Pembrokeshire', *T.H.S. Cymm.* (1946–7), pp. 216–20.
[7] BL Add. MSS 32686, f. 106.

1721 on behalf of the exiled Stuarts prior to the Atterbury Plot of the next year, the county being described as 'most inhabited by honest people and gentleman very well disposed'.[8]

In nearby Cardiganshire the dominant squire of the early eighteenth century, Lewis Pryse of Gogerddan, made little secret of his true allegiance. In 1709 or 1710 there took place a gathering of 'gentlemen of quality' at a private house in Aberystwyth. They included Pryse, William Powell of Nanteos, John Pugh of Mathafarn, and William Barlow of Slebech. Those present 'drank to the Pretender's health and return upon their knees'. The incident was reported to Lord Sunderland, Secretary of State in the Whig ministry, and a prosecution would have followed but for the fall of that administration in 1710.[9] At the time of the Fifteen Rising Pryse was expelled from the House of Commons for refusing to take an oath of loyalty to George I, and on 4 January 1717 the leading Cardiganshire Whig, Lord Lisburne, painted a dire picture of the county to Secretary of State Paul Methuen. Referring to his Tory rivals Lewis Pryse and William Powell, he commented that 'the one was expelled the House of Commons for refusing the oaths, the other never took them since the Revolution, and for their zeal against the government no men so famous in that part of his Majesty's dominions'. Rebels escaped from Chester gaol had been harboured by their agents, 'a party of which threatened to burn my house'. Intimidation of loyalists was widespread, by 'repeated insults and outrages offered and committed on all they thought in the least inclined to the government'. The dispatch of three companies of soldiers to Cardiganshire was essential: 'It would not only alter the face of affairs in that county, but affect the neighbouring ones, and prevent the further poisoning the minds of the people in so open and impudent a manner'.[10]

If Lisburne had but known, he might have been confronted with a rebellion. In a letter of 7 April 1717 from Innsbruck Pryse was informed by the Earl of Mar, leader of the Fifteen Rising and now Secretary of State to the Pretender, that a landing was intended that year in south Wales.

> I am ordered to acquaint you and other loyal men that a last push for the restoration of old England is to commence at about 30th October next. . .
> The expedition is to be regulated by our march from Milford to the west, under the command of Lord Ormond.[11]

---

[8] Stuart MSS 65/16.
[9] Penrice and Margam MSS L695.
[10] SP Dom. 35/8. f.68.
[11] Nanteos MSS, unnumbered. Copy of letter from Lord Mar to Lewis Pryse, 7 April 1717.

Nothing came of this plan to emulate the feat of Henry Tudor in 1485, and Pryse died soon afterwards, in 1720. The 1721 Stuart survey reckoned all the principal squires of Cardiganshire to be supporters, despite 'the death of the most worthy patriot Lewis Pryse of Gogerddan who ruled all this shire'.

Jacobitism in adjacent Montgomeryshire had been weakened at the local level by the decision of the first Marquess of Powis to accompany James II into exile. His son, styled Viscount Montgomery until his father's death in 1696, was imprisoned in 1689 on suspicion of treason, in 1696 at the time of the Fenwick Plot, and again during the rebellion of 1715. But there is no evidence that the second Marquess was openly Jacobite, and in 1722 he was restored to the Powis Castle estates.[12] Montgomeryshire was nevertheless reckoned a stronghold by Stuart agents; the survey of 1721 described the county as being under the influence of Lord Hereford, father of county MP Price Devereux, and of the borough MP John Pugh, 'both worthy men and fit to be relied on'. That was the customary unfounded optimism. According to a modern local historian 'Montgomeryshire Jacobitism was the stuff of rumour, malicious gossip and gesture', a judgement that might well be taken to apply to Welsh Jacobitism in general. In 1721 Lord Lisburne was manhandled by a Jacobite mob when passing through Llanidloes, and the next year John Pugh was again one of a group of squires accused of drinking to the Pretender on their knees.[13] These were protests of impotent discontent, not the basis for rebellion, and so too were the widespread manifestations of Jacobitism in north Wales.

Here the leading Jacobite in the early decades of the eighteenth century was the fourth Lord Bulkeley, whose opinions were notorious throughout north Wales. He nevertheless thought it politic to resent the open accusation of a local clergyman, Simon Langford, who declared on 24 June 1710, 'I will not vote for my Lord Bulkeley, because he abused Episcopacy and is for bringing in the Pretender.' When answer was made that Lord Bulkeley had taken the oaths to the government, Langford replied. 'He and his party may, when they please, have a dispensation for it, from the Pope.'[14] Lord Bulkeley complained of Langford's conduct, but could obtain no reprimand of the clergyman by the Bishop of Bangor, who himself called Lord Bulkeley 'an enemy to the Church'.[15] Whether or not these insinuations of popish tendencies had any foundation, Lord Bulkeley's personal papers leave no doubt of his political sympathies. They include two Jacobite songs, a Jacobite pamphlet of 1714, and copies of the

---

[12] *Complete Peerage*, IX, 563–4; X, 646–9.
[13] Humphreys, *Crisis of Community*, p. 189.
[14] Baron Hill MSS 5561.
[15] Baron Hill MSS 5566–9.

proclamations issued by the Pretender in 1714 and 1715.[16] They also contain correspondence of markedly Jacobite tone. In 1713 Lord Bulkeley was receiving unsigned letters which gave encouraging news of Stuart hopes. One of 30 May informed him that 'our parsons begin to call rebellion by its proper name, and not give it the new title of Revolution Principles'. Another of 18 June described Jacobite demonstrations on 10 June, the Pretender's birthday. One of 4 July held out the delusive hope that the main obstacle to another restoration would be removed.

A book is written and will be published on Monday next intitled a Dialogue between a Roman Catholic Nobleman and a Gentleman of the Church of England. It's said to be written for the confirmation of a certain Chevalier that either has or is upon changing his religion.[17]

The Pretender's refusal to abandon his Catholic faith doomed any hopes of his peaceful accession, and no coup was planned on Anne's death in 1714. Disgust at the unopposed Hanoverian Succession caused Lord Bulkeley to give up his parliamentary seat, but not his Jacobite views: also among his correspondence is a bundle of letters reporting in sympathetic manner the events and aftermath of the Fifteen Rising.[18]

There is much scattered evidence of Jacobite sentiment and activity in Wales during the generation after the Glorious Revolution. Thereafter, as such individuals as William Barlow, Lewis Pryse and Lord Bulkeley died off, north-east Wales became the focal point of Welsh Jacobitism with an organization centred on one of the most famous of all Jacobite clubs, the Cycle of the White Rose. This was founded on 10 June 1710, White Rose Day, the birthday in 1688 of the Old Pretender or 'James III'.[19] The early history of the Cycle is unknown, but some members may have instigated or encouraged the demonstration of Jacobite feeling in Wrexham at the time of the Fifteen Rising. A mob then wrecked the two Dissenting meeting-houses in the town, and the church bells were rung to celebrate the escape of a local man who had been taken prisoner with the rebels at Preston.[20] The first contemporary mention of the club is in a letter of 2 December 1720 from Cycle member Thomas Holland to Lord Bulkeley, written with reference to the election campaign already started in Anglesey for the contest of 1722.[21]

[16] Baron Hill MSS 6777–9, 6809–10.
[17] Bangor General MSS 1977.
[18] Baron Hill MSS 6781–91.
[19] Confirmation of the traditional date is provided by the existence of a badge bearing that date. Monod, *Jacobitism*, p. 296.
[20] Palmer, *History of Wrexham*, p.9.
[21] Baron Hill MSS 5620.

Last Tuesday was our day of monthly meeting . . . where your Lordship's health and success was very heartily drank. I proposed to exchange votes with all our members. Such an act would be worthy such a Society: but I fear most of them are too much wedded to their homes to undertake a journey to Anglesey though they are sincerely attached to your Lordship's service in their own country.

The Cycle of the White Rose began to flourish under the leadership of the first Watkin Williams Wynn, although since he was a schoolboy of seventeen in 1710 the legend that he was then its founder would seem to be improbable. Virtually all the information on the Cycle as a political organization comes from the years of Wynn's dominance of north Wales. Four membership lists survive for the period: fourteen names for 1721–2; seventeen for 1723–4; twenty-two for 1735–7; and twenty-seven for 1746–8.[22] Membership lists were in the form of circular rosters, on which there was written each member's name and the date of the meeting at his house. The names converged at the centre, where an inner circle contained the title of the club, 'The Cycle', written around a star, a favourite emblem of Stuart supporters. They met every three or four weeks in rotation, and during dinner the health of 'the king over the water' would be drunk in specially engraved glasses, decorated with the white rose adopted as the badge of the club. Membership was drawn from the Tory squires of Denbighshire, Flintshire and, later, Cheshire. It included, apart from Sir Watkin and his brothers Robert and Richard Williams, such other MPs as Thomas Eyton, Sir John Glynne, Sir Robert Grosvenor from Cheshire, and in 1735 even John Myddelton of Chirk Castle; but no member of the loyalist Mostyn family. In 1723 an elaborate set of formal rules was drafted, to specify the order, time, and attendance at the meetings.[23] At some time in these years a Cycle song was composed. The original verses were no more than a rallying cry against corruption typical of many opposition attacks on Walpole. But at the time of the Forty-Five Rising there was added this verse of overtly Jacobite views.[24]

> For the Days we've mispent
> Let us truly repent,
> And render to Caesar his due.
> Here's a Health to the Lad,
> With his Bonnet and Plaid,

[22] NLW General MSS 14941C; Leeswood MSS 2023; Francis, *Romance of the White Rose*, pp. 228, 230–1. Some lists are later copies, and there are duplicates of others.
[23] For a general account of the Cycle, see Francis, *Romance of the White Rose*, pp. 226–32.
[24] NLW General MSS 14941C.

For the World cannot stain his True Blue,
For the World cannot stain his True Blue.

Other Jacobite clubs flourished in Wales. Relics survive, for instance, of two in Montgomeryshire. And Anglesey diarist William Bulkeley made this entry for 3 May 1738. 'Today was the first meeting of the Jacobite club at Llanerchymedd for this year, where all the noted Tories and Jacobites of this country have constantly met once a month these two years.'[25] But the Society of Sea Serjeants was neither secret nor seditious, and must be removed from any list of Jacobite organizations. Contemporary suspicions, long echoed by historians, can now be seen as unjustified: indeed, the first question put to candidates for membership was 'Do you bear true allegiance to his majesty?'[26]

How secret these clubs were among contemporaries must remain a moot point: but in any case a man like Watkin Williams Wynn did not scruple, any more than earlier Jacobites, to make open display of his sentiments, as his new Whig neighbour John Meller of Erthig indignantly observed. In about 1721 not only was Wynn as a Denbighshire magistrate failing to prosecute those who drank the Pretender's health, but he himself had to flee from Shrewsbury for committing the same offence.[27] Worse followed during the election year of 1722. The time was one of widespread Jacobite activity, culminating in the crisis of the Atterbury Plot to restore the Stuarts. From Denbighshire Meller wrote this report on 27 February to his relation Philip Yorke, then Solicitor-General.

The Jacobites in our parts are strangely animated of late and they endeavour to carry their points by heat and fury, and they are so barefaced, as to drink the Pretender's health in public companys. But tho' we have intimation of it, yet we cannot prevail with any in company to prove it upon them. It is not long since that the Lord Buckley came hither out of Anglesea to keep up the spirit of the party, and he and Mr Watkin Williams audaciously burnt the King's picture and the several pictures of all the Royal Family.[28]

The clever exploitation of the Atterbury Plot by Sir Robert Walpole, who deliberately exaggerated the danger in order to strike at leading Jacobites in Britain, curbed for almost two decades active intrigues and open demonstrations on behalf of the Stuarts. In the meantime Jacobite

---

[25] Bulkeley Diary, I, 265; Thomas, 'Jacobitism in Wales', 292–3.
[26] F. Jones, 'The Society of Sea Serjeants', *T.H.S. Cymm.* (1967), p. 63.
[27] *Erthig Chronicles*, I, 231–2.
[28] Yorke, *Life of Hardwicke*, I, 76.

agents continued to attribute considerable significance to their Welsh supporters, and to exaggerate their strength. The 1721 survey had conceded the dominance of Hanoverian sympathizers in only three Welsh counties – Breconshire, Radnorshire and Carmarthenshire.[29] Even more sweeping and inaccurate was the assessment of the French envoy in 1743.[30]

> Monmouthshire. This county is completely under the influence of the Duke of Beaufort and his brother Lord Noel Somerset.
> Principality of Wales. The twelve counties of the Principality are entirely at the orders of the Dukes of Beaufort and Powis, Lord Bulkeley, Sir Watkin Williams, and those who think with them.

Stuart hopes increasingly came to be fixed on Watkin Williams Wynn. By 1730 he was already seen as one of the Jacobite leaders in the north and west of Britain.[31] In 1735 an assurance of his wholehearted support was conveyed to the Pretender through an intermediary, Colonel Cecil. 'Watkin Williams presents his duty to you, and desires I would let you know that you may command him in everything, and that he will be always ready to serve you, both with his life and fortune.'[32] Wynn gave generous financial assistance to George Kelly, the chief suspect in the Atterbury Plot, during his imprisonment in the Tower from 1722 until his escape in 1736. After Kelly arrived in France he urged that Wynn's wealth and his devotion to the Stuart cause made him the first man to contact in any negotiations with the Jacobites in Britain.[33] Perhaps a sense of obligation to Wynn may have led Kelly to overemphasize his importance, but there can be no doubt of his zeal. When Lord Sempill was dispatched in 1740 to sound out the Jacobites in Britain on their attitude to a project for a rising combined with a French invasion, he reported that, unlike such other friends as William Shippen, 'Watkin Williams is hearty and may certainly be depended on'.[34] Lord Sempill believed that Wynn and Lord Barrymore, the aged prospective military commander of any domestic rising, would exert themselves when James landed with an army.[35] The prestige Wynn enjoyed among the home Jacobites was underlined by the refusal of the other leaders to agree on any decision during his absence from London.[36]

---

[29] Stuart MSS 65/16.
[30] Cruickshanks, *Political Untouchables*, pp. 119, 122. Translated here from the French.
[31] Stuart MSS 133/151.
[32] Stuart MSS 178/6.
[33] Stuart MSS 194/10.
[34] Stuart MSS 221/109.
[35] Stuart MSS 222/33.
[36] Stuart MSS 234/165.

Thenceforth Sir Watkin was deeply involved in the Jacobite plotting that preceded the Forty-Five Rising. In 1742 he took part in London negotiations with Stuart envoy Lord Traquair concerning an invasion proposal for that year.[37] In May 1743 Wynn actually visited Louis XV at Versailles, when the French King expressed willingness to aid the Stuart cause.[38] In the ensuing summer there followed several London meetings between Traquair and other Stuart agents, and the home Jacobites like Wynn. The agents reported that Wynn and Barrymore were 'ready to embrace every opportunity but that the others were more shy'. Arrangements were discussed for a Jacobite rising supported by a French invasion early in 1744, but Wynn, like the others, refused to give any written pledge and stipulated the prerequisite of a French army. Then the need for finance was raised.

> Sir Watkin answered that it was natural to expect a large contribution from him, being possessed of a great fortune; but . . . observed, he was obliged to live at a great expense, and had it less in his power to be assisting that way, than if his income was smaller.[39]

The invasion date was fixed for the end of February, when any important parliamentary business would be over, and Wynn and his associates could leave London without arousing alarm. Several suspects were arrested, but not Wynn. This project of 1744, when a French army was ready for an invasion, was wrecked by bad weather in the English Channel. France nevertheless soon gave assurances that another expedition would be mounted, and Wynn, Barrymore and the Duke of Beaufort continued discussions with envoys of the Pretender.[40] They stipulated for 10,000 French soldiers, seeking to emulate the successful foreign invasion of 1688 rather than the abortive domestic rising of 1715. A nine-man Regency Council was devised, including Wynn.[41] In October, even though Britain and France were formally at war with each other, Sir Watkin again visited Versailles, seeking to extract a firm promise from Louis XV.[42] By the end of 1744 Wynn was conducting negotiations alone, for the other Jacobites refused to go to London, not 'inclining to put their persons a second time in the hands of the government'. The Pretender was therefore advised that

---

[37] Mahon, *History of England*, III, 441–2.
[38] McLynn, *France and the Jacobite Rising of 1745*, p. 14, citing Stuart MSS 251/12.
[39] Murray, *Memorials*, pp. 49, 55, 424–6, 451.
[40] Stuart MSS 259/199; McLynn, *France and the Jacobite Rising*, p. 27.
[41] Cruickshanks, *Political Untouchables*, pp. 38–49.
[42] McLynn, *France and the Jacobite Rising*, p. 29; Sedgwick, *House of Commons 1715–1754*, II, 544. Both cite Stuart MSS 260/6, 260/7.

any promises from Louis XV should be sent to Sir Watkin for transmission to his other supporters.[43] Wynn's contact in London was a physician, Doctor Peter Barry, who informed the Pretender that

> Sir Watkin Williams and Lord Barrymore both promised to join the Prince immediately upon his landing, that he has sent for the Duke of Beaufort and is certain that all your Majesty's friends will stand to the engagements of last year; upon that foundation good Sir Watkin is impatient for his Royal Highness's arrival with a body of troops and answers for his success.[44]

Barry himself assured the Pretender, 'You Majesty cannot have your own interests more at heart than Sir Watkin does', citing Wynn's recent rejection of a peerage offered by George II.[45] For this was the very time when Wynn and other Tories were negotiating with the Pelham ministry for offices and honours, and giving support in Parliament. At Westminster in January 1745 Wynn was arguing for the establishment of a British army in Flanders, thereby denuding Britain of soldiers at the very time he was urging the Pretender to launch an invasion.[46] In June, indeed, Sir Watkin sent a message suggesting an immediate attempt, for that very reason![47] This apparent double-dealing does not accord with the simple straightforward character customarily attributed to Wynn. Was it treachery? Or was Wynn hedging his bets by an orthodox role in Parliament? Certainly he refused to put all his political eggs in the Jacobite basket. Throughout these years of negotiations Sir Watkin had been careful never to commit any openly treasonable action, above all refusing to give any assurance in writing to the Pretender or his agents, an attitude explained by one of the Stuart agents in 1745.[48]

> The sentiments and inclinations of Sir Watkin, Lord Barrymore, and their friends are known to all. They intend they should [be], and even used means to manifest them; but they, with great reason, make a vast distinction between the owning of their principles, and being engaged in any direct or indirect correspondence with Your Majesty and the French Court, with the actual design of overturning the present government. The owning of their principles exposes them only to the hatred of an administration from which they neither expect nor desire any favour, but a

[43] Stuart MSS 260/108.
[44] Stuart MSS 261/54.
[45] Stuart MSS 261/48.
[46] Cobbett, *Parl. Hist.*, XIII, 1054.
[47] Cruickshanks, *Political Untouchables*, pp. 76–7.
[48] Stuart MSS 271/3.

correspondence of the nature I have mentioned, is an act of overt treason according to the present laws, the least suspicion of which would bring certain ruin upon them, and consequently render them insignificant and useless to Your Majesty's cause, whereas they have all along kept it awake, and can by their influence and example determine above two-thirds of the nation to act vigorously for it as soon as they see a possibility of success.

The assumption underlying all the negotiations and the promises of support was that the Young Pretender, Prince Charles Edward Stuart, would arrive with a French army as part of a concerted enterprise. But the Prince landed unexpectedly with a handful of men on the west coast of Scotland, in July 1745. Circumstances in Wales were singularly unfavourable. Sir Watkin found himself with only £200 in ready money at this emergency.[49] A zealous supporter had recently been lost with the death in February of the third Duke of Beaufort, though his brother and successor was also a Jacobite. Since the Young Pretender had arrived without a French army, Wynn and his friends made no move, while the Prince gained control of Scotland by September. Sir Watkin even launched a loyal Association in Denbighshire, but it was poorly subscribed.[50] Sir Watkin and other known Jacobites also deemed it prudent to avert suspicion by attending the emergency meeting of Parliament in October. This provided the opportunity to consult with London Jacobites, and it was from London that Wynn sent messages of support, conditional on the arrival of a French army. 'He and the King's friends will immediately upon the landing join the troops . . . He begs that arms and ammunition be brought with the troops.'[51] While in London Wynn was shadowed by government agents, and even taken in for questioning, but not actually arrested, though that course of action was being urged upon Secretary of State Newcastle.[52]

The anticipated arrival of a French army had not taken place before Prince Charles Edward began his march into England in November. That he chose the western route fuelled rumours that Wales might be his destination.[53] The Jacobite leadership, whose target was always London,

[49] Stuart MSS 310/139.

[50] Speck, *The Butcher*, p. 62.

[51] Cruickshanks, *Political Untouchables*, pp. 81–4; Thomas, 'Jacobitism in Wales', 296–7.

[52] Cruickshanks, *Political Untouchables*, pp. 82, 91; McLynn, *The Jacobite Army in England*, p. 79.

[53] For such rumours in London, Yorkshire, and Ireland see respectively Walpole, *Letters* (Toynbee), III, 352; BL Add. MSS 35598, ff. 126–7; *HMC Puleston*, p. 333. See also McLynn, *Jacobite Army*, pp. 2, 7, 8, 12, 54, 61, 62, 64, 65, 66, 70, 72, 78, 90, 96, 98, 104, 107, 115, 118. The wildest rumour was that the Jacobites would recruit up to 100,000 men in Wales, and then either march on London or await a French army. McLynn, *Jacobite Army*, p. 72.

perceived tactical advantages to be gained from spreading misinformation to that effect. It was readily swallowed by Lord Lonsdale, who hastened to inform Secretary of State Newcastle that 'they express in general great expectations of assistance from France when they get into Wales, where they also expect numbers to join them'.[54] The Duke of Richmond, serving with the Duke of Cumberland's army in Staffordshire, also thought that the arrival of the rebel army at Lancaster 'proves . . . they intend to take Chester and get into North Wales'.[55] The bridges over the River Mersey were therefore destroyed, forcing the rebel army to veer east to Manchester, a move that ironically assisted the Jacobite general Lord George Murray in his tactics of masking his real intention. Richmond commented to Newcastle on 30 November that the rebel army had five options – force a battle, retreat to Scotland, advance either south to Derby or west to Chester, or 'to push for North Wales. . . and that would be bad indeed, for . . . we can not get up time enough to stop them'.[56] Certainly there was confusion among ministers as to the Jacobite objective. Prime Minister Henry Pelham thought 'it seems out of doubt that they intend for Wales'.[57] But his brother the Duke of Newcastle remained sceptical. 'I can hardly believe it . . . I still think their design is to push for London'.[58]

The Welsh dimension of the Forty-Five was not merely the pretence that north Wales was the destination, but also the need to convince both opponents and supporters of the prospect of armed assistance from there. Prince Charles Edward claimed to have received a letter from Sir Watkin, brought by Wynn's servant Meredith, announcing Cycle preparations to raise a regiment of 300 horsemen, who with Wynn's armed tenants would join the Prince's army between Macclesfield and Derby.[59] It was in reply to this alleged missive that the Prince wrote to Sir Watkin from Preston.[60]

> The particular character I have heard of you, makes me hope to see you among the first. I am persuaded you will not baulk my expectations, and you need not doubt but I shall always remember to your advantage the example you shall thus have put to your neighbours and consequently to all England.

In a covering letter the Duke of Perth formally authorized Wynn to raise men and grant commissions, and urged him to attend the Prince if only

---

[54] Quoted in McLynn, *Jacobite Army*, p. 81.
[55] McCann, *Richmond–Newcastle Corr.*, p. 187.
[56] Ibid., p. 193.
[57] Quoted in McLynn, *Jacobite Army*, p. 118.
[58] McCann, *Richmond–Newcastle Corr.*, p. 194.
[59] McLynn, *Jacobite Army*, p. 80.
[60] Quoted in Thomas, 'Jacobitism in Wales', 297, and, more fully, in Cruickshanks, *Political Untouchables*, p. 87. The letter does not read like a reply to one received.

with 500 men or fewer. 'Whatever numbers you bring will be acceptable, though they were below that, and even though they were very small.' Evidently the propaganda impact, on both sides, of Wynn's arrival in the rebel camp was deemed more significant than his military contribution. But these messages never reached Wynn, the bearer being intercepted.[61]

The Welsh option was debated in a Jacobite Council of War at Manchester on 30 November, a march to Wales being urged by David Morgan of Penygraig in Glamorgan, who with William Vaughan of Courtfield in Monmouthshire had joined the rebel army at Preston. Morgan was legal adviser to the third and fourth Dukes of Beaufort, and so his adherence to the rebel cause seemed an omen of more important defections. Morgan was active in forming the so-called 'Manchester Regiment', though he refused its command, and his favoured position with Prince Charles Edward won him the name of 'the Young Pretender's Counsellor'.[62] Two days later, when the Jacobite army was at Macclesfield, the same matter was again discussed, with a new objection being raised that Wales was too mountainous for a march there to be practical. The decision to advance on London was confirmed, but a deliberate westward feint exploited the Welsh option by causing Cumberland to cover the move and so leave open the road to Derby.[63]

There on 5 December the fateful decision was taken to abandon the march on London. The Duke of Perth suggested that instead of a retreat to Scotland the rebel army should go to Wales, an idea supported by David Morgan and even the Prince himself as a last argument against withdrawal, but the proposal was rejected because of the obvious danger of being cut off from Scotland. Morgan is reputed to have then told William Vaughan, 'I had rather be hanged than go to Scotland to starve', and that was to be his fate. He left the Jacobite army and was arrested at Stone on his way back to Wales. In July 1746 he was tried, convicted, and executed for treason.[64]

News of the rebel retreat from Derby did lead Cumberland to think that Wales must be the destination, with Richmond confident that such a move could be intercepted.[65] Others also thought Wales the target of the rebel

---

[61] McLynn, *Jacobite Army*, p. 80.

[62] Thomas, 'Jacobitism in Wales', 297; Cruickshanks, *Political Untouchables*, pp. 91, 97; McLynn, *Jacobite Army*, p. 99.

[63] McLynn, *Jacobite Army*, p. 113.

[64] Llewellin, 'David Morgan, the Welsh Jacobite', *Transactions of the Liverpool Welsh National Society*, 10 (1894–5), 75–108.

[65] McLynn, *Jacobite Army*, pp. 126, 141; McCann, *Richmond–Newcastle Corr.*, p. 196. On 7 December Cumberland's army was at Coventry, a circumstance that would seem to refute the claim of some Jacobite historians that the road from Derby to London had been clear.

army, through Shrewsbury, for some Somerset Jacobites planned to join the Young Pretender there.[66] Prince Charles Edward tarried at Manchester, still hoping to see some Welsh Jacobites, as repeatedly promised by William Vaughan.[67] Vaughan stayed with the Pretender, fought at Culloden in April 1746, and then escaped to France.

The role played by Sir Watkin Williams Wynn during the Forty-Five Rising has conventionally been deemed inglorious. But his invariable stipulation of a French army had not been met, nor had the letters sent by the Young Pretender reached him. Two days after the retreat from Derby, however, Lord Barrymore's second son arrived there as a messenger from his father and Sir Watkin, to assure the Pretender that they were ready to join him 'either in the capital or everyone to rise in his own country'.[68] The letter had been sent from London, where, so it was stated, £10,000 was ready for the Pretender's arrival. Both men had remained there, presumably to await in safety a triumphant Jacobite entry into the capital, rather than risk participation beforehand. This behaviour was later cited by Jacobites as damning evidence of Wynn's insincerity. Why, it was soon being asked, was Wynn in London instead of going home to rally support as the Jacobite army approached? 'Why did not the famous Sir Watkin Williams Wynn show himself in North Wales when it was known that the Prince had marched as far as Derby?'[69]

'I stand the brunt and tell them there is no such thing for my countrymen are more loyal than to take up arms against their King.' So did a Welshman in Dublin refute rumours that Wynn and others intended to join the rebels.[70] Certainly there is no contemporary evidence to justify later legends that various Welsh squires had left to join the Pretender when news came of his retreat from Derby.[71] The only known instance of public disaffection was at Hawarden, where Flintshire MP Sir John Glynne drank the Pretender's health kneeling on the village green, in company with the local rector. Both men were arrested, but released after three months for lack of evidence: the witness had been intimidated.[72] The incident has a symbolic significance for Welsh Jacobitism. In the moment of crisis the sole action taken was yet another toast. The essence of Jacobitism in Wales was

---

[66] McLynn, *Jacobite Army*, p. 145.

[67] McLynn, *Jacobite Army*, p. 150.

[68] Stuart MSS 281/89. This source is a later letter from Prince Charles to his father, written on 12 February 1747. The message belatedly reached the Prince in Stirling in January 1746. Sedgwick, *House of Commons 1715–1754*, I, 618.

[69] Quoted in McLynn, *France and the Jacobite Rising of 1745*, pp. 196–7.

[70] *HMC Puleston*, p. 333.

[71] For some such stories, see *Archaeologia Cambrensis* (1856), pp. 181–2.

[72] Whittaker, 'The Glynnes of Hawarden', *Flintshire Historical Society Journal*, 4 (1906), 24–5.

epitomized in the reputed saying of Prince Charles Edward himself: 'I will do as much for my Welsh friends as they have done for me; I will drink their healths.'[73]

For the Tory squires of Wales kept their heads well down as the Jacobite storm approached. In south Wales many of them, Sea Serjeants included, joined loyalist Associations. In north Wales there was more of a passive resistance, refusal to subscribe to such Associations or to join the loyalist militia regiments Lord Cholmondeley was seeking to raise as lord lieutenant.[74] But in Flintshire, for example, Sir Thomas Mostyn could dismiss the idea of any support for the Rising, assuring the government that 'there is no one in this neighbourhood who has either the will or the ability to join the rebels with 20 men'.[75] In Denbighshire the southward progress of the Jacobite army was apprehensively monitored by former Cycle member John Myddelton of Chirk Castle. 'Thank God the rebels are gone from this part of the world', he was informed on 6 December. News of the withdrawal from Derby renewed the fear that Wales was the rebel target, and it was with relief that the Myddelton family greeted the news of the retreat back to Scotland.[76] How much popular opinion in nearby Wrexham had changed since 1715 was shown by the celebration in the town of the government defeat of the rebel army at Culloden. Sir Watkin's brother Robert, whose wife was 'a violent Jacobite', had his house windows broken for not putting out a light. Sir Watkin himself was more prudent and 'gave a crown to the mob to secure his windows'.[77] That was an appropriate postscript to his ignominious role in the rebellion.

The caution of Sir Watkin and his friends saved them from the penalties suffered by the more active Jacobites. No punishment of them was attempted even after John Murray of Broughton, former secretary to Prince Charles, had turned King's Evidence and revealed the negotiations since 1740. Two witnesses were required under the Treason Act of 1696, and the men implicated by Murray all denied complicity. Further evidence was lacking, even though papers captured after Culloden had already revealed to the government that five home Jacobites, including Sir Watkin and the Duke of Beaufort, had been in touch with the exiled Stuart court.[78] The care taken by Wynn and his associates to avoid direct correspondence and written assurances now proved to have been a wise precaution. The

---

[73] *Arch. Camb.* (1856), p. 181.

[74] Speck, *The Butcher*, pp. 62–3.

[75] Quoted in Baskerville, 'The Management of the Tory Interest in Lancashire and Cheshire 1714–1747', D. Phil. Oxford, 1976, p. 266.

[76] Chirk Castle MSS E22–4, 55, 117, 310.

[77] *Erthig Chronicles*, I, 279.

[78] McCann, *Richmond–Newcastle Corr.*, pp. 222–3.

Pelham ministry made no effort to arrest influential landowners who had not stirred, and contented itself with the public notoriety incurred by Sir Watkin and his friends through being mentioned in evidence at some trials.[79]

Not even the disaster of Culloden ended Wynn's contact with Stuart agents, and he still remained a key figure in any plan. A politic message was therefore sent by the Young Pretender to Sir Watkin and Lord Barrymore at the end of 1746, 'that the Prince is satisfied with their conduct when he was in England and takes in good part their sending to receive his orders for them, which he does not doubt but that they would have executed punctually'.[80] Before the end of 1747 Wynn sent a promise to Prince Charles of continued support.[81]

> The bearer . . . has authority from Sir Watkin Williams Wynn, who answers for himself and the whole body of your loyal subjects in England . . . If they failed joining Your Royal Highness in the time you ventured your sacred person so gloriously in defence of their rights, it was owing more to the want in them of concert and unanimity than that of real zeal and dutiful attachment.

In 1749 similar assurances were still being made by the Welsh Jacobite leaders, Wynn himself, the Duke of Beaufort, and Sir John Philipps; but such promises now brought little comfort even to the hitherto optimistic Stuart agents.[82] They were formal moves in a game that had lost all meaning before Wynn's death in 1749. With him died the spirit of Welsh Jacobitism, though the ghost lingered long. The Cycle of the White Rose survived as a social club for the gentry of Denbighshire and the neighbouring counties until 1869.[83]

Jacobitism in Wales was always a sentiment rather than a practical cause. The Cycle members who were unwilling even to journey to Anglesey for the election of 1722 would not prove of much assistance in more arduous and dangerous undertakings. Yet, because there was no practical motivation, sentimental support for the Stuarts survived the disappointment of the Forty-Five, specifically so in Anglesey, according to a letter of local Whig William Lewis of Llysdulas to Lord Herbert complaining about the appointment as magistrate of William Lewis of Trysglwyn.[84]

---

[79] Mahon, *History of England*, III, 336–7, 445–6.
[80] Stuart MSS 280/127.
[81] Stuart MSS 288/172.
[82] Stuart MSS 301/5.
[83] Francis, *Romance of the White Rose*, pp. 227–9; NLW General MSS 14941C.
[84] BL Add. MSS 35602, f. 299.

I apprehend . . . [him] not to be well affected to his Majesty for when rejoicings were made for our happy success at the battle of Culloden he run among the populace and making some of them drink 'Right to him that suffers wrong', his usual toast. He encouraged a Cocking the last 29th of May when unfit toasts were named, and a fiddler playing the tune 'When the King shall enjoy his own again', and money given by Mr Lewis and others for playing that tune particularly. His first child was christened the 5th of May last and a pin cushion on the occasion, of Scotch Plaid with a Rose and the words 'God preserve P.C.', 'Down with the Rump', and Mr Lewis fond of showing it. I could say more if he were not my sister's son.

The Baron Hill home of the Viscounts Bulkeley contained busts of Prince Charles Edward and his brother, Cardinal Henry of York, that must have been acquired in mid-century, and in 1760 the widow of the sixth viscount warned her Whig second husband, 'To now talk of party, whatever my real opinion is, I shall keep it to myself, only I must beg to be excused from drinking to the memory of either Georgites or Old Will.'[85] Such private avowals were matched by the public smears still bestowed by Whigs on political opponents, as when in 1755 William Powell of Nanteos was dubbed a Jacobite by the Cardiganshire Whigs.[86] But the advent to the throne in 1760 of young George III, born and bred in Britain, reconciled even old Jacobites to the alien dynasty. No longer were Stuart emblems on public display in private houses. Hence an incident recounted by J. Gardiner, a guest of Sir John Philipps at Picton Castle in 1763. Sir John ordered his servant to set out plain glasses on the table, but, so Gardiner told John Wilkes, 'he unluckily brought *me* one of the glasses with the White Rose and emphatical *Fiat* upon it. I held it up towards the light as if by accident, which Sir John perceiving, in an angry tone of voice called to the servant, "What is the reason you, Sir, you dont do as I order you? Bring a plain glass here".'[87] It was no longer respectable to be an open Jacobite.

---

[85] Baron Hill MSS 5736.
[86] *Morris Letters*, I, 353.
[87] BL Add. MSS 30867, f. 219.

CHAPTER 7

'The Prince of Wales':
Sir Watkin Williams Wynn (1693–1749)

'A simple Welsh knight of a vast estate, . . . from whence he was called Prince of Wales.' So wrote that famous chronicler of the Hanoverian age, Horace Walpole, on the first Sir Watkin Williams Wynn. Over forty years after Wynn's death Walpole recalled the mock title to a friend touring Wales in 1790.[1] It was seemingly long attached to the Wynnstay family, for as late as 1883 a *Punch* cartoon depicted the current Sir Watkin Williams Wynn as 'the Prince *in* Wales'. Another story indicative of the great prestige Sir Watkin enjoyed in Wales was that when he went up to London for the parliamentary session it was customary for the Welsh gentry resident in the capital to meet him at Finchley and form a procession to escort him into town.[2]

Wynn's estates straddled at least five Welsh counties and extended into Shropshire, with a reputed rent-roll of between £15,000 and £20,000 that made him one of the richest men in Britain. His contemporary reputation stemmed not merely from possession of wealth but from his lavish deployment of it. Wynn spent prodigiously on opposition politics, thereby leaving even such an estate heavily encumbered in debts, believed to amount to £120,000 at his death.[3] His electoral activities ranged over seven Welsh and four English counties. For decades he was a thorn in the flesh of government, not only in the constituencies but also in the House of Commons, where his prominence as an incessant critic of successive administrations gained him the offer of a peerage in 1744, one graciously declined. That ministerial approach was a superb irony, for at the very time it was made Sir Watkin was involved in the treasonable negotiations with the exiled royal house of Stuart that preceded the Forty-Five Rising, and he was seemingly a Jacobite all his life.[4]

---

[1] Walpole, *Corr.*, XVII, 234n, XXXIV, 95.
[2] *Byegones*, 1883, p. 232; Roberts, *Wynnstay and the Wynns*, p. 11.
[3] Bulkeley Diary, quoted in Ramage, *Portrait of an Island County*, p. 271.
[4] That facet of Wynn's career is discussed in the preceding chapter on Jacobitism. Here the concern is with his orthodox political role as electioneer and parliamentarian.

It was Watkin's grandfather William Williams who set the family on an upwardly mobile path. Son of an Anglesey vicar, he had married the heiress of the Glascoed estate in Denbighshire and purchased the substantial Shropshire estate of Llanforda. Williams was an able and successful lawyer, not overscrupulous in his political principles. He obtained a baronetcy from James II in 1688 despite having been Speaker of the House of Commons that between 1679 and 1681 had sought to exclude him from the throne. When that King fled abroad at the Glorious Revolution Sir William failed to win favour under William III and ended his political career as he had begun it, in opposition, a 'Country Whig' of the 1690s. His eldest son, also William, who succeeded him in title and estates in 1700, further improved the family fortunes by marrying another Denbighshire heiress, Jane Thelwall of Plasyward. This second Sir William Williams displayed little parliamentary ambition, only sitting as MP for Denbigh Boroughs between 1708 and 1710, as a Tory opponent of the Whig Junto ministry.[5] He remained nevertheless a paterfamilias, living mainly at Llanforda until his death in 1740, and Watkin's letters to him remained deferential in tone after he had become a great landowner and prominent parliamentarian.

Watkin was born in 1693, the eldest of four sons. He was educated at Ruthin School, whose headmaster Henry Price tactfully implied idleness in a letter of 1705. 'I would not have him without a whetstone for his industry, which hitherto hath been apt to be soon blunted.'[6] It may have been the rabid Jacobitism of Price that imbued the young Watkin with the same opinions; for in 1748 his former pupil erected a monument to a man who had resigned his post rather than take an oath of allegiance to the Hanoverian dynasty.[7] From Ruthin, Watkin went on to Jesus College, Oxford, being admitted on 18 December 1710 at the age of seventeen. At university he ran up debts all over the place, his college tutor Edward Thelwall making this reply in 1712 to his father's complaints.[8]

I was as much troubled as you could be at Mr Watkin's excursions, and as much concerned I could not prevent them. I did what was in my power, and as much perhaps as could reasonably be expected from me or the nature of my office required. I did not know . . . all the places where he owed money in; neither do I look upon it as my proper business to send you a particular account of what he owes. You charge me with not timely representing to you his extravagancies; you may remember, Sir, that I told

[5] Chirk Castle MSS E991.
[6] Wynnstay MSS Box C, 70/2.
[7] *Archaeologia Cambrensis* (1856), 180–2.
[8] Wynnstay MSS Box C, 70/5. An Edward Thelwall was Watkin's uncle. Griffith, *Pedigrees*, p. 274.

you a twelve month ago that he was not fit to live here, and since you were resolved to continue him here contrary to my desire, I dont know how I was to blame for [not] acting otherwise than I did.

Watkin was to be followed at Oxford by his brothers Robert, Richard, and Thomas, of whom nothing is known apart from his death there in 1719.[9] Robert subsequently pursued a legal career, training at Gray's Inn and becoming Recorder of Oswestry. Richard married well, acquiring from his second wife the Denbighshire estate of Penbedw. Both were to enter Parliament for brief spells at the behest of their eldest brother.

Watkin did not inherit the family baronetcy and the estates of Llanforda, Glascoed and Plasyward until his father died in 1740, but he had already become the greatest landowner in Wales some twenty years earlier. He was the designated heir of his mother's cousin, childless Sir John Wynn, owner of some family estates in Caernarfonshire, of Rhiwgoch in Merioneth, and, above all, of the Watstay estate in Denbighshire that he had gained by marriage to the heiress, and his home during his last years. Sir John evidently enlarged his estates by buying appropriate properties, for when nearby Erthig was on the market in 1716 it became known that 'Sir John Wynn will purchase no more'. It was then expected that Watkin's father would outbid everyone for the estate, but John Meller acquired it.[10] Sir John instead hoarded his money. At his death three years later, some £9,000 in ready cash was found at his house, mostly in the form of 8,000 golden guineas.[11] By 1713 Watkin was already living at Watstay most of the time, doubtless managing affairs for the old man. Sometime between then and 1719 it was renamed Wynnstay, perhaps when Watkin adopted the additional surname of Wynn as a condition of his inheritance: for a long while contemporaries were apt to refer to him still as Watkin Williams. Other estates were to come to him as a result of his marriage in 1715 to Ann, younger daughter of Montgomeryshire MP Edward Vaughan. Llwydiarth was second in Montgomeryshire only to that of Powis Castle; Glanllyn, near Bala, provided a second important estate in Merioneth; while Llangedwin was another substantial estate in Denbighshire. Within a decade Watkin had acquired all of them, through the deaths of his wife's father in 1718, her mother in 1722, and her sister in 1725.

Marriage brought Watkin happiness as well as wealth, his obituary notice describing him as 'a noble example of conjugal fidelity'.[12] But this

---

[9] Wynnstay MSS Box 6, 69/39.
[10] *Erthig Chronicles*, I, 145.
[11] Wynnstay MSS Box C, 70/9.
[12] *Gentleman's Magazine* (hereafter *Gent. Mag.*), XIX (1749), 430.

marital bliss was marred by the deaths of both their children. In September 1716 Watkin wrote a joyful letter to his father, announcing the birth of a son.[13] But this infant must soon have died, for there is no further reference to him, not even when Watkin wrote on 14 November 1717 to inform Sir William of the birth of a daughter.[14] Mary, as she was named, is mentioned in subsequent correspondence, as when Wynn informed his father of his mother-in-law's death in 1722. 'Babby is much concerned at the loss of her grandmama.'[15] Tragedy struck in 1735, and one Amos Meredith published a poem to Wynn on the death of his seventeen-year-old daughter.[16]

> Look up to Watkin, eminently blest. . .
> then see his only child in beautious pride,
> panting, expiring by her father's side.

Before his wife Ann died in the spring of 1748,[17] she is reputed to have urged him to marry his god-daughter Frances, daughter of George Shackerly of Holme in Cheshire. Certainly when he did so on 16 July, the seemingly indecent haste was publicly explained by an announcement that the marriage was 'at the request of his late lady under her hand'.[18] Marrying a wife who was thirty-one to his fifty-five, Wynn made provision for her future by giving her Llangedwin for life.[19] The apparent desire for a Wynnstay heir was promptly gratified by the birth of a son, later the second Sir Watkin Williams Wynn, on 8 April 1749.[20]

Watkin plunged into politics at the first opportunity after he came of age. At the general election of 1715 he was active in the Cheshire contest on behalf of the unsuccessful Tory candidate Charles Cholmondeley.[21] But there is no evidence of his participation in the Denbigh Boroughs contest

---

[13] Wynnstay MSS Box 6, 69/61.

[14] Wynnstay MSS Box 6, 69/22.

[15] Wynnstay MSS Box 6, 69/50. For other references to the little girl, see ibid., 69/35, 69/51.

[16] *Byegones*, 1880, p. 16.

[17] Her death is reported as having taken place on both 14 March and 24 May. *Gent. Mag.*, XVIII (1748), 139, 284.

[18] *Gent. Mag.*, XVIII (1748), 332. For the marriage articles, correctly identifying the bride, see Wynnstay MSS Box 105, no. 4.

[19] Wynnstay MSS Box 110, no. 29. She died on 19 May 1803, aged eighty-six. *Gent. Mag.*, LXXIII (1803), 387.

[20] *Gent. Mag.*, XIX (1749), 430. Some sources state that he was born in 1748 to Sir Watkin's first wife, but confirmatory evidence of his date of birth is provided by his coming-of-age party in April 1770: *Gent. Mag.*, XL (1770), 233. Sir Watkin had a second, posthumous, son, born on 19 April 1750, but he died in 1759: *Gent. Mag.*, XX (1750), 188. Griffiths, *Pedigrees*, p. 19. These biographical details of Sir Watkin and his family correct errors in sundry works of reference.

[21] Wynnstay MSS Box C, 69/42.

between the Myddelton and Cotton families, and he did not seek a seat himself. Sir John Wynn had sat for Merioneth and both Caernarfonshire constituencies, but Watkin sought none of these: Merioneth was represented by his Tory allies, the Vaughans of Corsygedol, while the control of Caernarfonshire politics by the Whig alliance headed by the Wynns of Glynllifon was a problem he was never to solve. His eyes were fixed on Denbighshire, where the shire seat had been held since 1685 by the county's foremost squire Sir Richard Myddelton of Chirk Castle. Watkin tactfully and tactically bided his time, and was rewarded with an unexpectedly early opportunity by Myddelton's death in 1716 at the age of sixty-two. The traditional dominance of Chirk Castle was defended not by Sir Richard's successor Sir William, who was to die childless in 1718, but by the latter's cousin and heir Robert. But the formidable collection of estates now under the direct control of Watkin Williams, doubtless cemented into a powerful interest by the energy and expenditure that characterized all his electioneering, enabled him to achieve a permanent political revolution in Denbighshire. Henceforth the Wynnstay interest, despite two Chirk Castle counter-attacks in 1722 and 1741, was to be foremost in that county until the overthrow of gentry power in the later nineteenth century.

Watkin Williams, capturing the county seat by a majority of 196 votes, in Parliament promptly joined the opposition to those he deemed 'the courtiers'.[22] In August 1717 he stuck to this principle by refusing to lobby the Lord Chancellor about a new commission of the peace for Denbighshire.[23] Since Sir Watkin Williams Wynn was to be the archetypal Tory of the Hanoverian era, that his own immediate declaration of political attitude should have been opposition to the court opens up the question as to how far Toryism at that time was anything more than reiteration of the 'country party' principles of the preceding half-century. For the views put forward by Wynn for thirty years at Westminster were of that ilk: disapproval of a large permanent army, as an unnecessary expense and an implicit threat to liberty; demands for more frequent elections, to secure the greater political purity of Parliament; and, also to serve that same aim, attacks on ministerial corruption by Place Bills to reduce the number of office-holders in the House of Commons. Nearly all Wynn's activities at Westminster were concerned with such matters; but it was not only his incessant opposition to Whig ministers that led him to be deemed and dubbed a Tory. There was, of course, his Jacobitism,[24] and, above all,

---

[22] Wynnstay MSS Box C, 69/17, 69/27.

[23] Wynnstay MSS Box C, 69/21.

[24] In this connection it is worth noting the anomaly that at the time of the Swedish Plot of 1717 Watkin should refer to 'the Pretender' in family correspondence. Wynnstay MSS Box C, 69/18.

his championship of the Church of England, that characteristic hallmark of the first Tory party. Watkin was a man for whom Christianity was part of the fabric of everyday life, and Anglicanism was its embodiment in this world. His obituary in the *Gentleman's Magazine* emphasized this aspect of Wynn's character.

> His piety towards his creator, was remarkable in his constant attendance on the service of the church. He revered religion, he respected the clergy, he feared God, the whole tenor of his conduct was one continued series of virtue. So prepared, he had little reason to be afraid of sudden death. Every day of his life was a preparation for heaven.[25]

Of immediate concern to Watkin on his entry into Parliament, therefore, was the scheme of the liberal-minded Lord Stanhope, head of the ministry from 1717 to 1721, to make concessions to Protestant Dissenters. The minimum proposal of the ministry was repeal of the coercive legislation at the end of Anne's reign, the Occasional Conformity Act of 1711 and the Schism Act of 1714. The latter had prohibited nonconformist schools, the former blocked a loophole in the 1673 Test Act that had sought to ban all non-Anglicans from office. Watkin, viewing the proposal from the perspective of a country squire, wrote on 4 April 1717 that by such a move 'the Presbyterians will be enabled to act as Justices of the Peace or any employment'.[26] The introduction of the legislation was postponed for nearly two years, until on 22 December 1718 Watkin found a summons at his Llangedwin home from William Shippen, a leading Tory MP notorious for his Jacobitism, 'to attend the House of Commons . . . when a Bill for repealing the Occasional Conformity and Test Acts is to be debated'.[27] The Stanhope ministry, after the Whig Schism of 1717, faced the opposition not only of Tories but of the Whig faction led by Walpole, himself a devout Anglican and champion of the privileged position of the established church. Stanhope accordingly soon dropped any idea of repealing the Test Act itself and wisely so, for even repeal of the Occasional Conformity Act was hard-fought. It was carried on second reading on 7 January 1719 by only forty-one votes, and two days later Watkin reported to his father the narrow defeat in Committee of an amendment 'to oblige Dissenters to own the Holy and undivided Trinity before they qualify'.[28]

In 1736 Wynn, by then a prominent figure in the Commons, was naturally in the forefront of opposition to a move to repeal the Test Act as

---

[25] *Gent. Mag.*, XIX (1749), 473.
[26] Wynnstay MSS Box C, 69/20.
[27] Wynnstay MSS Box C, 69/33.
[28] Wynnstay MSS Box C, 69/40, 69/41.

concerning Protestant Dissenters. Prime Minister Walpole himself opposed the measure, but Wynn thought only out of caution and expediency, writing this report to his father after the proposal had been defeated.[29]

> You are rightly informed of my being in the front of the battle . . . I was highly complimented by the ministry folks, whether they did in sincerity or not, I will not pretend to say. In this instance their sentiments and ours tallied though upon different principles. Theirs were founded in policy, ours upon the basis of our constitution in Church and State.

The downside of such strong opinions was Wynn's coercion of Dissenters and persecution of Methodists. In about 1720 his Whig neighbour John Meller noted that 'most of the Dissenters in our parts' had gone over to Wynn. 'They choose to fall in with the man whom they most fear, and who is most likely to hurt them.'[30] Dissenters at least enjoyed legal rights of worship, but Methodists Wynn deemed to have no such protection, and in the 1740s persecuted those in his neighbourhood under the Seditious Conventicles Act of 1661: wrongly so, as Howell Harris pointed out to Charles Wesley in 1748, because formally Methodists were still members of the Church of England. Wynn was levying fines of £5, £10 and £20, well beyond the capacity of poor men to pay. Preacher Peter Williams was among those summoned to Wynnstay and fined £20. Howell Harris apparently offered to remit such fines, for in 1750, after Wynn's death, he was reproached by one such sufferer for not having done so.[31] There is a story, suspect in its aptness, that on the day of Wynn's accidental death a Methodist meeting uttered the prayer, 'O Arglwydd cwmpa Ddiawl mawr Wynnstay', 'O Lord, humble the great devil of Wynnstay'.[32]

Apart from this religious dimension there was little to distinguish Wynn's electoral and parliamentary behaviour from that of other opponents of government, Whig or Tory, and he was to form tactical alliances with opposition Whigs in the 1730s and 1740s. That was not the case, however, in the general election of 1722, for the Whig party was re-united, with Robert Walpole as Prime Minister, and some historians have portrayed the election as a last attempt by the old Tory party to recover power. Wynn busied himself in several constituencies. It can be assumed that his family interest, based on his father's estate of Llanforda, helped to carry the

---

[29] Wynnstay MSS C97. The report of the debate in Chandler, *Debates*, IX, 161–72, does not mention Wynn.
[30] *Erthig Chronicles*, I, 233.
[31] *Trevecka Letters*, pp. 15, 16–17, 21, 34–5, 41.
[32] Roberts, *Wynnstay and the Wynns*, p. 12.

Tories to victory in a bitter Shropshire contest, a success that established Tory ascendancy in that county for the remainder of Wynn's life. Wynn himself was certainly drawn into the Chester election where Whig Thomas Brereton, challenging the Tory hold of the Grosvenor family, canvassed Wynnstay tenants without permission. An irate Wynn assured Sir Richard Grosvenor of his support, and the contest was another Tory success.[33] In north Wales Wynn had reason to be pleased with the election results. He himself successfully defended his Denbighshire seat against Robert Myddelton by a majority of 183. John Pugh's victory in Montgomery Boroughs was deemed a triumph for Wynn's vigorous support.[34] In that shire Wynn had returned Price Devereux at the 1719 by-election consequent on the death of his father-in-law Edward Vaughan, and kept him as county MP until he succeeded his father as Lord Hereford in 1740. Wynn's Jacobite ally Lord Bulkeley won back the Anglesey seat, and Cycle member Thomas Eyton held Flint Boroughs in a contest. Altogether north Wales returned nine Tories out of eleven MPs, Glynllifon-controlled Caernarfonshire being the sole base of Whig power. But on the national scene the Tory attack had failed, as Watkin reported to his father on 25 October. 'The Court have a greater majority I think in this House of Commons than the last.'[35] Twenty years of opposition to Walpole's ministry lay ahead.

Little is known of the debates of the Parliament of 1722 to 1727, and the only record of any speech by Wynn is when he seconded an opposition motion on 7 March 1727.[36] The death of George I later that year led to a general election earlier than had been anticipated. There resulted a serious setback to Wynn's influence when the Walpole ministry used its Parliamentary majority to disfranchise the out-boroughs in the Montgomery constituency after his brother Robert had had a majority of 475 to 128. Nor was the candidate favoured by Wynn in Flintshire, Cycle member Thomas Puleston, successful in his challenge to Hanoverian Tory MP Sir Roger Mostyn.[37] His main concern, however, was with the Anglesey seats. At the county by-election of 1725 it was Wynn who had arranged for his cousin Hugh, elder son of his lawyer uncle John Williams of Chester, to hold the seat for the Bulkeley of Baron Hill interest against the rival one headed by the Whig family, Meyrick of

[33] Baskerville, 'The Management of the Tory Interest in Lancashire and Cheshire 1714–1747', D. Phil. Oxford, 1976, p. 123.

[34] Wynnstay MSS C107.

[35] Wynnstay MSS Box C, 69/52.

[36] *Knatchbull Diary*, p. 66. A pamphlet-poem published on Wynn's death claims that he was an early and formidable critic of Walpole in Parliament, but little contemporary evidence of this survives for his first fifteen years as an MP. *Byegones* (1889), pp. 161–4.

[37] Mostyn MSS 7884.

Bodorgan.[38] In 1727, Williams successfully defended the seat. What is remarkable about Wynn's role was that Hugh Williams was as much a Walpole Whig as his opponent. Wynn himself was returned for Beaumaris as well as Denbighshire, a tactical manœuvre to ensure that the young Lord Bulkeley could take that borough seat when of age.

Wynn now emerged as one of the ministry's most frequent critics at Westminster, and his most enduring parliamentary achievement came in 1729, when he introduced a Bill 'for the more effectual preventing of bribery and corruption in the election of members to serve in Parliament'. Prime Minister Walpole was too wise to resist a measure with such a professed objective. It passed the Commons by 1 April, and was given permanent importance when the House of Lords added to it a Last Determinations clause, establishing that any decisions by the Commons on electoral franchises would henceforth be irrevocable. This amendment was confirmed by the Commons against the wishes of the ministry.[39]

So few reports of parliamentary debates for this period have survived that Wynn's known speeches, as when he spoke against the Address on 14 January 1730,[40] must constitute only a sample of his debating activity. One theme that he constantly reiterated was the need for a reduction in the size of the army, on grounds both of cost and the alleged threat to 'the liberties of the nation'. Wynn is recorded as speaking in this vein on the army estimates on 31 January 1730, 26 January 1732, and 5 February 1733.[41] On 4 February 1730 Wynn took part in the big debate over the hire of Hessian mercenary soldiers, speaking 'popularly but not much to the argument', thought the hostile Lord Egmont.[42]

Another topic close to the hearts of country squires was the restriction of Commons membership to landowners, as men of property who could resist the wiles of government. Wynn was prominent in a 1732 attempt to strengthen the 1711 Landed Qualification Act by the stipulation that this should be enforced by a formal oath before the Speaker, and not at the constituency election as specified in 1711. Prime Minister Walpole sought to undermine the whole principle of the legislation by a proposal on 16 March that possession of government financial stock should be regarded as an equivalent qualification to land. Wynn was among those who voiced such indignation at this idea that it was withdrawn, but on 23 March the

[38] Penrhos MSS 1335.
[39] *CJ*, XXI, 274–308, passim; Chandler, *Debates*, VII, 45–6, 49; *HMC Hastings*, III, 49.
[40] *HMC Egmont Diary*, I, 6.
[41] *HMC Carlisle*, p. 66; Chandler, *Debates*, VII, 104, 272; *Gent. Mag.*, II (1732), 881; III (1733), 353.
[42] *HMC Egmont Diary*, I, 26.

ministry defeated the whole measure, and a similar one failed in the next session, on 3 April 1733, after Wynn had led debating support of the proposal.[43]

By then Walpole was deep in trouble over his controversial Excise Bill proposals for duties on tobacco and wine. Even before the 1733 parliamentary session began Wynn was gleefully anticipating the minister's fall, assuring his father on 16 January that 'if Sir Robert attempts it, it must certainly end in his destruction'.[44] Wynn was one of fourteen Tories among thirty-one opposition politicians who dined with the lord mayor of London in March at the height of the political crisis.[45] It was surely no coincidence that Denbighshire and Denbigh Boroughs were the only Welsh constituencies to instruct their MPs to oppose the measure.[46] But there is no record of Wynn speaking on the topic in Parliament, and Walpole avoided political disaster by dropping the measure.

Memory of the Excise Bill was nevertheless to cost Walpole support at the general election due in 1734, and meanwhile the parliamentary opposition pressed the attack home in the last session of the expiring Parliament. The main thrust was a vain attempt to repeal the Septennial Act, on 13 March 1734, when Wynn made a well-reported speech. He opened with the assertion that

> His Majesty looks for the approbation of the generality of his people, as well as the majority of his Parliament; and while his measures are approved of by the generality of his people, frequent elections cannot surely bring any distress upon his government.

The restoration of triennial elections would reduce both disorder and bribery, for less would be at stake. His main theme was the standard opposition argument that the great increase in corruption at elections resulted from the longer duration of Parliaments and threatened the natural interest of country gentlemen.[47]

Opposition hopes were high at the general election of 1734, when Wynn was believed in north Wales to be a leading member of a nationwide electoral alliance against the Walpole ministry.[48] All his known electoral activity took place outside that area. Only one contest occurred there, in Flint Boroughs, where Cycle member Sir John Glynne fought a ministerial

---

[43] *HMC Egmont Diary*, I, 240, 346; Chandler, *Debates*, VII, 236.
[44] Wynnstay MSS C95.
[45] Stuart MSS 160/21.
[46] Langford, *Excise Crisis*, p. 52.
[47] Chandler, *Debates*, VIII, 165–70.
[48] Bulkeley Diary, I, 14.

candidate: no evidence of Wynn's presumed involvement has come to light. But from Cardiganshire Richard Lloyd wrote to claim credit with the Prime Minister that he had won the borough seat 'though Mr Williams Wynn's party exerted themselves with all their might'.[49] In the previous year Lord Barrymore, Jacobite MP for Wigan, had requested the presence there of 'his friend Watkin' to curb local Tory hotheads in order to preserve his electoral alliance in that borough with Whig Sir Roger Bradshaigh.[50] Already by then Wynn had again become involved in Chester politics. In 1732 he took charge of the Grosvenor interest there to prepare for a parliamentary by-election, essential to success in which would be victory at the preceding mayoral election of 13 October. Three days beforehand, a Whig mob destroyed the town hall. Next day Wynn took some 800 tenants into the border town, servants in Wynnstay livery, armed with pistols, at their head. The ensuing violence, directed against known Whigs and 'every man that declared for King George', was presided over by Wynn and his friends with drawn swords. After this display of force the Grosvenor interest won both the mayoral contest and the parliamentary by-election![51] Wynn also managed the successful Grosvenor interest in 1734, when one of the defeated Whig candidates was his cousin Hugh Williams, forfeiting as a Walpolite the Anglesey seat earlier secured for him by Wynn. Watkin himself became mayor of Chester in 1736, an office he treated not as a courtesy but as a post of political significance.[52] In 1739 the Whig Bishop of Chester warned the Duke of Newcastle how much 'the governing part here is influenced by Mr Watkin Williams Wynn'.[53]

Less successful was Wynn's intervention in the Bridgnorth contest in Shropshire, which he attended to support the challenge of the Tory Acton family to the dominant Whig interest of the Whitmore family, maintained by control of the borough corporation, which could create non-resident voters. Violence by a Tory mob, and Wynn's record in such matters would seem to point to him as instigator, was countered by the deployment of soldiers, and the Tory candidates lost by over 200 votes.[54] Whitmore control of Bridgnorth was not to be overthrown that century, yet how far Wynn had become an electoral bogey-man to Whigs in his area was shown by this comment on the borough the very next year. 'Almost the whole town belongs to Watkin Williams Wynn.'[55]

[49] Cholmondeley Houghton MSS 2212.

[50] NLW General MSS 3582E; Baskerville, 'The Management of the Tory Interest in Lancashire and Cheshire 1714–1747', D. Phil. Oxford, 1976, pp. 205–6.

[51] *Gent. Mag.*, III (1733), 87; Sedgwick, *House of Commons 1715–1754*, I, 203–4.

[52] *Gent. Mag.*, VI (1736), 677; Baskerville, 'Management of the Tory Interest', pp. 222–5.

[53] BL Add. MSS 32692, f. 448.

[54] Bulkeley Diary, I, 14; Sedgwick, *House of Commons 1715–1754*, I, 310–11.

[55] Walpole, *Corr.*, XL, 14.

Although the opposition hopes of 1734 were disappointed Wynn himself was undaunted. In 1735 he was reported to be speaking frequently in Parliament, and was one of six opposition MPs appointed to draft another unsuccessful Place Bill.[56] Watkin was now winning a national reputation for his role as an independent critic of government, as a thirty-line poem in the *Gentleman's Magazine* for 1736 testified.

> Amidst corruption, luxury and rage.
> Yet one true *Briton* shames a vicious age . . .
> Without hypocrisy, here reigns confest,
> the honest zeal in the bold patriot's breast.[57]

A different species of testimony to Wynn's personal influence came from the Prime Minister in 1737. It was known that opposition Whig leader William Pulteney intended to move that the Prince of Wales should be granted £100,000 from out of the King's Civil List, a proposal strongly resented by George II but popular in Parliament. Walpole therefore sought to strike a bargain with Wynn. If he would vote against the motion and persuade 'some of the Tories to do the same', Walpole would arrange for £20,000 to be paid to Lady Derwentwater, widow of a leader of the Fifteen whose estates had been forfeited. Wynn replied with the hope that such a payment would be made, but he would not seek it 'in so mean a manner'.[58]

Contemporary press reporting of Parliament was prohibited, and had to be disguised, Wynn appearing in 'the Senate of Lilliput' as 'Waknits Wimgal Ooynn'.[59] By no means all his known speeches were reported in these difficult circumstances. On 24 January 1738 he seconded Shippen's attack on the Address, criticizing the King's Speech for the expression, 'we will carefully avoid all heats and animosities'. On the contrary, Wynn declared, it was the hallmark of a free people that 'an opposition always must exist', and recalled that keeping a watchful eye on government had long been a Westminster tradition. 'In the true old Parliamentary method of proceeding redress of grievances was always insisted upon before any supplies were granted.' Wynn concluded with the claim, a remarkable one in the light of all the evidence of his Jacobite inclinations, that he was 'as forward as any gentleman here in . . . going the greatest lengths for securing the Crown in his Majesty's person and family'.[60]

[56] *HMC Puleston*, p. 318; Chandler, *Debates*, IX, 99–101; *Gent. Mag.*, V (1735), 744, 750.
[57] *Gent. Mag.*, VI (1736), 677.
[58] Parliamentary Journal of Edward Harley, 22 February 1737.
[59] *Gent. Mag.*, VIII (1738), 670–1, 676.
[60] Chandler, *Debates*, X, 5–6.

The next month Wynn was among opposition speakers arguing for a one-third reduction in the army, but his performance was deemed 'very weak' and is not recorded in the printed report of the debate.[61] Wynn was, however, the Tory who on 29 January 1740 seconded the motion of Whig Samuel Sandys for a Place Bill.[62] Later that year, the death of the acknowledged Tory Commons leader Sir William Wyndham suddenly catapulted Wynn into the limelight. The Tory lead fell to Wynn, now Sir Watkin, Sir John Cotton, and William Shippen, men of more zeal than ability, all suspect as Jacobites, and none possessing the stature of Wyndham, who had been a Chancellor of the Exchequer under Queen Anne. Their weakness was revealed on 13 February 1741 when opposition Whigs moved for the dismissal of Walpole. Wynn and other Tory leaders were unable to prevent a mass exodus of Tories disgusted by such a self-interested Whig proposal, and the Prime Minister triumphed by 290 votes to 106.[63]

That Tory fiasco rendered the episode meaningless as a guide to Walpole's political future. At the general election of 1741 the fate of his ministry was clearly at stake, and Wynn took his full part in preparing the way for the minister's parliamentary downfall. Sir Watkin himself faced an attack on his Denbighshire seat, a move also suggested by the Bishop of Chester in evident ignorance of the arrangement already made between the ministry and Wynn's Denbighshire rival John Myddelton of Chirk Castle.[64] That Denbighshire contest was linked with two by-elections of 1740, one of them in Caernarfonshire, where Wynn vainly attempted to exploit a Whig rift, 'which I dont find he has been able to accomplish, though [he] assumes as great a sovereignty there, as in any other parts of his Principality', so John Myddelton was informed.[65] Sir Watkin's attempt at a trade-off of interests to assist his Denbighshire campaign came to nought.[66] That contest took a bizarre turn when Cheshire Whig Sir Robert Cotton, the candidate originally chosen to challenge Wynn in the county, soon changed sides to ally with Sir Watkin as his candidate for Denbigh Boroughs. That arrangement was disapproved of by Wynn's old Tory friend Lord Barrymore, on the ground that a Whig like Cotton was even worse than a renegade Tory like Myddelton.[67] The Walpole ministry contrived to detach Cotton from Wynn, who was deprived of his Denbighshire seat in 1741

---

[61] *HMC Puleston*, p. 319; *HMC Carlisle*, p. 193; Chandler, *Debates*, X, 10–85.
[62] Parliamentary Journal of Edward Harley, 29 January 1740.
[63] Mahon, *History*, III, 380.
[64] BL Add. MSS 32692, ff. 448–9.
[65] Chirk Castle MSS E89–90.
[66] Chirk Castle MSS E903; BL Add. MSS 35600, f. 233.
[67] NLW General MSS 3582E; Baskerville, 'Management of the Tory Interest', p. 240.

by the disallowal of 594 of his votes after victory at the poll by 1,352 to 933.[68]

Sir Watkin had already taken the precaution of securing a seat in the House of Commons, as a result of a Montgomeryshire by-election in 1740. On news of a vacancy there, Wynn had written to the master of Powis Castle, judiciously addressed by his Jacobite title of Duke, assuming but not presuming on a continuation of their electoral alliance.[69]

My brother [Robert] having been formerly mentioned to your Grace and some few friends as a candidate whenever this event happened, I beg leave to assure your Grace that it is quite indifferent to me, who the person be, provided he is in the country interest and set up by the unanimous consent of men in it . . . The choice of members is important at this critical time, and will . . . determine whether we are to bend to the yoke or shake off that detestable influence, that flood of corruption. This possibly may be the last opportunity we may have . . . of saving the constitution.

Robert Williams was returned at the by-election, being replaced by Sir Watkin in 1741 after the Denbighshire return. In ministerial eyes, a stronger motive for the Denbighshire attack on Wynn than seeking to remove him from the Commons may have been the desire to curtail his troublesome electoral activities elsewhere. And only in two other constituencies is he known to have been involved. His brother Richard challenged Sir George Wynne in Flint Boroughs, reluctantly bowing to Wynn's command, and Sir George thereupon claimed credit with the Prime Minister for 'the present opposition that is now made to Sir Watkin' in Flintshire.[70] Wynne defeated Richard Williams by 320 votes to 280, but only after the rejection of seventy-five more for his opponent, and his return would obviously be challenged at Westminster. In Anglesey Sir Watkin canvassed on behalf of MP Nicholas Bayly as a safe opposition voter, albeit a Whig fighting a Tory, John Owen, but Bayly lost. The Welsh returns were disappointing for Wynn, but the overall result of the general election was so close as to afford hope to Walpole's opponents. In June Sir Watkin was named among eight MPs and six peers who therefore 'ought to meet with all convenient speed' to concert tactics, in the view of Whig opposition leaders.[71] Such a gathering may not have been arranged, for in October Sir Watkin was visited at Wrexham by William Pulteney, the foremost Whig opponent of Walpole in the Commons, and William Shippen, the leading Jacobite there.[72]

[68] Thomas, *NLW Journal*, 11 (1959), 113–18.
[69] Powis Castle MSS 1101.
[70] Cholmondeley Houghton MSS 3085.
[71] Coxe, *Walpole*, III, 575.
[72] Chirk Castle MSS E4832.

When the new Parliament met Sir Watkin took a prominent role in Walpole's fall. The first defeat of the ministry took place on 14 December over his own petition about the Denbighshire election, a motion to hear the case immediately being carried by 202 votes to 193, as the obvious injustice of the case tilted the balance in an evenly divided House.[73] Two days later Sir Watkin seconded the nomination of the opposition candidate, successful by 242 votes to 238, for the key post of chairman of the Committee of Elections. That was a blow from which Walpole never really recovered, and although he fought on his opponents scented victory, Wynn sending this complaint to a supporter on 29 December.[74]

We are now in a majority, and it is in the power of our friends to remain so, if they will but attend. It is that and that only that clogs the wheels . . . In all our late divisions our opponents have forced the lame, the halt and the blind to attend. A small fit of illness and slight fit of the gout cannot be a plea where there is an honest heart at this time, when the fate of the country may very possibly turn upon a single vote . . . We cannot therefore spare one man's attendance.

Sir Watkin played his part in the final onslaught on Walpole. On 21 January 1742 he was appointed to a Committee ordered to prepare a Place Bill, and the same day he made a well-reported speech in support of a motion by Pulteney for an enquiry into the conduct of the Spanish War. 'A minister is but a steward for the public.' Wynn reminded MPs that Charles I, 'an unfortunate prince', had fomented a republican spirit by protecting bad ministers.[75] Walpole won that day by 253 votes to 250 in a crowded House, but he had obviously lost his working majority, and resigned on 2 February.

Rumours flew thick and fast as to how the triumphant opposition would be rewarded, including one that peerages would be offered to Whig Pulteney and Tories Wynn and Cotton.[76] But only the Prime Minister had left office, and what ensued was a negotiation between his former colleagues, among them Henry Pelham and his brother the Duke of Newcastle, and some leading opposition Whigs, notably Lord Carteret and William Pulteney, for a ministerial reconstruction. This news led to discontent among those who had expected a complete change of the political system, and on 12 February a mass meeting took place of 230 MPs and 35 peers formerly in the opposition, both Tory and Whig. Six

[73] *CJ*, XXIV, 19.
[74] Quoted in Owen, *Rise of the Pelhams*, p. 28.
[75] Chandler, *Debates*, XIII, 70, 92–8.
[76] *HMC Egmont Diary*, III, 247.

days later the Tories, led by Wynn and Cotton, went to Court for the first time since the Hanoverian Succession.[77] These gestures were in vain. George II's deep aversion to Tories still barred them from office and, together with the Whigs excluded from the new ministry now headed by Carteret, they resumed parliamentary warfare on the government. On 19 February, the very next day after he had been to Court, Wynn spoke in favour of postponing the army estimates until grievances were redressed, citing the 1694 precedent of insistence on the Triennial Act before supplies had been voted for the ongoing French War. 'No administration had ever less title to be called just and wise than that which this nation has been under for twenty years past.'[78]

By this time Sir Watkin was being named first among 'the chiefs of the Tory party', and hostile observers noted that it was Wynn who on 23 March led a number of Tories out of the House of Commons to avoid voting on a loyal Address.[79] Sir Watkin's prestige and influence ensured priority consideration of the Denbighshire and Flint Boroughs election cases, and he was therefore soon joined in the House by his brothers Robert and Richard. But the hopes that the fall of Walpole would usher in a new political era of non-party and uncorrupt government had proved unfounded, and instructions from constituencies soon poured in to MPs, publicizing in effect their own views. That from Denbighshire on 8 April set out the standard 'country programme' of a Place Bill, repeal of the Septennial Act, and so on, and ended by calling for punishment of Walpole, but also made particular mention of the county election.[80]

The Grand-Corruptor distinguished you by exerting all the force of corruption against you; it is because he knew your attachment to the true interest of your country. He despaired of being able to prevail upon you to betray us by whom you was trusted, therefore were you honoured with his more particular malice.

The change of ministry did not lead to any move away from the strategy of fighting on the European mainland, and Tories soon came to think Carteret's enthusiastic pursuit of that policy worse than Walpole's half-hearted effort. When the next session of Parliament began on 16 November 1742 Wynn spoke in the debate on the Address. He suspected that 'our new ministers would not only tread the steps of the old, but

---

[77] Parliamentary Journal of Edward Harley, *sub*, 17 February 1742.
[78] Chandler, *Debates*, XIII, 122–30.
[79] *HMC Egmont Diary*, III, 254–5; NLW General MSS 1352, f. 52.
[80] *Gent. Mag*, XII (1742), 216.

would endeavour to improve every bad precedent introduced by any of their predecessors'. Sir Watkin then set up as a military strategist. He did not understand how sending a British army to Flanders could help Austria. It should have gone to Hanover, to coerce France in central Germany. Wynn also asked whether Hanoverians were the only soldiers in Europe for hire.[81] Behind Wynn's comments were antipathy to Hanover, which George II did not wish to see become a battle zone, and the old Tory hankering after a maritime war. 'We have always urged a sea war', Wynn was to be reminded in 1744.[82]

On 1 December 1742, in compliance with the wishes of his constituents, Sir Watkin seconded an unsuccessful motion for renewal of the inquiry into the last ten years of the Walpole ministry.[83] Two days later, he seconded one for a Place Bill. 'If a place does not induce a man to vote against his honour and his conscience, it at least biasses his judgement, and makes him think that to be wrong, which he before thought and declared to be right.' He concluded with the commonly professed fear of country squires, that a majority of the House would soon be placemen.[84] That Wynn failed later to speak on the Hanoverian soldiers was deemed noteworthy.[85] By now for the Duke of Newcastle Sir Watkin had come to personalize the opposition, for on 6 December he wrote to the Duke of Richmond. 'You have heard by what majorities we have demolished Watkin Williams, flung out the revival of the secret committee [on Walpole] and rejected the Place Bill.'[86]

Simultaneously Wynn was heavily involved in political bargaining over which election cases should be heard. On 29 November he 'complained loudly' in the House about postponement of the Pembrokeshire case. He later refused to give up the Denbigh Boroughs case in order to facilitate an arrangement for the four south-west Wales seats in dispute. But he was a witness when an agreement was made concerning them on 2 February.[87]

During 1743 the war seemed to prosper, the British highlight being George II's personal command at the fortunate victory of Dettingen. Wynn was scornful about celebrations of the event, observing to opposition Whig MP George Dodington, 'I trust our friends will not be so captivated with appearances as to "conster" escape into victory'.[88] Horace Walpole heard the story that he was loath to give the king any personal credit: 'Sir Watkin

---

[81] Chandler, *Debates*, XIV, 9–14.
[82] *HMC Various*, VI, 18.
[83] NLW General MSS 1352, f. 67; *HMC Trevor*, p. 84.
[84] Chandler, *Debates*, XIV, 33–6; NLW General MSS 1352, f. 72.
[85] NLW General MSS 1352, f. 87.
[86] McCann, *Richmond–Newcastle Corr.*, p. 94.
[87] NLW General MSS 1352, ff. 66C, 101, 121.
[88] *HMC Various*, VI, 18.

Williams at the last Welsh races convinced the whole principality (by reading a letter that affirmed it) that the King was not within two miles of the Battle of Dettingen.'[89]

Opposition confidence swelled as the new session approached. 'They say they are much superior', wrote Lord Hastings on 26 November 1743. 'They have two hundred and fifty staunch men of Sir Watkin's opinion and 'tis believed they will do great things this winter.'[90] The next month an opposition committee of six MPs was appointed to concert the Commons attack, comprising three Whigs and three Tories, Sir John Philipps, Sir John Cotton and Wynn, all of them members of a London Tory club, the Loyal Brotherhood.[91] Their presumption that they could act on behalf of the Tories with little consultation caused offence, and foreshadowed their failure the next year to take over to administration any significant Tory following.

Opposition hopes had proved optimistic even before the Jacobite invasion scare of February 1744 rendered such behaviour unpatriotic. As a suspect Jacobite Wynn was 'prudently silent', so Whig MP John Campbell noted, on a vote of credit to increase the army and navy.[92] Sir Watkin, however, was among the MPs who protested against the premature arrest of Lord Barrymore, in form rather than out of conviction, for Wynn knew that he was the intended leader of any domestic Jacobite army.[93] Nor did Wynn abandon what he deemed to be the role of constitutional opposition. On 19 March he was one of those who criticized a payment to Austria not sanctioned by Parliament.[94] Wynn's conduct distanced him from the power struggle now developing within the ministry between Carteret and the Pelham brothers, as he commented to a Welsh supporter on 1 March: 'You will easily perceive my interest is extremely low with the people in power. My own way of thinking leads me to defer . . . to see which of the competitors, Lord Carteret or Mr Pelham, gets the better.'[95]

It was at this moment of crisis, both military and political, that the House of Commons at last considered the case of the 1741 Denbigh Boroughs election. After a seven-day hearing, during which the House resolved, contrary to precedent and by the bare majority of one, 175 to 174, that the franchise lay only in resident burgesses, a motion confirming John Wynn's return was carried on 23 February by 193 votes to 167. The

---

[89] Walpole, *Corr.*, XVIII, 305–6.
[90] *HMC Hastings*, III, 40.
[91] Colley, *In Defiance of Oligarchy*, p. 74.
[92] NLW General MSS 1352, ff. 191–2.
[93] NLW General MSS 1352, f. 209; Cobbett, *Parl. Hist.*, XII, 670.
[94] Cobbett, *Parl. Hist.*, XIII, 677.
[95] NLW General MSS 12440E, f. 95.

partisan attitude is well conveyed by Horace Walpole. 'I am this moment come from the House, where we have carried a great Welsh election against Sir Watkin Williams by 26.'[96] Another ministerial supporter viewed the outcome as a significant triumph for administration over opposition.[97]

> If it had gone the other way, the enemies of the Government would certainly have given it a turn to their advantage both at home and abroad. Sir Watkin said a thing which was much taken notice of, that he hoped the year 1656 was not come round again, when none were admitted into the House, but whom the *Protector* and his *Council* pleased.

The political scene had clarified by the next parliamentary session. The summer of 1744 saw Carteret's war policy collapse in failure, and the Pelhams were able to force his resignation in November and to negotiate new arrangements with not only opposition Whigs but also Tories, a situation Wynn had failed to anticipate even in the autumn.[98] Lord Gower and Wynn negotiated for the Tories. Some, Philipps and Cotton as well as Gower, accepted office. Wynn was offered not a post but a peerage, a calculated move reflecting both his nuisance value in the Commons and his presumed lack of expertise in and distaste for routine administration.[99] Wynn rejected the offer. According to Lord Hastings,

> his answer was that as long as his Majesty's ministers acted for the good of their country, he was willing to consent to anything; that he thanked his Majesty for the earldom he had sent him, but that he was very well content with the honours he had and was resolved to live and die Sir Watkin.[100]

A Jacobite slant was put on the episode in a letter sent to the Pretender on 28 December. 'They have offered a title to Sir Watkin Williams which he rejected with indignation.'[101]

Wynn was true to his word. On 23 January 1745, in a debate over finance for an army in Flanders, 'Sir Watkin Williams, to the surprise of the generality, spoke for the question, and as he said himself, agreed with the Court for the first time in his life.'[102] The event was regarded as of such

---

[96] Walpole, *Letters* (Toynbee), II, 8.
[97] BL Add. MSS 35337, f. 53.
[98] *HMC Various*, VI, 18.
[99] Colley, 'The Tory Party, 1727–60', Ph.D. Cambridge, 1976, p. 224.
[100] *HMC Hastings*, III, 49.
[101] Stuart MSS 261/48.
[102] Cobbett, *Parl. Hist.*, XIII, 1054.

moment as to merit a detailed account to the British ambassador in Vienna.

> Sir Watkin Williams Wynn gave Mr Pelham great praise as to his abilities and his honesty: he said he was truly an English minister, and for that reason he would vote for the first time for the army, and that he did not doubt but all his friends would do the same.[103]

On 22 February Wynn led most Tories to support a payment for Hanoverian soldiers in Britain.[104] But Tory adherence to the Pelham ministry was to be short-lived. Wynn had accepted neither honour nor office, but he had expected that Tories would be rewarded by appointments to their county benches, the role of magistrates being dear to the hearts of many squires. Sir Watkin himself submitted lists for Denbighshire and Montgomeryshire.[105] The ministerial response on the issue had been disappointing, and meanwhile Wynn and his friends were publicly assailed for deserting the cause of liberty, notably in a pamphlet addressed to Sir Watkin personally, *An Expostulatory Epistle to the Welch Knight*. The Tories, so the charge went, had repeated Pulteney's error of 1742. 'Instead of coming in as conquerers, you are received as auxiliaries . . . You must serve on their own terms, or not at all.'[106] The pamphlet was promptly answered by another, *An Apology for the Welsh Knight*, but Attorney-General Sir Dudley Ryder believed the charge had struck home. 'Sir Watkin Williams Wynn who had joined the new ministry now deserts them . . . because of being abused in a late pamphlet.'[107]

Cherishing his role as the political conscience of the country gentlemen, Wynn was sensitive to the accusations of duplicity and folly, and soon reverted to his role of guardian of the public purse. When on 20 March Pelham moved for a £500,000 vote of credit, Wynn 'complained of the question being a surprise upon him, and of a want of light into the state of affairs abroad, particularly the dispositions of the Dutch: that he did not object to the thing itself so much as the manner of doing it'.[108] On the report next day, however, he was more forthright. 'Sir Watkin opposed it with more warmth than the day before, and fell into the old strain of talking of redress of grievances, and confining ourselves to the sea.'[109] By the end of the session the Tories were back in open opposition.

---

[103] Mahon, *History*, III, 429.
[104] Cobbett, *Parl. Hist.*, XIII, 1201–2.
[105] For these and applications for other Welsh counties, see BL Add. MSS 35602, ff. 38, 40, 42, 44, 54, 120.
[106] *Gent. Mag.*, XV (1745), 90.
[107] Harrowby MSS 21R 162 (March 1745).
[108] Cobbett, *Parl. Hist.*, XIII, 1218.
[109] Cobbett, *Parl. Hist.*, XIII, 1249–50.

The winter of 1744–5 was the high point of Sir Watkin's political career, for the peerage offer was not the only contemporary testimony to his importance. On 15 February 1745, when Sir Watkin was nominally an administration supporter, he was elected a Steward for the coming year by the self-styled Independent Electors of Westminster, an honour customarily reserved for men distinguished in opposition to government.[110] More practical testimony to the esteem in which Sir Watkin was held came in the Glamorgan by-election campaign during the last weeks of 1744. Opposition Whig MP Hans Stanley assured the Tory candidate Sir Charles Kemys Tynte that, if his Neath estate had been freehold and not leasehold, 'I should have undertaken in that case, to have waited on a friend of Sir Watkin Williams Wynn's, with the utmost readiness at whatever distance'.[111] Wynn was involved behind the scenes on behalf of Tynte, who requested his presence at the poll on 2 January 1745 'to keep the sheriff honest'. But the Duke of Beaufort and Lord Mansel, among others, failed to persuade Wynn to attend and Somerset MP Thomas Prowse wrote to explain his attitude to Tynte.[112]

> Sir Watkin has been very hearty in this affair, but in two or three instances when I pressed him to speak in your behalf, he declined doing it in person, as the election was out of his province (North Wales).

The next parliamentary session was dominated by the Forty-Five Rising. Wynn, in Stuart eyes professedly poised to join the rebellion at a suitable opportunity, nevertheless at Westminster adopted an orthodox opposition role. On 1 November 1745 he spoke against a proposal for the raising of private regiments to counter the threatened invasion of England.[113] But, as Lord Oxford noted in his diary, 'the country party' in that emergency acquiesced in financial proposals to strengthen the armed forces, and sought political concessions for their support. Sir Watkin and the Duke of Beaufort delivered proposals to Lord Gower, who had deserted the Tories to stay on in office, but the concessions promised were minimal, a few more Tory magistrates and some legislation concerning their qualifications and also county elections.[114] And so on 19 December Sir Watkin, deep in Jacobite negotiations, had the effrontery to demand in the House of Commons that Tory loyalty should be rewarded. 'He intended to move for [a] constitutional bill, as we had done so much for the Crown.'[115] In order to keep up the

---

[110] *Gent. Mag.*, XV (1745), 107.
[111] Kemys Tynte MSS D/DKT, 1/49.
[112] Kemys Tynte MSS D/DKT, 1/19, 22, 37, 42, 44, 47.
[113] Walpole, *Corr.*, XXVI, 17.
[114] Parliamentary Journal of Edward Harley, *sub* 27 November 1745.
[115] Harrowby MSS 21R 264. Notes of Sir Dudley Ryder.

pressure a circular of 31 December was sent to appropriate MPs, Wynn being the chief signatory among four. It began, 'As everything that is near and dear to us is now at stake', and urged attendance from 16 January 'for a fortnight or three weeks only'.[116] Nothing is known of what ensued from such preparations, but Wynn did make one major speech, seeking on 14 January 1746 to explain why he was now opposing what he had supported a year earlier, military and financial support for Britain's allies. Sir Watkin denied that he was an isolationist, accepting that Britain's interest was affected by the European balance of power and agreeing there was a close link with the Dutch. But they had let Britain down last year, furnishing only 15,000 out of 40,000 soldiers promised and being 'totally inactive' at the defeat of Fontenoy. Must we, he asked, defend those who will not help themselves? He wished 'to reduce the power of France', but could not perceive how to do so. 'We have now a rebellion on foot in the very heart of the kingdom . . . Threatened at the same time with an invasion from abroad.' Britain could not send her soldiers to Europe, and it would be 'madness' to hire foreign mercenaries. But Wynn's objection to blanket approval of ministerial policy secured only fifty-three votes as against 249.[117]

Sir Watkin Williams Wynn met with such scathing sustained criticism of his negotiations with the Pelham ministry whenever he visited Wales and the border counties that he was henceforth reluctant to embark on any further discussions with the administration, and his mood was shared by the Duke of Beaufort and Lord Barrymore. By the end of 1746 Wynn was back in wholehearted opposition.[118] But when the Jacobite contacts of Sir Watkin and his friends became public knowledge in the aftermath of the Forty-Five, the revelations temporarily destroyed any prospect of a coalition with opposition Whigs. All was soon forgiven if not forgotten when the Pelham ministry called a general election in 1747, a year earlier than necessary. Mutual self-interest led Frederick, Prince of Wales, who had reverted to opposition in 1746, to draft a political programme designed to appeal to Tory country gentlemen. Among other proposals he would 'abolish for the future all distinctions of party'; grant a Bill appointing as magistrates all gentlemen with landed estates worth £300 a year; and pass a Place Bill disqualifying all junior army and navy officers from being MPs. A meeting of Tory leaders, who included Sir Watkin, the Duke of Beaufort and Lord Windsor, responded with assurances of support.[119]

---

[116] NLW General MSS 1089B.
[117] Stowe MSS 354, f. 261.
[118] Colley, 'The Tory Party, 1727–60', pp. 249–50.
[119] BL Add. MSS 35870, ff. 129–30. For more detail, see Owen, *Rise of the Pelhams*, pp. 312–14.

The ensuing general election, from which the Pelham ministry emerged with a majority of 125, was a quiet one for Sir Watkin. Only one contest took place in north Wales, instigated by Wynn himself in Caernarfonshire. Perhaps he was seeking revenge on Glynllifon for the Denbigh Boroughs setback, when Sir Thomas Wynn's son John had been the successful candidate. Sir Watkin personally canvassed the county during the summer of 1746, as a public declaration of war; and local Tories discussed the preparation of 'leases among our friends to make a certain number of new voters for the county. Sir Watkin is well acquainted with such proceedings.'[120] The candidate named by Sir Watkin was a curious choice, Sir Thomas Prendergast, a stranger with ministerial connections. He was defeated by nearly a hundred votes, as Sir Watkin again burnt his fingers in Caernarfonshire politics. He himself met with no opposition this time in Denbighshire, but both his brothers left the Commons. Robert, hitherto an active MP, was replaced as Montgomeryshire MP by Shropshire squire Edward Kynaston. That reluctant MP Richard gave up his Flint Boroughs seat to his cousin Kyffin Williams, younger brother of the former Anglesey MP Hugh and also a Whig supporter of government. That Sir Watkin should support one Whig in Caernarfonshire and accept another for Flint demonstrates again that even for such a partisan Parliamentarian electoral advantage was more significant than political opinions.

Wynn was personally involved in two other constituencies. Thomas Pryse of Gogerddan on his death in 1745 had named Sir Watkin one of the trustees for his estate: that there had earlier been a link between Wynn and the Pryse family is suggested by his intervention in the 1734 Cardigan Boroughs contest. The role of the trustees was to preserve the Gogerddan electoral interest for the heir, but in 1747 they differed among themselves over who should be the candidate for the now safe borough seat. Wynn was among those who favoured Thomas Powell of Nanteos, but he accepted the objection of other trustees to a Cardiganshire candidate and acquiesced in the choice of John Symmons from Pembrokeshire.[121] Wynn's most active role at this general election was outside Wales, his part in the Tory attack on Lord Gower's interest in Staffordshire. Anger at his political apostacy led to the only county contest of the century, and there were rumours that Wynn might also instigate a challenge in Lord Gower's borough of Newcastle under Lyme.[122] The next year Staffordshire Tories organized their own race meeting as a snub to their former leader, in August 1748. It

---

[120] Brogyntyn MSS 35.
[121] Thomas, *Ceredigion*, 5 (1964–7), 409–10.
[122] Sedgwick, *House of Commons 1715–1754*, I, 318–20.

was attended by the Duke of Beaufort and Sir John Philipps as well as Sir Watkin, whose horse 'Old England' won a race.[123]

Wynn was in combative mood for the opening of the new Parliament, for the Duke of Beaufort told Cardiff MP Herbert Mackworth that Sir Watkin and other friends meant to attend early so as to support friends over disputed election cases.[124] But he left London for Wales on 20 November, presumably because of the illness of his wife, who died a few months later.[125] Domestic matters seem to have kept Sir Watkin away from the political scene until the spring of 1749, when, only a few days after the birth of his son, he was present on 13 April at the gathering of the Tory faithful for the opening of the Radcliffe Camera at Oxford. The highlight was a speech by the Public Orator Dr William King, one of the dons who gave Oxford the name of being a Jacobite stronghold, in sentiment if not in deed. Each of five prayers opened with the word *Redeat*, 'He will return', an obvious allusion to the exiled Pretender. Praise was lavished on the five trustees, Wynn being one of them: since he died before the text of the speech went to the printer, a Latin tribute to his memory appeared as a footnote.[126] The ministry briefly considered prosecution for treason, a threat that led to a *rapprochement* between the Tories and the party of the Prince of Wales. Over a hundred MPs and peers met on 1 May and agreed on an alliance for the next parliamentary session, Wynn being one of the speakers.[127] But Sir Watkin's political career was abruptly terminated that autumn. He died in a hunting accident on 20 September, when he struck his head on a stone as he fell off his horse.[128]

The sudden death of a prominent politician who was a man esteemed for his private and public virtues attracted considerable attention. There is a story that the Duke of Newcastle, who had found Wynn such a thorn in his flesh as an electioneer, rushed exultantly to inform George II, only to meet a royal rebuff. 'I am sorry for it', answered the King, 'he was a worthy man and an open enemy.'[129] Prime Minister Henry Pelham took a more measured view. Writing to Wynn's Denbighshire rival Richard Myddelton on 30 September, he made this comment. 'I can't but be sorry that my old acquaintance met with so unhappy a fate; for set aside his party zeal, which indeed governed him almost in everything, he was a generous, good natured man.'[130] To Lord Hartington the same day Pelham reflected more

[123] Colley, 'The Tory Party, 1727–60', p. 17.
[124] Mackworth MSS 1342.
[125] *Gent. Mag.*, XVII (1747), 542; XVIII (1748), 139, 284.
[126] Greenwood, *William King*, pp. 193–9.
[127] Walpole, *Letters* (Toynbee), II, 372–3.
[128] *Byegones* (1893), p. 245. 26 September is an alternative date.
[129] *Byegones* (1903), p. 140.
[130] Chirk Castle MSS E613.

generally on the political consequences. 'A great stroke it is for the King and his family.' He feared, however, that Sir John Cotton might now lead the Tories into an alliance with the Prince of Wales, 'which I am apt to think my old friend Watkin would not have done. Time however will open everything. The cause in general must be the better for the loss of such a man.'[131]

Wynn was buried at Ruabon on 3 October 'in a private manner', with the *Gentleman's Magazine* publishing an account of his funeral taken from a Chester newspaper.[132]

> At the park gate of Wynnstay the corpse was solemnly received by multitudes of people, whose outward gestures of affliction pathetically represented the inward sentiments of their hearts. Few men have ever deserved so general a lamentation! In his public character, he was resolute and unmoveable, in his private character, he was generous, and of exceeding good nature. He loved his country with a sincerity which seemed to distinguish him from all mankind. His morals were untainted. He had an utter detestation of vice. His manners, like his countenance, was open and undisguised. He was affable by nature. He knew how to condescend, without meanness. He was munificent, without ostentation. His behaviour was so amiable, as never to create a personal enemy. He was even honoured, where he was not beloved. In domestic life, he was the kindest relation, and truest friend. His house was a noble scene of regular, yet almost unbounded hospitality . . . He feared God, the whole tenor of his conduct was one continued series of virtue.

This eulogy was typical of several that promptly appeared. The same issue of the *Gentleman's Magazine* contained a seventy-eight-line poem on the death of Sir Watkin Williams Wynn, addressed to Edward Kynaston, praising Wynn as a champion of liberty and a benefactor of the poor.[133] This had appeared first in the *Chester Courant* for 3 October, and the same paper on 5 December published an appreciation of his character in Latin, with an English translation. 'Alas! How good, how great a man is dead!. . . He, who when living, had not an enemy, except who was a thorough enemy to the Constitution, and to the name of Britain . . . This excellent Patriot died in the fullness of reputation.' Before the end of the year there had been published a twenty-six-page quarto pamphlet, priced one shilling. 'A poem, sacred to the memory of the late Sir Watkin Williams Wynn, Bart, by Richard Rolt.'[134]

[131] Sedgwick, *House of Commons 1715–1754*, I, 76, 585; II, 545. Quotations from a letter in the Devonshire MSS.
[132] *Gent. Mag.*, XIX (1749), 473.
[133] *Gent. Mag.*, XIX (1749), 470.
[134] For details and extracts, see *Byegones* (1885), pp. 73–5; (1889), pp. 161–4.

There were contemporaries who would not have recognized in Wynn this paragon of private and public virtues. When John Meller, a Whig newly arrived in Denbighshire in about 1720, wrote that 'this whole country is governed by fear,' it was Watkin Williams Wynn he had in mind, and he went on to describe how Watkin and his father coerced all sections of the local community. 'Tis they who put the ordinary people upon offices, or excuse them as they think fit, and thereby gain a very great influence over them.' The same behaviour, Meller continued, gave Watkin's family the 'influence which they have over the middling gentry, who observing that at the Quarter Sessions the Bench of Justices is generally swayed by the Tory party and generally side with Sir William Williams' interest, they think it advisable to be of the strongest side.'[135] Meller himself suffered from their partisan violence. On 12 April 1721 Sir William Williams and his sons Watkin and Robert led a riding-party that cut down gates to the Erthig estate, and let their servants exercise horses there. The incident led Meller to challenge Watkin to a duel, but judicial intervention prevented the matter from being taken further.[136] Yet ten years later, when Wynn heard that Meller was in poor health, he sent him a key to Wynnstay Park so that he could ride there.[137]

Meller does not record a particularly nasty incident in the 1722 election campaign, when Wynn ejected from his estate and deprived of her small pension a crippled woman whose offence had been to give verbal encouragement to his opponent Robert Myddelton.[138] All this evidence is from the time when Watkin was a young man, and he may have mellowed with age, although the Methodists he persecuted in the 1740s would not have thought so. In any case coercion was as much a canvassing tactic as persuasion, and electioneering was a political technique in which Wynn acquired a formidable reputation. The Bishop of Chester commented to the Duke of Newcastle in 1739 on the influence possessed by Wynn, 'whose money and unwearied application keeps up an interest in too many places'.[139] It was an avowed electoral tactic of Sir Watkin to spare neither cost nor effort, as a Chirk Castle partisan noted in 1741. 'The policy of elections is to talk great and seemingly to carry everything on with the utmost vigour and spirit and to set forth they value no expense.'[140] Rueful testimony as to how lavishly Sir Watkin spent his money in this manner

---

[135] *Erthig Chronicles*, I, 230–1.
[136] *Erthig Chronicles*, I, 211–12.
[137] *Erthig Chronicles*, I, 247.
[138] *Chirk Castle Accounts*, II, 447.
[139] BL Add. MSS 32692, f. 448.
[140] Chirk Castle MSS C31.

came also from another quarter: Jacobite Aeneas Macdonald wrote this recollection in 1750.[141]

In 1745 when our affair broke out, . . . certain people began to examine their cash. The late Sir Watkin Williams Wynn had not two hundred pounds by him and you know lands are of no use nor credit to raise money on these occasions. . . This will appear less surprising when I tell you that by a very exact computation which I saw, it cost this man in his life-time in country elections no less than one hundred and twenty thousand pounds sterling so that very probably there was six times as much money thrown away upon such elections from first to last as would have restored the King.

Whig contemporaries like Sir George Wynne in Flint and Richard Lloyd in Cardigan claimed credit with Sir Robert Walpole for opposing such a redoubtable antagonist. Even a dozen years after Sir Watkin's death Sir John Wynn of Glynllifon thought worth recounting in 1761 to the Duke of Newcastle, then Prime Minister, his successful endeavours against this formidable foe.

I have stood three contested elections against the warmest efforts of Sir Watkin, at my own expense, and disappointed that Great Champion in every one of them. At the request of Sir R. Walpole I raised the opposition to Sir Watkin, which cost him above 20 thousand pounds.[142]

Yet even such an inveterate campaigner against government as Wynn was willing to bring his Whig cousins Hugh and Kyffin Williams into Parliament, and to support an opposition Whig against a Tory for Anglesey in 1741. Family interests, his own or those of his friends, took precedence over political affiliations.

Electioneering provided Wynn with a group of MPs of whom he was the leader. When Merioneth MP William Vaughan was persuaded by his Whig relative Thomas Wynn to vote with the ministry in an army debate of 1738, Wynn swiftly brought him back into the opposition ranks.[143] But it was not a personal following so much as his political zeal, buttressed by personal wealth and prestige, that gave Wynn an importance at Westminster that surpassed his talents. Sir Watkin was one of the few spokesmen of the

---

[141] Stuart MSS 310/139.

[142] BL Add. MSS 32919, f. 267. Two of these contests were Denbigh in 1741 and Caernarfonshire in 1747. The third may have been Caernarfonshire in 1740, though no poll took place. For Wynn's claim see also BL Add. MSS 32734, ff. 312–13; 33057, f. 523.

[143] Colley, *Defiance of Oligarchy*, p. 81.

inarticulate mass of country squires who thronged the back benches. That was the significance of his customary opening phrase. 'Sir, I am one of those', mocked by the sophisticated Horace Walpole. 'Sir Watkyn's *One of Those* when rhetoric fails, gives weight to nonsense, as the Prince of Wales.'[144] Wynn gave voice to all the standard country party criticisms of government power. By 1730 he was prominent in the parliamentary opposition, one of the patrons of Lord Bolingbroke's famous political weekly paper *The Craftsman*, and a member of that inner Tory council, The Board of Loyal Brotherhood.[145] Oxford University early acknowledged Wynn's importance in Tory circles by a DCL in 1732.[146] The extent of Wynn's involvement in metropolitan politics is unclear, and it may have been merely his parliamentary role that led to his 1745 choice as a Steward of the Independent Electors of Westminster, when his toast was 'That a Halter may bind those, whom Honour and Honesty cannot'.[147] In the 1740s the deaths of older and abler men, Sir William Wyndham in 1740 and William Shippen in 1743, meant that Sir Watkin perforce became a leading Tory, perhaps the foremost one in the Commons. To describe him as a Tory leader would be misleading, for, as the 1744–5 Tory fiasco revealed, Wynn and those who joined the ministry had little hold on their followers. A study of Wynn provides some explanation of the demise of the old Tory party. Integrity of character did not compensate for lack of those skills, oratorical and organizational, essential for success at Westminster and Whitehall. Sir Watkin was the archetypal politician 'in the country interest', his own self-description, though opponents dubbed him Tory. He did not seek the power and responsibility of office, nor was he suited to it.

[144] Walpole, *Corr.*, XXX, 292.
[145] Colley, *Defiance of Oligarchy*, pp. 211–12.
[146] *Gent. Mag.*, II (1732), 936.
[147] BL Add. MSS 32704, ff. 75–6; *Gent. Mag.*, XV (1745), 107.

CHAPTER 8

A Mid-Eighteenth-Century Tory: Sir John Philipps (1700–1764)

Hʜɪꜱᴛᴏʀɪᴀɴꜱ of Hanoverian Britain with peripheral vision know of Sir John Philipps. His name appears in books ancient and modern, from Archdeacon William Coxe writing in the reign of George III to the studies by Jonathan Clark, Linda Colley and Eveline Cruickshanks. He features prominently in Sir Lewis Namier's famous essay on 'Country Gentlemen in Parliament'.[1] His career exemplifies in one person the multi-faceted character of eighteenth-century Toryism. A Whig in his youth, a reputed Jacobite in middle age, when he was simultaneously and briefly a holder of government office, Sir John ended his days 'in very odour with his present Majesty' George III, as Horace Walpole recalled in 1784.[2] Leader of the Society of Sea Serjeants, a suspect Jacobite and certainly Tory organization in south-west Wales, Sir John was also an active participant in London politics, and for a time in the 1750s a parliamentary lobbyist for the port of Bristol. There was a political thread of consistency throughout all the twists and turns of his career, a country attitude of suspicion of the power of government. He did not shed this even when supporting the premierships of William Pitt and Lord Bute, and when he himself was currently exploiting that same patronage system of which he had long been a critic. Both Pitt and Bute found that they had to make concessions to a view of politics that was old-fashioned and impractical. For the country leopard did not altogether lose his spots. Sir John Philipps never became a court poodle.

Sir John's political career intertwines with that of Sir Watkin Williams Wynn in the 1740s, but thereafter ranges more widely on the national stage, though his Welsh roots were shallower.[3] It is a case-study in exploring the

---

[1] Printed in Namier, *Crossroads of Power*, pp. 30–45, and *Personalities and Powers*, pp. 59–77.
[2] Walpole, *Corr.*, XXXIII, 455.
[3] The accounts of his political career in the official *History of Parliament* are brief

changing nature of mid-century Toryism. His behaviour straddles two conflicting schools of thought: one that Jacobitism was the basis of Toryism, the other that hope of a return to office explains the alleged survival of a coherent Tory party.[4] Sir John fits into both hypotheses, or neither. Rather does he, like Sir Watkin, exemplify the 'country party' nature of Toryism, suspicion of the threat to liberty posed by government, in respect of both the old danger of military power and the new insidious menace of corruption. In the 1740s Philipps took this attitude of unreasoning and unreasonable suspicion further even than such contemporaries as Sir Watkin.

Why Philipps became a Tory is something of a puzzle, for his family tradition and personal connections were both Whig. His father Sir John Philipps, fourth baronet, of Picton Castle, had been a Whig MP under William III, and was one again when he represented Haverfordwest from 1718 to 1722. The younger John, born in 1700, and his elder brother Erasmus, were kinsmen of none other than Sir Robert Walpole himself, the Prime Minister from 1721 to 1742, being first cousins of his first wife Catherine.[5] In his early life John was on good terms with the Walpole family, to whom in 1724 he presented a family pedigree depicting their joint descent from the medieval Welsh prince Cadwallader. He also gave a little 'racing-mare' to young Horace Walpole, the future diarist.[6] In 1727 Lady Walpole was god-mother to his first son, another John.[7] As late as 1735 John and Erasmus exploited this family connection by persuading Sir Robert Walpole to kill an election petition against Erasmus, MP for Haverfordwest since 1726, twice waiting on the Premier at his levee.[8] This was despite the circumstance that Erasmus voted regularly against the ministry; John had already assured Sir Robert the previous year that this conduct of his brother did not betoken personal enmity, as Walpole had apparently been told.[9] Indeed, the two brothers may have remained on amiable terms with the Walpoles until Lady Walpole died in 1737. Her son Horace took a particular and often scathing interest in the activities of the

---

and unsatisfactory, being by two authors both ignorant of his Welsh background and failing to consult his family papers. Sedgwick, *House of Commons 1715–1754*, II, 344–5 (Eveline Cruickshanks); Namier and Brooke, *House of Commons 1754–1790*, III, 274–5 (John Cannon).

[4] For these interpretations, see respectively Cruickshanks, *Political Untouchables*, and Colley, *In Defiance of Oligarchy*.

[5] Walpole, *Corr.*, XIX, 310N.

[6] NLW General MSS 23274, p. 175; Walpole, *Corr.*, XXXIII, 454.

[7] NLW General MSS 23274, p. 192. This son, born 2 January 1727, died of smallpox in 1733. Ibid., p. 264. The heir was a second son, Richard, born in about 1742.

[8] Picton Castle MSS 1673.

[9] Sedgwick, *House of Commons 1715–1754*, II, 343.

man he first knew as 'Jack Philipps',[10] his own first cousin once removed. He is the source of the story that John became a Tory only because Sir Robert had not honoured what in that age of patronage might almost have been deemed a family obligation, by refusing an application to appoint him to the Customs Board, a coveted and lucrative post.[11] Horace Walpole was in a position to know such matters, and it is certainly true that in 1727 John Philipps did request an official appointment. As soon as he was admitted a barrister in November, John, accompanied by Erasmus, called on the Lord Chancellor to request a place as a Commissioner of Bankruptcy, without success.[12]

Such offices would have been incompatible with a parliamentary career, and John Philipps may not at first have cherished personal political ambitions. For he was a practising barrister with a living to earn, a younger son whose sole patrimony was the minor family estate of Kilgetty, worth a mere £400 a year, given to him by his father when he married in 1725.[13] Yet whether or not he had been infected with Toryism while at Oxford in the early 1720s,[14] John Philipps soon became involved in electoral politics. Much of the motivation for his active role against Sir Arthur Owen in the 1727 Pembrokeshire election was personal antipathy. Owen had shown some of John's private correspondence to his father. John denounced Sir Arthur's conduct as 'bad and rascally', offering the choice of a public apology or a duel. The quarrel was patched up, but resentment lingered, and John's deployment of Picton Castle votes turned the election against Owen. Erasmus Philipps noted the consequent high feeling. 'Was assured by several that as my brother John . . . was going the report of a pistol was heard. People did talk of some design against him'.[15]

Since Owen's successful rival John Campbell was also a Whig, the episode did not betoken the conversion of John Philipps to Toryism. More significant as a pointer to his political future was his role as key personality in the Society of Sea Serjeants, secretary at its foundation in 1726 and president from 1752. This was a Tory or 'country party' electoral organization as well as a social club, but not a Jacobite one. John Philipps himself became at some time a Stuart sympathizer, for he did possess glassware marked with the White Rose, but it is doubtful whether he was the 'John Philips' whom the Pretender thanked for a message of support in 1726.[16]

---

[10] Walpole, *Corr.,* XVII, 418.
[11] Walpole, *Corr.,* XXXIII, 454–5.
[12] NLW General MSS 23274, 211.
[13] Picton Castle MSS 320.
[14] As suggested by Colley, *In Defiance of Oligarchy,* p. 86.
[15] NLW General MSS 23274, pp. 201–6.
[16] BL Add. MSS 30867, f. 219; Stuart MSS 91/13.

He was not involved or even mentioned in all the correspondence and plotting that preceded the Forty-Five, and his name was not then given to the exiled Stuart court as a possible supporter.

By the general election of 1741 Sea Serjeants had gained control of Carmarthen, and John Philipps won that borough seat, defeating the local Whig leader Griffith Philipps, who submitted a petition to Parliament. Already a man of mature years and experienced at the Bar, Philipps at once became one of the foremost Tory spokesmen in the Commons. His opening remark on 19 February 1742, 'I never trouble you long on any occasion', shows that only three months into the new Parliament he was already a regular speaker. In this, his first recorded speech, Philipps adopted the old constitutional argument that grievances should be redressed before finance was voted for government.[17] Three days later Philipps had the Palace of Westminster searched for MPs to attend a debate on army estimates. Their disgruntlement led to noise, about which he complained, and then he announced he would not oppose the motion.[18] When on 9 March the famous motion for a secret Committee of Inquiry into the alleged malpractices of the Walpole ministry was debated, Philipps scorned the claim that the secret service money had been used to pay British spies abroad. The service had been 'performed rather in this House than in foreign courts'.[19] The motion was successful, and Philipps was one of seven Tories on the opposition list for the ballot for the Committee on 26 March, but the Walpolites contrived to exclude the three most virulent Tories – Philipps, Wynn and Sir John Cotton.[20] A month later, on 29 April, Philipps was the first to oppose the transfer of 4,000 soldiers from Ireland to Britain. He scoffed at the argument of the danger of invasion. 'Our navy must be in a profound sleep, and our ministers void of intelligence, if they suffer Spain to approach our coasts.' He then mounted a favourite hobby-horse. 'Whoever advises a British King to delight in a standing army, is an enemy to his country, as it tends to enslave the people.'[21]

Such opinions were not only out-of-date, but also inappropriate in a time of national crisis, a period of unsuccessful war against Spain and then France as well as of a Jacobite threat. Yet Philipps persisted in them even when other critics of government, Tory as well as Whig, held their fire. His intemperate lack of judgement was displayed on the opening day of the next session, 17 November 1742. 'After the Address was agreed to, Mr Philipps of Kilgetty stood up and moved for the House to go into a

---

[17] Chandler, *Debates,* XIII, 117–18; Cobbett, *Parl. Hist.*, XII, 428–9.
[18] Chandler, *Debates,* XIII, 131.
[19] Chandler, *Debates,* XIII, 149–50; Cobbett, *Parl. Hist.*, XII, 460–1, 522–3.
[20] Walpole, *Corr.,* XVII, 383–4; Owen, *Rise of the Pelhams,* pp. 106–8.
[21] Chandler, *Debates,* XIII, 227–9.

Committee on the State of the Nation [on] 17 January.' So his Pembrokeshire foe John Campbell informed his son Pryse, describing how the ministry rejected the motion without debating it.[22]

> His action was I suppose his own, for had it been concerted the Party would doubtless have spoke to support it; a man shows want of judgement, a meddling busy temper, and hurts his character by doing such things without the knowledge or approbation of his friends, for no party can do any thing to purpose, but when they act in concert. Kilgetty was for granting no Supply Bill till the State of the Nation was known, and yet would put off that enquiry for two months. How absurd, unless he would confess he would destroy the government by putting a full stop to all measures.

For this new session his political zeal led John Philipps to live in Westminster itself. John Campbell on 10 December saw him in the House of Commons claiming a seat at 8.30 a.m. 'in his slippers. I am told he has taken a lodging close by. I am apt enough to believe the Tories will bring him in for some borough if he loses Carmarthen', to the petition from Griffith Philipps: that did not happen. The occasion was the debate that day in the Committee of Supply over voting finance for Hanoverian soldiers, a ministerial decision that defied popular prejudice against the Electorate, and approved only after fierce debate. Campbell noted that Philipps was 'up to speak, once or twice, but prevented by others, so kept his speech, perhaps for Monday', when the resolution would be reported to the House proper.[23] Philipps then contended that Britain was being over-charged, paying £392,000 for a cost to Hanover of £100,000, and attacked the political folly of the Carteret ministry by a contrast with Sir Robert Walpole. 'The late minister was too wise a man, and too faithful a subject to advise the King to employ Hanoverians, to render him odious to his British subjects.'[24]

Philipps had already spoken twice earlier that month, as on 3 December for an unsuccessful motion for a Place Bill. Such a measure was necessary to maintain 'freedom within these walls . . . A bill therefore of this nature, that so evidently tends to lead men out of temptation, must necessarily deliver them from evil.'[25] In a Committee of Supply on 6 December he argued that Britain's ally Austria should be assisted with money, not by

---

[22] NLW General MSS 1352, ff. 128–9.
[23] NLW General MSS 1352, ff. 87–8.
[24] Chandler, *Debates*, XIV, 190–4. This is printed as for the debate of 10 December.
[25] Chandler, *Debates*, XIV, 53–4.

an army in Flanders. 'Our naval force is our natural strength'.[26] John Campbell thought that the House was not 'so attentive to him as decency and the regard due to his merit and abilities required'.[27]

But in Tory circles Philipps, now Sir John after he succeeded his bachelor brother Erasmus as baronet and master of Picton Castle in October, was held in high esteem. Already a member of the elitist Loyal Brotherhood, in December 1743 he was one of three Tories chosen to concert tactics with opposition Whigs.[28] When in February 1744 there was a French invasion attempt on behalf of the Stuart cause, Philipps yielded not an inch in his criticism of emergency measures. He complained of the arrest of MP Lord Barrymore before the House was informed, and twice, on 23 and 29 February, spoke against suspension of the Habeas Corpus Act.[29] On 24 February he was alone in opposing an Address promising support to the Crown, moved by Commons Leader Henry Pelham. 'Sir John Philipps was extremely sorry he could not agree with him, for whom he had the greatest respect, but he could not agree to this Address, which he called a vote of credit. He could not put such a high trust in ministers.'[30]

The ironic sequel to all this obstruction was that before the end of the year Sir John Philipps took office under Pelham, as he constructed a 'broad-bottom administration' on the fall of Carteret. Philipps became a Lord of Trade, as one of several Tories entering the ministry, but he avowedly refused to accept that the implicit obligation of office-holding was to support the ministry in Parliament. On 16 January 1745 he seconded an opposition obstructionist motion over finance for the Ordnance Department, 'resolved to give us an early specimen that he would be as troublesome a placeman as a patriot', tartly observed Lord Chancellor Hardwicke's son Philip Yorke.[31] On 29 January Sir John spoke in favour of an Annual Parliament Bill, a stock opposition measure, and frankly announced that office would not alter his parliamentary conduct. 'The late change in my circumstances has produced no change in my way of thinking, nor shall produce any change in my way of voting in this House'.[32] Little over a fortnight later, on 15 February, Philipps led the toast to annual Parliaments when he attended a mass meeting of the Independent Electors of Westminster, the first evidence of his involvement in metropolitan politics.[33] In the House of Commons Sir John continued in the same vein.

---

[26] Chandler, *Debates*, XIV, 71–4.
[27] NLW General MSS 1352, f. 78.
[28] Owen, *Rise of the Pelhams*, p.199; Colley, *Defiance of Oligarchy*, p. 74.
[29] NLW General MSS 1352, ff. 209, 223; Cobbett, *Parl. Hist.*, XIII, 670, 673.
[30] NLW General MSS 1352, ff. 215–17.
[31] BL Add. MSS 35337, f. 87.
[32] Almon, *Debates*, II, 46–63.
[33] BL Add. MSS 32704, ff. 75–6.

On 1 February he raised frivolous objections to a subsidy grant already agreed the previous year.[34] Three weeks later, on 22 February, Philipps objected to a grant to Hanoverian soldiers, customarily made on their discharge from British service, being in a minority of 40 against a majority of 181 that included Sir Watkin Williams Wynn.[35] Finance for foreign soldiers was always a sensitive issue, and on 20 March Sir John was among those Tories who protested about a grant for the Dutch regiments that had served in Britain in 1744.[36] On the same day, and the next, he spoke and voted against a motion by Pelham for a £500,000 vote of credit, designed especially to meet the cost of a possible future alliance with Russia.[37] Sir John Philipps had personified the incompatibility of country attitudes with ministerial office, and by the end of the month he had accepted the inevitable, as Horace Walpole reported to a correspondent on 29 March. 'My wise cousin, Sir John Philipps, has resigned his place.'[38]

Sir John's decision symbolized the Tory disillusionment with the ministry, especially over its failure to make any significant concessions over what to many squires was the key issue, the appointment of substantial numbers of Tory magistrates. Hitherto only leading Tories like Sir John himself and Sir Watkin Williams Wynn had been magistrates. On 8 March Sir John submitted to Lord Chancellor Hardwicke lists of proposed magistrates for Cardiganshire, Carmarthenshire, Haverfordwest, and Pembrokeshire, a total of 96 names.[39] Twelve days later the Duke of Beaufort warned Hardwicke of the unease among Tory peers and squires that nothing had been done for 'the six counties', lists having been submitted also for Denbighshire and Montgomeryshire by Sir Watkin. He asked that new commissions be issued for them 'for the present, as an earnest of what should be done in other counties', with a clear threat that otherwise 'the coalition' would be broken off.[40] It may already have been too late, for on 22 March over one hundred Tories voted in the Commons against the ministry, and only about forty for.[41] The Pelham cabinet made no attempt to save the situation, resolving on 5 April only that 'when any new commissions of the peace shall be issued, all proper regard shall be had to gentlemen of figure and fortune, well affected to His Majesty's

---

[34] Cobbett, *Parl. Hist.*, XIII, 1125.
[35] Cobbett, *Parl. Hist.*, XIII, 1201–2.
[36] BL Add. MSS 35337, f. 101.
[37] BL Add. MSS 35337, ff. 101–3.
[38] Walpole, *Corr.,* XIX, 26–7.
[39] BL Add. MSS 35602, ff. 38–45.
[40] BL Add. MSS 35602, ff. 46, 54.
[41] BL Add. MSS 32804, ff. 286–7.

Government, without distinction of parties'.[42] This concession of principle, without any practical implementation, did not suffice to prevent the mass return of Tories to opposition.

The episode, moreover, had weakened Tory morale. Many were cynical about the way some of their leading spokesmen had sought office at the first opportunity. One such was George Barlow, who had succeeded Sir Erasmus Philipps as Haverfordwest MP. Early in 1745 he commented to John Campbell 'that Sir J.P. and some others having accepted places had made him think very differently of politics from what he did before; he thought it was plain they only opposed in order to get the places they now had'.[43] That was a harsh judgement on Sir John himself, but damage had been done. And for Tories matters went from bad to worse. The Forty-Five Rising gave parliamentary opposition in the session of 1745–6 the taint of disloyalty, though that did not deter Philipps. In the debate of 17 October on the Address he complained of 'the arbitrary power established in our present Royal Family and supported by a corrupt Parliament and a mercenary standing army'. He was answered by George Lyttelton, who spoke pointedly of 'concealed Jacobites' arousing animosity against the government, and the Address passed without a vote.[44] Sir John was one of nine Tories appointed to a Commons Committee that ordered the Pretender's Proclamation to be burnt.[45] But after that public demonstration of loyalty he obstructed emergency measures to meet the crisis. On 1 November Sir John so vehemently opposed the suggestion that several noblemen should raise regiments to counter the rebellion, calling the proposal 'a job', that William Pitt reprimanded him for 'such coarseness of language'.[46] Nevertheless, on 4 November Philipps objected to the subsequent motion for finance to cover the costs incurred.[47]

The consolidation of the Pelham ministry during February 1746 enabled the administration to dispense with the need for Tory support, though Philipps scored a debating point off Pitt, now in office, for his change of opinion when finance for Hanoverian soldiers was again voted, on 11 April.[48] More directly damaging to the Tories were the suspicions and revelations of involvement in Jacobite plotting. Although Philipps was not personally involved in any such accusations, Horace Walpole a few years

---

[42] BL Add. MSS 35602, ff. 50–1.
[43] NLW General MSS 1352, f. 256.
[44] Almon, *Debates*, II, 336–9, 343.
[45] Colley, *Defiance of Oligarchy*, p. 251.
[46] Walpole, *Corr.*, XXVI, 13–19.
[47] Almon, *Debates*, II, 386–90; Coxe, *Pelham Administration*, I, 277.
[48] Owen, *Rise of the Pelhams*, p. 306.

later put forward this explanation as to why he left the Commons at the general election of 1747.

> Sir John was a man of worse character than parts, though they were not shining. He had quitted Parliament on the desperate situation of the Jacobite cause, after having attempted during the last Rebellion to get the Subscriptions and Associations for the King declared illegal; and was now retired to Oxford, the sanctuary of disaffection.[49]

Sir John certainly did decide to quit Parliament, for the *London Evening Post* of 25 June 1747 announced that he had declined to stand for any constituency, even though he had been invited to contest Westminster. In his native Pembrokeshire he preferred to help William Owen of Orielton to turn out John Campbell rather than seek the county seat himself. Neither had he intended to defend his seat for Carmarthen, where in any case his Whig opponents had won control the previous year. It was a piquant touch that he should be replaced by Admiral Thomas Mathews, for Sir John had taken part in a parliamentary vendetta against him in 1745. Mathews, obnoxious to Welsh Tories as victor in the bitter Glamorgan by-election of January that year, had been vulnerable as commander of the British fleet at an unsuccessful battle off Toulon in 1744. During the parliamentary inquiry into this setback it was Philipps who on 12 March proposed that Mathews be examined, and on 10 April he spoke in favour of a court martial.[50]

Sir John Philipps may have temporarily quitted Parliament, but he remained an active and prominent politician in several spheres of activity. It must have been about this time that he sent to the Pretender the assurance of support mentioned by a Jacobite agent in 1749 – a singular piece of mis-timing and a move apparently not followed up by any further action.[51] Philipps now became involved in London politics, being so prominent in 1748 in metropolitan agitation against a Bill to naturalize foreign Protestants that a pamphlet on the subject was addressed to him personally.[52] Sir John never lost his London connections. Shortly before his death he spoke, on 27 January and 16 March 1764, in favour of an unsuccessful City of London petition for money to complete London Bridge.[53]

---

[49] Walpole, *Memoirs of George II*, I, 114.
[50] Cobbett, *Parl. Hist.*, XIII, 1250–4, 1268.
[51] Stuart MSS 301/5.
[52] Sedgwick, *House of Commons 1715–1754*, II, 345.
[53] Malmesbury MSS, Harris Diary, 27 January, 16 March, 1764.

Nor was Philipps out of the national scene. Towards the end of 1748 he was involved in Tory negotiations for a parliamentary opposition alliance with the Prince of Wales.[54] A list for a new Parliament on the Prince's accession, drawn up soon afterwards by Lord Egmont, therefore assumed that Philipps, whose election for Haverfordwest was anticipated, would be 'for a time with us - he talks loudly for us now'.[55] Nothing came of this planning, as the Prince predeceased his father, in 1751.

In 1751 Sir John re-assumed his legal persona to move successfully in the Court of King's Bench for a writ of habeas corpus for one Alexander Murray, a former Jacobite agent, who had been committed to Newgate Prison by the House of Commons for contempt, his refusal to kneel at the Bar of the House, in circumstances arising out of a bitterly fought Westminster by-election of the previous year.[56] His speech was published as a pamphlet, The Argument of Sir John Philipps, Bart.[57] According to Horace Walpole, then an MP, 'there was a disposition' in the House of Commons to commit to prison also 'my worthy cousin Sir John Philipps' for his temerity in implicitly challenging its authority.[58]

During these years Philipps developed a connection with the Beckford brothers, also busy in London politics. The eldest, William, held political opinions, variously deemed Tory or radical by historians, similar to those of Sir John. Inheritor of a West Indies fortune, William Beckford had entered Parliament in 1747 as MP for Shaftesbury, but had since played such an influential role in City politics that he was to sit as MP for London from 1754 until his death in 1770. It was in association with the Beckfords that Sir John in 1754 brought an unsuccessful legal action against Princess Amelia, a daughter of George II, for closing Richmond Park to the public, thereby 'presenting themselves as tribunes of the people', as Horace Walpole caustically commented.[59]

This Beckford link was to be important in facilitating Sir John's return to Parliament in 1754. Meanwhile he engaged in high-profile politics in both Oxford and Pembrokeshire as well as London. He was present in Oxford to receive a D.C.L. at the opening of the Radcliffe Camera in 1749; but he did not live there as much as Horace Walpole had suggested. Sir John's

---

[54] Coxe, *Pelham Administration*, II, 50; Walpole, *Corr.,* XX, 3.

[55] Newman (ed.), 'Leicester House Politics', *Camden Miscellany,* XXIII, p. 165.

[56] Thomas, *House of Commons*, pp. 337–8; Sedgwick, *House of Commons 1715–1754*, I, 287. See *Grenville Papers*, III, clxviii note, for an account of this celebrated case sent by Philipps to Lord Temple in about 1763. The Court granted the writ, but sent Murray back to Newgate because his committal was for contempt of Parliament. For the episode, see Almon, *Debates,* IV, 238–46.

[57] Colley, *Defiance of Oligarchy*, p. 337.

[58] Walpole, *Corr.,* XX, 249–50.

[59] Walpole, *Memoirs of George II*, I, 402.

personal papers show that he spent most of his time in Pembrokeshire, as the leading personality in the Society of Sea Serjeants.[60] These multifarious activities made him an idol of those opposed to the Whig ministry, and he was the candidate chosen by the Tory Steadfast Society of Bristol to fight their borough in 1754.

The outcome of the ensuing contest was unlucky for Philipps. The Bristol Tories were seeking both seats, their second candidate being Richard Beckford, absent in Jamaica but with brother William running his campaign, while the rival Whig organization of the Union Club sponsored Robert Nugent. The Bristol Whigs evidently regarded Philipps as the more obnoxious of their two opponents, and made much of the alleged Jacobitism of the Sea Serjeants, of the role Sir John had played in the Murray case, and even of his supposedly pro-Jacobite record in the Forty-Five. With only one candidate and marginally superior in numbers, the Bristol Whigs could decide which Tory would be elected, and opted for Beckford, in defiance of the pressure of the Duke of Newcastle, now head of the ministry on the death of his brother Henry Pelham. The Duke had informed George II, 'As I find all the Whigs wish to have Sir John Philipps, a broken Jacobite, rather than Mr Beckford, a wild West Indian, I have humbly presumed to say that Your Majesty would not be against it'. The King endorsed this preference, 'You did very right my Lord, to declare for Sir John Philipps against Beckford'.[61] Josiah Tucker, the leading Whig election manager, commented privately that 'it would be quite inconsistent in us first to rouse the people against Philipps as a Jacobite and then choose him ourselves'.[62] At the poll Nugent had 2,592 votes, Beckford 2,245, and Philipps 2,160. However, all was to be well for Sir John. William Beckford, unsure of election for London, had also secured a seat for the Hampshire burgage borough of Petersfield. This Philipps now inherited, as the Steadfast Society paid William Beckford £2,200 on his behalf. Sir John had been their first choice, and they wanted him in the Commons for their own purposes. The Duke of Newcastle was told that 'great matters are to be brought on . . . this Parliament in regard to commerce so as to make Sir John's having a seat in it, necessary in several capacities'.[63] The backbone of the Steadfast Society was the Society of Merchant Venturers, and it was to be on their behalf that Philipps in February 1755 unsuccessfully proposed the abolition of the press-gang system that raided merchant crews to man

---

[60] Picton Castle MSS 591. Account Book of Sir John Philipps, 1746–1763.
[61] BL Add. MSS 32735, f. 50. The King put 'not' after 'right', but this would seem to be confusion of mind or error of writing.'
[62] BL Add. MSS 4319, ff. 246–7.
[63] BL Add. MSS 32736, f. 139.

the Royal Navy.[64] In the previous month Philipps and the Beckfords vainly opposed a Bristol Night Watch Bill, because it gave too much power to the Whig corporation.[65]

The parliamentary scene to which Sir John Philipps had returned was very different from the one he had left only seven years before. Jacobitism was dead, and the political atmosphere was dominated by the contest with France for trade and empire. That was an issue over which even independent MPs of Tory tradition could support administration; but on 25 March 1755 Sir John Philipps and William Beckford opposed a vote of credit.[66] That may have been simply a reaction against a procedural device of which Philipps always disapproved. But it was apparent that warm Tory support even for a French war would be conditional on a shift of policy away from a continental campaign, a change being urged by William Pitt.

In 1755 Tories had matters of more immediate interest to engage their attention, two election cases being disputed in the Commons. In the celebrated Oxfordshire matter, the Tories fought a long and unsuccessful struggle against the Whig majority. Sir John was a close friend of the Tory candidates and spoke up for their cause in debate.[67] The other contest, over the Mitchell borough election, offered the Tories a rare opportunity to deploy their voting strength, for the Whig majority was split between Commons Leader Henry Fox and Prime Minister Newcastle. Sir John Philipps, at a private meeting of Tory MPs, suggested the anti-Whig stroke of voiding the election by voting against each pair of candidates in turn. The meeting refused to endorse this plan, deciding to judge the case on its merits, and Sir John's persistence with his idea was defeated in the House.[68] Once again his partisan zeal went too far even for his fellow Tories.

The next year saw the political change that finally altered Sir John's parliamentary stance. William Pitt became virtual head of the ministry as Southern Secretary in November 1756, as the Duke of Devonshire took the Treasury when Newcastle resigned amid a catalogue of war disasters. Philipps and Beckford were the most important of the independents, styled Tories by Newcastle and Horace Walpole, who flocked to support a ministry with an apparently more patriotic policy. Philipps wrote to Pitt on 21 November, presumably a pledge of support.[69] Pitt needed the backing of such men, for Newcastle remained effective master of the Commons. Care

---

[64] Colley, *Defiance of Oligarchy*, p. 140.
[65] Cobbett, *Parl. Hist.*, XV, 470–5.
[66] BL Add. MSS 32853, f. 480.
[67] Robson, *Oxfordshire Election*, pp. 8, 109, 139, 166.
[68] Clark, *Dynamics of Change*, pp. 146–7, quoting the diary of Sir Roger Newdigate.
[69] Picton Castle MSS 572, p. 131. Sir John Philipps's Letter–Book, 17 August 1753–21 December 1756. There is no indication of the letter's content, and no record of any reply or other such letters.

was therefore taken to show Philipps the King's Speech on the morning of 2 December, before it was read out to Parliament that afternoon, a formal courtesy and not a genuine consultation.[70] Two days later, Sir John was one of eleven Tory MPs who, with two peers, signed a circular asking their political friends to attend Parliament.[71]

Even after Pitt's parliamentary weakness was remedied by his coalition with Newcastle in the summer of 1757, he deemed it expedient to cater for the personal needs and political whims of the independent MPs of Tory lineage now in the unfamiliar guise of ministerial supporters. Although Pitt himself was notorious for his lack of hospitality, Sir John was entertained to dinner during the ensuing session by two of his friends, Lord Lyttelton on 19 December 1757 and Lord Temple on 12 February 1758.[72] Soon afterwards the same social device was employed to resolve a political crisis, after Pitt had signed a subsidy treaty with Britain's new ally Prussia. Tory indignation threatened a Commons revolt against this, headed by Philipps, who was already disgruntled over the failure of a Shorter Parliaments Bill moved on 20 February by Sir John Glynne. Philipps had spoken in favour of annual elections when seconding this, and the ministry had rejected such an extreme proposal, though Pitt had taken care to absent himself. Philipps and Beckford were invited to dine with Pitt's brothers-in-law, Lord Temple and George Grenville, on 15 April, and a few days later the Commons agreed to the Prussian subsidy without a vote.[73]

At the beginning of the next session, on 23 November, Philipps was appointed to the Committee that drafted the Commons Address welcoming the Prussian alliance, though he made a gibe against Newcastle by expressing the hope that 'no ministry would ever rob us' of Cape Breton, the island restored to France by the Duke at the peace of 1748 and now again conquered.[74] Horace Walpole noted other occasions when Philipps did not scruple to embarrass ministers. In March 1758 he complained of the cost of work carried out at Gibraltar. In March 1759 he accused Pitt of favouring Hanover. In November of that year he complained of the expense and patronage involved in the creation of new militia regiments, and in December drew attention to George II's parsimony.[75]

This behaviour did not inhibit Sir John from making patronage requests, now that he was a supporter of government. On 24 June 1757 he solicited

---

[70] *Grenville Papers*, I, 184.
[71] Colley, *Defiance of Oligarchy*, pp. 277–8.
[72] Picton Castle MSS 589.
[73] Colley, *Defiance of Oligarchy*, pp. 75–6, 282–4.
[74] Walpole, *Memoirs of George II*, III, 150; *CJ*, XXVIII, 318.
[75] Walpole, *Memoirs of George II*, III, 109, 179, 233–4, 238.

George Grenville, then Treasurer of the Navy, concerning the appointment of a navy victualler at Milford Haven.[76] On 6 August Sir John thanked Pitt himself for having acceded to an unknown request, expressing the hope that the war would go better under Pitt's guidance.[77] His most important application to Pitt, on 29 April 1761, was that he should press the First Lord of the Admiralty, Lord Anson, to fulfil a promise made to 'the gentlemen of Wales about a year ago' that a large naval ship would be built in Milford Haven.[78] Philipps was evidently successful in his request, for construction of a ship-of-the-line, to carry 74 guns, commenced there shortly afterwards. In 1762 Sir John obtained the consent of the then Prime Minister Lord Bute that it would be named *The Prince of Wales*, 'being the first ship of that magnitude built in Wales, set in the stocks about the time his Royal Highness the Prince of Wales was born, and built chiefly of Welsh timber'. But on a visit to Milford in 1763 Sir John discovered that the name had been changed to *Hibernia*, a decision he supposed to have been made by the new First Lord of the Admiralty Lord Egmont, and which on 2 August 1763 he asked Lord Bute to have reversed.[79] It would seem that the ship may never have been completed, for on 6 April 1764 parliamentary diarist James Harris noted 'a talk about Milford Haven. £27,000 had been laid out there, and nothing finished. Sir J. Philipps moved it. After much talk, the affair was dropped, and nothing done.'[80]

Even when he was thus exploiting the patronage system of court politics Philipps retained the country party instincts to which Pitt had occasionally to pander. What especially characterized Sir John was his concern for the political power of the landed interest. In 1758 he was allowed to pass the Freeholders' Qualification Act. This measure, intended to restrict the county franchise to genuine freeholders, arose out of a Tory reaction against Whig deployment of copyholders in the 1754 Oxfordshire election.[81] Two years later, at the beginning of 1760, Philipps and Beckford demanded a further reward from Pitt. 'That they had supported the government and that they expected in return that something might be done for the country.' Their request was the revival of an idea advocated in the 1730s by Sir Watkin Williams Wynn, that the oath prescribed by the Landed Qualification Act of 1711 should be taken by MPs in the House of Commons as well as at the election. Pitt promised to support this, and

---

[76] BL Add. MSS 57820, ff. 142–3.
[77] PRO 30/8/52, ff. 89–90.
[78] PRO 30/8/52, ff. 94–5.
[79] Bute MSS(Cardiff), no. 99.
[80] Malmesbury MSS, Harris Diary, 6 April 1764.
[81] Almon, *Debates*, V, 222–3. For the background, see Colley, *Defiance of Oligarchy*, pp. 70–1, 284.

persuaded the Duke of Newcastle, well aware of George II's hostility to the measure, to permit its passage.[82] Pitt himself spoke for the Bill in a debate of 21 April after its committal had been moved by Philipps, who was 'willing to alter any part of it that should be found improper'. So Newcastle was informed by MP James West, who reported that Pitt had justified the measure as 'a small return to gentlemen who had assisted in all measures for support for their country in carrying on the war'.[83] Horace Walpole was characteristically sardonic about the whole episode.[84]

> A man, whose pretensions to virtue were as equivocal as Whitefield's to sanctity, took it upon him about this time to lay stricter obligations on Members of Parliament. The plan, like that of hypocrites of all denominations, was, by coining new occasions of guilt. Sir John Philipps brought a bill into the House of Commons, to oblige the Members to give in particulars of their qualifications, *and to swear to the truth of them*. A known Jacobite, who and whose friends had taken the oath to King George, ought to have been sensible that perjury was *not* the crime at which most men stuck in that age.

Sir John Philipps, quirky in behaviour and old-fashioned in his country attitude to government, had by now come to symbolize the independent MPs in the House of Commons. It was therefore Sir John who, seconded by Chancellor of the Exchequer Henry Legge, moved the official vote of thanks on 18 March 1761 to Speaker Arthur Onslow, retiring from the Chair after serving the House there throughout the reign of George II. Horace Walpole drily reported to a correspondent that Philipps had 'forgot his speech, and though in his hat, could not read it'.[85] In his subsequent memoirs Walpole recorded the scene more fully, that Sir John had moved the Address of Thanks 'so wretchedly, that the sensibility the House showed on the occasion flowed only from their hearts, not from any impression made on them by the eloquence of their spokesman'.[86]

The accession in 1760 of young George III created a new political climate, by ostentatious removal of the proscription of Tories from favour and office that had hitherto characterized the Hanoverian period, the 1744 negotiation having been unique in this respect. But during the Seven Years War these Tories, or independent country gentlemen as they themselves preferred to be designated, had already flocked to support Pitt. Not all

---

[82] *Devonshire Diary,* p. 35.
[83] BL Add. MSS 32905, ff. 14–16.
[84] Walpole, *Memoirs of George II*, III, 278–9.
[85] Walpole, *Corr.*, XXX, 164.
[86] Walpole, *Memoirs of George III*, I, 40.

transferred their allegiance to the new King's favourite Lord Bute when the time came to make a choice, in October 1761 when Pitt and Lord Temple resigned from the ministry over the Cabinet refusal to accept their demand for a Spanish war. That Sir John then stayed with Pitt is the implication of a conversation with George Grenville, who had remained in government to replace Pitt as Commons Leader, that Lord Hardwicke reported to the Duke of Newcastle on 15 October. 'Mr G . . . did not imagine that Mr. Pitt would have any great following of the Tories, that Ald. Beckford and Sir John Philipps pretended to answer for them, but could not.'[87] Before the end of the year, George III gleefully believed Sir John was no longer a Pitt man:[88] but the reports of his speeches during the session of 1761–2 throw no light on his political allegiance. On 18 November he proposed a Committee to consider methods of enforcing an earlier start to the Parliamentary day, and returned to the same theme on 4 December. On 18 November, in a debate on army estimates, Philipps obtained an assurance that soldiers in Britain would be distinguished from those in Germany. Twice he spoke in favour of a Militia Bill, on 14 December 1761 and 12 March 1762.[89] None of these topics were matters of controversy as between administration and opposition. All were of concern to country squires, who would, for example, welcome an earlier parliamentary hour than office-holders or merchants.

Whether or not Sir John's allegiance to Lord Bute was merely unrecorded before, it became manifest when Bute became Prime Minister in May 1762; for on 23 May Philipps wrote to him this adulatory letter which is a classic revelation of how and why independent country gentlemen chose to support the new King and his chosen minister as men who would clean up the old Whig system of corruption.

> I look on your Lordship as our Guardian Angel; you my Lord, by dispensing your favours to those who only merit them, by firm but economical measures, by encouraging enquiries into past extravagancies, and by your own good and great example, will check that spirit of venality that has so long fatally prevailed, and restore that confidence which ought always to subsist between the King and his People.[90]

Bute replied that it was his duty to save the kingdom from ruin.[91]

---

[87] BL Add. MSS 32929, f. 332.

[88] BL Add. MSS 32932, ff. 82–3.

[89] Malmesbury MSS, Harris Diary, 14 December 1761, 12 March 1762. Philipps also spoke on the Lichfield election, 1 February, 1762; an infant mortality Bill, 4 February, and the Bridport election, 2 March.

[90] Bute MSS (Cardiff), unnumbered.

[91] BL Add. MSS 36796, f. 143.

Philipps was now high in favour with the new regime. Two days later, the *London Chronicle* named him as one of seven expected new peers.[92] That rumour was false, but his standing with the Bute ministry was signified by his choice as seconder of the Address when the new parliamentary session began in November. Lord Temple made this sharp comment on this news about 'that quintessence of dulness, Sir J.P.; which shall I admire most, his dulness, or the infamy of standing out foremost in the support of B-'.[93] But Philipps became ill and could not perform the duty, as Bute informed his Commons Leader Henry Fox on 23 November. 'Sir John Philipps is grown worse, and cannot come to town. This is very unlucky.'[94] Lord Temple thereupon erroneously deduced a change of mind. 'Sir John is again grown, in my opinion, a man of some parts, and even vivacity, from not seconding the motion.'[95]

Sir John Philipps was soon afterwards offered junior ministerial office, as a Lord of the Admiralty, with a promise of promotion to the first vacancy at the Treasury Board.[96] He refused the post, but accepted the honour of appointment to the Privy Council, being sworn in on 10 January 1763.[97] Symptomatic of Sir John's transformation into a supporter of government was his behaviour when an issue was revived on which he had spoken in 1758. On 11 February in that year the Commons had debated the Spanish seizure in 1756 of a British ship, the *Anti-Gallican*, and Philipps had then favoured a strongly-worded resolution.[98] Now, when the same matter was raised on 7 February 1763 by an opposition MP, it was Philipps who promptly moved an adjournment to prevent discussion, agreeing to withdraw it only in order to ensure its rejection instead.[99]

Later in the session Sir John apparently gave support to the controversial cider tax, despite its unpopularity in south Wales as well as south-west England. Journalist John Almon records the story that Bute vainly sought to appease the City of London by authorizing Philipps to promise repeal of the tax the next year.[100] There is no report of any speech by Sir John on the tax, but on his journey back to Pembrokeshire for the summer he was mobbed at Monmouth, reporting afterwards to Bute:[101]

[92] Walpole, *Corr.*, XXXVIII, 159.
[93] *Grenville Papers*, II, 6.
[94] BL Add. MSS 51379, f. 113.
[95] *Grenville Papers*, II, 8.
[96] BL Add. MSS 32946, ff. 104–5.
[97] Picton Castle MSS 125, 589.
[98] BL Add. MSS 32877, ff. 422–3.
[99] Malmesbury MSS, Harris Diary, 7 February 1763.
[100] Almon, *Chatham Anecdotes*, I, 370.
[101] Bute MSS (Cardiff), no. 99.

I had the honour to be burnt in effigy with your Lordship at Monmouth. It gave me no concern, except the fright it put my wife and daughter into, by breaking the windows of the house and keeping an uproar all night.

But if Sir John now incurred unpopularity as a government supporter, his 'country' heart still beat inside his 'court' exterior. Already on 2 February 1763 he had objected to an increase of the navy estimate, even though it was incurred by the expense of laying up ships at the end of the war.[102] He then decided on a parliamentary initiative likely to embarrass members of the administration and opposition alike. This was for a Commission on Public Accounts, a clumsy and antiquated procedure of a permanent body that had long since been replaced by Commons Committees of Inquiry. When his intention became known, at the beginning of February, it seemed to the Duke of Newcastle to confirm his long-held suspicion that Bute would seek to embarrass him by an enquiry into the financial management of the Seven Years War.[103] But the idea was that of Sir John himself, who, after he gave notice of his intention in the House of Commons on 7 February, sent a message to Newcastle, by way of Lord Barrington, disavowing any personal motives.

I beg leave to assure your Lordship that my motion is not levelled at any particular person or persons, minister or ministers, and so I shall acquaint the House. But I think Parliament is and ought to be a check on all Ministers, and those who have the disposition of public money, granted by Parliament, are accountable to it for such money. I have no reason to suspect the noble Duke... of any misapplication of public money. But as the sums expended are very large and the accounts not explicit, many gentlemen think it necessary, they should in several instances be explained.[104]

Such unexceptionable sentiments put the ministry in a predicament. Refusal to permit the inquiry would offend many independent MPs, and the principle accorded with the King's professed aim of honest and efficient government. But George III himself thought Sir John's proposal 'very silly';[105] and Leader of the House Henry Fox feared an investigation into his own accounts as Paymaster of the Forces during the Seven Years War. It was too late to prevent Sir John's motion on 11 February, as Fox

[102] Malmesbury MSS, Harris Diary, 2 February 1763.
[103] BL Add. MSS 32944, f. 364; 32947, f. 182.
[104] BL Add. MSS 32946, f. 369.
[105] *Bute Papers*, p. 190.

evidently hoped to do.[106] Philipps then produced precedents for the reigns of William III and Anne, and despite doubts raised by both ministerial and opposition speakers, only John Campbell was against proceeding.[107] On 22 February Sir John formally moved the appointment of a Commission to examine the public accounts of the previous twenty years, but in the course of a long debate he was persuaded by his friend Sir Francis Dashwood, a country gentleman who was then Chancellor of the Exchequer, to accept instead a Committee of Inquiry.[108]

The next day Dashwood proposed, on the argument of efficacy, a Select Committee chosen by ballot.[109] This decision accomplished the ministerial aim of neutering Sir John's initiative, while accepting the principle of accountability. The Committee chosen on 1 March corresponded exactly with a Treasury list, and achieved no more than examination of the finance of the Board of Ordnance.[110] In the following session, on 27 January 1764, Philipps moved to revive the Select Committee, and it was re-appointed with the same membership after George Grenville, by then Prime Minister, had seconded Sir John: but this concurrence was even more of a token gesture.[111]

While the Bute ministry had been seeking to resolve that problem, Sir John started another 'country' hare, also with a political pedigree dating back to at least the seventeenth century – the fear of a large standing army as a perceived threat to liberty. On 17 February Philipps sent a long letter to Bute, writing as a loyal supporter to warn him that the projected size of the peacetime army had aroused just such an apprehension.

Nothing but the strict duty I owe to, and cordial affection I have for, his Majesty, and my profound regard for your Lordship, could induce me to take this liberty with you. The proposed regulation of the army I find gives very great uneasiness to many Members of Parliament with whom I have conversed, as they judge it unconstitutional to keep up an army consisting of so large a number of corps in time of peace, a measure they have always opposed and therefore cant think of giving their assent to now.

The army proposed, almost double that of any previous force 'in time of peace, and of such a peace that is so likely to continue', would, Sir John

---

[106] Bute MSS (Cardiff), no. 125.
[107] Malmesbury MSS, Harris Diary, 11 February 1763.
[108] Malmesbury MSS, Harris Diary, 22 February 1763.
[109] Malmesbury MSS, Harris Diary, 23 February 1763; BL Add. MSS 32947, f. 88.
[110] BL Add. MSS 32947, ff. 138–40, 176; 32948, f. 42; *Bedford Papers*, III, 220.
[111] Malmesbury MSS, Harris Diary, 27 January 1764; BL Add. MSS 32955, f. 277.

feared, be thought a design by George III 'to make himself an absolute monarch and your lordship an absolute minister'. Philipps then pitched the issue very high. 'I look upon this to be the very crisis of your Lordship's administration, and indeed of his Majesty's Government.'[112] The King's private comment to Bute on all this nonsense was scathing.

I am not in the least surprised at the attack of Sir J. Philipps. It is very like him. If government is to yield in everything to men who only rebel because they have never been accustomed to act by any rule but passion, tis not worth while to consider two minutes what is to be done. I deny every reason Sir John gives.[113]

Bute nevertheless had to pay heed to Sir John's prejudices, and in his reply on 23 February stated that the size of the army had now been reduced. 'I yield respecting your opinion, and that of your friends, but I am by no means convinced by any argument I have heard.'[114] This soft answer turned away Sir John's wrath. At a meeting of ministers and country gentlemen next day, Philipps and all but one of the other squires present accepted the reduced army estimates.[115] When they were proposed to the Commons on 4 March Sir John spoke warmly in support, extolling the ministry's economy to his fellow squires.[116]

A month later George Grenville was appointed Prime Minister on the surprise resignation of Lord Bute, and Sir John Philipps was among those who feared that he lacked the ability and experience to survive against an opposition comprising the factions of both William Pitt and the Duke of Newcastle. He took literally his duty as a Privy Councillor to advise the King, sending Grenville himself an account of how at 'a private audience of his Majesty' he had warned George III against reliance on the opposition groups. 'His Majesty said he was sensible of the truth of what I told him, . . . and when I took my leave His Majesty said, Remember, Sir John, when you see me next, you will find me the same firm man you leave me.' It was therefore with concern that during the summer Philipps, home at Picton Castle, heard the news that George III was negotiating with Pitt, and he expressed satisfaction to Grenville when he knew that Prime Minister was to remain in office.[117]

---

[112] Bute MSS (Cardiff), no. 98.
[113] Bute MSS (Cardiff), no. 274.
[114] BL Add. MSS 36797, f. 34.
[115] *Bute Letters*, p. 191.
[116] Nicholas, 'Lord Bute's Ministry, 1762–3', Ph.D. Wales, 1987, p. 301.
[117] *Grenville Papers*, II, 117–19.

Now safe at Court, Grenville next faced a major challenge in Parliament over the ramifications of the *North Briton* case. On 23 April, in the forty-fifth issue of that weekly paper, John Wilkes had seemingly libelled the King. Most MPs were not concerned about the personal fate of the dissolute Wilkes, and Sir John still bore resentment for a personal attack on himself in an earlier issue. Having believed himself on friendly terms with Wilkes, Sir John had been so upset as to ask him publicly in the House of Commons whether he had written the offending piece, receiving a negative answer.[118] But considerable alarm had been aroused by the threat to individual personal liberty implied by the use of a general warrant to arrest Wilkes and his associates, for this device permitted the seizure of unnamed persons. An early indication of unease over this matter among independent MPs occurred on 23 November, when Sir John Philipps was among those voting against the ministry.[119] Early in 1764 the issue became the centre of dispute, and on 6 February Philipps condemned the use of general warrants in principle. Charles Townshend, that famous maverick politician, waxed sarcastic on Sir John's new 'zeal for liberty', reminding MPs of his role in the Murray case of 1751.[120] By 17 February the Grenville ministry faced the prospect of parliamentary defeat. Philipps may well have been its saviour, for near the end of the debate he promised MPs that he would introduce legislation on the matter. Even so, Grenville won by only fourteen votes, 232 to 218, in a division for which Sir John acted as a ministerial teller.[121] Four days later Philipps introduced a Bill to limit the use of general warrants, having taken prior advice from Grenville; but he met such a cool reception that he withdrew the proposal. Opposition journalist John Almon deemed it 'a sham offer' by a ministerial dupe.[122]

That was Sir John's last political action of note, for he 'died suddenly' on 23 June 1764.[123] To the end he remained a mixture of new courtier and old Tory. He was high in favour with the government of George III: 'Sir John Philipps was well with Mr. Grenville', Lord Holland reminded John Campbell in November.[124] Lord Bute referred to Philipps as having been 'a very warm friend of mine and who I knew to be zealously devoted to the King, and who was greatly esteemed by him for this reason'.[125] Yet his older Tory roots remained. Still a member of the Loyal Brotherhood, it was as

---

[118] BL Add. MSS 30867, f. 219.

[119] Fortescue, *Corr. of George III*, I, 62; Walpole, *Memoirs of George III*, I, 258.

[120] Malmesbury MSS, Harris Diary, 6 February 1764; Walpole, *Memoirs of George III*, I, 283.

[121] Malmesbury MSS, Harris Diary, 17 February 1764.

[122] Malmesbury MSS, Harris Diary, 21 February 1764; Almon, *Debates*, VI, 292–3.

[123] Dynevor MSS Parcel Four, A. Davids to [G. Rice], 28 June 1764.

[124] BL Add. MSS 51406, ff. 81–2.

[125] Bute MSS (Cardiff), no. 599.

that club's registrar that in 1764 he informed Sir John Glynne of his admission to the society.[126] And almost his last known move was his key role in obtaining a pension of £200 from the Grenville ministry for Dr John Shebbeare, a political journalist notorious in the reign of George II for his anti-government writing: he had been once sentenced to the pillory and twice sent to prison. But in the new political climate other such writers as Samuel Johnson and Tobias Smollett had already obtained financial rewards before a memorial signed by fourteen MPs asked Grenville on 29 February that Shebbeare be given a similar recompense to those given to the other 'men of letters'. Philipps was one of them, and followed up this plea by successful lobbying.[127]

Back home in Wales Sir John Philipps had been president of the Society of Sea Serjeants since 1752.[128] But in the last decade its political edge had become dulled, with Serjeants sometimes at odds with each other in parliamentary elections. The last known meeting of the Society, at Pembroke in July 1763, epitomized the change in political atmosphere since 1726, the year of its foundation and of Sir John's emergence as an active politician. It was attended by the leading local Whig, Sir William Owen of Orielton; and the range of toasts offered shows how far the members, like Philipps himself, had departed from their old 'country' principles. Sir John gave Lord Bute as his toast, and another member William Pitt, the great war hero. But old Tory prejudices were still reflected in spontaneous protests at the names of such partisan Whig leaders as the Duke of Devonshire and Lord Temple, while that of John Wilkes was simply deemed unacceptable.[129]

Sir John Philipps was one of the foremost Welsh politicians of the eighteenth century. His role as a spokesman for independent MPs gave him consequence, and in the last decade of his life made him a man to whom ministers had to pay ostentatious attention, whatever their private opinions of his out-of-date attitudes, doubtless much the same as that of George III, 'silly'. Whig contemporaries dubbed him a Tory on account of his Jacobite label. He was a leading figure among the loose grouping of independent MPs, of country attitude, many of Tory family tradition, though Philipps himself was not, that some modern historians have dubbed a Tory party. But the career of Sir John Philipps, a man determined to go his own way, and often more extreme than most in attitude and behaviour, weakens rather than strengthens the idea of any such entity.

---

[126] Glynne of Hawarden MSS 561.

[127] *Grenville Papers*, II, 270–1.

[128] His account–book shows how he personally financed the meetings. Picton Castle MSS 591.

[129] BL Add. MSS 30867, f. 218.

CHAPTER 9

A New Political Era? (1760–1789)

T HE accession of George III in 1760 no longer possesses the key political significance that it once did. Much of the change formerly attributed to that event had already happened. The mid-century instability of government began not with a new sovereign supposedly determined to rule himself but at the death in 1754 of Henry Pelham. It was in 1756 that opposition MPs labelled Tory by supporters of administration rallied to the support of Pitt as war minister. Men like Sir John Philipps were seeking and receiving favours before the new young King made it clear that there was no longer any proscription of such 'country' gentlemen from the patronage system.

Nevertheless the arrival on the throne of a young sovereign determined to play a more positive role than his grandfather did alter the rules of the political game, and one immediate consequence of the change of sovereign was the importance of Lord Bute, the new King's favourite, for he personified the extra dimension added to the political scene by the determination of George III to have a say in the appointment of his ministers. The Duke of Newcastle remained First Lord of the Treasury until May 1762, and managed the general election of 1761, which in many respects was conducted as before. Lord Powis supervised matters for government in north Wales and Shropshire, writing to Newcastle on 25 September 1760,

> as to elections, the event of them, in all those places, where I am concerned will put matters on the same footing they are now, in respect to members for the ensuing Parliament, I know of no difference as yet, nor do I apprehend any.[1]

---

[1] BL Add. MSS 32912, ff. 106–7.

That was too sanguine an approach. Newcastle had to take cognisance of Bute's wishes, and politicians often turned to the new sun, by-passing the Duke by direct applications to Lord Bute for appointments or electoral assistance. One Welsh politician who had a foot in both Newcastle and Bute camps was George Rice. He was already the ministry's political manager for south Wales, and in December 1760 sent Newcastle a survey of the electoral situation in thirteen constituencies there, those exclusive of Monmouthshire.[2] But in 1756 he had married a daughter of Lord Talbot of Hensol, a man high in favour at the Leicester House court of the then Prince of Wales, and now named at his accession as Lord Steward of the Royal Household. George Rice himself was appointed to the Board of Trade and Plantations in 1761, and even when he moved to a Court office in 1770 as Treasurer of the Chamber remained one of the government's colonial experts. Another Welsh MP also appointed to be a Lord of Trade at the behest of Lord Bute was Sir Edmond Thomas of Wenvoe, who was now chosen for Glamorgan. Formerly, when MP for Chippenham, an official in the households successively of the new King's father and mother, and out of Parliament since 1754, Thomas canvassed his native county in 1759, with the support of Lord Talbot and of Sir Charles Tynte. He was confident of success even before the change of sovereign assured him of official support, and Thomas Mathews, who had at first intended to defend his seat, withdrew a month before the election.[3]

His electoral success owed little to Bute, and neither was the royal favourite's influence necessarily decisive in the success in Radnorshire of another former Leicester House partisan Lord Carnarvon, son of the Duke of Chandos. He had long resented the lack of regard for his claims to the shire seat and the county lieutenancy, both of which had gone to Howell Gwynne in 1755, and as early as 1756 had told Newcastle that he would fight the next election there.[4] Now in November 1760 he informed the Duke that his Radnorshire candidature had George III's approval. He secured the support of Lord Oxford, and threatened Thomas Lewis with a wealthy candidate for the borough. George Rice offered to act as intermediary, and the Duke of Newcastle and Lord Powis, who regarded himself as Gwynne's patron, put forward a compromise proposal in December; that Lord Carnarvon could have the shire seat if Gwynne was given a parliamentary seat elsewhere and Lewis met with no opposition in the borough.[5] But Lord Carnarvon held out for the lieutenancy, and not until 2 March, after a series of meetings involving Newcastle and Bute, was

[2] BL Add. MSS 32916, ff. 404–5.
[3] Kemys Tynte MSS 1/86, 87.
[4] BL Add. MSS 32861, f. 481; 32862, f. 3.
[5] BL Add. MSS 32918, f. 200.

it agreed that Gwynne should retain this for five years. Carnarvon was then returned unopposed for Radnorshire, and Gwynne for Old Sarum, but the agreement came too late to prevent a borough contest. The candidate Lord Carnarvon had conjured up there, a London merchant Edward Lewis, who had recently bought the local estate of Downton, persisted in his challenge, being encouraged by Chase Price of Knighton, whose family were old rivals of that of Harpton. At the poll Edward Lewis obtained 544 votes and Thomas Lewis 513, and the result was a double return.[6] Edward Lewis afterwards sought Bute's help;[7] but that he was awarded the seat by the House of Commons was due to the professed unwillingness of Thomas Lewis to prolong local animosities by a tedious contest in the House. The real reason, he later told Newcastle, was the carelessness of Harpton partisans in not stamping burgess admissions.[8] Chase Price, moreover, retaliated against Lord Powis for his part in the Radnorshire compromise by setting up a candidate, an unidentified Governor Roberts, in his pocket borough of Montgomery: though no poll was forced against Richard Clive, the campaign caused Lord Powis trouble and expense.[9]

One current MP who would have been a Bute supporter had he not lost his Anglesey seat in 1761 was Sir Nicholas Bayly, once a follower of Frederick Prince of Wales, for Bute gave him the county lieutenancy, a new appointment.[10] Until 1760 it was anticipated that Bayly, as in 1754, would have little difficulty retaining his seat, with the support of the Dowager Lady Bulkeley of Baron Hill, against another challenge by Owen Meyrick of Bodorgan. But in the autumn of that year Bayly forfeited local goodwill by seducing the young sister of a local squire. Lady Bulkeley, anxious to deny the seat to Meyrick, chose as her candidate Hugh Owen, son of Pembrokeshire magnate Sir William Owen of Orielton, since the small Bodeon estate could not become the basis of any rival new interest, as Plas Newydd had done after Baron Hill support to Bayly from 1734. Contrary to expectations, Bayly persisted in his candidature, but shortly before the poll threw dice with Owen to decide which of them should fight Meyrick. Owen won the toss, but not all Bayly's supporters would vote for him, and Meyrick was elected by 202 votes to 160.[11]

It was not a good election for Orielton. In Pembrokeshire Sir John Philipps, aware that the Owen family would no longer have the support of

---

[6] *Gloucester Journal*, 7 April 1761.

[7] BL Add. MSS 5726, f. 205.

[8] BL Add. MSS 32932, f. 208; 32985, f. 413. For more detail on Radnorshire politics, see Namier, *Structure of Politics*, pp. 268–78.

[9] BL Add. MSS 32921, ff. 252–3, 268–9.

[10] Bute MSS (Cardiff), nos 14, 80.

[11] For details and documentation, see Thomas, 'The Rise of Plas Newydd', *WHR*, 16 (1992), 167–71.

government that had been so invaluable a buttress to their electoral interest since 1714, now decided to seek the county seat himself, and thereby launched an electoral rivalry of Orielton and Picton Castle that was to outlast the century. As a tactic to coerce Sir William Owen into surrendering the shire seat he had held since 1747, Sir John used the weapon Orielton always dreaded, the claim of Wiston to participate in the Pembroke Boroughs constituency. The man prepared to fire this weapon was that maverick politician Charles Townshend, later the Chancellor of the Exchequer who imposed the fateful tea tax on the American colonies. It so happened that Townshend had not yet found a seat for the general election, and that he was a friend of John Wogan, a Sea Serjeant and current patron of Wiston. Since Townshend had influential connections in government, and was prepared to spend lavishly in his quest for a seat, his prospective candidature was an alarming threat to the hitherto safe Owen hold on the constituency, which might be overthrown for ever if the right of Wiston was now established. Sir William Owen therefore capitulated. At a Pembrokeshire county meeting on 4 December 1760 the candidature of Sir John Philipps was proposed by Haverfordwest MP William Edwardes, seconded by Sir Thomas Stepney, endorsed by Sir William Owen, and unanimously accepted.[12] Stepney himself again sought the Carmarthen seat and asked Lord Bute for support, somewhat naively citing as a reference Lord Talbot, father-in-law of George Rice, the close ally of MP Griffith Philipps.[13] In the event Philipps sold the seat to Lord Verney, a wealthy Buckinghamshire landowner.[14]

Charles Townshend was not involved in this Pembrokeshire arrangement, and persisted in his borough candidature, despite efforts of Wogan and Sir John Philipps to deter him. Sir William Owen therefore asked Newcastle to dissuade him from his 'bad scheme' of creating 1,000 new voters at Wiston and establishing their validity by a decision of the House of Commons.[15] Townshend, already promised a safe government seat, expressed disapproval of the way in which he had been let down by his original sponsors but desisted from forcing a contest against Owen.[16]

Sir John Philipps, successful in his Pembrokeshire strategy, was outwitted in Cardiganshire. Here the obvious tactic of recreating the traditional Tory interest by an alliance of Gogerddan and Nanteos had been forestalled by the 1755 by-election coup of William Vaughan of Crosswood in joining with William Powell of Nanteos that had then

---

[12] *Public Ledger*, 11 December 1760.
[13] Bute MSS (Cardiff), no. 141.
[14] *Additional Grenville Papers*, p. 128.
[15] BL Add. MSS 32919, ff. 222–3.
[16] Namier and Brooke, *Charles Townshend*, pp. 62–7.

secured him the county seat. By 1761 Sir John Philipps, as manager of the Gogerddan interest, had a stronger hand to play. The Gogerddan heir John Pugh Pryse, already a Sea Serjeant, had come of age, and the other two county factions vied for Gogerddan support. Sir John Philipps accepted the offer of Vaughan's Whig rivals, Thomas Johnes of Llanfair and Herbert Lloyd of Peterwell, that Pryse should stand for both Cardiganshire seats, and if successful in both would give the borough to current MP John Symmons. Vaughan indignantly denounced this 1759 arrangement to the Duke of Newcastle as a Whig sell-out to the local Tories.[17] But the offer was a trap, too good to be true. Once the aim of dividing Gogerddan from the Crosswood–Nanteos alliance had been achieved, Herbert Lloyd announced that he would stand for the county unless he was given the borough himself. Since Vaughan intended to defend his seat this threat sufficed, and Lloyd displaced Sir John's long-term ally John Symmons as borough MP.[18] Vaughan did not in the end take the county contest to a poll, when he found that Newcastle had failed to obtain a favourable sheriff for him.[19]

It was a sign of changed times that such 'old Whig' families as the Vaughans of Crosswood and the Owens of Orielton could no longer rely on government support at elections. It was another that Thomas Wynn, son of Sir John Wynn of Glynllifon, should thank Bute for being given the new lieutenancy of Caernarfonshire.[20] For despite the apprehension of the Duke of Newcastle about Bute's electoral role, in Wales it had done little to restore old Tory interests. The solvent of Newcastle's political power was to be his desertion by traditional Whigs who saw their future lay with a young sovereign rather than an old minister. Typical was the reaction of Sir Hugh Williams, a Whig army officer who was the new second husband of Lady Bulkeley. He had his eye on the Baron Hill pocket borough of Beaumaris when he wrote to his wife. 'Lucky is he who gets into the present Parliament for it will certainly be the seat for promotion.'[21] Sir Hugh was to be disappointed, for his father-in-law persuaded his wife to retain Richard Price.

The 1761 general election itself was not to be of importance in determining the political future, and in Wales passed off quietly. Although several MPs were pushed out of their seats against their will, the only two polls were those in Anglesey and Radnor Boroughs. Altogether eighteen of the twenty-seven previous MPs were returned, two changing seats. One was

[17] BL Add. MSS 32893, f. 300; 32901, f. 359.
[18] NLW General MSS 14215C, ff. 1–2.
[19] BL Add. MSS 32918, f. 248.
[20] Bute MSS (Cardiff), unnumbered, Wynn to Bute, 26 June 1761.
[21] Baron Hill MSS 5697.

Sir John Wynn, who in Caernarfonshire moved to the borough from the more troublesome county, where his son Thomas for a time faced a canvass from a young local squire Thomas Kyffin of Maenan.[22]

The Parliament elected in 1761 was to support five different ministries in seven years, and this constant state of political flux renders impossible any simple classification of MPs. The old Whig government party split into two, being divided into those whose allegiance was to the King's government, whoever the minister might be, and those who followed Newcastle on his resignation in 1762 and from 1765 his political heir the Marquess of Rockingham, briefly in power again then for a year. As the wartime coalition disintegrated, factions developed around such other political leaders as George Grenville, Prime Minister from 1763 to 1765, and the elder William Pitt, who headed a ministry as Earl of Chatham from 1766 to 1768. Former Whigs and Tories alike went in all political directions. Contemporary political leaders themselves were confused and deceived about the allegiance of individual MPs. But it can be discerned that most Welsh MPs were supporters of government, with both political traditions, Whig support of the new system and Tory loyalty to the Crown, pulling politicians in that same direction, unless they were adherents of organized factions.

In 1762 seven Welsh Whig MPs remained loyal to Newcastle and then Rockingham: the three Morgans of Tredegar, their Monmouthshire ally Capel Hanbury, Lord Verney, and two recent converts from old Tory families, Sir Roger Mostyn and Richard Myddelton. The last, and doubtless others, had resisted efforts to win him over to the Court party. Sir John Wynn, long a friend of Henry Fox, the man appointed to create a ministerial majority for Bute in 1762, sought to win over Myddelton. 'Whatever friendship you profess, Mr Fox will meet you more than half way.' Fox also wrote to Myddelton, to no avail.[23] Three Welsh MPs, two former Tories and one Whig, went in the end with Grenville, Sir John Glynne, Edward Kynaston and Richard Clive, following the lead of his famous son. All the others were supporters of government, albeit varying in their assiduity and loyalty, except for Benjamin Bathurst, who maintained an independent opposition attitude until his death in 1767, being classed variously as 'Tory' and 'country gentleman'. In a political list of 1766, Rockingham dubbed eight of these Welsh MPs 'Swiss', Switzerland being the famous recruiting ground for mercenary troops: they included the two Glynllifon Wynns, who voted for every administration, including that of Rockingham himself; some others of Whig tradition like

---

[22] Baron Hill MSS 5699, 5711, 5714.
[23] Chirk Castle MSS E210, 4443.

Lord Carnarvon, Sir Lynch Cotton, Owen Meyrick and Sir William Owen; and also Edward Lewis and, with a query, William Vaughan. Attributed to Bute were George Rice and Sir Edmond Thomas, while three were marked 'Tory Bute' – Richard Price, John Pugh Pryse and Sir Richard Philipps, son and by then successor to Sir John. But Sir Herbert Lloyd, who had been created a baronet by Bute, was ascribed to Lord Powis.[24]

By the general election of 1768 the political scene had been both stabilized and clarified. Bute was no longer an active participant, and his followers had been merged with the general body of government supporters. Lord North was already the key figure as Leader of the House and Chancellor of the Exchequer even before he began his twelve-year spell as Prime Minister in January 1770. Until then, though Chatham was nominally head of the ministry to October 1768, the Duke of Grafton was in effective command. This consolidating administration was confronted by the Rockingham party, in permanent opposition from 1766 to 1782, and by the Grenville party from 1765 until Grenville's death in 1770 ended it; while the Chatham party gradually moved over to opposition between 1768 and 1770.

None of this had a direct impact on the Welsh elections, although in some constituencies candidates received government help. Local disputes were as yet unrelated to the national scene, and there were few of them. Nineteen out of the twenty-seven MPs from the old Parliament were to sit again, one for a different seat, after election petitions had been resolved in the Commons. The five contests taken to a poll all arose from local power struggles, most notably in Pembrokeshire. Here at a 1765 by-election consequent on the death of Sir John Philipps his son Sir Richard had defeated a vigorous challenge by Hugh Owen, son of Sir William Owen of Orielton, by 778 votes to 701.[25] Owen, because he was a Newcastle–Rockingham man, blamed government choice of a partisan sheriff, and in 1768 stood again on the 'Whig interest', so he told Newcastle.[26] Philipps again won, by 850 votes to 737, but that Owen had a justifiable grievance against the sheriff became evident when the case was heard by the Commons in 1770. Philipps gave it up on 6 March, when the election was declared void, and even agreed not to oppose Owen at the by-election, a concession to save the sheriff from punishment.[27] Picton Castle did put up John Symmons of Llanstinan, namesake son of the former Cardigan MP,

---

[24] Wentworth Woodhouse MSS R86. For all known Commons division-lists for the Parliament of 1761 to 1768, see Ginter, *Voting Records*, V, 2–43.

[25] Tredegar MSS 143/63.

[26] BL Add MSS 32968, f. 19; 32985, ff. 272–3. *CJ*, XXX, 207–8.

[27] NLW General MSS 6108; *London Evening Post*, 8 March 1770; *CJ*, XXXII, 755–6.

but he decided not to force a poll.[28] Hugh Owen, perhaps because of this electoral treatment, was to enter the Commons as an opposition MP, even though his father, as Pembroke Boroughs MP, supported government.

Two other contests corresponded to the parliamentary divide of administration and opposition – Carmarthen and Radnor Boroughs, and both were decided by the House of Commons in favour of the ministerial candidates. In 1764 Griffith Philipps, with the aid of George Rice, obtained a new charter for Carmarthen that gave him control of the borough.[29] Even so Philipps, seeking to reclaim the seat himself, faced a contest when retiring MP Lord Verney set up a fellow Rockinghamite Joseph Bullock, who obtained a majority at the poll of sixty-two to fifty-three. But twenty of his voters were 'old burgesses', admitted before the new charter. They were disallowed, and Griffith Philipps was returned, a decision subsequently upheld on appeal to the House of Commons. The borough poll-book reveals a voting alignment that might have been reflected in the county, where for a long time Rice also faced the prospect of a poll. If he and Howell Gwynne voted for Philipps, supporters of Bullock included Richard Vaughan of Golden Grove, Sir Thomas Stepney, William Powell of Nanteos, and James Philipps of Pentypark.[30] Richard Vaughan, still resentful about his 1754 county defeat, wrote on 15 December 1766 to William Powell recommending as a candidate there, Robert Banks Hodgkinson, who had acquired Edwinsford by marriage to a niece of Sir Nicholas Williams: 'The county has long been oppressed.'[31] Hodgkinson was canvassing early in 1768, and Rice was still afraid of a contest in a letter he dated '30 February'; but no evidence of one has survived.[32]

Radnorshire as usual faced the prospect of contests in shire and borough. In September 1767 Howell Gwynne announced his county candidature, stating that Lord Carnarvon was not seeking re-election.[33] Presumably as an administration candidate he obtained the support of both Lord Oxford and Lord Powis, a piquant situation that demonstrated how much politics had changed even at the local level, for in the reign of George II they had been respectively heads of the old Tory and Whig interests. But Chase Price was already in the field, with a trump card to play. 'It is a long time since a native of Radnorshire has presumed to offer himself to represent you. Permit me therefore to recall that idea, and at the

---

[28] Nanteos MSS L130. For more detail on these elections, see Thomas, 'Orielton versus Chirk Castle', *Pembs H.S. Journal*, 6 (1994–5), 35–43.

[29] Cawdor MSS 5826; Cwmgwili MSS 102, 104.

[30] Cawdor MSS 5530; *CJ*, XXXII, 762–3.

[31] Nanteos MSS L132.

[32] Dolaucothi MSS v2, 17; BL Add. MSS 38457, ff. 181–2.

[33] *Gloucester Journal*, 14 September 1767.

same time to make use of it as a recommendation.'[34] Price was confident of success even before his old enemy Thomas Lewis put the Harpton interest at his disposal, through anger that on the death of his brother Henry Lewis in January 1768 the Stewardship of Cantref Maelienydd, with control of three out-boroughs, had been given to Lord Oxford. Price now expected to win by a two to one majority, and Gwynne declined a poll on election day. In the borough Edward Lewis was challenged by John Lewis, nephew of Thomas.[35] Oxford's new appointment came too late for him to create any burgesses, and John Lewis was returned after winning the poll by 547 to 440, defeating 'the united power of the opposite party, and permit saying, ministerial influence', so the jubilant Thomas Lewis told Newcastle.[36] John Lewis sided with opposition in Parliament, but he was unseated on petition on 7 March 1769; for Henry Lewis had failed to have his patent as Steward enrolled again after George III's accession, and burgesses made since then in the Harpton interest were struck from the poll.[37] Again, as in 1761, technical carelessness had cost the Harpton family the seat.

Matters were also complex in Cardiganshire. Here John Pugh Pryse of Gogerddan reversed the electoral strategy of Sir John Philipps, and allied with the Nanteos–Crosswood interest of William Powell and Lord Lisburne, as Wilmot Vaughan had become in 1766. The key to the local political situation was the unpopularity of borough MP Sir Herbert Lloyd, notorious as a petty tyrant.[38] By the end of 1766 Pryse had responded to this feeling by creating 1,000 new burgesses at Cardigan and Aberystwyth, but Lloyd retaliated by making 1,200 at his borough of Lampeter between January and March 1767. Pryse then astounded Cardiganshire opinion when he announced at a county meeting on 22 August 1767 that he would give up his safe shire seat to fight Lloyd in the borough; and, in a vain attempt to break the alliance Lloyd had with Thomas Johnes, Pryse offered Johnes the county seat. Far from being attracted by the offer Johnes refused, deeming Pryse a fool who had 'sacrificed his interest to the resentment and passion of others', and hoped that Lloyd would defeat him.[39] In any case the offer was in the nature of a poisoned chalice of a contest, for Lisburne had already decided to fight the county even 'to a poll', because although he was back in Parliament since 1765 as MP for Berwick, his tenure of that seat was uncertain.[40] He was now adopted

---

[34] *Gloucester Journal*, 1 February 1768.
[35] *Gloucester Journal*, 7 and 14 September 1767.
[36] BL Add. MSS 32989, ff. 272–3.
[37] Harpton MSS 2150; *CJ*, XXXII , 293–4.
[38] On this, see Phillips, *Peterwell*, passim.
[39] Dolaucothi MSS v10, 40.
[40] NLW General MSS 14215C, f. 2.

unanimously, and returned without a contest. Retaining the seat until 1796 Lisburne launched into an active career in government, serving a year at the Board of Trade from 1769 and then twelve years at the Board of Admiralty until the end of North's ministry. In the end Pryse chose not to stand for the borough, offering the seat to his relative Pryse Campbell, grandson of former MP Lewis Pryse and son of John Campbell of Stackpole Court. Sitting for Scottish seats since 1754, he had been a Lord of the Treasury from 1766. The Gogerddan pedigree and the prospect of ministerial support over any election petition formed a combination of circumstances that caused even Sir Herbert Lloyd to abandon the contest on the day of election.[41]

Pryse's decision to withdraw his candidature was caused by the offer of the seat for Merioneth, where William Vaughan was intent on retirement and his younger brother Evan unwilling to succeed him. Pryse, who held the Rug estate there, was elected with widespread acclaim.[42] But the death of Pryse Campbell in December 1768 posed an unexpected problem for him in Cardigan Boroughs, that of finding a candidate to fight Sir Herbert Lloyd. He brought in a complete stranger, Ralph Congreve of Aldermaston in Berkshire, whose primary qualification was sufficient wealth to stand the contest. Although Congreve did not even attend the election he won by 1,950 votes to 1,704 in January 1769, only about 5 per cent of the electorate being resident; and Lloyd died in May before his petition was heard.[43]

North Wales saw contests taken to a poll in Anglesey, where Owen Meyrick defended his seat against the indefatigable Sir Nicholas Bayly by 259 votes to 155,[44] and in Caernarfonshire. Here Sir John Wynn retired from the borough seat in favour of his younger son Colonel Glyn Wynn, but his elder son Thomas, holder since 1756 of a lucrative post as Auditor of Land Revenue in Wales, faced a challenge in the county from a local squire William Wynne of Wern, supported by such traditional enemies of Glynllifon as the Brogyntyn, Mostyn and Wynnstay families. Thomas Wynn, with the support of most of the lesser squires and freeholders, won by 250 votes to 130 in a poll both orderly and courteous. The two candidates started it by voting for each other, and then polled their supporters in alternate groups of ten.[45]

---

[41] For more detail and documentation, see Thomas, 'Eighteenth-Century Elections in the Cardigan Boroughs Constituency', *Ceredigion*, 5 (1964–7), 412–14.

[42] Rug MSS 1225.

[43] *CJ*, XXXII, 177–8; Thomas, 'Eighteenth-Century Elections in the Cardigan Boroughs Constituency', 414–15.

[44] Pantperthog MSS 1113.

[45] Porth-yr-Aur MSS 12511–2; Peniarth MSS 416D.

At this election Sir Hugh Williams, now retired from the army, prevailed on his wife to give him the Beaumaris seat. The only other Welsh seat to change hands was that for Glamorgan. Here George Venables Vernon, a Rockinghamite MP for Bramber in his native Sussex, aspired to win the county by a revival of the old Mansel interest. Proprietor of Briton Ferry through his wife, Vernon secured the support of the Talbot family of Margam, and opened his campaign in 1766. Sir Edmond Thomas vigorously canvassed to defend his seat, but died on 10 October 1767. Lord Talbot, his chief ally, thereupon sponsored John Aubrey of Llantrithyd, grandson of the MP in Anne's reign, as part of his persistent challenge to the clique of Glamorgan magnates, and much the same alignment ensued that in 1745 had been Whig versus Tory. Vernon was denied the Chiltern Hundreds to fight the by-election, but found a stop-gap candidate to keep the seat warm for him, Richard Turbervill of Ewenni, who was returned in December 1767 after Aubrey withdrew. Vernon was unchallenged at the general election, but celebrations may have become subdued after one voter died of an excess of food and drink![46]

This Glamorgan situation illustrates the continuing dichotomy between local and national politics. Courtier Lord Talbot headed the traditional Whig alliance there, but his candidate John Aubrey was to sit as an opposition MP for English constituencies from 1768, voting on the same side in the Commons as his putative opponent Vernon. Such opposition men were soon a small minority among Welsh MPs, though ten voted in opposition in 1769 over the popular issue of the Middlesex Election, the expulsion of John Wilkes.[47] Yet Treasury Secretary John Robinson listed only four as 'con' before the next general election, in 1774. One was ironworks proprietor John Hanbury, an independent but zealous Rockinghamite who had come in for Monmouthshire in 1766 on the death of his father Capel. The others were Hugh Owen, Chase Price, and Evan Lloyd Vaughan, newly elected for Merioneth on the death of John Pugh Pryse, who had also been a steady opposition voter. Three others were deemed 'doubtful' by Robinson, as likely to oppose, Ralph Congreve, Sir Roger Mostyn and Sir Hugh Williams. Robinson erred when deeming as 'hopeful' Watkin Williams, whose cousin, the second Sir Watkin Williams Wynn, had brought him in for Montgomeryshire on the death of Edward Kynaston in 1772; for his voting record, both before 1774 and when he later returned to Westminster, was consistently one of opposition.

---

[46] On this, see Thomas, 'Glamorgan Politics 1688–1790', in *Glamorgan County History*, IV, 420–1.

[47] For division-lists in the Commons from 1768 to 1774, see Ginter, *Voting Records*, V, 43–116.

That only eight out of twenty-seven Welsh MPs were likely to oppose Lord North's ministry by 1774 exemplifies his success in winning over independent-minded MPs, for the classification of the others by John Robinson as 'pro' or 'hopeful' was sometimes at variance with their earlier political behaviour.[48] The most conspicuous example is that of the archetypal Whig family, Morgan of Tredegar, which moved over to administration in about 1769. Contemporaries thought that the Morgans deemed themselves obligated to government for preference over the Duke of Beaufort in Monmouthshire patronage; but a more immediate motive may have been to ensure that the elder Thomas Morgan, Judge-Advocate-General from 1741 to 1768, would be succeeded, as he was in 1769, by his deputy and son-in-law Charles Gould. The personnel of the Morgan family group altered considerably during this Parliament. The elder Thomas Morgan died in 1769, when his second son Charles succeeded him as Breconshire MP. The third son John took over the Brecon seat, but moved to Monmouthshire when his eldest brother Thomas died in 1771. The Tredegar interest there faced, for the first time since 1727, a Beaufort candidate in Valentine Morris of Piercefield, whose father had purchased the estate with money made in the West Indies. John Morgan won this 1771 Monmouthshire by-election by 743 votes to 535, despite a suspicious delay of the writ that caused the transference of the poll from Newport to Monmouth. The Morgans then brought in their brother-in-law Charles Van for Brecon. John Robinson's judicious evaluation of all three as 'hopeful' reflected some recent Morgan votes in opposition, but was unduly cautious about Van. He had recently made fiery anti-American speeches that earned notoriety for the ministry in the colonies, even suggesting that the town of Boston should be destroyed as punishment for the Boston Tea Party of December 1773. 'Demolish it. Make it a mark that shall never be restored.'[49]

Other Welsh MPs moved from opposition to administration at a later date than the Morgans, but change a number of them did during the early years of Lord North's ministry. Perception that he was there to stay enhanced genuine appreciation of his attitudes and policies. All the recorded votes during the Parliament elected in 1768 of Herbert Mackworth, Richard Myddelton and Sir John Stepney were cast for opposition, yet all were rated ministerial supporters by 1774; while George Venables Vernon, with a similar record, was deemed 'hopeful'. Herbert Mackworth, proprietor of the Gnoll Copper Company, had succeeded his

---

[48] John Robinson's 1774 lists may be found in BL MS Facs. 340 (3). His two analyses by constituencies (ff. 8, 13, 18, and 24, 29, 36) are more accurate than that in his nominal rolls (ff. 43–51).

[49] Quoted in Thomas, *Tea Party to Independence*, pp. 55–6.

father as Cardiff Boroughs MP in 1766. He was a frequent speaker in Parliament, and when voting against government over the Middlesex Election in 1769 declared, 'My mind is distressed to give a vote. . . I shall go against his Majesty's ministers, but my principle is to support them.'[50] An independent, discriminating supporter of North's ministry, Mackworth was given a baronetcy in 1776. Sir John Stepney, son of Sir Thomas and brought in for Monmouth by the Duke of Beaufort in 1767, was likewise now deemed a government supporter, and was to serve abroad as a diplomatic envoy from 1776 to 1784. Most Welsh MPs voted regularly for government, including former Grenvillites Sir John Glynne and Edward Kynaston even before Grenville's death in 1770. The ministry gained also when an elderly former naval officer Frederick Cornewall replaced the deceased Richard Clive as a stop-gap MP for Montgomery in 1771, and when in 1770 Sir Nicholas Bayly, on the death of Owen Meyrick, returned for a final spell as Anglesey's MP. For the first time he was usually, if not always, a ministerial supporter.

The general election of 1774 was called early by the North ministry so that there would be no interruption to the subsequent conduct of American policy. The colonial crisis had not yet become a matter of public concern, and was mentioned in only two Welsh constituencies, Montgomeryshire and Radnorshire. In that sense 1774 was the last of the old-fashioned general elections when national issues and the political alignments of candidates at Westminster impinged little on local rivalries. The atmosphere was to be very different in the next two general elections, 1780 and 1784, and then, of course, the French Revolution opened up a new political environment.

Treasury Secretary John Robinson's election notes for 1774 were compilations of information rather than campaign plans, certainly with respect to Wales. Here he expected seven contested elections, in Caernarfonshire, Caernarfon Boroughs, Cardigan Boroughs, Merioneth, Montgomeryshire, Pembrokeshire and Radnorshire. In these last two he hoped, vainly as it transpired, for the defeat of opposition MPs.[51] He was wrong on three counts. There were no contests in Caernarfon Boroughs or Pembrokeshire, and he failed to anticipate the one in Radnor Boroughs. In three of the six Welsh contests the prevailing interests were defeated – Glynllifon in Caernarfonshire, Gogerddan in Cardigan Boroughs, and Wynnstay in Montgomeryshire; but the overall impression is one of dominant oligarchy. Nineteen MPs were returned again for the same seats, though three after polls and one of them on petition, while five changes were all the results of decisions by patrons.

---

[50] BL Egerton MSS 217, p. 241.
[51] BL MS Facs. 340 (3), ff. 18, 36.

In north Wales the long minorities at Baron Hill and Wynnstay had ended, and their young masters were eager to claim traditional family seats and otherwise exercise electoral power. The seventh Viscount Bulkeley did contemplate fighting Caernarfonshire on the long dormant Baron Hill interest, but he was anticipated by Thomas Assheton Smith of Vaynol, a newcomer to that county and proprietor of slate quarries there. Lord Bulkeley therefore reverted to his first idea of representing Anglesey, where old Sir Nicholas Bayly gave way without difficulty, and an early rumour of the candidature of Owen Putland Meyrick of Bodorgan, son of the MP who had died in 1770, proved to be false. Lord Bulkeley was elected without opposition, while his step-father Sir Hugh Williams retained the Beaumaris seat.[52] In Caernarfonshire the position of the Glynllifon family had greatly deteriorated, though Glyn Wynn retained the borough without the contest John Robinson had expected. Sir John Wynn had died in 1773, and his heir, now Sir Thomas and county MP since 1761, had made himself personally unpopular. Smith was supported not only by Lord Bulkeley, Sir Roger Mostyn and Sir Watkin Williams Wynn, whose family interests had always been pitted against Glynllifon since the era of Whig–Tory conflict, but also by many local squires whose families had hitherto supported Glynllifon. Smith won by 200 votes to 117.[53] The next year Sir Thomas Wynn, as a faithful placeman, was found a seat by Lord North at St Ives, and in 1776 was further rewarded by an Irish peerage as Lord Newborough.

The second Sir Watkin Williams Wynn never gave politics the absolute priority his father had done. He was a man interested in art, drama and music, and had his own private theatre at Wynnstay. But he nevertheless conceived it his duty to be in Parliament, and displayed considerable political zeal from time to time. Even before 1774 he sat two years for Shropshire, and now took the predestined Denbighshire seat tactfully vacated by MP Sir Lynch Cotton.[54] The Cotton family's participation in Denbighshire politics thereby came to an end. Sir Lynch died in 1775, and a year later his son, who was to represent Cheshire from 1780 to 1796, sold the Lleweni estate to Thomas Fitzmaurice, younger brother of Lord Shelburne, political lieutenant and heir of the Earl of Chatham. Untroubled in Denbighshire, Sir Watkin nevertheless played an active part in the 1774 general election. Quite apart from his anti-Glynllifon role in

---

[52] Llanfair and Brynodol MSS C253; *Adams Weekly Courant*, 11 and 25 October 1774.

[53] Porth-yr-Aur MSS 12513–23; Thomas, 'The Parliamentary Representation of Caernarvonshire in the Eighteenth Century: Part II, 1749–1784', *Transactions of the Caernarvonshire Historical Society*, 20 (1959), 76–7.

[54] *Adams Weekly Courant*, 11 and 25 October 1774.

Caernarfonshire he was heavily involved in the Montgomeryshire and Merioneth contests, the only ones of the century in either constituency.

The Montgomeryshire campaign was one of the century's great Welsh elections, the first clash between Powis Castle and Wynnstay. Since the later seventeenth century, the masters of the Llwydiarth estate, now seated at Wynnstay, had either themselves been the county members or had named them, with the acquiescence of Powis Castle an apparent formality; and the re-election of Watkin Williams, Sir Watkin's cousin and MP since 1772, was at first taken for granted. But Lord Powis, the former Henry Arthur Herbert, had died in 1772, and the Dowager Lady Powis decided to revitalize the electoral interest of Powis Castle on behalf of her under-age son. Powis Castle agents canvassed Montgomeryshire from April 1774, nearly a year before the election was due, and without at first a candidate, until, after several refusals, William Mostyn Owen of Bryngwyn was declared in May. The Powis Castle propaganda claim was to be restoring 'the independency' of the county from the yoke of Wynnstay, and many freeholders responded to this appeal to support a local squire. The great landowners of North Wales, headed by Richard Myddelton and Sir Roger Mostyn, rallied to the Wynnstay cause, while Owen found assistance from Lord Clive and other Shropshire allies of Powis Castle. Both sides entertained lavishly but they also used coercion, especially Wynnstay. Owen publicly voiced his concern that threats and menaces had been deployed to influence voters against him.[55] It was, however, established practice for dependants to vote in accordance with their squire's wishes: hence Mrs Victoria Kynaston, widow of the previous MP and a Wynnstay partisan, reproached a tenant. 'You refused me your vote . . . It is always customary for tenants to go along with their landlords and landladies. No obligation that you can owe Mr Owen can authorise you to go from this known rule.'[56]

Late in the campaign a political content was injected into the contest by Wynnstay exploitation of the ministerial support enjoyed by Powis Castle: it was at this election that Whitshed Keene, who had married a step-sister of Lord North himself, began a forty-four-year tenure of the Montgomery Borough seat. An 'Old Montgomeryshire Freeholder' asserted in a local newspaper that if Owen was elected

he may prove serviceable to the junto that promotes his interest, in voting with the Ministry; which to strengthen the Quebec and Boston Bills, every tool will be found necessary . . . The Powis Family are well known friends

---

[55] Powis Castle MSS 18086.
[56] Peniarth MSS 418D.

to the Ministry, and he who joins that party is an enemy to the constitution in general. Therefore detest the Espouser of Popery and his measures.[57]

Lady Powis was a Roman Catholic, and this attack sought to exploit popular prejudice against the Quebec Act, which had legalized Catholic worship in that colony.

Six months of campaigning by propaganda, coercion and entertainment was troublesome and expensive, and both sides doubtless welcomed the ministry's decision to hold an autumn election. The poll began at Montgomery on 14 October and lasted three days, Owen being returned by a majority of 700 to 624. Powis Castle costs amounted to £5,400, those of Wynnstay to £4,800.[58] All this effort culminated in a double irony. Owen, despite his Powis Castle sponsorship, soon went over to opposition. 'He acted as a friend to government for some time, but of late has taken a most hostile part', noted John Robinson in 1780, and his voting record confirms a change of allegiance from 1777.[59] Watkin Williams, moreover, did not have to wait long for a seat. In 1777 he was returned at a by-election for Flint Boroughs on the death of Sir John Glynne, a constituency his father Richard had represented and for which he sat until 1806.

It was doubtless in retaliation for Vaughan of Corsygedol assistance to Wynnstay in Montgomeryshire that in October an army general, Henry Arthur Corbet, who owned the Ynysymaengwyn estate in Merioneth, was nominated with Powis Castle support to oppose MP Evan Vaughan for that county. Like Owen in Montgomeryshire he claimed the support of the small freeholders against the great landowners backing Vaughan, alleging the creation of leasehold voters. After Vaughan's victory in November by 342 votes to 258, this charge was refuted by a published analysis of the poll, demonstrating a majority for Vaughan among the freeholders of 244 to 208: but even this defence tacitly conceded some substance to the allegation by showing that seventy-eight leaseholders had voted for Vaughan as against twenty for Corbet.[60]

The expectation of John Robinson that Sir Richard Philipps might mount a successful challenge to Hugh Owen in Pembrokeshire was ill-founded. Hugh Owen was, so he boasted, 'unanimously re-elected'.[61] But, since he now became an administration supporter, it is possible that ministerial intervention averted a contest, for Philipps was brought into

---

[57] Glansevern MSS 14076.
[58] Powis Castle MSS 18328–509; Wynnstay MSS 122, L1249.
[59] Christie, 'John Robinson's State . . . 1780', *Camden Miscellany*, XXX, p. 471.
[60] *Adams Weekly Courant*, 15 and 22 November 1774.
[61] *London Evening Post*, 3 November 1774.

Parliament for the government borough of Plympton Erle, and, moreover, two years later, given an Irish peerage as Lord Milford. There was a change in Pembroke Boroughs where Sir William Owen now retired from Parliament after fifty-two years unbroken service, his successor being his nephew Hugh Owen of Great Nash, also a ministerial voter. Orielton was another 'old Whig' family now in support of the North ministry.

But in Radnorshire Robinson's hopes equated with the fears of Chase Price, well aware that the Harley family was intent on removing him from the shire seat. It was at first anticipated that Price would be challenged by Walter Wilkins, who had recently purchased the Maesllwch estate with a fortune amassed in India. But the Harley family, after early negotiations with Wilkins and doubtless aware that Price was expected to defeat him easily, proposed the candidature of Thomas Johnes, the Cardiganshire squire who had acquired by marriage the Croft Castle estate in Herefordshire, and that of Stanage in Radnorshire. Confident that Wilkins, on promise of future support, would not join Price, the Harleys believed Johnes would win easily. There were even rumours that Price would withdraw, and return to the Leominster seat he had previously held.[62] But Chase Price confounded all such expectations by winning the county, with the help of both the Harpton family and Wilkins, whose role was thought to have decided the result. After the first day's poll on 25 October, Price led Johnes by 430 votes to 349, and had another 150 freeholders ready to vote next day. Johnes declined to continue, and went off to Cardiganshire, where his namesake son was fighting the borough seat.[63] That this Radnorshire election was a contest between administration and opposition supporters was signified by the promise of Chase Price that he would seek to 'restore and preserve that harmony between the legislature and the people which is declining in the more distant parts of the British Empire', a rare mention of the American crisis at this general election.[64]

In the Radnor Boroughs constituency Lord Oxford, as Steward of Cantref Maelienydd, had created 426 burgesses in Rhayader, all but seventeen non-resident; and when rumours of a Harley family candidate proved false, it was evident that they would be deployed on behalf of MP Edward Lewis.[65] The response of the Harpton family to this situation was to contend, contrary to precedent, that only resident burgesses could vote. At the election the bailiff of New Radnor, as always a Harpton nominee, in

---

[62] Tredegar MSS 66/81–2; Harpton MSS C90, 91, 138, 168.

[63] Harpton MSS C131, 176, 189; *Gloucester Journal*, 31 October 1774. For more detail, see Adams, 'The Parliamentary Representation of Radnorshire 1536–1832', MA Wales, 1969, pp. 374–83.

[64] *Hereford Journal*, 10 November 1774.

[65] Harpton MSS C83, 90; *CJ*, XXXVII, 399.

an ostensible display of impartiality prolonged the poll for several days to give time for Edward Lewis to bring voters from 'seven or eight different counties' to achieve a majority of 619 to 201. He then disallowed all non-resident burgesses and returned John Lewis by a majority of 201 to seventy. The Election Committee, created under the Election Act of 1770, on petition from Edward Lewis awarded him the seat but without making any decision on the franchise.[66]

Another Welsh contest that ended in an Election Committee was that for Cardigan Boroughs. The MP, Ralph Congreve, had long been failing in health, and by 1773 it was correctly anticipated that he would not stand again. John Pugh Pryse, abroad at the time and without consulting his electoral allies William Powell of Nanteos and Lord Lisburne of Crosswood, offered the seat to a distant relative, Sir Robert Smyth, who lived in Essex but was a native of Cardiganshire.[67] His behaviour in 'setting the whole county in a flame' so long before the election was widely resented.[68] Thomas Johnes, already intent on putting forward his son, sought to break the electoral coalition of Nanteos and Crosswood with Gogerddan, denouncing Pryse's behaviour as arrogant and Smyth's candidature declaration as 'unpardonable' in 'a person totally unknown in Cardiganshire . . . without any other introduction than a mandate from Mr Pryse.' Mindful of how Pryse had in 1769 introduced a complete stranger in Ralph Congreve, he asked for the co-operation of Powell and Lisburne to show that 'the right of election for that town is not a mere burgage tenure.'[69] But the masters of Nanteos and Crosswood, although annoyed by Pryse's presumption, decided to support his choice to preserve 'the peace of the county'.[70] Not even the death of Pryse on 13 January 1774 changed their minds after the new owner of Gogerddan, Lewis Pryse of Woodstock, confirmed Smyth's candidature. Thomas Johnes then suggested to Lisburne a cost-sharing alliance with his son, and on his refusal threatened his own candidature in the county, a menace Lisburne perceived to be a bluff.[71]

The younger Thomas Johnes had the support of John Adams, nephew and successor of Sir Herbert Lloyd in the Peterwell estate, who himself became MP for Carmarthen in 1774 as its patron Griffith Philipps finally withdrew from Parliament. Several hundred new burgesses were created at

---

[66] Harpton MSS C.92; *Gloucester Journal*, 10 October 1774; *London Evening Post*, 27 October 1774; *CJ*, XXXV, 134–5.

[67] Nanteos MSS L117, 126, 154–6.

[68] Nanteos MSS L107.

[69] Nanteos MSS L102. The most notorious pocket boroughs of the time were those where the votes were attached to pieces of property or 'burgages'.

[70] Nanteos MSS L156.

[71] Crosswood MSS III, 24.

Lampeter early in 1774, and over 4,000 at Cardigan between May and October; but all their votes were invalidated by the decision to hold an autumn election, since the Durham Act of 1763 forbade any burgesses to vote within a year of admission. The poll began on 20 October and continued until 31 October. On 30 October, a Sunday, the older Thomas Johnes reported to his brother John.

> On Friday we finished polling our men, which amount to about one thousand. They continued the poll all day yesterday and do not propose closing it till tomorrow. They are now upwards of 400 men before us . . . I hope I shall be able to disappoint them, though it will be a dear bought victory.

How far the old West Wales Tory alignment had survived even the demise of the Sea Serjeants Society is shown by his final comment. 'The whole party attended the whole week, Sir Richard Philipps, Symmons, Edwardes, . . . etc, etc.'[72]

The mayor of Cardigan, a Gogerddan nominee, returned Smyth with a majority of 1,488 to 980. Not until near the end of 1775 did an Election Committee consider the petition submitted by the younger Johnes. It struck off 566 votes for Smyth, but allowed all those for Johnes on the ground that they had been accepted after scrutiny at the election, despite suspicious circumstances about many Lampeter admissions, and he was awarded the seat on 7 December 1775.[73] How far this result was due to Gogerddan mismanagement or to malpractices at Lampeter is unclear, but Smyth was concerned that he would be held responsible, and on 11 December offered to stand again next time,

> although the contest has been tedious and expensive to myself . . . I have not the least doubt but the gentlemen of the county will exert themselves to prevent a paltry contributory borough from imposing a representative upon them, against the general sense of the county.[74]

No other Welsh seat changed hands at the general election, and after the Cardigan and Radnor elections had been decided, the ministry had the support of all but seven Welsh MPs; for new members John Adams, Whitshed Keene and the younger Thomas Johnes were ministerial men.

---

[72] Dolaucothi MSS V14/12.

[73] Douglas, *Elections*, III, 173–229.

[74] Nanteos MSS L128. For fuller details and documentation, see Thomas, 'Eighteenth-Century Elections in the Cardigan Boroughs Constituency', *Ceredigion*, 5 (1964–7), 416–19.

Johnes soon became a placeman, enjoying a secret-service pension of £500 until he succeeded Lord Newborough as Auditor of Wales in 1781, a post worth £1,000 a year.[75] Those in regular opposition from 1774 were John Hanbury, Chase Price, Thomas Assheton Smith, Evan Lloyd Vaughan, George Venables Vernon, Sir Watkin Williams Wynn, and, probably, Sir Hugh Williams. His step-son Lord Bulkeley voted for opposition over the revival of the Middlesex Election case in 1775, but was reckoned an administration supporter, and Sir Watkin Williams Wynn became one when a local patronage request was granted in 1775. At the time, George III commented to Lord North, 'I consent to Sir Watkin Williams being Lieutenant of Merioneth if he means to be grateful, otherwise favours granted to persons in opposition is not very political.'[76]

The comfortable parliamentary majority the North ministry enjoyed after the general election of 1774 was gradually to dissolve during the War of American Independence, until Lord North resigned in 1782. This process can be identified and exemplified from the Welsh experience, but the political situation should not be misunderstood as a popular reaction. Political responses in Wales at this time were not spontaneous outbreaks of public opinion, but instigated by local MPs or other landed magnates to demonstrate support for their own political attitudes. Even the occasional election campaigns for 'independency' of the freeholders were orchestrated by families otherwise outweighed in local politics, like Orielton in Pembrokeshire, Glynllifon in Caernarfonshire, and in 1774 even by Powis Castle in Montgomeryshire. Political consciousness at a lower social level than that of county freeholders, who after all were by definition men of a little landed property, was a plant of slow growth, apart from mere riots, and there was scant sign of it in Wales before the French Revolution.

The few Welshmen who embraced radical political views gravitated to London, writers like Richard Price and David Williams, and such activists as Watkin Lewes and Robert Jones of Fonmon Castle, both members of the Bill of Rights Society formed to support John Wilkes in 1769, of which another Welshman, Robert Morris from the Swansea area, was the first secretary.[77] All three men were to involve themselves in popular Glamorgan politics of the 1780s, but earlier they virtually ignored Wales, apart from a demonstration of Welsh support for the Wilkite movement organised as an ego-trip by Watkin Lewes. In 1771 he contrived to take advantage of his Welsh connections by arranging Addresses from the counties of Cardigan, Carmarthen and Pembroke to demonstrate their solidarity with the City of

---

[75] Fortescue, *Corr. of George III*, V, 232.
[76] Fortescue, *Corr. of George III*, III, 205–7.
[77] Thomas, *John Wilkes*, pp. 111–12, 142.

London officials imprisoned during the dispute over parliamentary reporting. A contemporary print depicted Lewes presenting the Addresses, over this piece of doggerel verse.[78]

> The Ancient Britons, generous, bold and free,
> Untaught at Court to bend the supple Knee,
> Corruption's Shrine with honest pride disdain,
> And only bow to Freedom's Patriot Three.

How far ostensible displays of public opinion were manipulated by local politicians was to be underlined by the only overt Welsh responses to the coming of the American Revolution. This Welsh reaction comprised three loyal Addresses in 1775, all from the very same area, south-west Wales, whence Lewes had drawn his Wilkite Addresses only four years earlier. The man behind them was evidently Carmarthenshire MP George Rice, one of the ministry's parliamentary spokesmen on America. On 25 October he presented to George III a Carmarthenshire Address with 160 signatures, and borough MP John Adams one from Carmarthen with 167 signatures; while on 13 November MP William Edwardes and Sir Richard Philipps jointly handed in one from Haverfordwest with 207 signatures.[79]

At that time majority political opinion in Britain did support the principle of the American war, assertion of parliamentary sovereignty over the colonies, and in 1775 the King received altogether 126 such Addresses of support, as against only 26 petitions of protest.[80] It was only when, from 1778 onwards, the war proved both unsuccessful and expensive that criticism of the administration began to gain ground. Aware that the North ministry would not yet be defeated over a direct challenge to the war, the parliamentary opposition sought to exploit alleged government extravagance and corruption by a campaign for so-called Economical Reform: and it so happened that on 20 November 1778 the ministry, short of money, issued a Treasury Warrant setting up an inquiry into the diminution of royal revenue in Wales.[81] The real threat of any such investigation, as many Welsh landowners perceived, was that it would reveal long-term encroachments on royal lands in Wales.[82] A storm of protest, portraying the scheme as an attack on liberty and property in

---

[78] Reproduced in Treloar, *Wilkes and the City*, at p. 120. The last word is actually 'trois'. The three were Mayor Brass Crosby, Alderman Richard Oliver and John Wilkes, who was not imprisoned at all.

[79] PRO, HO55/10/13; 55/11/14, 30.

[80] Thomas, *Tea Party to Independence*, p. 276.

[81] NLW General MSS 9072E is a collection of papers relating to the whole episode.

[82] Nanteos MSS L110.

Wales, was instigated by Lord Bulkeley and Sir Watkin Williams Wynn. Sometimes this was generalized into a broad attack on the North ministry, as by 'A Freeholder of Denbighshire' in a public letter of 30 January 1779. 'I am very apprehensive that the Welsh (like the Americans) will very soon be stigmatised with the opprobrious epithet of being a factious, seditious people . . . It behoves us to be upon our guard, and diligently to watch the actions of the rapacious Minister.'[83] Nine county meetings and two London ones of Welsh landowners resulted in a formal memorial presented to the Treasury on 23 February 1779 by every Welsh MP bar one, presumably Whitshed Keene, and the Treasury Board dropped the plan on 5 March.[84]

The episode nevertheless cost the ministry some parliamentary support. Lord Bulkeley, Sir Watkin Williams Wynn and Sir Roger Mostyn were so influenced by this Welsh example of dubious government practice that henceforth they embraced the opposition cause of Economical Reform, and Lord Bulkeley proved a zealous convert. He took with him Caernarfon Boroughs MP Glyn Wynn and his father-in-law Sir George Warren, MP for Lancaster. By January 1780 he had organized his own 'little Parliamentary phalanx' of these two and his step-father Sir Hugh Williams, to whom he commented, 'If the people of England are in earnest, now is the moment for contracting the enormous influence of the Crown.'[85] Lord Bulkeley, with Sir George Warren, attended the initial meeting in February 1780 of the Westminster Committee for political reform.[86] But in 1780 there was no reaction in Wales over Economical Reform comparable to the outcry a year earlier over the Treasury Warrant. Whereas in England twenty-six of forty counties petitioned over Economical Reform, only three Welsh counties did so. A Breconshire meeting on 9 February decided 'with only two dissentient voices' to petition the House of Commons, and also to ask for a parliamentary enquiry into the possibility of abolishing sinecures, both to save money and to reduce 'the unconstitutional influence' of the ministry. But a correspondent in the *Gloucester Journal* of 21 February claimed that most freeholders were against the petition, stating that only twelve magistrates signed it whereas thirty-one had refused to attend. Doubtless aware of this controversy MP Charles Morgan, a ministerial supporter but who voted for Economical Reform in 1780, assured MPs when presenting the petition

---

[83] NLW General MSS 9072E.

[84] *St James's Chronicle*, 27 February 1779; *Gloucester Journal*, 15 March 1779. For more detail and documentation, see Thomas, 'A Welsh Political Storm: The Treasury Warrant of 1778 concerning Crown lands in Wales', *WHR*, 18 (1997), 430–49.

[85] Baron Hill MSS 5885.

[86] BL Add. MSS 38593, ff. 1–2.

that it was 'the general sense of the county'.[87] Denbighshire voted a petition which was presented by Sir Watkin Williams Wynn on 5 April. Flintshire held a meeting at Mold on 17 February, instigated by Dean William Shipley and chaired by Thomas Pennant of Downing, and voted a petition complaining of the 'multitude of extravagant salaries, useless places, sinecures and pensions', which both lessened 'the respect and independence of Parliament', and reduced the financial capacity to fight France and Spain, now both in the war on the American side; this petition was presented to Parliament on 17 March.[88]

The nationwide petition campaign formed the backdrop to the parliamentary session of 1780 that was dominated by opposition attempts to reduce government patronage by implementing its programme of Economical Reform. All the specific efforts failed, but the House of Commons responded to the popular movement by voting a general resolution of principle proposed by John Dunning on 6 April 1780 that deplored the influence of the Crown. Fifteen Welsh MPs voted for it, and ten against. Among the habitual supporters of the administration who rebelled on this issue were Charles and John Morgan of Tredegar, the two Hugh Owens from Pembrokeshire, and Sir Herbert Mackworth.[89] By the time a general election was called in the autumn of that year the government's election manager, still John Robinson, reckoned all five to be among the sixteen ministerial supporters from Wales, but not those who had broken with government over the 1778 Treasury Warrant. Their change of attitude explains the increase to eleven of opposition voters from Wales in the House of Commons at the dissolution of Parliament.[90]

Despite all the national excitement the general election proved to be the quietest of the century in Wales. Only two polls were forced, in Pembrokeshire and a formal one in Radnor Boroughs. Twenty-three of the twenty-seven MPs were returned for the same seats, none of the four changes resulted from a contest, and the political balance of the Welsh representation was unaltered. John Robinson proved to be woefully ignorant of the Welsh political scene, optimistically anticipating gains in three prospective contests. He believed a report that in Montgomeryshire Lord Powis and Sir Watkin Williams Wynn had made an improbable alliance to put forward John Kynaston, nephew of former MP Edward, to fight William Mostyn

---

[87] *Gloucester Journal*, 24 January, 7, 14, 21 February 1780; Almon, *Parl. Reg.*, XVII, 441; Walpole, *Last Journals*, I, 265.

[88] NLW General MSS 5502E; *Adams Weekly Courant*, 22 February and 9 March 1780; *CJ*, XXXVII, 730; Almon, *Parl. Reg.*, XVII, 424.

[89] For the known votes of MPs in the Parliament of 1774 to 1780, see Ginter, *Voting Records*, V, 116–203: for those on Dunning's motion, ibid., 180–90.

[90] Christie, 'John Robinson's State . . . 1780', *Camden Miscellany* XXX, pp. 444–78, passim (constituencies in alphabetical order).

Owen, who was standing 'at the head of the independent gentlemen'. On the contrary, Wynn seized the opportunity of Owen's defection to the parliamentary opposition to re-assert the Wynnstay interest by promising him assistance, and Lord Powis reluctantly accepted his unopposed re-election.[91] Robinson for a time also hoped for a challenge to Lord Bulkeley in Anglesey. Two possible candidates he had in mind were Sir Nicholas Bayly, now over seventy, and Sir John Stanley, a courtier in the sense of being a personal attendant on George III. Stanley, by his marriage in 1773 to Margaret Owen, heiress of the Penrhos estate, had acquired an important interest in the county. Neither was prevailed upon to stand.[92] Robinson's third hope of a ministerial gain was based on Lord Newborough's candidature in Caernarfonshire. Although in 1784 Lord Newborough was to complain of 'my ministerial persecutions for not voting, and for writing against the ruinous and disgraceful American war',[93] and he may have been deprived of his St Ives seat for some such reason, Robinson still reckoned him an administration supporter in his election prognosis, whereas current MP Thomas Assheton Smith was an opposition man: 'Lord Newborough ought to have the best interest, but he is personally disliked for some slights to the gentlemen and therefore although he thinks he shall succeed yet it is very doubtful.'[94] The threat to Lord Newborough was not so much Smith as a third candidate, lawyer John Parry of Wernfawr, who opened his canvass in May with the support of Lord Bulkeley.[95] The latter's concern was to promote the Baron Hill interest in Caernarfonshire, and he therefore rejected the request of his step-father Sir Hugh Williams to support his candidature there, even though he was forcing Sir Hugh to surrender his Beaumaris seat to Sir George Warren.

> With respect to Caernarvonshire politics, I can only say, that as there would be no doubt of a contest in case of your standing I will freely confess, that however my inclination might lead me, my purse would not allow of my embarking, and I know the jealousy of many individuals would take fire at my endeavouring to fix so near a relative as yourself in that county.

---

[91] Christie, 'John Robinson's State . . . 1780', 471; Wynnstay MSS 128; *Adams Weekly Courant*, 12 September 1780.
[92] Christie, 'John Robinson's State . . . 1780', p. 444.
[93] Plas Newydd MSS II, 199.
[94] Christie, 'John Robinson's State . . . 1780', p. 453.
[95] Brogyntyn MSS 1448; Baron Hill MSS 5886.

Parry had stood on his own initiative, Lord Bulkeley stated, but would have his support since Smith had 'scandalously neglected both his friends and the country in general'.[96] When Smith discovered that Lord Bulkeley had transferred his support to Parry he withdrew his candidature, but voiced his indignation to Sir Hugh. 'Now to own the truth I did not expect to have been approved of by the common freeholders. Yet I thought people of another description . . . would at least have consulted me before they either canvassed or adopted another candidate'.[97] During the campaign John Parry won such support, as from the Brogyntyn and Plas Newydd interests, as to put his success beyond doubt. Lord Newborough persevered in his canvass until the day of election, 20 September, when 'as the sheriff was going into the hall, he declined the poll'. Parry reckoned his majority would have been six to one.[98] Parry joined Lord Bulkeley's little parliamentary group, but it was deserted in 1781 by Caernarfon Boroughs MP Glyn Wynn when the North ministry bought back his allegiance with the office of Receiver-General of North Wales. Personal disaster now struck his brother Lord Newborough. Deprived of parliamentary immunity from his creditors, he was imprisoned by them before the end of the year, and in 1782 went to live in Italy.[99]

Radnorshire had no contest at the general election only because there had been one earlier in 1780. When Chase Price had died in 1777 his former opponent of 1774, the elder Thomas Johnes, had succeeded him without a contest. But he died himself in May 1780, and his namesake son and successor thereupon resigned his Cardigan Boroughs seat to prevent Walter Wilkins of Maesllwch taking advantage of the vacancy. With the support of Richard Price, brother of Chase, Johnes defeated Wilkins in June by 528 votes to 372, in a three-day poll, and although Wilkins canvassed for the general election he withdrew his candidature in September.[100] In the borough constituency, although Thomas Lewis had died in 1777, his nephew John made one last effort to restore Harpton control. The poll was stopped by mutual consent, so that the franchise could at last be decided. John Lewis had an agreed majority of fifty to thirty among the resident burgesses, but Edward Lewis one of sixty to fifty altogether, and a double return was submitted to the House of Commons. Once again the seat was awarded to Edward Lewis without any decision on

[96] Baron Hill MSS 5887.
[97] Baron Hill MSS 5889, 5891.
[98] Brogyntyn MSS 1454; Plas Newydd MSS, II, 198.
[99] Porth-yr-Aur MSS 12608.
[100] Dolaucothi MSS, unnumbered. T. Johnes to J. Johnes, 31 January 1777; Richard Price to J. Johnes, 23 May 1780; *Hereford Journal*, 31 August and 14 September 1777; *Gloucester Journal*, 4 and 25 September 1780; Adams, 'The Parliamentary Representation of Radnorshire', MA Wales, 1969, pp. 386–8.

the franchise.[101] The Harpton family thereupon gave up the struggle, and the constituency came under the control of Lord Oxford, as Edward Lewis discovered to his cost in 1790.

Resignation of his hard-won Cardigan Boroughs seat still left Thomas Johnes with the leading voice in the constituency.[102] His former ally John Adams, patron of Lampeter and due to lose his Carmarthen seat at the general election, came forward at the by-election, hoping Johnes would repay the help given him in 1774, and it was widely assumed that he would do so. Lord Lisburne commented to William Powell on 22 May, 'it seems as if Adams would have no competitor, and in that respect he is fortunate, having so keen an appetite for Parliament'.[103] But the new MP was John Campbell, son of Pryse Campbell and since 1777 owner of the Stackpole Court and Cawdor estates inherited from his namesake grandfather. He owed his seat to Johnes rather than to his family link with Gogerddan, and was to retain it until he obtained a peerage in 1796 as Lord Cawdor.

It is not clear why Adams, who never spoke in Parliament, was so anxious to be an MP, but financial ruin, which caused him to sell Peterwell in 1781, explains both the reluctance of Johnes to support him and his loss of the Carmarthen seat in 1780.[104] Control of that borough now lay firmly with Griffith Philipps of Cwmgwili, who was open to offers since he was unwilling to serve again himself and his son John George was under age. He was therefore much sought after at a summer ball given by the Vaughans of Golden Grove. Here is an account by one observer.

> It was truly laughable to see how the old gentleman felt his consequence, and with what servile attention the three candidates addressed him, for as soon as one had done speaking to him, the other immediately paid him his regards, so that wherever you saw Mr P. there you were sure to see one or other of these three candidates.

It was thought he would favour an old friend and local squire George Philipps of Coedgain, and so it proved.[105] His hosts presumably preferred another candidate, Sir Cornelius Maude, for his daughter married the Vaughan heir John in 1781. In 1779 John Vaughan had succeeded the deceased George Rice as county MP. Both he and Philipps were supporters of the North ministry.

[101] *Hereford Journal*, 7 September and 5 October 1780; *CJ*, XXXVII, 12, 136, 156.
[102] For evidence of his control, see NLW General MSS 14215C, ff. 55–6, and *Gloucester Journal*, 11 September 1780.
[103] Nanteos MSS L157.
[104] Phillips, *Peterwell*, pp. 214–19.
[105] Cwmgwili MSS 131.

There was only one genuine poll in Wales that election, in Pembrokeshire, and here John Robinson feared a ministerial loss. The absence of a contest in 1774 had been misleading, for the Orielton–Picton Castle rivalry remained as bitter as ever, and it was now given a political edge. Lord Milford had joined the parliamentary opposition in 1779, honourably resigning the Devonshire borough seat Lord North had given him in 1774. Owen was nevertheless clearly taken by surprise when Lord Milford announced his candidature in July 1780, and Robinson soon noted, 'there is a warm contest for this county'.[106] In contrast to their previous contests it was now Owen who enjoyed government favour, and thereby the tactical advantage of the election being held at Pembroke, not the usual venue of Haverfordwest. That borough's MP, Lord Kensington, though a ministerial voter, maintained the Edwardes family alliance with Picton Castle in return for support in his own constituency, and 'most of the gentlemen of great property' also supported Lord Milford.[107] But Owen evidently won over many of the small squires and freeholders, for he triumphed in the poll in September by 1,089 votes to 912, boasting that his majority had been 'obtained without threats or promises, and without the paltry aids of subscriptions, abuse or insult . . . The principal interest of this county is now so clearly established . . . as to admit of neither doubt or dispute.'[108]

The general election saw a last-minute flurry in Glamorganshire, for MP George Vernon, who was expected to retain the seat, succeeded his father as Lord Vernon in August. A minor squire, Thomas Pryce of Dyffryn, at once declared his candidature, evidently hoping for the support of the old Whig interest, headed by Lord Talbot and the Morgans of Tredegar, which earlier in the century had sometimes successfully challenged the dominant electoral coalition, once deemed Tory and still in alliance, of the Raglan interest of the Duke of Beaufort, the Cardiff Castle interest now held by Lord Mountstuart, and the former Mansel interest, currently shared by Thomas Talbot of Margam and the new Lord Vernon of Briton Ferry. Their nominee for the vacancy was Charles Edwin of Llanfihangel, and he was returned without a contest: but this episode foreshadowed the successful challenge to the dominant oligarchy in 1789.[109]

---

[106] Christie, 'John Robinson's State . . . 1780', p. 475; *Gloucester Journal*, 3 and 10 July, 7 August 1780.

[107] Cwmgwili MSS 131.

[108] *Gloucester Journal*, 9 October 1780.

[109] *Gloucester Journal*, 11 and 18 September, 9 October 1780; John, 'The Parliamentary Representation of Glamorgan, 1536–1832', MA Wales, 1934, pp. 104–11. For more detail, see Thomas in *Glamorgan County History*, IV, 422–4.

Since Edwin was to vote in opposition, the political balance of Welsh parliamentary representation remained exactly the same as before the general election at sixteen to eleven in favour of the North ministry. The next eighteen months saw a parliamentary battle that culminated in the resignation of Lord North on 20 March 1782 as his Commons majority finally vanished. Only two Welsh MPs changed from administration to opposition, John Vaughan and Richard Myddelton, although the absence of Sir Herbert Mackworth from the crisis votes of February and March 1782 was doubtless deliberate: it left exactly thirteen Welsh MPs on each side. On the one occasion when the North ministry was defeated, 27 February on the ending of offensive war in America, Charles and John Morgan were among the MPs who then switched to vote against government before reverting to its support.[110]

The two years following the fall of Lord North witnessed a whirligig of ministerial changes and political re-alignments; and examination of any group of MPs, such as those from Wales, reveals the political complexity of this period and dispels any notion of a two-party system. On North's resignation, the two opposition factions headed by Lord Rockingham and Lord Shelburne, who had inherited Chatham's following in 1778, formed a coalition ministry, with the former as Prime Minister. But when he died in July most of the former Rockinghamites, led by Charles James Fox, refused to serve under Shelburne, George III's choice, and returned to opposition. In February 1783 the Foxite and Northite factions united to defeat the Shelburne ministry over the peace terms with America, causing the King unwillingly to accept the Fox–North Coalition as his ministry in April. Eight months later, in December 1783, George III dismissed it and appointed a minority administration under the Younger William Pitt, with the subsequent general election of 1784 producing a decisive majority for Pitt over his opponents. The political paths pursued by individual MPs during this period were motivated by individual opinions, private friendships, and personal interests, as well as political allegiances. At least three Welsh family interests were divided politically – Baron Hill, Tredegar and Wynnstay.

As in 1762 with regard to the Duke of Newcastle, so in 1782 the MPs who had supported North divided into those who were his personal followers and those, whether office-holders or independents, whose loyalty was to the King's government. Seven Welsh MPs were among the Northites. Two had held political office under North – Whitshed Keene, at the Board of Trade from 1774 to 1777 and Surveyor-General of the Board of Works from 1779

---

[110] For votes of MPs in the Parliament of 1780 to 1784 see Ginter, *Voting Records*, V, 203–81.

to 1782, and Lord Lisburne. Promoted to an Irish Earldom in 1776, he served twelve years at the Board of Admiralty, declining in 1780 an offer of promotion to be Comptroller of the Household, including appointment to the Privy Council, and blossoming into a Commons spokesman during the last two years of North's ministry.[111] The other Welsh Northites were the professional diplomat Sir John Stepney, Edward Lewis, as a recipient of lucrative war contracts, John Campbell, and two men of impeccable Whig ancestry, the Hugh Owens, Sir William's son having succeeded him in baronetcy and the Orielton estate in 1781.

Four Welsh members can be identified as belonging to the Court party, three as office-holders. Sir Charles Gould, MP for Brecon since 1778, owed his seat to the Tredegar interest; but he was Judge-Advocate-General and, unlike the Morgans, always voted for government. So did Thomas Johnes, Auditor of the Land Revenue in Wales, and Glyn Wynn, Receiver General of Land Revenue in North Wales. Lord Kensington, hoping for a British peerage, was equally faithful to government.

Of the MPs who had voted against the North ministry, five proved to be Foxites – John Hanbury, Sir Roger Mostyn, William Mostyn Owen, Sir Watkin Williams Wynn and Sir George Warren. About the last Lord Bulkeley who, with John Parry, sided with Shelburne and then Pitt, confessed to Shelburne, 'I have no hold upon him, although I bring him into Parliament'.[112] Sir Watkin might almost have said the same about Watkin Williams, who voted for Shelburne and Pitt. Many independents voted for Shelburne only in February 1783, as a protest against the Fox–North Coalition's attempt to browbeat the Crown. Among Welsh MPs they included five who later supported the Coalition in office – Sir Herbert Mackworth, Charles and John Morgan, and Foxites Sir Roger Mostyn and John Hanbury; and others who later absented themselves from Westminster, through illness, lack of interest or caution, such as George Philipps, John Vaughan and Evan Lloyd Vaughan, casting perhaps his only pro-ministerial vote ever.

The general election of 1784 was deliberately called early, after only half the possible lifetime of the 1780 Parliament, in order to give the Pitt ministry a Commons majority. The calculation of John Robinson, now acting on behalf of Pitt, was correctly that at the dissolution Wales was represented by ten Pittites and seventeen Coalitionists. But his forecast for Wales was wildly and optimistically wrong. He anticipated that after the election the ministry would have a majority from Wales of twenty to seven

---

[111] NLW General MSS 14215C, f.63. For Lisburne's speeches, see Almon, *Parl. Reg.*, VIII, 128–9; Debrett, *Parl. Reg.*, I, 90–1, 92, 202–3, 205–6, 232–3; III, 479–80; V, 71, 97, 98, 422; VII, 161, 209.
[112] Quoted in Namier and Brooke, *House of Commons 1754–1790*, III, 609.

MPs.[113] He was actually wrong in forecasting the future behaviour in the new Parliament of ten who sat at the dissolution. After the general election there were only nine Pittite MPs from Wales as against eighteen opposition members.[114]

It was just as well for Pitt that Robinson's forecasts were more accurate for the rest of Britain! For the first time since 1710 government influence and popular opinion were on the same side, with the additional thrust of the political reformers, since Pitt had made himself the Commons champion of Parliamentary Reform. The result was that almost one hundred MPs who had supported the coalition failed to secure re-election, but only one of them came from Wales: in his pocket borough of Beaumaris Lord Bulkeley replaced his own father-in-law Sir George Warren, a Coalitionist, by Pittite Hugh Fortescue.[115] Evidently the electoral power of the Welsh magnates was more firmly based than in England, where long-established interests tumbled everywhere. Only in Flintshire and Cardiganshire did opposition MPs in Wales suffer concern or alarm before re-election.

The most bitter contest, paradoxically, was a duel between Pittite patrons, in Anglesey. The two main protagonists, Lord Bulkeley and Lord Paget, were both to be rewarded by Pitt after the election with promotions in the peerage. North Wales opinion had long held that the Baron Hill hegemony in the island county was deceptive, owing much to the age of Sir Nicholas Bayly of Plas Newydd and the pusillanimity of Owen Putland Meyrick of Bodorgan. In 1782 local gossip had it that Lord Bulkeley would be 'turned out of the county' at the next election;[116] and John Robinson noted that 'Lord Bulkeley comes in with the support of his friends but has a strong interest against him in Lord Paget'.[117] The eldest son of Sir Nicholas Bayly, Lord Paget, who had inherited that British peerage from a cousin in 1769, had succeeded him at Plas Newydd in 1782. In December 1783, with an election imminent, Lord Bulkeley sounded out Meyrick, who after hard bargaining was offered the Baron Hill interest for the county 'with no conditions as to his Parliamentary conduct'.[118] Lord Bulkeley presumably knew by then that he was to receive a British peerage, and he was actually to make that announcement before the election to

---

[113] Laprade, *Parliamentary Papers of John Robinson*, pp. 68, 74, 94–8.

[114] See Ginter, *Voting Records*, V, 281–334, for the voting of MPs in the Parliament of 1784 to 1790.

[115] Cannon, *Fox–North Coalition*, pp. 244–5, names ninety-six such MPs, but omits Warren.

[116] Nannau MSS 613; Plas Newydd MSS II, 4.

[117] Laprade, *Parliamentary Papers of John Robinson*, p. 44.

[118] Plas Newydd MSS II, 1–2.

explain his own withdrawal.[119] Lord Paget put forward his younger brother Colonel Nicholas Bayly, and deployed the Paget wealth derived from Anglesey copper mines, for Plas Newydd spent £8,400 on this election.[120] The contest was finally turned by Lord Paget's coup in securing the Bodeon interest of Sir Hugh Owen, a Foxite faced with a choice between two Pittite interests.[121] For Bayly won by a mere seven votes, 370 to 363, in a poll protracted over a fortnight.[122]

Lord Paget also won another contest, in the Caernarfon Boroughs constituency. MP Glyn Wynn, aware that his elder brother Lord Newborough would wish to re-enter the Commons, took steps to secure that safe Glynllifon seat for himself. He allied with Lord Paget, and his nominee as constable of Caernarfon Castle, and so mayor of the borough, admitted 329 new burgesses there in 1782, 362 in 1783, and sixty-four in 1784, many of them Paget tenants from Anglesey. Lord Bulkeley, concerned about the threat of Paget ambitions in both Anglesey and Caernarfonshire, retaliated by allying with the agent of the absent Lord Newborough, still in Italy. Sixty new burgesses were then admitted in the Glynllifon borough of Nefyn, and 435 in Cricieth, controlled by the Owen family of Brogyntyn, long-term allies of Baron Hill. But early in 1784, after Wynn had gone over to the Pitt ministry, official pressure was put on Lord Bulkeley not to oppose him. In February, with apparent reluctance, he authorized Pitt's cousin Lord Temple to inform Lord Paget that 'he would not molest or impede Colonel Wynn in his election for Caernarvon. That the Colonel having of late voted so uniformly in the way that Lord Bulkeley wished it had materially abated his Lordship's resentment.'[123] Lord Newborough was still put forward as a candidate, perhaps without his consent, but lost to his brother by 490 votes to 410 in a poll that lasted from 9 to 20 April, ten voting days.[124] Newborough had a majority of resident burgesses by ninety-three to forty-one, but the petition put forward was not on that ground. Wynn's success cost the Glynllifon family control of the constituency. Lord Paget had spent £1,150 at the election;[125] but more important was the enrolment of hundreds of Paget tenants as burgesses. Lord Paget, by then Earl of Uxbridge, completed the takeover by becoming constable

[119] *Adams Weekly Courant*, 13 April 1784.
[120] Plas Newydd MSS I, 1–2; IV, 5266.
[121] Plas Newydd MSS I, 3356; PRO 30/8/164, Lady Owen to Pitt, 13 August 1786.
[122] *Adams Weekly Courant*, 11 May 1784. For a fuller account, see Thomas, 'The Rise of Plas Newydd', *WHR*, 16 (1992), 173–6.
[123] Plas Newydd MSS II, 216.
[124] *Hereford Journal*, 6 May 1784.
[125] Plas Newydd MSS I, 197–9.

of Caernarfon himself in 1785, and henceforth, from the general election of 1790, Pagets held the seat until 1830.[126]

That Lords Bulkeley and Paget were Pittites put them in a minority among the dominant Welsh families. The most famous confrontation between the tide of Pittite sentiment and an entrenched family interest occurred in Flintshire. MP Sir Roger Mostyn faced an immediate challenge from Sir Thomas Hanmer of Bettisfield, who sought to revive his old family interest by announcing his county candidature in January.[127] Local Pittites summoned a county meeting at Mold for 28 February to vote a loyal Address to the Crown, only to meet a crushing defeat. That proposal was rejected by 212 votes to eighty-two, a resolution was carried condemning such Addresses as divisive, and then the meeting displayed entire confidence in Mostyn and scorned his critics.[128]

> *Resolved.* That this county, placing the most perfect reliance in the integrity and abilities of our present representative, are satisfied that his Parliamentary conduct is governed by the purest principles of honor, and is directed, on all occasions, to the best of his judgement, to the support of our glorious constitution.
>
> *Resolved.* That for any set of men to obtrude their private opinions as a test to direct the public conduct of their representative, is a general insult to the county, as the sentiments of the freeholders are only to be collected at a county meeting. That the delegate of a free people should be no less free than themselves. And that from a man who is mean enough voluntarily to bow to the shackles of slavery – independence and integrity can never be expected.

There were rumours that this overwhelming display of support for Mostyn had been produced by coercion of freeholders.[129] Hanmer persisted in his candidature, writing on 27 March to Sir Edward Lloyd of Pengwern. 'I hope the County of Flint will exert itself upon this occasion and show its loyalty to the King by making a fresh choice.' Lloyd, canvassed also by Mostyn, would promise only neutrality, and Hanmer soon withdrew.[130] Lloyd was torn between personal and political considerations, as more famously was Mostyn's own brother-in-law, the celebrated naturalist Thomas Pennant of Downing, whose anonymous pamphlet, *A Letter from*

---

[126] For more detail and documentation, see Thomas, 'The Parliamentary Representation of Caernarvonshire in the Eighteenth Century: Part II, 1749–1784', *T. Caerns. H. S.*, 20 (1959), 81–5.

[127] Mostyn MSS 7891.

[128] *Adams Weekly Courant*, 2 March 1784, reprinted in *Morning Chronicle*, 6 March 1784.

[129] *Chester Chronicle*, 26 March 1784.

[130] Mostyn MSS 7892–4.

a Welsh Freeholder to his Representative, was written by 10 February and published on 1 April, with this declaration. 'There is not a wish to change our representative provided he acts consonant to our wishes; but none of us ought to give up principle for affection.' Five days later, Pennant wrote privately to Mostyn. 'I have done my duty to my country by using every argument to withdraw you from a party disapproved of by the majority of your constituents . . . *It is the cause* not the man that will ever be my firm consideration. Others will be *less delicate*, and attend you at your election. I cannot.'[131] As Pennant anticipated, Mostyn met no opposition to his re-election later that month.

In nearby Denbighshire a Ruthin meeting on 13 February voted a pro-Pitt Address, that was presented by Lloyd Kenyon, then Pitt's Attorney-General, and signed only by the chairman, Thomas Fitzmaurice of Lleweni, brother of Lord Shelburne. This thanked George III for exercising his

> undisputed prerogative of dismissing from the public service, the late Ministers of the Kingdom. A set of men, who, separated in principle, were united only in that lust for power and employment, which they grasped at with deceit and obtained by violence.[132]

But a subsequent Ruthin meeting on 10 March condemned this as the opinion of only fourteen persons, and then voted an Address calling for the appointment of 'a broad, firm, efficient, popular administration, such as may deserve the confidence of every branch of the legislature', asking the King 'to listen to the voice of your faithful Commons'. This Address, presented by Sir Watkin Williams Wynn, and with 303 signatures, was also printed in the official *London Gazette*, unusually so for an opposition statement.[133] The meeting thanked Sir Watkin, and also Richard Myddelton, the only evidence that this absentee borough MP was a Coalition supporter.[134]

Even more remarkable for forthright sentiments was the Address voted on 6 April by the constituents of Pembrokeshire and Pembroke Boroughs when re-electing their MPs, Sir Hugh Owen and Hugh Owen; for in the emphasis on the libertarian tradition of the Owen family is a condemnation of the behaviour of William Pitt.[135]

---

[131] Mostyn MSS 8432.
[132] *London Gazette*, 21 February 1784.
[133] *London Gazette*, 3 April 1784.
[134] *Morning Chronicle*, 19 March 1784.
[135] *Hereford Journal*, 15 April 1784.

We unanimously return you our warmest thanks for your upright conduct in the late Parliament, and have given you the strongest proof of approbation, by as unanimously re-choosing you this day to represent us in this. We have not dictated to nor required any test of you. Let those, who distrust their candidates, have recourse to such an unusual mode. The family of Orielton have always been remarkable for their loyalty to their Sovereign, and no less for their fidelity to their constituents. We are perfectly satisfied that you will boldly persevere in maintaining the dignity of the House of Commons, that corner stone of the Constitution; and not suffer us to be enslaved by the Back Stairs Influence of the Minister, and his train of new made Lords. Let the Parliament be dissolved as often as an ambitious and inconsiderate youth may be rash enough to recommend so ill-judged a measure, we solemnly assure you that we will as often re-choose you, and that we are firmly determined, that our liberties and our lives shall stand and fall together.

These Welsh reactions were out of line with the wave of Pittite sentiment in England, where only a few constituencies voiced similar opinions, as against over two hundred loyal Addresses.[136] The contrast was noted by the *Morning Chronicle* of 24 March when commending the Flintshire and Denbighshire Addresses as indicative of a Welsh spirit of independency. 'It is remarkable that the Cambro-Britains are the only inhabitants of this Empire who have had courage enough to speak out like Britons.' In reality, of course, these reactions were the views of a few dominant landowners, most of whom in Wales happened to be anti-Pitt. Even from Wales six loyal Addresses were voted, including the one of dubious antecedents from Denbighshire.

The loyal Addresses from Anglesey and Caernarfonshire, after meetings at Beaumaris on 5 March and Caernarfon on 15 March, were signed only by the sheriffs, and presented respectively by the Bishop of Bangor and Lord Bulkeley, and by John Parry. Both thanked the King for dismissing the Coalition ministry, with the Caernarfonshire one pointedly describing the Pitt administration as 'men of high reputation for public virtue, love of freedom, and distinguished attachment to the British constitution'. The Anglesey one assured George III that 'we hold the due exertion of your royal prerogative no less sacred than the constitutional rights of your subjects'.[137]

---

[136] Cannon, *Fox–North Coalition*, p. 187.
[137] Plas Newydd MSS I, 3351; *Adams Weekly Courant*, 2 March 1784; *Morning Chronicle*, 24 March 1784; *London Gazette*, 13 and 24 March 1784.

The Address from New Radnor was an evident attempt to embarrass the Northite MP Edward Lewis, for, signed by 283 persons, it was presented by his old rival John Lewis as recorder, though he did not again contest the parliamentary seat.[138] In Carmarthenshire several leading squires were Pittites, and a loyal Address was voted by the Grand Jury at the Great Sessions on 24 March, and signed by Sir William Mansel of Iscoed as chairman.[139] Mansel had married the niece of borough MP George Philipps, and became county MP at the general election when John Vaughan, instead of seeking to maintain the pre-eminence of the Golden Grove interest, inexplicably retired from Parliament. Mansel came in on the rival interest, the old alliance of Rice of Newton, now Dynefor, with Philipps of Cwmgwili, even though John George Philipps, who had inherited Cwmgwili from his father in 1781, was a zealous Foxite.[140] Old electoral tradition could still override new political alignments.

In Carmarthen George Philipps, who died on 17 April, had made way twelve days earlier for John George Philipps. The Pitt ministry lost another MP when Lord Milford, accepting that he would not unseat his fellow Foxite Sir Hugh Owen in Pembrokeshire, deployed the powerful but long dormant Picton Castle interest to displace the indignant Lord Kensington from Haverfordwest.[141]

Such strong family interests were impervious to the tide of Pittite sentiment, but there may have been one Welsh constituency, Glamorgan, where, at least in a negative sense, it influenced the election result. In 1780 MP Charles Edwin and his clique of magnate sponsors had all inclined to opposition; but in 1784 Edwin was a Pittite, whereas all his patrons except the Duke of Beaufort were Foxite. Public opinion in the county, as reflected in the self-styled 'independent freeholders', was strongly in favour of Pitt, and Edwin presented George III with a loyal Address bearing 697 signatures.[142] This display of popular feeling may have deterred the magnates from any idea of replacing him.

Direct government intervention, that ministerial weapon in the Pitt armoury, threatened only one Welsh MP, Lord Lisburne in Cardiganshire. In January 1784 he anticipated hostility from Edward Loveden, Pittite MP for Abingdon, and current proprietor of Gogerddan on behalf of his wife Margaret, heiress of Lewis Pryse, who had died in 1779. Lisburne feared that Loveden would join with Thomas Powell, who in 1780 had inherited

[138] The *Gazette* mistakenly at first stated that Edward Lewis was responsible for the Address, an error later corrected. *London Gazette*, 23 March and 6 April 1784.
[139] *London Gazette*, 6 April 1784.
[140] Cwmgwili MSS 157, 174.
[141] NLW General MSS 6106D.
[142] *London Gazette*, 1 May 1784.

Nanteos but not his father William's friendship with the master of Crosswood. By 9 March Lisburne was among the opposition MPs targeted for removal by the Pitt ministry. 'I have not escaped notice', he wrote to his ally James Lloyd of Mabws, believing that Pittite Thomas Johnes had been persuaded 'to raise an opposition in the county'. The danger may have been imaginary. Loveden had already assured Lisburne that he would not cause him trouble, and Johnes also soon gave him a promise of support. Powell remained hostile and called a meeting of his supporters on 5 April, but did not pursue the challenge further.[143]

Despite the national excitement the impression is of a quiet general election in Wales. For once both MPs from Radnorshire, Thomas Johnes and Edward Lewis, were able to boast of unanimous elections.[144] Two MPs were even re-elected in their absence abroad. It was an ironic anomaly that Pittite Thomas Johnes should issue a Cardigan Boroughs election address 'in the name of my absent friend . . . Mr Campbell being at this time out of the kingdom', for John Campbell remained a staunch Northite. John Morgan's advertisement for Monmouthshire included 'my worthy colleague Mr Hanbury, who though at present abroad I am certain will be ambitious of again tendering his services'.[145] Lord Nevill, son of Lord Abergavenny, and son-in-law of election expert John Robinson, had sounded Hanbury about his intentions and made known his hopes more widely, but did not press the matter when the Duke of Beaufort decided to support the sitting members, who were re-elected on 8 April at a combined expense of £351. When news soon came that Hanbury had died at Rouen two days before, the Duke of Beaufort sponsored Lord Nevill. John Hanbury Williams, Hanbury's cousin, also came forward, but withdrew when Charles Morgan of Tredegar informed him that 'to preserve the peace of the county' he would support Lord Nevill.[146] The latter's election redressed the overall loss of a seat in Wales suffered by the Pitt ministry at the general election, and also marked the revival of the Beaufort claim to nominate to one county seat. Yet Beaufort had retained Northite Sir John Stepney as Monmouth MP, just as the opposition Morgans had left Pittite Gould in his Brecon seat. Even in 1784 family interests or mere personal friendships took priority over political considerations.

*　　　*　　　*

---

[143] NLW General MSS 14215C, ff. 77–8, 81–3, 86, 91–2.
[144] *Hereford Journal*, 8 and 22 April 1784.
[145] *Hereford Journal*, 1 April 1784.
[146] Tredegar MSS 261–2; 53/50–57; Laprade, *Parliamentary Papers of John Robinson*, pp. 68–9.

The story of Welsh politics in the century between the Glorious Revolution of 1688 and the French Revolution of 1789 is one of the tightening grip on the electoral system of an ever smaller group of powerful landowners. The control of parliamentary representation in Wales had fallen into the hands of a score of great families. It was essentially based on the voting-power of their estates, or the control of borough machinery, strengthened over the course of time by tradition and by the deployment of the local patronage that customarily accrued to MPs. The oligarchy became a self-perpetuating one. No single estate could provide an overall majority in any county, as Gogerddan discovered in Cardiganshire in 1710, but it was almost invariably the largest one in each shire that provided the basis of the dominant interest, attracting friends and allies by persuasion and patronage, controlling tenants and dependants by coercion.

The existing power structure was buttressed by the difficulty and expense of mounting a challenge. The reputed intention of Tredegar to spend £10,000 in the 1771 Monmouthshire by-election highlighted the problem facing opponents of dominant interests. It cost Plas Newydd over £8,000 to wrest Anglesey from Baron Hill in 1784 by the barest of margins. When two major interests clashed, as in Montgomeryshire in 1774, the contest cost over £10,000 between them. Sir John Glynne and Sir Thomas Mostyn complained that a shared expenditure of £4,000 in Flint Boroughs in 1734 was too great a burden even for leading squires. Since a poll itself accounted for much of the expenditure of a contest, through the cost of the transport, accommodation and entertainment of voters, it was no coincidence that several challenges were dropped on the day of election itself, after having otherwise caused the maximum of inconvenience. Many canvasses were abandoned much earlier, and prospective candidates would often do no more than take soundings among the local gentry. It was often customary to await the opportunity of a vacancy, for one factor in the electoral situation was the frequently professed reluctance to 'disturb the peace of the county'. The hustle and bustle of a contest, creating bad feeling as well as causing expenditure, was a circumstance genuinely deplored among the gentry. Even if the balance of power in an area was still undecided, rival interests usually deemed compromise wiser than conflict, as did the Morgans of Tredegar and the Dukes of Beaufort in south-east Wales, and Baron Hill and Plas Newydd in north-west Wales after 1784. Contests were increasingly rare, and often decisive for decades.

This dead hand of oligarchy left little scope for popular opinion. Occasional appeals to and demonstrations of 'independency' at election times concerned the role of county freeholders, for borough contests centred on the creation of obedient burgesses. Such appeals were essentially tactical weapons used by squires otherwise overmatched in the local power structure, and sometimes achieved success, as for the Owens of Orielton in Pembrokeshire and the Rices of Newton in Carmarthenshire. That magnate power underlay elections was true even of the famous Glamorganshire by-election of 1789, sometimes hailed as the dawn of a new political era. Certainly the control of the ruling county oligarchy was overthrown, but by an alliance of other powerful interests rather than through the popular campaign. Radical Robert Morris might state in a pamphlet that the issue was 'whether a few non-resident Lords shall name, or the freeholders elect, a member to represent the county of Glamorgan in Parliament';[147] and to the contemporary observer it could seem that the torrent of such propaganda had carried the day. But the underlying reality of the situation was demonstrated by the circumstance that the successful popular candidate, himself a wealthy landowner and son of the retiring MP, was proposed by Thomas Mansel Talbot of Margam and seconded by John Morgan of Tredegar.[148]

Earlier in the century the apparent demonstrations of public opinion were conjured up by parliamentary politicians and other local magnates for their own purposes. That had been so with respect to the 'Church in danger' cry of 1710, the furore over the Excise Bill in 1733, the excitement over the fall of Sir Robert Walpole in 1742, and the occasional outbreaks of Jacobite sentiment. While there must have been some bases of popular sentiment, in Wales those occasions were stage-managed affairs.

The political movements of the later eighteenth century, even before the French Revolution, are often seen as being somewhat different in character, as harbingers of a more genuinely popular opinion. There is some validity in this interpretation. The targets were less vague, not so much immediate grievances, or naive ones like 'corruption'. There was more concern with major political issues, like the American Revolution or the matters raised by the career of John Wilkes, and also with such long-term objectives as Parliamentary Reform. But the orchestration of local public opinion in Wales on such matters was still a matter of initiatives by local MPs or other squires. In 1769, when Denbighshire celebrated the first re-election of John Wilkes after his expulsion from Middlesex, the lead was taken by borough MP Richard Myddelton, who illuminated the bridge of Llangollen with 136 lamps, the supposed number of the minority voting against the

---

[147] Tredegar MSS 72/77.

[148] For more detail on this by-election, see John, 'The Parliamentary Representation of Glamorgan, 1536–1822', MA Wales, 1934, pp. 118–20, and Thomas in *Glamorgan County History*, IV, 425–7.

expulsion of Wilkes on 3 February.[149] Neither, as has been seen, was spontaneous public feeling the motive of the other manifestations of political opinion in Wales: the three pro-Wilkes petitions of 1771, and the three anti-American ones of 1775, all from south-west Wales; the protests against the Treasury Warrant of 1778; the three petitions of 1780 on Economical Reform; and the 1784 meetings voting resolutions for or against Pitt.

None of this threatened the political structure of contemporary Wales. The nascent movement for Parliamentary Reform was quite another matter, for it intended to alter constituencies and widen electorates. As early as 1780 a Denbighshire county meeting at Ruthin on 1 May voted for Parliamentary Reform in principle: 'the unequal representation of the people is a grievance that stands in need of a remedy'.[150] And in national plans of that year for Parliamentary Reform, Wales was not forgotten. In the scheme for representation formulated by the Westminster Committee the number of Welsh MPs would have been increased from twenty-seven to thirty.[151] Christopher Wyvill's movement proposed four extra county seats, for Carmarthenshire, Denbighshire, Glamorgan and Montgomeryshire, presumably the shires deemed to have the largest electorates.[152]

It was only in 1782 that Wyvill, the Yorkshire leader of the nationwide reform movement, was able to give priority to Parliamentary Reform over Economical Reform, and that year the cause found a Commons champion in young William Pitt. In Wales the campaign barely got under way. Only in Caernarfonshire and Denbighshire, so it would seem, were Reform Committees established, being chaired respectively by MP John Parry and Thomas Kyffin of Maenan. In the spring of 1782 Caernarfonshire voted reform resolutions suggested by Wyvill, but the lack of enthusiasm in Denbighshire deterred Kyffin from attempting the same step. On 7 May Pitt introduced his first reform motion, and that John Parry was among the minority of 141 in favour is evident from a resolution passed by a Caernarfonshire county meeting of 18 May thanking him for supporting it. Pitt's move was evidently premature, but Wyvill hoped to take advantage of a supposedly sympathetic ministry by a national campaign of petitions later in 1782 when, he told Kyffin, he hoped to have 'the approbation and

---

[149] *Baldwin's London Weekly Journal*, 4 March 1769. The minority was 137, plus two tellers – Myddelton himself had been absent! Forty-five bonfires were lit on hills in the county, that being the symbolic Wilkes number – that of the issue of the *North Briton* for which Wilkes had first been prosecuted. For an account of celebrations in Bala, Merionethshire, see *Gazetteer*, 27 February 1769.

[150] *Chester Chronicle*, 12 May 1780.

[151] BL Add. MSS 38593, f. 43.

[152] *Wyvill Papers*, II, 588.

support of the independent gentlemen of Wales'.[153] On 1 November Wyvill issued a circular seeking the views of local reformers. Only two Welsh responses are known. Dean William Shipley, who, as chairman of the Flintshire Committee had already sent Wyvill a copy of resolutions it passed on 18 September, reported that a committee meeting on 27 November had put a Welsh angle on the issue of rotten boroughs by proposing that instead of disfranchisement they could be grouped as in Wales.[154] The Mayor of Tenby, Laurence Cook, suggested that those electors disfranchised in rotten boroughs should be allowed to vote in counties instead.[155] Three reform petitions from Wales were presented to the House of Commons, voted by Caernarfonshire, Denbighshire and Flintshire.[156] When on 7 May 1783 Pitt put forward another reform motion, a division-list shows that eight Welsh MPs were among the 149 voting for it. Politically they were a mixed bag, and evenly split between supporters and opponents of the future Pitt ministry. The former were Lord Bulkeley, despite his ownership of the pocket borough of Beaumaris, John Parry, John Vaughan and Watkin Williams. The latter were Northite Hugh Owen, Foxites John Hanbury and Sir George Warren, and independent Sir Herbert Mackworth.[157] There is nothing here to suggest that advocacy of reform won Pitt political support. Nevertheless that his commitment to Parliamentary Reform was an electoral asset to him in 1784 was clearly implied by the Caernarfonshire Address of 15 March.[158]

We therefore humbly take this occasion to shew to your Majesty our firm reliance, that from your Majesty's paternal attention to the welfare of your people, the abilities, zeal and integrity of your Ministers, and the widest necessity of the measure impressed in the minds of your faithful subjects, such Reformation of Parliament will take place, that in all circumstances the genuine voice of a free and loyal people shall be fairly and fully expressed by their representatives.

Yet Parliamentary Reform was a cross-party cause, and when on 18 April 1785 Pitt made his third and last reform proposal, four of the six Welsh MPs voting in support were opposition men, Lord Milford, absent from the previous Parliament, and three who had not hitherto done so – Evan Lloyd Vaughan and the two Tredegar Morgans, Charles and John.

---

[153] *Wyvill Papers*, I, 407–11.
[154] *Wyvill Papers*, II, 86–7; IV, 192–4.
[155] *Wyvill Papers*, II, 78–81.
[156] *CJ*, XXXIX, 251, 290–1, 360–1; *Wyvill Papers*, II, 210–12.
[157] *Wyvill Papers*, II, 253–7.
[158] *London Gazette*, 23 March 1784.

The two Welsh Pittites in favour were John Parry and new MP Nicholas Bayly.[159] Altogether, in 1783 and 1785, thirteen out of a possible thirty-three Welsh MPs who might have voted for Parliamentary Reform had done so, a greater than average proportion of the House of Commons membership.

All this was a false dawn of popular politics. The stirrings of political opinion in Wales before 1789 were slight and superficial, virtually confined to the gentry and freeholders. Reaction against the French Revolution would cut short the incipient reform movements, and the Industrial Revolution, with its social and economic consequences, would be a necessary precursor to the achievement of political reform. Even then it would take nearly a century before the complete overthrow of the gentry rule that was the characteristic of eighteenth-century Wales, a situation implicitly emphasized by the circumstance that the very two parliamentary families most associated with industrial development, Hanbury of Pontypool and Mackworth of the Gnoll, had by the end of the century both lost their share in the parliamentary representation that they had enjoyed for most of the period.

It was the social structure of Wales that provided the distinctive political ambiance of opposition to government, rather than any sense of national identity; although displays of such feeling were occasionally hailed as praiseworthy examples of the independent spirit of 'Ancient Britons'. A 'country' attitude towards government was characteristic of the squire-archy in England, and in Wales their dominance was more firmly rooted, as Horace Walpole observed even before their electoral power to resist government was confirmed by the 1784 election. It was not coincidental that at the times of high political temperature the ruling class of Wales provided a clear majority against the government of the day. The 1784 election invites comparison with the reign of Queen Anne, when the overwhelming Tory majority was essentially 'country' in outlook. Such spontaneous responses were muted in quieter times, and in mid-century most of the Welsh squires were drawn into the contemporary patronage system, becoming more 'court' than 'country'. For detailed study of both the constituencies in Wales and the behaviour of Welsh MPs at Westminster points to that political distinction as being more significant than the traditional party divide of Whig and Tory.

The first age of party before 1714 had witnessed the formation of local electoral alliances bearing that party terminology, at least in the minds of their respective opponents, both within counties and across shire boundaries, for the estates of many squires were geographically scattered.

[159] *Wyvill Papers*, II, 433–5.

Some of these electoral coalitions survived for generations, hallowed by tradition, long outliving their original party political purposes though not their practical advantages. The mid-century alliance in Cardiganshire of Whig Crosswood and Tory Nanteos was an exception even then in breaking with such customary practice. By that time most electoral alignments in Wales bore little relation to national politics at Westminster. In some instances they never had done so, for personal friendships outweighed political differences in the scales of most men, and so did tactical advantages, as in Cardiganshire during Anne's reign.

After 1714 it suited families of Whig tradition to claim electoral assistance and political patronage from Whig ministers by branding as Tory opponents who themselves accepted no such designation, preferring that of 'country party', one esteemed in contemporary opinion as denoting opposition to government, and genuinely used by a man like the future first Sir Watkin Williams Wynn from his entry into Parliament early in George I's reign. If supporters of government after 1714 sought for their own purposes to portray the political scene as Whig versus Tory, opponents of government perceived it in a context of honest 'country' against corrupt 'court'. Detailed studies, as of the evidence from Wales, destroy simplistic notions of a two-party system. Constituency politics were often divorced from events at Westminster.

Select Bibliography

Primary Sources

(A) Manuscripts

(i) British Library (cited as BL)

Eg[erton] MSS 215–63	Parliamentary Diary of Henry Cavendish 1768–1774.
Harleian MSS 7556	Various Matters relating to Parliament.
Stowe MSS 223	Hanover State Papers.
Stowe MSS 354	Collections Relating to Parliament.
Add[itional] MSS. 4319	Letters to Dr Birch.
Add. MSS 5726	Sir William Musgrave's Autograph Collection.
Add. MSS 29548–96	Nottingham Papers.
Add. MSS 30865–96	Wilkes Papers.
Add. MSS 32686–3072	Newcastle Papers.
Add. MSS 35349–6278	Hardwicke Papers.
Add. MSS 36796–7	Bute Papers.
Add. MSS 38190–468	Liverpool Papers.
Add. MSS 38593–4	Minutes of Westminster Committee 1780–83.
Add. MSS 39707–56	Welsh Pedigrees.
Add. MSS 46397–400	Puleston Papers.
Add. MSS 51318–2254	Holland House Papers.
Add. MSS 57804–37	Grenville Papers.
Add. MSS 61101–710	Blenheim Papers.
Add. MSS 70001–523	Portland Papers.
MS Facs. 340 (1–5)	John Robinson Papers.

(ii) Public Record Office

Home Office Papers (cited as HO).
State Papers Domestic (cited as SP).
Chatham Papers (cited as PRO 30/8).

(iii) National Library of Wales
NLW General MSS
341F	1741 Denbighshire Poll-Book.
1352	Letter-Book of John Campbell.
1548	Anglesey and Caernarvonshire Papers.
5502E	Thomas Pennant Papers.
66106–8	C. F. E. Allen Collection on Pembrokeshire Elections.
6575E	Glamorgan Election Papers 1767–1826.
7705D	1715 Monmouth Boroughs Poll-Book.
9070–2	Panton Papers.
12356E	Welsh Pedigrees.
12440E	Miscellaneous Correspondence.
14215C	Letters to James Lloyd of Mabws.
14941C	Cycle Club Minute Book.
23273–5	Journals of Sir Erasmus Philipps.
23276	Letter-Book of Sir Erasmus Philipps.

Peniarth MSS 416A Diary of Mrs Elizabeth Baker of Dolgelley 1728–86.
        418D Miscellaneous Letters.
Bettisfield MSS.
Brogyntyn MSS.
Chirk Castle MSS.
Crosswood MSS.
Dolaucothi MSS.
Edwinsford MSS.
Glansevern MSS.
Glynllifon MSS.
Glynne of Hawarden MSS.
Gogerddan MSS.
Harpton MSS.
Leeswood MSS.
Llanfair and Brynodol MSS.
Nanteos MSS.
Pantperthog MSS.
Penpont MSS.
Penrice and Margam MSS.
Picton Castle MSS.
Powis Castle MSS.
Rug MSS.
Tredegar MSS.
Wynnstay MSS.

(iv) Library, University of Wales, Bangor
Bangor General MSS.
Diary of William Bulkeley of Brynddu 1734–1760.
Baron Hill MSS.

Bodorgan MSS.
Mostyn MSS.
Nannau MSS.
Penrhos MSS.
Plas Newydd MSS.
Porth Yr Aur MSS.
Presaddfed MSS.

(v) Carmarthenshire Archives Service, County Hall, Carmarthen
Cawdor MSS.
Cwmgwili MSS.
Dynevor MSS.

(vi) Cambridge University Library
MS 6851   Parliamentary Journal of Edward Harley
                                    1734–1751.
Cholmondeley Houghton MSS.

(vii) In other repositories or in private possession

Bute MSS (Cardiff group)	In the possession of the Marquess of Bute.
Chandos Letter-Book 1721–2	Northamptonshire County Record Office.
Harrowby MSS	In the possession of the Earl of Harrowby.
Kemys Tynte MSS	Glamorgan Record Office.
Mackworth MSS	Library, University of Wales, Swansea.
Malmesbury MSS (photocopies)	Hampshire County Record Office.
Stuart MSS	Royal Archives, Windsor Castle.
Wentworth Woodhouse MSS	Sheffield Archives, Sheffield City Libraries.

(B) Printed Sources

(i) Parliamentary Proceedings
Journals of the House of Commons (cited as *CJ*).
Journals of the House of Lords (cited as *LJ*).
Almon, J., *The Debates of the British House of Commons from 1743 to 1774* (11 vols., London, 1766–75). Cited as Almon, *Debates*.
Almon, J., *The Parliamentary Register . . . 1774 to . . . 1780* (17 vols., London, 1775–80). Cited as Almon, *Parl. Reg.*
Chandler, R., *The History and Proceedings of the House of Commons . . . 1660 to . . . 1743* (14 vols., London, 1741–4). Cited as Chandler, *Debates*.
Cobbett, W., *Parliamentary History of England from . . . 1066 to . . . 1803* (36 vols., London 1806–20). Cited as Cobbett, *Parl. Hist.*
Debrett, J., *The Parliamentary Register . . . 1780 to . . . 1796* (45 vols., London, 1781–96). Cited as Debrett, *Parl. Reg.*

Select Bibliography

(ii) Contemporary Correspondence and Memoirs

Reports of the Historical Manuscripts Commission (cited as *HMC*).
Carlisle MSS (15 Report, App. Part VI, 1897).
Diary of John Perceval, 1st Earl of Egmont (3 vols., 1920–3).
Hastings MSS III (1934).
Kenyon MSS (14 Report, App. Part IV, 1894).
Portland MSS IV–V (15 Report, App. Part IV, 1897–9).
Puleston MSS (15 Report, App. Part VII, 1898).
Various MSS VI (1909).

Correspondence of John, Fourth Duke of Bedford . . . with an introduction by Lord John Russell (3 vols., London, 1842–6). Cited as *Bedford Papers*.
The Diaries of John Bird of Cardiff, Clerk to the First Marquess of Bute 1790–1803. Ed. H. M. Thomas (Cardiff, 1987).
Letters from George III to Lord Bute 1756–1766. Ed. R. Sedgwick (London, 1939). Cited as *Bute Letters*.
Correspondence of William Pitt, Earl of Chatham. Ed. W. S. Taylor and J. H. Pringle (4 vols., London 1838–40). Cited as *Chatham Papers*.
Anecdotes of the Life of the Right Hon. William Pitt, Earl of Chatham . . . 1736 to . . . 1778. Ed. J. Almon (3 vols., London, 1810). Cited as *Chatham Anecdotes*.
Chirk Castle Accounts 1666–1753. Ed. W. M. Myddelton (Manchester, 1931).
The Devonshire Diary: William Cavendish Fourth Duke of Devonshire. Memoranda on State of Affairs 1759–1762. Ed. P. D. Brown and K. W. Schweizer (London, 1982).
The History of the Cases of Controverted Elections. Ed. Sylvester Douglas (4 vols., London, 1802). Cited as Douglas, *Elections*.
'Leicester House Politics, 1750–60, from the papers of John, Second Earl of Egmont'. Ed. A. Newman, *Camden Miscellany XXIII*, Royal Historical Society (London, 1969), pp. 85–228.
Chronicles of Erthig on the Dyke. Ed. A. L. Cust (2 vols., London, 1914). Cited as *Erthig Chronicles*.
The Correspondence of King George the Third from 1760 to December 1783. Ed. Sir John Fortescue (6 vols., London, 1927–8).
The Grenville Papers: Being the Correspondence of Richard Grenville, Earl Temple, K.G., and the Right Honourable George Grenville . . . . Ed. W. J. Smith (4 vols., London, 1852–3). Cited as *Grenville Papers*.
Additional Grenville Papers, 1763–1765. Ed. J. Tomlinson (Manchester, 1962).
The Works of the Right Honourable Sir Chas. Hanbury Williams, K.B. (3 vols., London, 1827).
The Parliamentary Diary of Sir Edward Knatchbull 1722–1730. Ed. A. N. Newman (London, 1963).
Narcissus Luttrell. A Brief Historical Relation of State Affairs from September 1678 to April 1714 (6 vols., Oxford, 1857). Cited as Luttrell, *State Affairs*.
The Letters of Lewis, Richard, William and John Morris, 1728–1765. Ed. J. H. Davies (2 vols., Aberystwyth, 1907). Cited as *Morris Letters*.

Memorials of John Murray of Broughton. Ed. R. F. Bell (Edinburgh, 1898).

The Correspondence of the Dukes of Richmond and Newcastle 1724–1750. Ed. T. J. McCann (Lewes, 1984).

The Parliamentary Papers of John Robinson 1774–1784. Ed. W. T. Laprade (London, 1922).

'John Robinson's "State" of the House of Commons, July 1780'. Ed. I. R. Christie, *Camden Miscellany XXX*, Royal Historical Society (London, 1990), pp. 441–97.

Thraliana. The Diary of Mrs Hester Lynch Thrale 1776–1809. Ed. K. C. Balderston (2 vols., Oxford, 1951).

Selected Trevecka Letters 1747–1794. Ed. G. M. Roberts (Caernarfon, 1962).

The Letters of Horace Walpole, Fourth Earl of Orford. Ed. P. Toynbee (16 vols., Oxford, 1905). Cited as Walpole, *Letters* (Toynbee).

The Yale Edition of Horace Walpole's Correspondence. Ed. W. S. Lewis (48 vols., Oxford, 1937–83). Cited as Walpole, *Corr.*

Horace Walpole. Memoirs of the Reign of George II. Ed. Lord Holland (3 vols., London, 1847).

Horace Walpole. Memoirs of the Reign of King George the Third. Ed. G. F. R. Barker (4 vols., London, 1894).

The Last Journals of Horace Walpole, during the reign of George III from 1771 to 1783. Ed. A. F. Stewart (2 vols., London, 1910).

Calendar of Wynn of Gwydir Papers 1515–1690 (Aberystwyth, 1926).

Political Papers, chiefly respecting the attempt of the county of York . . . to effect a reformation of the Parliament. Collected by the Rev. Christopher Wyvill (6 vols., York, 1794–1802).

(iii) Contemporary Periodicals and Pamphlets

(a) Periodicals
Adams Weekly Courant
Baldwin's Weekly Journal
Chester Chronicle
The Flying-Post
The Gazetteer
The Gentleman's Magazine
Gloucester Journal
Hereford Journal
London Evening Post
London Gazette
Middlesex Journal
Morning Chronicle
Morning Herald
The Post-Boy
The Public Ledger
St James's Chronicle

(b) Pamphlets

A Collection of White and Black Lists . . . (1715).

A Letter from a Welsh Freeholder to his Representative (1784).

Secondary Works

(A) Books

(i) General

Baxter, S. B., *William III* (London, 1966).

Brooke, J., *King George III* (London, 1972).

Browning, A., *Thomas Osborne, Earl of Danby and Duke of Leeds* (3 vols, Glasgow, 1951).

Cannon, J., *The Fox–North Coalition: Crisis of the Constitution 1782–4* (Cambridge, 1969).

Cannon, J. (ed.), *The Whig Ascendancy: Colloquies on Hanoverian England* (London, 1981).

Christie, I. R., *The End of North's Ministry 1780–1782* (London, 1958).

—— *Wilkes, Wyvill and Reform: The Parliamentary Reform Movement in British Politics 1760–1785* (London, 1962).

Clark, J. C .D., *The Dynamics of Change: The Crisis of the 1750s and English Party Systems* (Cambridge, 1982).

—— *English Society 1688–1832* (Cambridge, 1985).

Cokayne, G. E. (ed.), *The Complete Peerage* [14 vols., London, 1910–59].

Colley, L., *In Defiance of Oligarchy: The Tory Party 1714–60* (Cambridge, 1982).

Coxe, W., *Memoirs of the Life and Administration of Sir Robert Walpole, Earl of Orford* (3 vols., London, 1798).

—— *Memoirs of the Administration of the Right Honourable Henry Pelham* (2 vols., London, 1829).

Cruickshanks, E., *Political Untouchables: The Tories and the '45* (London, 1979).

Dickinson, H. T., *The Politics of the People in Eighteenth-Century Britain* (London, 1995).

Ditchfield, G. M., Hayton, D., and Jones, C. (eds.), *British Parliamentary Lists 1660–1800: A Register* (London, 1995).

Feiling, K., *A History of the Tory Party 1640–1714* (Oxford, 1924).

Foord, A. S., *His Majesty's Opposition 1714–1832* (Oxford, 1964).

Francis, G. R., *Romance of the White Rose* (London, 1933).

Ginter, D. E., *Voting Records of the British House of Commons 1761–1820* (6 vols., London, 1995).

Greenwood, D., *William King, Tory and Jacobite* (Oxford, 1969).

Harris, R., *A Patriot Press: National Politics and the London Press in the 1740s* (Oxford, 1993).

Hill, B. W., *The Growth of Parliamentary Parties 1689–1742* (London, 1976).

Holmes, G., *British Politics in the Age of Anne* (London, 1967).

—— *The Trial of Doctor Sacheverell* (London, 1973).

Horwitz, H., *Parliament, Policy and Politics in the Reign of William III* (Manchester, 1977).

Jones, C. (ed.), *Party and Management in Parliament 1660–1784* (Leicester, 1984).

Langford, P., *The Excise Crisis: Society and Politics in the Age of Walpole* (Oxford, 1975).

McInnes, A., *Robert Harley: Puritan Politician* (London, 1970).

McLynn, F. J., *France and the Jacobite Rising of 1745* (Edinburgh, 1981).

—— *The Jacobite Army in England. 1745: The Final Campaign* (Edinburgh, 1983).

Mahon, Lord, *History of England from the Peace of Utrecht to the Peace of Versailles 1713–1783* (7 vols., Leipzig, 1853–4).

Monod, P. K., *Jacobitism and the English People 1688–1788* (Cambridge, 1989).

Namier, Sir Lewis, *The Structure of Politics at the Accession of George III* (2nd edn, London, 1957).

—— *England in the Age of the American Revolution* (2nd edn, London, 1961).

—— *Personalities and Powers* (London, 1955).

—— *Crossroads of Power* (London, 1962).

Namier, Sir Lewis and Brooke, J., *Charles Townshend* (London, 1964).

—— (eds.), *The House of Commons, 1754–1790: The History of Parliament* (3 vols., London, 1964).

O'Gorman, F., *The Rise of Party in England: The Rockingham Whigs 1760–82* (London, 1975).

—— *Voters, Patrons and Parties: The Unreformed Electorate of Hanoverian England 1734–1832* (Oxford, 1989).

Oldfield, T. H. B., *An Entire and Complete History, Political and Personal, of the Boroughs of Great Britain* (3 vols., London, 1792).

Oldmixon, J., *History of England under King William and Queen Mary, Queen Anne, and George I* (London, 1735).

Owen, J. B., *The Rise of the Pelhams* (London, 1957).

Porritt, E. and Porritt, A.G, *The Unreformed House of Commons* (2 vols., Cambridge, 1909).

Sedgwick, R. (ed.), *The House of Commons 1715–1754: The History of Parliament* (2 vols., London, 1970).

Robson, R., *The Oxfordshire Election of 1754* (London, 1949).

Rubini, D., *Court and Country 1688–1702* (London, 1968).

Speck, W. A., *The Butcher: The Duke of Cumberland and the Suppression of the '45* (Oxford, 1981).

Thomas, P. D. G., *The House of Commons in the Eighteenth Century* (Oxford, 1971).

—— *Lord North* (London, 1976).

—— *Tea Party to Independence: The Third Phase of the American Revolution 1773–1776* (Oxford, 1991).

Thomas, P. D. G., *John Wilkes: A Friend to Liberty* (Oxford, 1996).

Thorne, R. G. (ed.), *The House of Commons 1790–1820: The History of Parliament* (5 vols., London, 1986).

Treloar, W. P., *Wilkes and the City* (London, 1917).

Walcott, R., *English Politics in the Early Eighteenth Century* (Oxford, 1956).

Yorke, P. C., *The Life and Correspondence of Philip Yorke Earl of Hardwicke, Lord High Chancellor of Great Britain* (3 vols., Cambridge, 1913).

(ii) Relating to Wales

Barlow, M., *Barlow Family Records* (London, 1932).

Clement, M., *The SPCK and Wales 1699–1740* (Cardiff, 1954).

Coxe, W., *Historical Tour Through Monmouthshire* (London, 1801).

Dodd, A. H., *Studies in Stuart Wales* (Cardiff, 1952).

—— *A History of Wrexham* (Wrexham, 1957).

—— *A History of Caernarvonshire 1284–1900* (Caernarfon, 1968).

Evans, G. E., *Aberystwyth and its Court Leet* (Aberystwyth, 1902).

—— *Lampeter* (Aberystwyth, 1905).

Fenton, R., *A Historical Tour Through Pembrokeshire* (Brecon, 1903 reprint of 1810 edition).

Griffith, J. E., *Pedigrees of Anglesey and Caernarvonshire Families* (Horncastle, 1914).

Herbert, T. and Jones, G. E. (eds.), *The Remaking of Wales in the Eighteenth Century* (Cardiff, 1988).

Howell, D. W., *Patriarchs and Parasites: The Gentry of South-West Wales in the Eighteenth Century* (Cardiff, 1986).

Howells, B. (ed.), *Pembrokeshire County History: Volume III. Early Modern Pembrokeshire 1536–1815* (Haverfordwest, 1987).

Howse, W. H., *Radnorshire* (Hereford, 1949).

Hughes, J., *A History of the Parliamentary Representation of the County of Cardigan* (Aberystwyth, 1849).

Humphreys, M., *The Crisis of Community: Montgomeryshire 1680–1815* (Cardiff, 1996).

James, A. J. and Thomas, J. E., *Union to Reform: A History of the Parliamentary Representation of Wales 1536–1832* (Llandysul, 1986).

Jenkins, G. H., *The Foundations of Modern Wales 1642–1780* (Oxford, 1987).

Jenkins, P., *The Making of a Ruling Class: The Glamorgan Gentry 1640–1790* (Cambridge, 1983).

Jones, T., *The History of Brecknockshire* (4 vols., Brecon, 1898–1930).

Lloyd, J. E. (ed.), *A History of Carmarthenshire. Volume II* (London, 1939).

Locke, A. A., *The Hanbury Family* (2 vols., London, 1916).

Meyrick, S. R., *History and Antiquities of the County of Cardigan* (London, 1808).

Moore, D. (ed.), *Wales in the Eighteenth Century* (Swansea, 1976).

Palmer, A. N., *History of the Town of Wrexham* (Wrexham, 1893).

Phillips, B., *Peterwell: The History of a Mansion and its Infamous Squire* (Llandysul, 1983).

Phillips, J. R., *Memoirs of the Ancient Family of Owen of Orielton* (London, 1886).

Ramage, H., *Portraits of an Island: Eighteenth Century Anglesey* (Llangefni, 1987).

Richards, M., *Welsh Administrative and Territorial Units: Medieval and Modern* (Cardiff, 1969).

Roberts, A., *Wynnstay and the Wynns* (Oswestry, 1876).

Roderick, A. J., (ed.), *Wales Through the Ages, II* (Llandybie, 1960).

Williams, D., *The History of Monmouthshire* (London, 1796).

Williams, G. (ed.), *Glamorgan County History: Volume IV, Early Modern Glamorgan* (Cardiff, 1974).

Williams, J., *The History of Radnorshire* (Tenby, 1859).

Williams, W. R., *The Parliamentary History of the Principality of Wales 1541–1895* (Brecknock, 1895). Cited as Williams, *Parl. Hist.*

—— *The History of the Great Sessions in Wales 1542–1830* (Brecknock, 1899). Cited as Williams, *Welsh Judges.*

(B) Essays, Articles and Chapters

(i) General

Browning, A. and Milne, D. J., 'An Exclusion Bill Division List', *Bulletin Institute of Historical Research* (*BIHR*), 23 (1950), 205–25.

Burton, I. F., Riley, P. W. J., and Rowlands, E., 'Political Parties in the Reigns of William III and Anne: The Evidence of Division Lists', *BIHR Special Supplement No. 7* (November 1968).

Cannon, J., 'Polls Supplementary to the *History of Parliament* volumes 1715–90', *BIHR*, 47 (1974), 110–16.

Clark, J. C. D., 'The Decline of Party, 1740–1760', *English Historical Review*, 93 (1978), 499–527.

Colley, L. J., 'The Mitchell Election Division, 24 March 1755', *BIHR*, 49 (1976), 80–107.

—— 'The Loyal Brotherhood and the Cocoa Tree: The London Organisation of the Tory Party, 1727–1760', *Historical Journal* (*HJ*), 20 (1977), 77–95.

Cruickshanks, E., Ferris, J., and Hayton, D., 'The House of Commons Vote on the Transfer of the Crown, 5 February 1689', *BIHR*, 52 (1979), 37–47.

De Beer, E. S., 'Division-Lists of 1688–1715. Some Addenda', *BIHR*, 19 (1942–3), 65–6.

Dickinson, H. T., 'The October Club', *Huntington Library Quarterly*, 32 (1969–70), 155–73.

Hayton, D., 'The "Country" Interest and the Party System, 1689-c.1720', in Jones, *Party and Management*, pp. 37–85.

—— 'The Country Party in the House of Commons 1698–1699: A Forecast of the Opposition to a Standing Army?', *Parliamentary History*, 6 (1987), 140–67.

Jones, J. R., 'Shaftesbury's "Worthy Men": A Whig View of the Parliament of 1679', *BIHR*, 30 (1957), 232–41.

Ransome, M., 'Division-Lists of the House of Commons 1715–1760', *BIHR*, 19 (1942–3), 1–8.

—— 'The Parliamentary Career of Sir Humphrey Mackworth', *Birmingham Historical Journal*, 1 (1948), 232–54.

Snyder, H. L., 'Party Configurations in the Early Eighteenth Century House of Commons', *BIHR*, 45 (1972), 38–72.

Speck, W. A., 'The Choice of a Speaker in 1705', *BIHR*, 37 (1964), 20–46.

—— ' "The Most Corrupt Council in Christendom": Decisions in Controverted Elections 1702–1742', in Jones, *Party and Management*, pp. 107–22.

Thomas, P. D. G., 'Party Politics in Eighteenth-Century Britain: Some Myths and a Touch of Reality', *British Journal for Eighteenth Century Studies*, 10 (1987), 201–10.

Walcott, R. R., 'Division-Lists of the House of Commons 1689–1715', *BIHR*, 14 (1936–7), 25–36.

(ii) Relating to Wales

Archaeologia Cambrensis (*Arch. Camb.*), passim.

Byegones relating to Wales and border counties, passim.

Cragoe, M., 'The Golden Grove Interest in Carmarthenshire Politics, 1804–1821', *Welsh History Review* (*WHR*), 16 (1993), 467–93.

Dodd, A. H., 'The Pattern of Politics in Stuart Wales', *Transactions of the Honourable Society of Cymmrodorion* (*T.H.S. Cymm.*), (1948), pp. 8–91.

—— 'Tuning the Welsh Bench, 1680', *National Library of Wales Journal* (*NLWJ*), 6 (1949–50), 249–59.

—— 'Flintshire Politics in the Seventeenth Century', *Flintshire Historical Society Journal*, 14 (1953–4), 22–46.

Howells, J. M., 'The Crosswood Estate, 1547–1947', *Ceredigion*, 3 (1956–9), 70–88.

Howse, W. H., 'The Harley v. Lewis Affray at New Radnor in 1693', *Radnorshire Historical Society Transactions*, 26 (1956), 50–3.

—— 'A Family Feud at New Radnor and Its Results', ibid., 28 (1958), 17–23.

Jenkins, D., 'The Pryse Family of Gogerddan', *NLWJ*, 8 (1953–4), 81–96, 176–98, 353–68.

Jenkins, P., 'Jacobites and Freemasons in Eighteenth-Century Wales', *WHR*, 9 (1979), 391–406.

—— 'Tory Industrialism and Town Politics: Swansea in the Eighteenth Century', *HJ*, 28 (1985), 103–23.

—— 'Party Conflict and Political Stability in Monmouthshire 1680–1740', *HJ*, 29 (1986), 557–75.

Johnson, A. M., 'Bussy Mansell (1623–99): Political Survivalist', *Morgannwg*, 20 (1976), 9–36.

Jones, F., 'Disaffection and Dissent in Pembrokeshire', *T.H.S. Cymm.* (1946–7), pp. 206–31.

—— 'The Society of Sea Serjeants', *T.H.S. Cymm.* (1967), pp. 57–91.

Llewellyn, W., 'David Morgan, the Welsh Jacobite', *Transactions of the Liverpool Welsh National Society*, 10 (1894–5), 75–108.

Lloyd-Johnes, H. J., 'The Cardigan Boroughs Election, 1774', *Ceredigion*, 7 (1972–5), 50–5.

Morgan, W. T., 'County Elections in Monmouthshire, 1705–1847', *NLWJ*, 10 (1957–8), 167–84.

Richards, T., 'The Anglesey Election of 1708', *Transactions of the Anglesey Antiquarian Society (TAAS)* (1943), pp. 23–34.

Roberts, G., 'Parliamentary Representation of the Welsh Boroughs', *Bulletin Board of Celtic Studies (BBCS)*, 4 (1927–9), 352–60.

—— 'The County Representation of Anglesey in the Eighteenth Century', *TAAS* (1930), pp. 60–78.

—— 'The Parliamentary History of Beaumaris, 1555–1832', *TAAS* (1933), pp. 97–109.

—— 'Political Affairs from 1536 to 1900', *A History of Carmarthenshire*, II, 1–86.

Roberts, P., 'The Merioneth Gentry and Local Government', *Journal of the Merioneth Historical and Record Society (Merioneth HJ)*, V (1965), 21–38.

Shankland, T., 'Sir John Philipps of Picton Castle, the Society for Promoting Christian Knowledge, and the Charity School Movement in Wales 1699–1737', *T.H.S. Cymm.* (1904–5), pp. 74–216.

Taylor, H., 'Flint Boroughs Election, 1697', *Flintshire Historical Society Journal*, 11 (1925), 88–90.

Thomas, P. D. G., 'The Parliamentary Representation of Merioneth during the Eighteenth Century', *Merioneth HJ*, 3 (1958), 128–36.

—— 'The Parliamentary Representation of Caernarvonshire in the Eighteenth Century: Part I, 1708–1749', *Transactions of the Caernarvonshire Historical Society (T. Caerns. H.S.)*, 19 (1958), 42–53.

—— 'The Parliamentary Representation of Caernarvonshire in the Eighteenth Century: Part II, 1749–1784', *T. Caerns. H.S.*, 20 (1959), 72–86.

—— 'Wynnstay Versus Chirk Castle: Parliamentary Elections in Denbighshire 1716–1741', *NLWJ*, 11 (1959), 105–23.

—— 'Parliamentary Elections in Brecknockshire 1689–1832', *Brycheiniog*, 6 (1960), 99–113.

—— 'Jacobitism in Wales', *WHR*, 1 (1960–2), 279–300.

—— 'Glamorgan Politics 1700–1750', *Morgannwg*, 6 (1962), 52–77.

—— 'Sir George Wynne and the Flint Borough Elections of 1727–1741', *Flintshire Historical Society Journal*, 20 (1962), 43–57.

—— 'Anglesey Politics, 1689–1727', *TAAS* (1962), pp. 35–54.

—— 'County Elections in Eighteenth-Century Carmarthenshire', *The Carmarthen Antiquary*, 4 (1962), 32–8; (1963), 124–30.

—— 'The Montgomery Borough Constituency, 1660–1728', *BBCS*, 20 (1963), 293–304.

—— 'The Montgomeryshire Election of 1774', *The Montgomeryshire Collections*, 59 (1965–6), 116–29.

—— 'Eighteenth-Century Elections in the Cardigan Boroughs Constituency', *Ceredigion*, 5 (1964–7), 402–23.

Thomas, P. D. G., 'The Cardigan Boroughs Election of 1741', *Ceredigion*, 6 (1968–71), 128–9.

—— 'Glamorgan Politics 1688–1790', *Glamorgan County History*, IV, 394–429.

—— 'County Elections in Eighteenth-Century Cardiganshire', *Ceredigion*, 11 (1991), 239–57.

—— 'The Rise of Plas Newydd: Sir Nicholas Bayly and County Elections in Anglesey, 1734–1784', *WHR*, 16 (1992), 160–76.

—— 'Sir Hugh Williams and Lady Bulkeley: Love and Politics in Mid-Eighteenth-Century Anglesey', *TAAS* (1992), 51–62.

—— 'Orielton Versus Picton Castle: County Elections in Pembrokeshire 1765–1786', *Pembrokeshire Historical Society Journal*, 6 (1994–5), 35–46.

—— 'A Welsh Political Storm: The Treasury Warrant of 1778 Concerning Crown Lands in Wales', *WHR*, 18 (1997), 430–49.

Thorne, R., 'The Political Scene 1660–1815', *Pembrokeshire County History*, III, 333–59.

Vaughan, H. M., 'Welsh Jacobitism', *T.H.S. Cymm.* (1920–1), pp. 11–36.

Whittaker, W. E. B., 'The Glynnes of Hawarden', *Flintshire Historical Society Journal*, 4 (1906), 1–36.

Williams, D., 'Cardiganshire Politics in the Mid-Eighteenth Century', *Ceredigion*, 3 (1956–9), 303–18.

Williams, J. G., 'Sir John Vaughan of Trawscoed, 1603–74', *NLWJ*, 8 (1953–4), 33–48, 121–46, 224–41.

(C) Unpublished University Theses

Adams, D. R. L., 'The Parliamentary Representation of Radnorshire, 1536–1832' (MA Wales, 1969).

Baskerville, S. W., 'The Management of the Tory Interest in Lancashire and Cheshire, 1714–1747' (D.Phil. Oxford, 1976).

Colley, L. J., 'The Tory Party, 1727–60' (Ph.D. Cambridge, 1976).

David, I. W. R., 'Political Electioneering Activity in South-East Wales, 1820–52' (MA Wales, 1959).

Elis-Williams, D. M., 'The Activities of Welsh Members of Parliament, 1660–1688' (MA Wales, 1952).

Havill, E. E., 'The Parliamentary Representation of Monmouthshire and the Monmouth Boroughs, 1536–1832' (MA Wales, 1949).

Isaac, D. G., 'A Study of Popular Disturbances in Britain, 1714–1754' (Ph.D. Edinburgh, 1953).

John, L. B., 'The Parliamentary Representation of Glamorgan, 1536–1832' (MA Wales, 1934).

Jones, M. E., 'The Parliamentary Representation of Pembrokeshire, the Pembroke Boroughs and Haverfordwest, 1536–1761' (MA Wales, 1958).

Nicholas, J. D., 'Lord Bute's Ministry, 1762–3' (Ph.D. Wales, 1987).

Rees, R. D., 'The Parliamentary Representation of South Wales, 1790–1830' (Ph.D. Reading, 1962).

Roberts, G., 'The Boroughs of North Wales: their Parliamentary History from the Act of Union to the First Reform Act, 1536–1832' (MA Wales, 1929).

Wager, D. A., 'Welsh Politics and Parliamentary Reform, 1780–1835' (Ph.D. Wales, 1972).

Index